The SUMMER TRADE

La collection Louis J. Robichaud/The Louis J. Robichaud Series

Directeur de la collection/series editor: Donald J. Savoie

Collaboration entre l'Institut Donald J. Savoie et McGill-Queen's University Press, la collection « Louis J. Robichaud » regroupe des publications en français et en anglais, évaluées par des pairs et qui portent sur les politiques publiques canadiennes, le régionalisme et des sujets connexes. La collection est ouverte aux chercheuses et chercheurs de toutes les universités du Canada atlantique et offre une plus grande visibilité aux travaux universitaires qui s'intéressent aux enjeux fondamentaux de politique et comprennent des analyses rigoureuses, pertinentes et non partisanes à forte valeur sociale et contribuant à des débats publics éclairés. La collection rend hommage à l'ancien premier ministre néo-brunswickois Louis J. Robichaud, reconnu comme l'un des grands leaders politiques du XXe siècle au Canada et l'un des fondateurs de l'Université de Moncton.

A collaboration between the Donald J. Savoie Institute and McGill-Queen's University Press, the Louis J. Robichaud Series publishes peer-reviewed scholarship on Canadian public policy, regionalism, and related subjects in both English and French. The series welcomes books by researchers at all Atlantic Canadian universities and offers widespread visibility to Atlantic university research that focuses on the stakes of public policy, informed by rigorous, relevant, and non-partisan analysis that is socially engaged and aims to contribute to transparent and informed public debate. The series honours Louis J. Robichaud, a New Brunswick premier widely recognized as a leading light of twentieth-century Canadian politics and a founder of the University of Moncton.

1 The Summer Trade
  A History of Tourism on Prince Edward Island
  Alan MacEachern and Edward MacDonald

The SUMMER

A History of Tourism on Prince Edward Island

TRADE

ALAN MACEACHERN *and* EDWARD MACDONALD

MCGILL-QUEEN'S UNIVERSITY PRESS

Montreal & Kingston • London • Chicago

© Alan MacEachern and Edward MacDonald 2022

ISBN 978-0-2280-1089-0 (cloth)
ISBN 978-0-2280-1211-5 (ePDF)

Legal deposit first quarter 2022
Bibliothèque nationale du Québec

Printed in Canada on acid-free paper

This book has been published with the help of a grant from the Canadian Federation for the Humanities and Social Sciences, through the Awards to Scholarly Publications Program, using funds provided by the Social Sciences and Humanities Research Council of Canada. Funding was also received from the J.B. Smallman Publication Fund, Faculty of Social Science, University of Western Ontario.

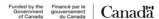 

We acknowledge the support of the Canada Council for the Arts.
Nous remercions le Conseil des arts du Canada de son soutien.

Images from Prince Edward Island Visitors Guides used with permission of the copyright holder, Tourism PEI.

LIBRARY AND ARCHIVES CANADA CATALOGUING IN PUBLICATION

Title: The summer trade : a history of tourism on Prince Edward Island / Alan MacEachern and Edward MacDonald.
Names: MacEachern, Alan, 1966– author. | MacDonald, George Edward, 1957– author.
Description: Series statement: La collection Louis J. Robichaud = The Louis J. Robichaud Series ; 1 | Includes bibliographical references and index.
Identifiers: Canadiana (print) 20210344385 | Canadiana (ebook) 20210344520 | ISBN 9780228010890 (hardcover) | ISBN 9780228012115 (PDF)
Subjects: LCSH: Tourism—Prince Edward Island—History. | LCSH: Tourism—Social aspects—Prince Edward Island—History. | LCSH: Prince Edward Island—Description and travel.
Classification: LCC G155.C2 M33 2022 | DDC 338.4/79171704—dc23

Dedicated to

Jim and Helen Larkin, who have
made a life in the summer trade,

and

Meredith and Arnold MacEachern,
who cultivated the land and
way of life that cultivated
the summer trade.

Contents

Tables, Figures, and Plates   ix

Acknowledgments   xv

INTRODUCTION ▪ A Summer Place   3

CHAPTER 1 ▪ The Seaside Beckons / *to 1905*   17

CHAPTER 2 ▪ Of Boosters and Knockers / *1905–40*   55

CHAPTER 3 ▪ Escape Velocity / *1940–60*   97

CHAPTER 4 ▪ Great Expectations / *1960–80*   139

CHAPTER 5 ▪ Laws of Attraction, Rules of Engagement / *1980–2000*   203

EPILOGUE ▪ A Delicate Balance / *since 2000*   253

Notes   271

Index   319

Tables, Figures, and Plates

TABLES

5.1 Position of the tourism portfolio within provincial government, 1940–99.   209

6.1 Estimated number of tourists, 1925–2019.   256

6.2 Number and acreage of farms, 1901–2016.   267

FIGURES

i.0 Miniature Green Gables, Rainbow Valley, Cavendish. Courtesy Ed McKenna.   2

i.1 Map of northeastern North America. *Prince Edward Island, the England of Canada*, PEI Travel Bureau, 1941.   5

i.2 Cartoon map of PEI. *Vacationland of Heart's Content*, PEI Travel Bureau, 1939.   6

i.3 MV *Holiday Island* life preserver. Prince Edward Island Museum and Heritage Foundation.   15

1.0 Cover *Prince Edward Island as a Summer Resort: Where It Is and How to Get There*, Acadia Hotel, 1893.   16

1.1 Seaside Hotel group, Anglo Rustico. PARO PEI 34661.HF72.66.4.8 (2).   18

1.2 Island Park Hotel, Summerside, 18 July 1890. PARO PEI 2301/246.   19

1.3 Advertisement for Bovyer's Sea-side Establishment, *Haszard's Gazette*, 20 July 1852.   23

1.4 Shaw's Hotel, Brackley, August 1891. PARO PEI 3466/HF78.72.20.   24

1.5 "Beach at Tracadie." S.G.W. Benjamin, *Cruise of the Alice May*, 1885.   27

1.6 Guest register, Seaside Hotel, Anglo Rustico, 1875. PARO PEI 3466/HF 79.15.3.   28

1.7 Pastoral scene. *Picturesque Canada*, vol. 2, 1882.   33

1.8 Robert Harris sketches, McCallum's resort, Brackley, 1894. Collection of Confederation Centre Art Gallery, Gift of Robert Harris Trust, 1965.   37

1.9 Summer visitors, Mutch's Hotel, 1897 and Cliff Hotel, 1896. Courtesy Earle MacDonald.   42

1.10 Souvenir playing cards, Intercolonial and PEI Railway. Collection of Alan MacEachern.   45

1.11 "The Cape House" of C.P. Flockton, Abells Cape, Fortune Bay. *Prince Edward Island Magazine*, December 1901.   51

2.0 Cover *Prince Edward Island: Visit Canada's Garden Province*, PEI Travel Bureau, 1937.   54

2.1 "Evening Shadows" postcard, W.S. Louson. Postcard collection, Prince Edward Island Museum and Heritage Foundation.   60

2.2 Mi'kmaw encampment. Postcard collection, Prince Edward Island Museum and Heritage Foundation.   61

2.3 Robert Harris sketch, Sheepcote Cottage, Holland Cove, 1917. Collection of Confederation Centre Art Gallery, Gift of Robert Harris Trust, 1965.   66

2.4 Views of the ss *Prince Edward Island.* William Notman and Son Collection, McCord Museum, Montreal.   68

2.5 Tourist cars loading for PEI. Postcard collection, Prince Edward Island Museum and Heritage Foundation.   69

2.6 "Green Gables," the Macneill homestead, 1910s. Collection of Alan MacEachern.   70

2.7 Advertisement for Avonlea Restaurant, Cavendish. *Guardian*, 30 June 1928.   71

2.8 Judge Aubin E. Arsenault. PARO PEI 2301/137. Jim and M.K. "Minnie" MacFadyen. Courtesy the family of Mrs Minnie MacFadyen.   73

2.9 Victoria Hotel. PARO PEI 3535/12.   81

2.10 Advertisement for reduced ferry rates. *Official Motor Guide to Prince Edward Island*, PEI Motor League, 1935.   83

2.11 Advertisement for Dalvay-by-the-Sea. *Official Guide of Prince Edward Island Auto Routes*, 1931.   85

2.12 Map of Prince Edward Island National Park. General Information and Map, Department of Mines and Resources, 1940.   89

2.13 "Green Gables," the Webb house in Cavendish, 1936. Library and Archives Canada C146799.   92

3.0 Cover *Prince Edward Island*, PEI Travel Bureau, 1942.   96

Tables, Figures, and Plates

3.1 "The Romance of Canada" historical pageant parade, 1939. Courtesy family of the late Mary MacNutt MacRae.   100

3.2 Cover *Prince Edward Island: The England of Canada*, PEI Travel Bureau, 1941.   106

3.3 Tourist information booth, Aulac, New Brunswick. *Prince Edward Island: The England of Canada*, PEI Travel Bureau, 1941.   107

3.4 Horseracing at the Charlottetown Driving Park. CN Images of Canada Collection.   109

3.5 Advertisement for Northumberland Ferries Ltd. *Prince Edward Island: The England of Canada*, PEI Travel Bureau, 1941. Postcard of the MV *Prince Nova*. Courtesy Ed McKenna.   110

3.6 Logo of the PEI Innkeepers Association. Logo of the Tourism Industry Association of PEI.   113

3.7 MV *Abegweit* postage stamp, c. 1946. Library and Archives Canada, RG3, Accession number: 1989-565 CPA. © Canada Post Corporation, 1946.   117

3.8 "Where Your Tourist Dollars Go" pie chart. *PEI Innkeepers Association*, 1951.   120

3.9 George V. Fraser. Courtesy Jeannine Fraser.   122

3.10 Stanhope Beach postcard. Courtesy Ed McKenna.   123

3.11 Green Gables Bungalow Court. PARO PEI 4500/54778.   128

3.12 Stanhope Campground postcard. Postcard collection, Prince Edward Island Museum and Heritage Foundation.   129

3.13 Woodleigh Replicas. Courtesy Earle MacDonald.   132

3.14 Charlottetown Centennial souvenir currency. IslandArchives.ca.   133

4.0 Cover *Prince Edward Island, Canada*, PEI Travel Bureau, c. 1966.   138

4.1 *Come to Prince Edward Island*, PEI Travel Bureau, 1960. *Come to Prince Edward Island*, PEI Travel Bureau, 1968.   142

4.2 Martin Mitchell and Micmac Indian Village. Postcard collection, Prince Edward Island Museum and Heritage Foundation.   147

4.3 Maps of tourist accommodations and summer cottages, 1965. Acres Research and Planning, *Tourism Study, vol.2*, Robertson Library, UPEI.   152

4.4 Fathers of Confederation Memorial Buildings. Postcard collection, Prince Edward Island Museum and Heritage Foundation.   160

4.5 Bob Chambers cartoon, Halifax *Chronicle-Herald*, 8 August 1966. Courtesy family of Bob Chambers.   167

4.6 Concept drawings, PEI Causeway, 1966. PARO PEI RG 25.26/1967-1968/Box5/1063c.   169

4.7 Patsy Glover, Kitten Club Lounge, Brudenell Resort. Ottawa *Citizen*, 23 October 1971. 178

4.8 Map of provincial and private camping sites and trailer parks. Ed McKenna Collection, Robertson Library, UPEI. 181

4.9 Logo of Brothers and Sisters of Cornelius Howatt. *Cornelius Howatt: Superstar!* 1974. 184

4.10 PEI Centennial licence plate, 1973. Collection of Simon Lloyd. 188

4.11 Abegweit Sightseeing Tours postcard. Postcard collection, Prince Edward Island Museum and Heritage Foundation. 191

4.12 Boundaries of proposed East Point National Park, c. 1970. Map adapted by Josh MacFadyen from original in Parks Canada files, Ardgowan National Historic Site, Charlottetown. 195

5.0 Cover, *Prince Edward Island Visitors Guide, 1996.* Tourism PEI/ John Sylvester. 202

5.1 Concept drawing for Prince Edward Hotel. Charlottetown *Evening Patriot*, 5 July 1980. 204

5.2 Theme promotions, 1988 to 1991. Tourism PEI. 221

5.3 Map of planned development, Greenwich Peninsula. Map from M.D. Simmons, "Environmental impact assessment proposed Greenwich development, St. Peter's Bay," Halifax: Maritime Resource Management Service, 1981. 222

5.4 Map of Confederation Trail. Tourism PEI. 224

5.5 Mi'kmaw basket, c. 1980s. Courtesy of the Prince Edward Island Museum and Heritage Foundation. 229

5.6 Founders' Hall, promotional pamphlet. Courtesy Natalie Munn, City of Charlottetown. 231

5.7 Golf course expansion, 1965–2003. Maps by Josh MacFadyen. 241

5.8 Confederation Bridge. "Pont de la Confédération/Confederation Bridge" by Phil Grondin, licensed with CC BY-ND 2.0. 249

6.0 *Prince Edward Island Visitor's Guide*, 2020. Tourism PEI/Stephen Harris. 252

6.1 Elephant Rock photo. *Prince Edward Island Visitors Guide*, 1996. Tourism PEI/Camera Art. Souvenir coaster. Collection of Edward MacDonald. 254

6.2 Cavendish Beach Music Festival promotional image. Courtesy Whitecap Entertainment. 258

6.3 MSC *Meraviglia* at Charlottetown, 2019. Photo by Edward MacDonald. 259

PLATES

1 Robert Harris oil sketches. *Brackley Beach*, 1907. Public domain. Untitled, undated landscape near Holland Cove. Courtesy Stewart and Rita MacRae.

2 Summer tourist accommodations, c. 1879. *J.H. Meacham's Illustrated Historical Atlas of Prince Edward Island*, 1880.

3 Prince Edward Island souvenirs. Clamshell painting, courtesy Michael Murphy. Centennial token, 1964. PARO PEI RG44/S1/44. Whiskey decanter, collection of Alan MacEachern. All other objects, courtesy Prince Edward Island Museum and Heritage Foundation.

4 *Anne of Green Gables* memorabilia. Green Gables, postcard collection, Prince Edward Island Museum and Heritage Foundation. Lover's Lane postcard, courtesy Ed McKenna collection, Robertson Library, UPEI. Cover *Anne of Green Gables*, 1st ed., Robertson Library, UPEI. Cover, *Anne of Green Gables* 1956 Polish ed., courtesy KindredSpaces.ca.

5 Tourist information booths. Top left and right, postcard collection, Prince Edward Island Museum and Heritage Foundation. Bottom right, courtesy Ed McKenna.

6 Promotional images of Prince Edward Island by federal agencies. Three in dunes, Chris Lund, National Film Board of Canada, Still Photography Division, Library and Archives Canada, e010949047. Water temperature 76°, Library and Archives Canada, TCA 01185/K2939. Two with bicycles, courtesy Earle MacDonald.

7 Anne of Green Gables promotional applications. Program cover for *Anne of Green Gables – The Musical*, courtesy Confederation Centre of the Arts. Anne licence plate, collection of Linda Berko. "Topless Anne" T-shirt, courtesy Dale McNevin and Anne Putnam. *Annekenstein* brochure, collection of Donald Moses.

8 *Visitors Guides* and *Visitor's Guides* images. Cover of French-language edition, 1988. Tourism PEI, Barrett & MacKay (couple in buggy), John Sylvester (field), Gordon Johnston (woman). Cover of English-language edition, 2010. Tourism PEI/Russell Monk. Child with ice cream cone, from 2006 edition. Tourism PEI/John Sylvester. Cover of English-language edition, 2021. Tourism PEI/Sander Meurs.

9 Scenic drives and regions maps. Tourism PEI.

Acknowledgments

This book flickered into possibility decades ago, the authors saying, "We should!" and "Let's!" countless times over coffee, over the telephone, over Skype, over Zoom, and over the years since then. Finally, we did, and the story is better for taking its time to develop. That is in no small part thanks to the help of others.

Early on we benefited from University of Prince Edward Island student researchers who are now deep into other careers. Thank you, Alanna James, Michele McDonald, Rosemary Driscoll, Matthew MacKinnon-Gray, and Kyle Murnaghan. Colleagues have been extraordinarily generous with material and insights. Thank you, Ben Bradley, for always keeping your eye out for us. Thank you, Matthew McRae and Josh MacFadyen, for generously letting us read work that you had yet to publish. Thank you, Catherine Hennessey, for sharing your files. Thank you, Barbara MacDonald of Parks Canada, for allowing unfettered access to yours. Thank you, our friends at the Robertson Library, University of PEI, for building up your tourism holdings, making a hundred helpful suggestions, and granting a hundred small favours, and to our friends at the Public Archives and Records Office of PEI for guiding us through your indispensable tourism materials and accommodating our requests. Thank you, Confederation Centre Art Gallery, not only for supplying us with visuals but also for asking us to curate a major tourism exhibit in 2022; thank you, PEI Museum and Heritage Foundation, for partnering with us on that exhibit and sharing your collection with us. Thank you, Tourism PEI and the Tourism Industry Association of PEI, for helping without steering. Thank you, colleagues at both the University of PEI and Western University, for supporting us along the way. Thank you, Canada's Awards to Scholarly Publications Program and Western University's J.B. Smallman Research Fund, for publication support. And thank you, Kyla Madden, Kathleen Fraser, Elli Stylianou, and everyone at MQUP, for making a manuscript a book.

Thank you, too, to the many Islanders who have shown an interest in our project over the years and often translated interest into material assistance. Megan Skinner helped us get to know Dolph and Bertha Fleming, who feature in chapter 3. The hosts of two fantastic Facebook sites, Earle MacDonald of Earles Picture Restoration and Ed McKenna of Historic PEI, generously helped in tracking down obscure images. Jeanine Fraser shared memories and material relating to her father, George V. Fraser, tourism's first deputy minister. Don Cudmore, at the time director of the Tourism Industry Association of PEI, gave us access to unarchived files from its recent past. His predecessor, Jim Larkin, answered questions and read parts of the manuscript. So did Shauna Sullivan Curley, long-time deputy minister with the provincial government. The late Boyde Beck commented on chapter 3 and assisted with statistics. David Weale and the late Harry Baglole offered feedback on parts of chapter 4. Josh MacFadyen made us maps and Sandra MacFadyen found us a photo we badly wanted. The indefatigable Katherine Dewar brought us to the Macnutt MacRae photo album, and Rita and Stewart MacRae then graciously shared their collection with us. Thank you, specially, Harry Holman, for a steady stream of early tourism nuggets from your back files and for your superb blog, *SailStrait*. Thank you Anita Chambers and Robbie Shaw and Natalie Munn and Michael Murphy and Anne Putnam and Dale McNevin and – the list stretches out like an Island summer, too many people to list them all by name, but not too many to forget their assistance or to be grateful for it. Thank you all.

And, finally, thank you to our travel companions these many years, Genevieve and Sadie, and Sheila. "Are we there yet?" Yes.

The
SUMMER
TRADE

INTRODUCTION

A Summer Place

In September 1864, Anne Brown of Toronto received a long letter from her husband, George, who was in the Maritimes for a conference. Recounting his cruise down from Quebec to Prince Edward Island on the government steamer *Queen Victoria*, he wrote,

> I was up at four in the morning! – Thursday morning – to see the sun rise & have a saltwater bath. We had just reached the westerly point of Prince Edward & were running along the coast of as pretty a country as you ever put your eye upon. The land all along this shore rises gradually up from the sea for a space of two or three miles, & this slope all round the island is well cultivated & when we passed was clothed in bright green verdure.

The ship soon landed "amid most beautiful scenery" at Prince Edward Island's capital, Charlottetown, launching Brown into a hectic week of mixing business with pleasure. Following a five-hour meeting on their first full day on the Island, Brown and his fellow conference goers were treated to oysters, lobsters, and champagne. "This killed the day," he noted, "& we spent the beautiful moonlight evening in walking, driving or boating as the mood was on us." Before retiring to bed, Brown spent some time simply "looking out on the sea in all its glory." Meetings continued throughout the weekend and into the next week, as did the festivities, reinforced by what seemed a boundless supply of Island food and Central Canada liquor. On the conference's sunny final day, delegates took carriages to the Island's north shore, walking the sand and drinking in the air of Brackley Beach. They returned to the capital for a closing banquet that ran long into the night – although, George assured Anne, he himself turned in early. At almost five in the morning, the visitors stumbled back to the *Queen Victoria* and sailed for Nova Scotia.[1]

Figure i.0 (facing) ▪ A 1970s postcard view of the miniature Green Gables house at Rainbow Valley in Cavendish.

George Brown and the other Fathers of Confederation did not gather in Charlottetown in 1864 principally as tourists: they were there to discuss the union of colonies that would ultimately result in the creation of the Dominion of Canada, with Prince Edward Island its smallest province. Yet they enjoyed many of the elements that we still associate with tourism on PEI: beautiful pastoral scenery, welcoming beaches, friendly locals, and delicious seafood. And what's more, they would have recognized that they were playing tourist. Certainly, by 1864 some Islanders were becoming aware of leisure travel to their shores, and some were already hoping to attract more of it. With "our climate, water, beaches, roads, &c.," the local *Ross's Weekly* newspaper had argued a few months earlier, "We believe that PE Island will yet become a 'watering place' and be yearly visited by hundreds, if not thousands, of the better-class." Like countless subsequent Prince Edward Island tourism promoters, the editor imagined visitor growth would come from the United States, not Canada.[2]

Now, more than 150 years later, the more than 150,000 citizens of Prince Edward Island welcome more than 1,500,000 travellers each year, a business worth almost $430 million annually to the province. Tourism has been the province's second leading industry for the past half century, trailing only agriculture, and by 2019 – before the lost tourism summers of COVID-19 – seemed ready to overtake it. How this happened and what effects, good and bad, tourism has had on Prince Edward Island is the subject of this book, the first comprehensive history of tourism in any province of Canada.

A standard definition of tourism has it as the set of activities engaged by people while temporarily, voluntarily away from home for personal reasons other than employment, such as leisure or the betterment of health or spirit.[3] Most importantly, the definition makes clear that tourism is not simply a thing but rather a set of transactions within a web of relationships. Tourism scholar Stephen L.J. Smith contends that "Tourism is something that people do, not something that businesses produce" – that is, it is a practice that the tourist calls into existence.[4] To be a tourist, an individual must combine an inclination to travel with the leisure time and money to act on that desire. Personal prerequisites overlap with more global considerations such as convenient, reliable, affordable means of travel; political and economic stability; and an accepted medium of exchange. What tourists then "do" is consume a destination: its scenery, its architecture, its culture, its local foods, its souvenirs, its accommodations, its amusements and attractions, its art and heritage, its

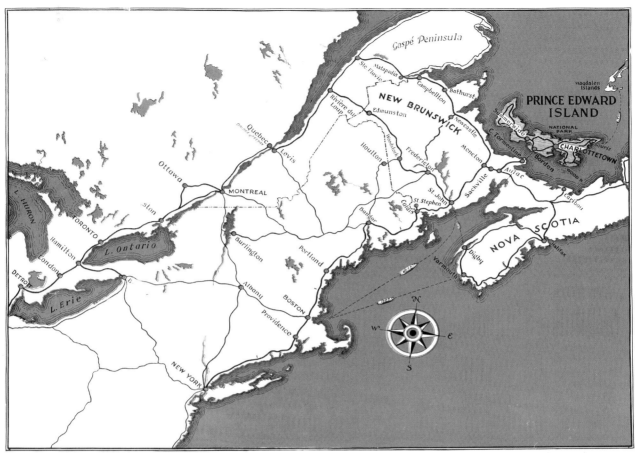

Paved Trunk Highways from everywhere connect by Car Ferries with the Paved roads on Prince Edward Island.

felt uniqueness. All this requires a destination and, typically, a host. Tourists may make tourism but not in conditions of their own choosing.

Whereas tourism has long attracted the attention of sociologists, cultural geographers, and business and leisure studies scholars, historians came to it relatively late – and historians of Canada later still.[5] What has been written of tourism in Canada has mostly been at the provincial level and even then focusing on subregions, eras, and themes. Moreover, tourism has typically been used as an interpretive vehicle or frame of analysis, as a way to get *at* a thing rather than a subject in its own right. Historians know well the danger of identifying "firsts" – an earlier example can always be found – but Ian McKay's highly influential 1994 *The Quest of the Folk: Antimodernism and Cultural Selection in Twentieth-Century Nova Scotia*, on how tourism refashioned the character of the province and its people, heralded a spate

Figure i.1 ▪ This map, like many that illustrate how to reach Prince Edward Island, emphasizes the primary market for its tourism: the northeastern United States, central Canada, New Brunswick, and Nova Scotia.

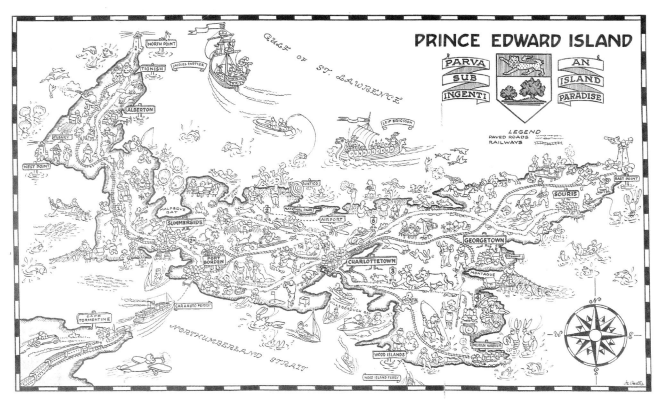

Province of PRINCE EDWARD ISLAND, *Canada*

Figure i.2 ▪ In this 1939 map, every corner of Prince Edward Island offers attractions to the active tourist. Or Viking.

of Canadian scholarly works exploring the misalliance of tourism, heritage, capital, and the state. James Overton's collection of essays examining tourism in Newfoundland and Labrador produces a pointed exposé of class conflict and power imbalance. Karen Dubinsky's *The Second Greatest Disappointment* is a masterful dissection of Niagara Falls as a honeymoon destination, as interested in sexual mores as in nature and tourism per se. In books on British Columbia, Michael Dawson adopts a consumer-culture perspective on the development of the tourism industry, while Ben Bradley explores how tourism was shaped for and by the automobile. In *Time Travel*, Alan Gordon examines that curious construct, the living history museum, as a culturally revealing conjunction of tourism and public memory. Recently, Nicole Neatby has tracked the reorientation of tourism promotion and imagining in Quebec between 1920 and 1967. What's missing from this catalogue of scholarship is a Canada-wide history of tourism. The closest approximations are two recent collections of essays on the topic, both associated with J.I. Little: "The History of Tourism in Canada," a special issue of *Histoire sociale / Social*

History that Little coedited with Ben Bradley, and his own *Fashioning the Canadian Landscape: Essays in Travel Writing, Tourism, and National Identity in the Pre-Automobile Era.*[6]

The tourism trade has also made appearances in Prince Edward Island's historiography – unsurprising given its longtime importance to the province. Judith Adler's pioneering 1982 account of postwar tourism traces the state's attempts to rationalize and professionalize the trade in the 1960s and '70s. Several scholars, particularly Shelagh Squire, have connected L.M. Montgomery's *Anne of Green Gables* to the maturation of the Island's pastoral tourism image. In a pair of perceptive essays, Matthew McRae examines PEI's tourism-inspired assertion of its role as Birthplace of Confederation.[7] Tourism also figures significantly but selectively in our own individual books and more directly in articles we have written separately and together.[8] But as in the case of Canada writ large, there has been no overarching history of tourism in the province. If we are to build a history of tourism in Canada from the ground up, province-by-province, then tourism on Prince Edward Island is a great place to start.

Perhaps the absence of such comprehensive histories is rooted in a belief that every destination's experience with tourism is essentially alike. Indeed, there is a certain sameness to many histories of tourism around the world: a place doesn't have tourists, and then it does, and the principal dramas concern whether it keeps them and whether they ruin it. There are three reasons for such predictability. First, tourism history, not surprisingly, tends to focus on places that have become tourism destinations. Second, this narrative, in the broadest terms, *is* the history of tourism globally over the past two centuries. And third, a reason can always be found to explain a specific destination's existence: its water, its mountains, its proximity to something, its distance from something, something. Canadian geographer R.W. Butler's classic articulation of the standard narrative was the Tourism Area Life Cycle, or TALC. Butler posited that tourism destinations move through relatively predictable stages of exploration, involvement, development, consolidation, and stagnation – at which point they move towards either rejuvenation or decline.[9] It would be easy enough to categorize PEI tourism history in just such terms, arguing that the province has arrived at the stage of consolidation if not stagnation – where the populace is dependent on a tourism economy that has slowed and likely peaked – and that it must now think carefully about how to proceed.

Yet Prince Edward Island's experience is also distinct. Because it is a small island, all of its land and all of its people became enmeshed with tourism – more or less at the same time, and more or less in the same way – and because it has been a full-fledged political jurisdiction for all its tourism history, it developed its own particular homegrown commercial, political, and cultural responses to the trade. Taken together, these two factors make Prince Edward Island unique in continental North American terms. What makes PEI's example so valuable, in other words, is that it offers a single, self-contained history of tourism – even as the topic itself refutes the very notion of any place in modernity being truly "self-contained." No island is an island.

In the process of cowriting this book long distance, the two authors developed shorthands that saved time when talking over big issues. We eventually realized that these prompts constituted the book's themes: concepts that are intrinsic to the Island's tourism history and may also contribute to tourism studies generally. The first of these is *the Island imagined*, the remarkably stable image Prince Edward Island has presented to tourists the past 150 years. What sets travellers on the road does not determine where they will go; rather, a destination must possess something the traveller craves and believes they will find there. There is no way of knowing what attracted the first, anonymous tourist to Prince Edward Island, but it is almost as difficult to know exactly what attracted later tourists, given that "push" factors such as travel writing and "pull" factors such as advertising and promotional literature muddy the integrity of their intentions. Yet the elements of PEI's image for tourism have been so consistent that it is reasonable to conclude they are a fusion of elements that visitors sought, that Islanders *believed* visitors sought, and that the Island could actually provide. The first element is simply the Island's islandness.[10] Consciously and implicitly, tourism promotion has played to literary traditions that portray islands as places of escape and refuge, and the passage to PEI itself became an integral part of the tourist experience. A second element is Prince Edward Island's landscape: rolling agrarian countryside with a backdrop of ocean. Beyond being of mere aesthetic appeal, such scenery has claimed to improve the visitor's physical and psychological health; even if doctors no longer actually prescribe the temperate climate and salt air to escape the miasmas of city living, as they did in the nineteenth century, the underlying belief in their benefits persist.[11] The third element is the pastoral people who inhabit this pastoral landscape. Bolstered by antimodernism, tourism has presented Island society and the "Island way of life" as authentic relics of an earlier, simpler time and an attraction in their own right.[12] One or more of these three generic elements have been made manifest in specific market lures: golf mecca, birthplace of Canadian Confederation, and – most apropos, most famously, and most beneficially – the setting for

L.M. Montgomery's beloved novel *Anne of Green Gables*. A 1988 survey asked Islanders why they thought tourists chose to visit the Island, and the five most common responses were the scenery, the quiet way of life, the beaches, the friendly people, and the uniqueness of it being an island.[13] A survey a century earlier might well have yielded the same results – as might a survey today.

But such continuity does not just happen, it must be continuously produced – retaining Prince Edward Island's identification with pristine nature, pastoral farming, and premodernity against the relentless pressure of a changing world. (As in F. Scott Fitzgerald's line "And so we beat on, boats against the current, borne back ceaselessly into the past," we can miss the degree to which heavy rowing is required.) This leads to our second major theme: that tourism and the form it takes are never inevitable, that "*destinations are not destined.*"[14] They are the product of work. The arc of the industry in a particular place, once launched, develops out of an ever-changing dynamic between guests and hosts, so the histories that rise out of these circumstances are necessarily distinctive. They are also contingent: that is, the existence and form of later events are dependent on the existence and form of earlier ones. It might seem "natural" today that tourists crowd Cavendish beach, for example, because the beach exists and visitors enjoy their time there, but the Island's rivers once attracted as much or more attention from visitors as did its shores. The example of Cavendish is particularly useful in showing that tourism has no magnetic north – or, rather, that like magnetic north, it moves. When beach tourism did arise, it was Rustico that had the strongest claim to being the heart of PEI tourism until the 1910s when Cavendish's association with *Anne of Green Gables* began drawing tourists there. Even then, both Cavendish and Park Corner claimed credit for author L.M. Montgomery, and by the 1930s both had placed signs proclaiming their community to be home to the model for *Anne*'s Lake of Shining Waters. Montgomery noted with some amusement in her journal that some Cavendish boys apparently sneaked into Park Corner one night and destroyed its sign.[15] Working to ensure one tourism timeline over another is not usually so violent, but the episode speaks to the fact tourism does not just develop organically.

In fact, as tourism grew in importance to Prince Edward Island, it was less and less left to chance. Our book's third theme is the *professionalization* of the trade. From 1900 onward, both private enterprise and the state have been increasingly involved in organizing for tourism: creating government agencies and associations of private operators; building infrastructure; supporting accommodations, attractions and activities; developing licensing and rating systems; and relentlessly refining the Island's image and messaging. A diversion became a true industry. Of course, Prince Edward Island was not the first, let alone the only place that sought to tame and direct tourism nor is our book the first to explore that process. Almost thirty-five years ago, Scott Lash and John Urry identified mass tourism as paradigmatic of "organized capitalism" and dated its emergence to the rise of the mid-nineteenth century British travel company Thomas Cook and Son; more recent scholarship has pushed the commodification of American travel back towards 1800.[16] But Prince Edward Island's distinct experience offers some cautionary lessons about the professionalization of tourism. Seduced by success in attracting the masses in the postwar decades, the Island's industry grew more intent in supporting boomer families' desire for convenient vacationing and so in producing a consistent, repeatable experience. The result was a more generic tourism, questionable commercial developments that ran counter to PEI's deeply rooted image, and the threat of what has since been dubbed "overtourism." And so, modern tourism on Prince Edward Island, as elsewhere, confronts a central contradiction: the visitor's experience must be commodified and neatly packaged yet still judged "authentic" – all without the visitor actually having the opportunity or even desire to accurately assess the authenticity of their experience.

This leads to our fourth theme, which we have come to call "*hospitility*": the strand running through this history of locals expressing ambivalence, displeasure, or outright hostility towards tourists, tourism, and the promotion of tourism. Antipathy to tourism is practically universal, of course, and many tourism scholars have gleefully cited American novelist Henry James's line that "Tourists are vulgar, vulgar, vulgar." (Although this is in fact a paraphrase, and James was calling vulgar the *American* travellers he met in Europe, not tourists per se.)[17] But evidence of this negative attitude is often anecdotal, and its effect hard to measure, so the subject is everywhere and nowhere rather than systematically explored in tourism literature.[18] All the more reason to consider it when it does appear. On Prince Edward Island such sentiment emerged only occasionally in the public sphere – such as during the 1908 banning of the automobile or following the 1973 tourism department's publication of advice on how Islanders should behave with visitors – but its continued reappearance in private correspondence and letters to the editor suggests its constant presence.[19] Some Islanders resented tourists' display of wealth and leisure. Some felt that tourism distracted from the more familiar, reliable, and "real" industries of farming and fishing.[20] Some were xenophobic. Some bristled against an industry that directed them to maintain their traditional way of life, even as it encouraged the wider world to their door. Some felt that, thanks to tourism, an authentic Island way of life was morphing into the contrived.

This leads to the fifth and final theme, which gives title to our book: *the summer trade*. This is an old, occasional name for tourism, including on Prince Edward Island. It nicely captures not merely when the business occurs but that summer and everything it invokes is the commodity being sold. We also mean the term in the sense of a transaction: that the Island gains from the trade but also gives something away.[21] This is not always how tourism has been presented to Prince Edward Islanders. In the mid-1920s, for example, tourism revenue was described as "found money," and the head of the new Tourist Association assured citizens that "the ground is fertile ... the crop is sure, the land cannot be depleted."[22] But tourism requires more of a place than that it just be itself because the place discovers value in conforming to the desires of the broader world. (In physics this is called "the observer effect," in which a system cannot be observed without changing that which is being observed.) Tourism is ultimately a relationship between host and visitor, observing one another. The visitor looks for what they wish to find in the landscape and people of the destination – and sees what they wish to see. The host is looking, too. It may be said, accurately, that tourism has helped Prince Edward Islanders better understand their home and society by allowing them to see how others perceive them. But, because the tourist pays for what they want, this is as much a market survey for Islanders as it is an act of cultural self-discovery. Over the course of its tourism history, Prince Edward Island has simultaneously sought to change to accommodate visitors' needs and stay unchanged to accommodate visitors' desires. Tourism has encouraged the development of a service-based economy, while discouraging development that would threaten the Island's image of peaceful, pastoral simplicity.

As these five themes suggests, the perspective here is principally that of the producer rather than the consumer. Although we periodically gaze through the eyes of tourists, our view is often second hand, filtered by consultants and survey-takers. For the most part, this is the story of Prince Edward Island tourism as experienced by its Prince Edward Island providers, promoters, enablers, regulators, funders, and, sometimes, victims. Their changing understanding of what tourism is and how it works, of who tourists are and what they want, is central to our narrative.

"Tourism! Tourism! What good are tourists anyway?" a cabinet minister is said to have sputtered in the Prince Edward Island legislature in the 1930s. "They bring home an old shirt, and then they go back to the States with all your strawberry jam!"[23] Why tell this history of tourism at all, he might well have asked. Aside from the fact that tourism is the world's fastest growing industry and so begs our understanding? Aside from the fact that it consistently contributes a greater percentage to the GDP of Prince Edward Island than in any other province? That it speaks so eloquently to nuanced issues of identity? That it casts a long shadow across every culture and society it touches? That all of us have been both tourist and host and so personally part of the phenomenon we study? Aside from that, no reason at all.

The Summer Trade opens in the middle of the nineteenth century, as tourism edged up North America's eastern seaboard, and the mild summer climate, sea breezes, and pastoral scenery of Prince Edward Island began to attract attention. Chapter 1 winds its way through the second half of the century, when distant travel writers raised the Island's profile and helped refine the image it presented visitors, while improved steamer and rail transportation made such visiting possible. A few entrepreneurial minds recognized the burgeoning trade's potential. But a lack of private capital, the competing priorities of cash-strapped provincial governments, and perhaps above all, widespread obliviousness to tourism's existence – let alone its prospects, let alone that these prospects could be purposely fashioned – meant the trade ran at a low ebb for a long time. The 1905 establishment of both a provincial tourist association and a provincial Old Home Week meant to entice expatriates signalled the first concerted attempt to promote tourism and the end of PEI's decades-long tourism prehistory.

Chapter 2 traces Prince Edward Island's homegrown efforts to advance tourism between 1905 and 1940. Certainly it was an undertaking made no easier by a provincial automobile ban, world war, global pandemic, provincial economic stagnation, and global economic crash. But almost as damaging was a lack of vision among private and government boosters as to what Prince Edward Island tourism should be; there should just, perhaps, be more of it. But slowly the Island's tourism image assumed greater definition, as the Garden of the Gulf also pronounced itself the Birthplace of Confederation, and it rode the wave of its association with *Anne of Green Gables*. The 1936 creation of Prince Edward Island National Park – annexing the Island's most popular resort area, some of its best beaches, and its most famous literary home – was the capstone of this process. It gave tourists to Prince Edward Island a destination within the broader destination and, for the first time, a clear something to *do*. It also firmly entrenched the provincial and federal governments' role in PEI tourism planning, simultaneously validating and repudiating the decades of private boostering work that had come before.

Chapter 3 covers the period from 1940 to 1960, when the Island's tourism industry achieved lift-off. Following the interlude of another world war, with tourism booming worldwide and budgets inflated by federal transfers, Island governments took greater control of the industry's direction, something pointedly emphasized in the naming of the new Department of Tourist Development in 1960. The private sector also grew more organized and deliberate as the postwar Innkeepers Association evolved into a new tourist association. Meanwhile, tourism numbers ballooned, from fewer than 40,000 visitors in 1950 to a quarter of a million a decade later.

These trends accelerated during the ambitious, fractious years of the Comprehensive Development Plan (1969–84), which forms the backbone of chapter 4. Tourism was by then too important, it was felt, to be left to its own devices: it must be studied, understood, scientifically managed, and planned. Within the Development Plan's detailed blueprint for the province's economic transformation, tourism was tagged as a key catalyst, and planners set out to attract more tourists, and have them stay longer, spend more money, and spread out across the seasons and the province. Some strategists feared that catering to baby boom families seeking affordable, convenient "mass" tourism experiences might run counter to the Island's reputation as an unspoiled, bucolic "class" destination. Such considerations catalyzed state intervention to keep tourism providers on message and to model the sort of development it felt the industry needed. As tourism's shadow lengthened, critiques of the industry sharpened as well. Where many Islanders had once wondered why tourism should even matter, they now worried that it mattered too much, that it threatened to subvert their conservative, self-reliant ethos.

By the time the Development Plan dwindled to a convenient vehicle for federal transfer payments in the early 1980s, tourism's mushroom growth had slowed as well. Chapter 5 sees the provincial government learning that "control" had certain practical limits that did not necessarily translate into perpetual growth. Like the weather, tourism does not take dictation. And because it was built around discretionary rather than necessary travel, it was also subject to larger forces well beyond the control of provincial planners. In the new era of supply-side economics a maturing partnership between the private and public sectors steered tourism across a series of economic crests and troughs in the last two decades of the millennium. Tourism promotion relied still on longstanding tropes and traditional markets, but imaging and analysis became increasingly sophisticated. And even as tourism boosters doubled down on familiar lures such as *Anne of Green Gables* and Confederation, they gambled on new infrastructure, such as the Confederation Trail and a slew of new golf courses. The biggest infrastructural investment of all was the Confederation Bridge, the long sought "fixed link," which opened amid much fanfare in the spring of 1997.

Literally and figuratively, the Confederation Bridge brought tourists to Prince Edward Island like never before, and our Epilogue peers over its humpbacked span to examine how the summer trade has evolved in the new millennium. (For one, it has become somewhat more of a spring and fall trade, thanks largely to the influx of cruise ships.) Globally, there have been a press of more people, more people travelling, and people travelling more often, and

Prince Edward Island is just one of countless tourism destinations that has both benefited from and fought to manage that reality. As a place that relies heavily on its association with the past and the pastoral, the Island has little room to manoeuvre in a fast-changing tourism landscape and can at best tack incrementally in response. A looming long-term game-changer, like the climate crisis, or a sudden catastrophic shock to the system, such as COVID-19, can make Islanders feel that they are rearranging deck chairs on the *Titanic*. And yet how can they not? Prince Edward Islanders can hardly step away from the tourism trade. Both in terms of contributing to the economy and defining the image of their home, for more than 150 years tourism has helped make them who they are.

Figure i.3 ▪ Tourism as life saver. "Holiday Island" was, from the mid-1950s on, one of PEI's tourism slogans and, as of 1971, the name of one of the ferries that brought tourists there.

PRINCE EDWARD ISLAND
AS A SUMMER RESORT

WHERE IT IS AND HOW TO GET THERE

CHAPTER 1

The Seaside Beckons

to 1905

Tourism was just getting started on Prince Edward Island in the mid-1870s, which is why it is so remarkable the Island already boasted two of the finest tourist resorts it would ever have. On Rustico Beach — today, Anglo Rustico — John Newson and family ran the Seaside Hotel. When the Seaside had opened in 1871 as the Ocean House, it was the Island's first summer-run hotel. In style the Seaside was a classic beach hotel, both simple and grand, a three-story rectangular wooden box measuring sixty feet by thirty-five. Its first floor consisted of a series of halls connected by folding doors, to be thrown open to create one large ballroom. There were twenty-one bedrooms upstairs, and a third-floor smoking room offered views out over the countryside and the Gulf of St Lawrence.[1] The Seaside also had its own wharf, where visitors were ferried out to the hotel's bathhouses on the sand hills of nearby Robinsons Island.[2] The hotel sent coaches twice-weekly to Charlottetown to pick up guests, and met every train that arrived at Hunter River station.

As well appointed as the Seaside was, the Island Park Hotel, situated on its own island in Summerside Harbour, was even grander in style and ambition.[3] James L. Holman is said to have spent the enormous sum of $80,000 constructing it in 1872, fitting it with bowling alleys, billiards rooms, croquet grounds, a carriage road around the island, and a ferry to run guests to and from Summerside. He also fitted it with 125 rooms, in an era when most Prince Edward Island hotels had fewer than a dozen.[4] In 1875, PEI's correspondent to the Toronto *Globe* reported that a considerable number of Canadian and American travellers were beginning to find their way to the Island, and the Seaside and Island Park hotels helped explain why: "We have an invigorating and bracing atmosphere with health-inspiring sea breezes, throughout the summer. Both the Rustico and Island Park watering places afford excellent opportunities for surf bathing."[5]

Figure 1.0 (facing) • The Acadia Hotel in Grand Tracadie produced this guidebook of the entire Island in 1893 and even included within it ads for other summer hotels.

Figure 1.1 ▪ The Seaside Hotel in Anglo Rustico was Prince Edward Island's premier beach resort in the late nineteenth century. "This is a beautiful place," said Canada's governor general, the Marquis of Lorne, at the end of his 1879 visit. "I am not at all surprised at its popularity – everything is so tasteful and clean."

But the fortunes of the two hotels quickly diverged. The Seaside became a mainstay of the Island's travel trade for the next generation. It was a fine hotel but not so high-priced that only the very wealthy could stay there. Yet the wealthy did stay. When Canada's governor general the Marquis of Lorne visited the province in 1879, Premier Sullivan selected the Seaside as the most suitable destination for an excursion into the countryside. When the party arrived, they ate a carnivorous bill of fare, including nine choices of meat plus lobster and chicken salads, all washed down with champagne, port, and claret.[6] On one of just a few occasions in which a Prince Edward Island scene ever adorned the *Canadian Illustrated News*, the Seaside is shown overlooking an improbably hilly landscape, with visitors strolling its grounds and boating its waters.[7] The Seaside expanded a number of times throughout the late nineteenth century, ultimately to around seventy-five rooms, becoming Prince Edward Island's premier Victorian summer resort.[8]

The Island Park Hotel was not so fortunate. It never reached full occupancy, except with mosquitoes, and in 1877 its owner died and no one stepped into the breach.[9] Just three years later, a travel writer would derisively point out "the deserted Island Park Hotel and grounds, where $50,000 were

expended by an enterprising man on permanent improvements that can now be purchased for $10,000."[10] The hotel lived on only in guidebooks that throughout the next decade continued to recommend it. As late as 1900, the Baedeker Guide thought it necessary when discussing Summerside to add, "The large summer-hotel on an island in the harbour has been long closed."[11] When American travel writer S.G.W. Benjamin visited the once-majestic hotel in 1885, he could say only that "standing on the islet, empty and deserted, [it] adds a tinge of dreariness to an otherwise pleasing picture."[12] To a travel writer such as him, the moral of the Island Park story was not that it was possible to overextend into the burgeoning tourism industry but that Islanders had not yet extended enough.

Two Prince Edward Island resort hotels, born at the same time, both relying on summer traffic to the sea. One a swift failure, one a steady success. Yet the *Globe* writer who discussed them in 1875 was not wrong to place them on equal footing because, at that moment, that is what they were. Destinations are not destined; their fortunes are contingent, and on factors too numerous to determine let alone predict. Nothing made the Seaside's success or the Island Park's failure inevitable, but once these began to occur, they helped

Figure 1.2 ▪ In 1873, local entrepreneur James L. Holman opened the Island Park Hotel on a small island in Summerside Harbour. He may have overestimated Prince Edward Island's tourism potential. After his sudden death in 1877 no one was willing to take on the hotel, although its imminent reopening was announced several times. Before it finally burned down in 1904, the R.T. Holman family used the 125-room hotel as the Island's largest summer home. The photograph here dates from 1890.

The Seaside Beckons

set the boundaries of what might follow. The Seaside, for example, helped solidify the North Shore beaches as the focus of the Island's tourist trade, with Rustico its heart. As early as 1880, Island MP Frederick Brecken stood in Parliament to ask that a branch line of the PEI Railway be built from Hunter River, seeing that "Rustico and vicinity are rapidly becoming favourite resorts, owing to the health-giving and invigorating climate, affording also the luxury of sea-bathing to an extent not surpassed by any place in the Dominion."[13] Cavendish's proximity to Rustico in turn helped it displace its neighbour as the heart of Prince Edward Island tourism in the 1910s. By comparison, as Holman's Island reverted back into spruce, Summerside made no inroads at becoming a leading resort destination again.

So it is worth understanding what drew early tourists to Prince Edward Island and Islanders to tourism – which paths were chosen, which rejected – as a first step to determining how those paths have travelled down to today. This chapter examines the Island's summer trade from its hazy beginnings to 1905. It traces how tourism emerged in the mid-nineteenth century, aided by the simultaneous growth of the North American population, a middle class, and leisure time, as well as improved transportation. It then explores early travel literature, much of it American, which introduced tourists to the Island while simultaneously teaching Islanders how they were perceived and how they might adapt to suit tourists' needs. The Island embodied it, so writers described it, so tourists expected it, so operators provided it, so the Island embodied it – the wheel kept turning, until it was impossible to remember what had started it turning and to imagine what the Island would have been like without it.

While the chapter highlights the outsized significance in this history of American visitors both real and notional (as their appearance a few times already in this narrative attests), it also shows that by the end of the nineteenth century PEI was also beginning to realize the tourist value of expatriate Islanders – many of them Americans. Outmigration had created ambassadors for the province as well as a potential market returning home for visits. (The critical role that "intramural" tourists – Islanders travelling the Island – played in supporting fledgling resorts and restaurants went entirely unnoticed.) The year 1905, then, stands as both culmination and turning point to the opening era of PEI's tourism history. The staging of the first provincial Old Home Week signalled a recognition of how important expatriates and other outsiders had become to the Island's society and economy, while the creation of a provincial tourist association suggested Islanders' growing desire to control the trade's fate for themselves and not leave their destination to destiny.

Pinpointing the dawn of tourism is a mug's game. As soon as one dates it to an early resort, attraction, or tourist association you realize there were antecedent tourists who helped justify the establishment of those things in the first place. When the Fathers of Confederation visited Prince Edward Island's north shore in 1864, they were following what was already clearly a well-worn path. There is mention of a few souls "travelling for pleasure" in 1851.[14] As early as 1840, a Charlottetown newspaper spoke of the need of a hotel to accommodate "the influx of strangers who visit the island in pursuit of business or amusement and which may be expected greatly to increase."[15] Precursor yields precursor, and soon politicians' references to sixteenth-century explorer Jacques Cartier as Prince Edward Island's "first tourist" begin to sound almost plausible.[16] But although there has likely been the occasional traveller visiting the Island for pleasure for as long as there has been an Island, they were for the longest time few in number, attracted little attention, and left little mark.

The birth of tourism on Prince Edward Island required first the birth of tourism. The trade began to achieve something of a critical mass first in Great Britain and then across the Western world in the first half of the nineteenth century, not coincidentally during the glowing heart of the Industrial Revolution. The new machine- and factory-based form of industry separated the workplace from home life and work time from leisure time. It encouraged urbanization, improved wages, and resulted in the rise of a working class, which all allowed for more social mobility. Industrialization also ran on steam engine technology that was soon used in the development of railways and steamships, which allowed for more spatial mobility. In short, the Industrial Revolution provided the means, motive, and opportunity for tourism. Add to that a Romantic movement that taught an affinity for nature – including, of relevance to Prince Edward Island's story, for the sea – and the result was increasing travel for leisure purposes. In Britain, Thomas Cook's spectacular success in launching a travel agency and then package tours and then guidebooks, all in the 1840s, is often seen as heralding a new industry there.[17] In North America, tourism's rise was more gradual, more distributed, but no less apparent. Whereas in the 1820s the wealthy were already speaking of an "American Grand Tour" modelled on the European one, by the 1850s the term was passé precisely because there was no longer a single "tour": travellers seemed to be spreading everywhere.[18]

The conditions for Prince Edward Island tourism started to coalesce in the first half of the nineteenth century, well before tourists themselves arrived.

Perhaps most importantly, the potential market grew: the population of British North America and the United States quintupled in that half century and tripled again in the next. The Island also became better known and more accessible to the outside world. Beginning in the 1830s, there was regular steamship service between it and the adjacent mainland, which linked with stage lines to Saint John and Halifax, which in turn linked by steamer to New England and Canada.[19] The same decade also saw New England mackerel fishers plying their trade in Island waters and landing at Island ports. These were hardly tourists in the traditional sense – although 1,500 American fishermen did come ashore at Malpeque for an agricultural fair in 1851 – but they deepened "the Boston States'" connections with the colony.[20] More steamship lines in the 1850s connecting New England to Quebec by way of the Maritimes opened up the possibility of summer traffic even more.[21]

By midcentury there were the first rumblings that a few tourists were finding their way to the Island and that, with a little effort, more might come. *Haszard's Gazette* stated in 1856, "We are perfectly satisfied that if the public in the adjoining provinces and ... the United States were convinced, that they could rely on punctuality coming to, and returning from the Island, it would operate as an inducement to great numbers to make the trip. And when once the purity of the atmosphere and the beauty and variety of the landscapes, the cheapness of living, and the facilities for sea-bathing came to be thoroughly known, the Island would become a favourite watering place with those whom pleasure or the quest of health induce to travel."[22] The American consul in Charlottetown confirmed this assessment, telling his Washington superior that once transportation routes became better known between the United States and the Island, "I will venture to say that our citizens can come here and spend three months in summer in as pleasant and healthy a country as exists in any part of the world."[23] Others on the Island began to anticipate this, too. With "our climate, water, beaches, roads, &c.," *Ross's Weekly* argued in 1864, "We believe that PE Island will yet become a 'watering place' and be yearly visited by hundreds, if not thousands, of the better-class inhabitants of the cities of the Atlantic States of the American Union."[24] But such references to tourism were exceedingly rare, almost as rare as tourists themselves. The judgment by British writer, naturalist, and explorer – and tourist – Isabella Bird in 1856, that Prince Edward Island "has not been tourist-ridden, like Canada or the States, and is a *terra incognita* to many," was undoubtedly an accurate one.[25]

The earliest instance we have found of Islanders providing a service that seems aimed at tourists are two advertisements by William and George Bovyer in 1852. That July, the two publicized a "House of Entertainment" in Covehead (see figure 1.3), and the following month William ran a longer ad

22

The Summer Trade

Figure 1.3 ▪ William and George Bovyer's 1852 advertisement is a very early example of a notice directed at the summer trade and listing the seaside attractions the Island had to offer. Notably, it is directed first and foremost to Prince Edward Islanders themselves.

Sea-side Establishment.

THE undersigned having just completed building and furnishing a new HOUSE OF ENTERTAINMENT at Cove Head, on the North Coast of this Island, are ready to accommodate visitors desiring to remain there for a time, or making merely a day visit. The situation is very beautiful, on a fine open sea and beach, which, with the advantages of sea-bathing it affords, renders it a very pleasant retreat in the summer season. Pic Nic and other Parties also accommodated. As this is the first enterprize of the kind in that neighborhood, the Subscribers hope to meet with encouragement from the Inhabitants of the Island in general.
WILLIAM BOVYER.
GEORGE BOVYER.

Cove Head, July 19, 1852.

about a "Cottage" for pleasure-seekers in Stanhope – "the first enterprise of the kind, that has ever been established in this part of the Island." That the Bovyers boasted explicitly of being the first to accommodate this market gives them even greater claim to primacy in the summer trade. "The facilities for sea bathing, shooting, fishing, cricket games, and other amusements, cannot be surpassed," William wrote. "A most beautiful and expansive sheet of Water lies open to its view, where may be seen the stately and gallant ship, passing by with all the pride imaginable, and on every side may be seen reposing on its glassy bosom, the white flowing sails of the beautiful American schooners, together with many other charms which orender [sic] it the most delightful retreat that can be found any where on the Island." But as attractive as Bovyer's cottage might have been to tourists, his advertisement was aimed directly at "the Ladies and Gentleman of Charlottetown," not off-Islanders.[26] These were certainly tourists of a sort – ones who were crucial, we will argue, in their support of the nascent tourist trade – yet the fact that Bovyer did not even mention the possibility of customers from away is striking. In any case, the Bovyers never advertised their enterprises again, suggesting either that their ventures were unsuccessful or so successful with return Island customers that they no longer needed to be promoted.

A few Islanders slowly waded into the travel trade in the 1860s. The family of Neil Shaw of Brackley is generally credited with opening the first tourism establishment on Prince Edward Island, having started taking summer guests on their family farm in 1860; today, Shaw's Hotel is the oldest family-owned hotel in Canada.[27] But as a business it started slowly, and in its early days was likely not an inspiration to other Islanders. In 1866, John C. Keefe launched the Commercial House in Alberton with advertisements that, while not mentioning off-Island tourists explicitly, certainly seem directed at them: "Ho! Ye

Figure 1.4 ▪ The gradual transition from farm home to summer resort is nowhere better illustrated than in Shaw's Hotel at Brackley. Neil Shaw began taking summer guests in the 1860s and by 1890, when this photo was taken, had added a three-storey mansard-roofed wing. Shaw's is still in business, the oldest family-owned hotel in Canada.

who wish to leave the heat and dust of cities! Come where the air is pure and bracing! Come where you'll get good bathing! Come where you'll have fishing and shooting in plenty! Come where you can find an appetite before breakfast!" Keefe not only explained where Alberton was, he located it in reference to "the centre of the Mackerel Fishing Grounds," which was in that era awash in American fishers.[28]

This is a useful reminder that Island tourism has always been shaped by events having little to do with tourism or the Island. For example, the 1857 extension of the European and North American Railway from Saint John to Pointe-du-Chêne, near Shediac, and the 1867 extension of the Nova Scotia Railway to Pictou made it much easier for summer travellers to reach Prince Edward Island from the Maritimes and New England, without those railways being built expressly for that purpose.[29] And, of course, just as the US Civil War undoubtedly discouraged Island tourism in the early 1860s, Canadian Confederation in 1867 probably encouraged it.

John Nelson's 1871 opening of the Ocean House in Rustico – sold three years later to John Newson and renamed the Seaside Hotel – may be said to herald the real birth of the Island's tourist trade. Nelson was a Charlottetown hotelier formerly of Gloucester, Massachusetts, itself a popular coastal resort area, who apparently had a keen sense of what upscale summer travellers of the day were seeking.[30] The Ocean House/Seaside was, if not lavish, substantial enough to satisfy the resort traveller, and its beaches were first-rate. Just two years after the hotel's opening, a Halifax newspaper reported that "All of this season the 'Ocean House' has been crowded with visitors from abroad."[31] It swiftly became PEI's foremost summer hotel, even more so after the failure of the Island Park in Summerside.

In 1878, the *Patriot* ran a feature on the Seaside, unusual in its detail. The newspaper called it "the favorite resort, not of the pleasure-seeker only, but also of the more sober, earnest and thoughtful men of business, farmers, and others who can afford to spend a day or two from their offices, farms, or counting-houses for purposes of recreation" – underscoring once again the importance of Island tourists to the early Island tourism trade. The article described the Seaside's garden, its lawn for croquet and other games, its pleasant walks, its broad veranda with easy chairs overlooking the gulf, and its "waiters and attendants, both in-doors and on the outer premises … selected with great judgment by the proprietor." In an exceptionally rare move, the reporter even laid out what a Victorian bather looked for in an Island beach, describing the hotel's bathing grounds on nearby Robinsons Island in great detail:

On the seaward side, the furious beating of the surf is destructive to vegetation, and nothing greets the eye but a sloping wall of pure silicious glistening granules all along the ridge, and along the shore to low water mark. Here is the bathers' paradise. The shore bed feels as soft and grateful to the naked foot as Brussels carpet, and is yet sufficiently firm to resist the weight of the heaviest body. An indentation of half an inch or so in the sand is all the impression that remains, and that but for a moment, to mark the course of the acquatic [*sic*] sportsman. The waters are pure and limpid and when their surface is rippled by a gentle surf, the operation of bathing here must be experienced in order to convey an adequate idea of the pleasurable sensation it affords.

The writer then matter-of-factly recounted how a young visitor to the Seaside had drowned there earlier in the month.[32] It is a jarring reminder to the modern reader that many if not most Victorians did not swim and that they were drawn to the seashore for other reasons. Prince Edward Island was attractive for more than just its beaches per se. It had miles and miles of sandy beach for walking, cliffs for viewing, healthy sea air to breathe in, and cool, bracing water to bathe in.

The Seaside was both a measure of the Prince Edward Island tourist trade having reached a certain level and an inspiration for more businesses like it. Even at the hotel's 1871 launch, a Charlottetown newspaper noted that "Farmers residing on the North Shore, who have comfortable residences, and would be disposed to accommodate, during the summer season, tourists seeking the cool air and sea bathing, &c., of the Island, would, no doubt, find lots of applicants."[33] Later that decade, the *Patriot* reported that in Stanhope alone, "Messrs. Leich [John C. Leitch, owner of the Glencourse], Shaw [Neil Shaw, whose home by this point could accommodate ten families], and [?] Auld have been 'receiving' tourists and health seekers from the States and Canada for years past. David Carr, this season, advertises for a share of this patronage. We think the accommodation will always keep pace with the demand. Mr. Angus McMillan has extended his domicile [renaming it the Point Pleasant Hotel] so that he can now take in and board some 25 people."[34]

By the publication of *Meacham's Atlas* in 1880, there were expensive advertisements for a number of seasonal accommodations along the north shore: Lorne Summer Hotel on Tracadie Beach (its name perhaps inspired by the Marquis of Lorne's visit to PEI in 1879), North Shore House in Princetown, Seaside Hotel in Rustico, Neil McCallum's in Brackley Point, Glencourse Summer Resort, and Point Pleasant Summer Hotel in Stanhope. None of these had existed a decade earlier. That John Newson was moonlighting from his profession as cabinetmaker to run the Seaside signals how tourism was originally taken up – and, in many cases, still is – by Prince Edward Islanders. All of the lodgings advertised in *Meacham's* were run part-time; the popular Lorne and Point Pleasant hotels, for example, were both owned by farmers.[35] And these were the more-established businesses; there were almost certainly other farm homes taking in summertime guests, such as Shaw's in its early days, which did not advertise in *Meacham's Atlas* or anywhere else. As a result, they left little trace, their number and influence in the growth of early tourism impossible to gauge.

But even as good tourist lodgings were popping up along the north shore, hotels in Charlottetown, the Island's premier port of call, were universally criticized as being inadequate in number and wanting in quality. The inability of the Fathers of Confederation to find lodging in Charlottetown in September 1864 was in part because the circus was in town but fundamentally because the capital was woefully short of accommodations. The situation did not improve in the years that followed. One writer arriving in Charlottetown "received a palpable corroboration of the statement made to me on the journey, that there was not a comfortable hotel in the place," while another called

26

The Summer Trade

Figure 1.5 ▪ A windblown beach scene at Tracadie, from American travel writer S.G.W. Benjamin's *Cruise of the Alice May* (1885).

the town's hotels small, mean, and expensive, chiding that "this is not the way to attract tourists to go that distance from home."[36] Visitors were known to hop off steamers, look fruitlessly for lodging, and hop back on.[37] But critics ignored the fact that Charlottetown hotels had been built largely to cater to an entirely different clientele: rural Islanders seeking cheap lodgings when they had to stay overnight in the capital for business or to coordinate with train or ship schedules. Such hotels could not simply expand to accommodate summer travellers without expecting the rooms to sit idle much of the year save for the occasional commercial traveller. A seasonal seaside resort, by comparison, could thrive on a correspondingly lower investment. Beyond that, the lure of a summer holiday by the sea made all the difference. Time and time again throughout the nineteenth century, commentators lamented the lack of first-class Charlottetown hotels but predicted they would soon be built and that when they were, Prince Edward Island would be one of the foremost summer destinations on the continent.[38]

Figure 1.6 ▪ A page from the Seaside Hotel guest register for 1875. Note that the preponderance of visitors are from Prince Edward Island and the Maritimes, although there are also guests from Quebec and England. And from Boston, travel writer S.G.W. Benjamin.

28

The Summer Trade

All that is left of the Seaside Hotel today is its brown leather guest register, now residing in the provincial archives. Used for almost all of the hotel's twenty-eight summers, it is filled with thousands upon thousands of signatures. Some, likely all, have their stories. Beside the signature of "Capt. E.A. Walsh & wife," there is a note in the proprietor's hand: "A fraud detected." Bored staff doodled their own names over and over. Cheeky locals claimed to be "Dicky Redhead" or "George Boarder – hit him with a boarde – Rusty Co."[39]

And on 5 September 1875 there is "S.G. Wheeler Benjamin Boston, U.S.A." Benjamin was an American travel writer visiting the Island as research for a piece that would eventually appear in *Harper's Magazine*. His review of the Seaside would be favourable – "although the rooms are small, they are neat, cheerful, and clean, and the table is excellent" – as would his assessment of the Island overall. In fact, he ended up devoting a chapter to the province in his paean to islands, *The Atlantic Islands as Resorts of Health and Pleasure* (1878), concluding that it "in point of scenery, and equability, and moderation of temperature, is surpassed by no other island on the American coast as a summer resort."[40]

But perhaps Benjamin's opinion of the Island didn't matter so much as the fact that he gave one. In a 1911 Boston *Sunday Globe*, Thomas F. Anderson recounted the ongoing debate as to whether Cabot or Cartier had discovered PEI but concluded that "The real discoverer of Prince Edward Island was that intrepid explorer of a later date, Charles Dudley Warner."[41] Warner was an American travel writer who in his 1874 *Baddeck and That Sort of Thing* had introduced his countrymen to a little-known world, the Maritime provinces of Canada. Anderson, himself a travel writer, knew that his fellow "intrepid explorer" had written about the Island but either forgot or thought it irrelevant that Warner had been unimpressed with it, dismissing its landscape as "flat from end to end as a floor" and stating that the capital Charlottetown had "the appearance of a place from which something has departed."[42] Anderson knew that all publicity was good publicity.

It was certainly good for Prince Edward Island. The nineteenth century saw the blossoming of travel literature across the Western world, both to support the blossoming tourist trade and to allow armchair travellers the vicarious enjoyment of other lands.[43] Travel writers visited Prince Edward Island from Great Britain and Canada, but more came from the United States. A booming magazine industry there allowed freelance writers the opportunity to travel, tell of what they saw, have their work published in serial form, and in time perhaps turn this into a book. The industry did not exist at nearly the same scale in Canada nor was the Island as novel to Canadians as Americans, while few British writers made the side-trip to PEI when touring North America. And since Islanders were already fascinated by the United States, accounts from the Great Republic were not only the most numerous but also the most heeded.

Travel literature provides a snapshot of what tourism to Prince Edward Island was like in its earliest, purest form – before the province began actively shaping its image. But more than this, the literature itself affected tourism in two distinct ways. Most directly, articles in newspapers, magazines, and books publicized the province to millions of readers who might otherwise not have known of its existence. Since the demographics of those who read for pleasure and those who travelled for pleasure closely overlapped, there can be little doubt that these accounts attracted some of the earliest tourists to PEI. But travel literature was also a mirror in which Islanders enjoyed looking at themselves. Island newspapers were sure to reprint passages or full articles that spoke good or ill of the province. Here could be found judgments of the Island's landscape, economy, towns, and society made by ostensibly unbiased observers. (Of course, they *were* biased: by their preformed expectations, their necessarily hurried grasp and the chance nature of what they experienced on the Island, and their entrenched ideas as to what a tourist destination should be.) Travel accounts thus helped Islanders understand what outsiders hoped to find there and what might be done to make sure they found it.[44]

Prince Edward Island was not alone as either a subject for travel literature or a place of growing interest to tourists, of course. As James Doyle states in *Yankees in Canada*, "the nineteenth century appears to have been the great age of American imaginative interest in Canada."[45] A growing network of ships and trains was making Canada's distant reaches more accessible but had not yet brought the homogenization of North American society. Canada of the late nineteenth century was still very much a foreign land to Americans: more British, more French, and less industrialized. It was a fisherman's delight, a hunter's heaven, a wild frontier for which Americans were already becoming nostalgic. And, as many visitors noted, it was pleasantly cool in the summer. Canada was beginning to be interested in attracting tourists, and the Maritimes in particular faced many of the same issues as PEI: insufficient and unsatisfactory accommodations, being relatively out of the way, spotty transportation links, and a perceived lack of go-gettingness.

But the Island had one thing that set it apart for tourists: it was an island. The sea defined Prince Edward Island far better than any manmade boundary ever could and made it particularly coherent as a destination. An island guaranteed otherness; to visit one meant to give up one world for another, with the intermediate sea voyage a sort of decompression chamber.[46]

All visiting travel writers were sure to describe their approach to the Island and their initial impression of it. Charles Dudley Warner, for one, found it surprisingly welcoming, that it "has a pleasing aspect, and nothing of that remote friendlessness which its appearance on the map conveys to one."[47] He seemed almost disappointed that the Island was not as aloof as he had imagined. For others, arrival had an otherworldly quality. Benjamin wrote, "We were surrounded by the red cliffs of Governor's, St. Peter's, and Prince Edward Islands, mirrored on the glassy surface of the water with absolute fidelity, or half lifted in the air by a partial mirage. Here and there a schooner lay idly over the quivering reflection of its own spars and sails. Overhead the sky was cloudless azure ... and no sound disturbed the magical stillness of this peaceful scene but the far-reaching quavering cry of the loon throbbing over the water."[48] There were no people or even landscape to spoil the image: the Island existed only in relationship with the water surrounding it.

Not surprisingly, travel writers were sure to describe the Island's weather. "Genial," "moderate," and "equable" were the sort of adjectives they chose, words that assured readers that the Island's climate was almost immoderately moderate.[49] Calm was called for because what motivated much North American seaside travel of the time was a panicked desire to flee the unhealthy air of overcrowded, industrialized cities, in an age when medical science believed diseases were spread by "miasmas" or bad air.[50] As early as 1868, the Summerside *Journal* would base the Island's potential as a tourist destination on its ability to attract city dwellers "all eager to exchange the pestilential air which issues from the back slums and overcrowded alleys, together with other unwelcome arrangements too frequently met with in the city, for the green fields and an invigorating atmosphere."[51] A Boston newspaper in 1873 essentially agreed, noting that one of Prince Edward Island's great advantages was "its summer climate, too delicious to be described, nearly hot, never chilly, never foggy, always soft, healthful and strength-giving. No epidemic has ever been known in the Island, except the epidemic of monstrous chignons, which still rages frightfully."[52] At the turn of the century, a trainload of American travellers would be described as "fleeing to Prince Edward Island to escape the heat which was terrifying the inhabitants of the larger American cities."[53]

The Island's pure ocean air was not just for avoiding sickness but for becoming well. Introducing Prince Edward Island in his *Atlantic Islands as Resorts of Health and Pleasure*, for example, Benjamin wrote of "the manifold attractions it offers to the tourist and invalid."[54] Islanders themselves believed this or at least believed that tourists believed it. As early as 1866, John C. Keefe was already advertising his Commercial Hotel as having air that was "always COOL AND BRACING, and has a peculiarly beneficial effect upon Consumptives, restoring them to health and vigor in a short time."[55] A later travel brochure would likewise describe the province as "notable as a health spot, surrounded as it is by ocean and strait ... Its breezes are nothing but pure ones, bearing all of the healthful tonic and ozone of old ocean itself."[56] While such testimonials complimented the entire province, they drove tourists towards the coast. As evidence that sea air was thought the healthiest – and city air unhealthy no matter how small the city – the first guest in Shaw's Hotel is said to have been a sick child from Charlottetown who stayed the summer to be cured.[57]

Such were the benefits of Prince Edward Island – in summer. In *Picturesque Canada*, Rev. R. Murray concluded his essay on the Island by saying explicitly, "We advise our readers to visit this garden of the Sea Provinces in summer," but generally it was assumed that no one would try visiting at any other time of year.[58] Nevertheless, the province's winter isolation was put to best advantage in travel literature. Accounts invariably included engravings and lengthy descriptions of the small iceboats that carried mail and passengers through the ice floes of the Northumberland Strait. Many writers continued to speak of these boats as if they were the sole means of traversing the strait even after the introduction of icebreaker service once Prince Edward Island joined Confederation in 1873. (Although the icebreaker service was so inadequate they might be pardoned that assumption. Early twentieth-century postcards abound in images of iceboat crossings and winter steamers imprisoned in ice.) Presenting Islanders as icebound, isolated folk gave them a certain romance, one that travel writers may well have felt they needed. "Think of a civilized and enlightened people," Benjamin wrote, "in this age, shut off from the rest of the world by such a frightful siege of ice and tempest and snow! ... Were it not for this drawback, the Island might be a paradise."[59] It is strange to read travel writers' fascination with a scene they neither experienced for themselves nor intended their audience to. The only awesome spectacle that PEI offered the reader, of man doing battle with nature on the ice, had by the tourist season long since melted away. For those seeking a pulse-quickening confrontation with nature's sublime power – the feelings that a pilgrimage to the Alps or Niagara Falls could raise – there was little about PEI to inspire, and so the world-renowned Baedeker Guide could dismiss its landscape in a sentence: "It scenery is hardly of a nature to repay a veteran traveller."[60]

Instead, the Island offered pastoral scenery that was "natural," pretty, serene, and unthreatening, the very embodiment of the picturesque landscape aesthetic. Indeed, *Picturesque Canada*'s Murray was the most demonstrative in praise of this landscape, gushing that "The face of the country is gently undulating, like a sea which has sobbed itself to rest, but has some remembrance still of a far-off storm. These low-lying hills which rib the country from north

Figure 1.7 ▪ Nature as pastoral: the Island countryside, engraved for *Picturesque Canada* (1882). The pleasing blend of rolling hills, farm fields, stream, and ocean was already a part of the province's tourism signature.

The Seaside Beckons

to south are but the slumbering waves of that quiet sea."[61] The Island was even picturesque in the strict sense of the word – fit to be painted. "Nowhere very striking," Benjamin decided, the scenery was "charmingly rural and picturesque, everywhere pleasing, and offering quiet little bits that the artistic eye might transfer effectively to canvas."[62] Everything was picture perfect. In Murray's words, "No mountain, no stubborn hills nor barren wilderness, no stony land nigh unto cursing, no desolate heath" marred the view.[63] Admittedly, there was a slippery slope beyond which Prince Edward Island's lack of slopes became a detriment, that the pretty and serene became the banal, and some travel writers believed its landscape slid past that point. Charles Dudley Warner's line that the Island was as flat as a floor was, in landscape aesthetic terms, the most damning of judgments.[64]

Prince Edward Island could be described as an idyllic pastoral land largely because of, well, pastureland: fields with livestock grazing on them.[65] But farming was treated in travel writing not as an industry, let alone a leading industry in the province, but simply as evidence of how richly the province had been blessed. By at least the 1870s, Prince Edward Island was routinely being called a garden, particularly "the Garden of Canada" or "the Garden of the Gulf," a nickname it has retained. But it was nowhere evident in the literature that farmers had created and cultivated this garden or that the landscape was as it was for anything but the tourist's pleasure. In this way, neither the Island nor Islanders were fully realized characters in works that were ostensibly about them.

Many travel writers shared the sentiment of W. Fraser Rae, who in *Newfoundland to Manitoba* stated that "In traversing this Island and visiting the private houses and living in the hotels, one is pleasantly reminded of the Old World; there is not much bustle and there is much more comfort."[66] Where in the old world didn't much matter. After crossing the province by carriage, an American author wrote, "Peasant life in France was suggested by the farm scenes that met our eyes almost the entire distance."[67] But more compared Prince Edward Island to Great Britain. Benjamin wrote of farmland "resembling some of the most beautiful portions of Old England,"[68] whereas Murray weighed in that "Not Ireland itself is clad in richer green than our lovely Island when summer has bestowed on it the crown of glory."[69]

Such comparisons were convenient shorthand for writers, allowing them to describe one place in terms of another with which readers were already familiar, whether by experience or reputation. Put cynically, they turned PEI into a relatively inexpensive, relatively accessible knock-off for tourists. Put more favourably, they granted PEI an ethereal, bygone quality, as the term "old world" suggests. Of course, there was a reason why the Island could stand in for the old world: it had experienced little of the industrialization that had blighted the old world's landscape. S.E. Dawson proclaimed that "Prince Edward Island is an Arcadian province without manufactures – the ideal country of Mr. Ruskin, where no tall chimneys vomit soot and blacken the herbage."[70] Or as John Rowan wrote in *The Emigrant and Sportsman in Canada* (as its name implies, more than strictly a travel book), Prince Edward Island was like England but "not indeed an England of to-day, with its numerous smoky cities and enormous wealth, but an England where wealth is evenly distributed, or rather where there is no great wealth, but universal competence."[71] Authors were not above idealizing the Britain of yesteryear in the act of idealizing the Prince Edward Island of the day.

It took just a small step to equate this Arcadia with the Acadia made famous in Longfellow's 1847 poem "Evangeline: A Tale of Acadie," which offered a romantic telling of the Acadian deportation. Though the late nineteenth-century cult of Evangeline was centred in Grand Pré, Nova Scotia,[72] PEI received substantial overflow interest. The removal of the consonant was explicitly performed when writer Moses Sweetser's description of the Island as "a sort of Arcadia, in which Shenstone would have delighted" was recycled by Withrow as "a sort of Acadia, in which Shenstone would have delighted."[73] But more often, authors settled for calling to mind "Evangeline" by referring to woods on the Island as "the forest primeval," a phrase made famous in Longfellow's first line.[74] Surprisingly, travel writers of this era seldom drew attention to the Acadian people actually living on the Island.

As much as tourists might have wished it, they could not be transported directly to the rustic charms of rural Prince Edward Island. Charlottetown and Summerside were discussed in travel literature almost by default, since it was at these two main towns that travellers would arrive and first seek accommodation. But if these towns were all the Island had to offer, few visitors would have been encouraged to go. As part of his generally underwhelmed account of Prince Edward Island, Warner dismissed Charlottetown as "a wooden town, with wide and vacant streets, the air of waiting for something." The drabness was, to his mind, as much a reflection of the citizens' laziness as their economic condition: "Tasteful residences we do not find nor that attention to flowers and gardens which the mild summer would suggest."[75] Charlottetown was constantly berated in travel literature for not trying hard enough, and would be nicknamed "Sleepy Hollow" well into the twentieth century.[76] The best that a later *promotional* brochure could say was that it "was attractive to visitors, although its pleasures and sights are soon exhausted."[77] Such dissatisfaction with the capital was almost comical, considering the purple prose with which the countryside was praised. Travel writers demanded the best of both worlds: the rural was applauded for not yet being drawn into modern life, while the urban was criticized for the same thing. An

1887 account demonstrates the contradiction. Following a lengthy criticism of Charlottetown, the author admitted, "There is, however, something quaint and taking in its appearance. It reminds one of the old parts of large towns in other countries."[78] Charlottetown could be forgiven as long as it was associated with the past, with no pretensions to modernity.

Summerside, having risen out of the shipbuilding boom of the 1860s, was by contrast thought a young, progressive town – at least at first. Tourists would land there from the steamship that linked New Brunswick to the Island and find a small town swollen with summer activity. One writer contrasted conservative Charlottetonians to Summersiders, who are "more democratic and have more of the American 'snap' about them."[79] Writing in 1878, Benjamin praised the vibrant young town, reining in his exuberance only by adding drily, "It has not grown quite as rapidly as Chicago."[80] And yet just eight years later he painted Summerside as a failed community: "It is a new place which sprang up mushroom-like, and soon threatened with its bustling prosperity to overtop every other port on the island. But its growth stopped."[81] Shipbuilding had tanked, and the failure of the Island Park Hotel was as symbolic of Summerside's fortunes in the 1880s as its creation had been in the 1870s. With the town's promise seemingly gone, travel accounts resorted entirely to pleasantries: "Summerside is pleasantly situated and has a fine harbour with numerous pleasant islands of its own" and is but "a pleasant morning walk" to the nearest beach.[82]

It was faint praise, but it was praise. Travel writers were capable of appreciating the Island's rustic rural scenery and rustic urban societies just as long as those conditions could be interpreted as the province having been bypassed by modernity – or, as it would later be formulated, having outright rejected modernity – rather than having failed at modernity. How writers assessed the Island ultimately depended on why they thought it was as it was. As a result, there could be wide disagreement as to what would seem a relatively objective standard, the Island's economic condition. An account in the New York *World*, for example, portrayed Islanders as "Rather a poor class – shiftless and ignorant Kentucks. Men, women and children work together in the fields. Some live in houses patched with mud, on barren hillsides or shelves of granite. The windows are commonly broken and the empty panes are stuffed with old hats, rolls of rags, old quilts, carpets, and bundles of all descriptions."[83] Such a vivid image was bound to discourage readers who had no way of knowing the Island has no granite or, for that matter, houses patched with mud. Yet other travel accounts of the era would say, "The people are mostly in good circumstances"; "There are no poor districts, and there is no poverty in the country places"; and "When commercial failures spread ruin over the continent, little Prince Edward Island never feels the shock, but jogs on as usual."[84]

Figure 1.8 ▪ Artist Robert Harris sketched his stay at McCallum's farm resort in Brackley in August 1894, providing a tourist's-eye view of the accommodation. The setting is conspicuously rural and restful.

Ultimately, the citizens of Prince Edward Island could be described just as their landscape and towns were, either as charming relics of a simpler, better age or as simply backward. Benjamin's descriptions of Islanders demonstrate this tension. "Of the people," he wrote following his first voyage there, "so far as personal observation goes, I can speak favourably," and "Of the hospitality of the Islanders I can speak in high terms." And yet their indifference to punctuality drove him crazy: "it will not do in this age and in the Western World ... for those who desire to rise in the world."[85] Similarly, after his second voyage to the Island, he praised "the genial hospitality of its people, especially in the kind folk of Charlottetown" – but within ten pages was complaining that, in trying to find a cook, "we were not prepared to meet such a gang of shiftless, shuffling, vacillating, prevaricating, self-complacent, exorbitant, and utterly good-for-nothing varlets as those who applied for the position, or whom we discovered after chasing through the lanes, sailors' boarding houses, and purlieus of Charlottetown."[86] They were hospitable, they were rude. They were rustic, they were backward. Lacking further details, it is hard to know what to make of Benjamin's changes of heart. His may have been a common tourist reaction: delight when strangers treat you kindly, mixed with a paranoia that they hope to gain by you.

Of course, it is the nature of tourism that the host *does* want to gain from the visitor. As tourists began to come to Prince Edward Island and travel writers to describe the experience, Islanders began to see both the potential financial value of the tourist trade and what visitors wanted and expected. In the decades that followed, Island society would take up and expand upon models that travel writers and tourists had developed.

Who were these travellers making their way to Prince Edward Island? As the many references to Americans already in this chapter indicates, Islanders expected tourists to be Americans and in practice found them to be Americans – or, at least, as shorthand labelled them all as Americans. The Island was advertised in terms of its distance from New York and Boston. Hotels ran on the American plan, with a single rate for room and meals. Travel accounts and early promotional literature compared the Island to places Americans would know, cited tourist operators' connections to the United States, and even mentioned individual Americans one might meet. The Intercolonial and PEI Railway's 1892 *Forest, Stream and Seashore*, for example, commended the Brackley Beach Hotel as being "well filled throughout the season with boarders from the United States. Close to the hotel is the well-appointed summer cottage of Mr. G.A. Crane of New York."[87] The Acadia Hotel advertised that its chef was "a normal Graduate of the famed Boston Cooking School" and that summer guests would be entertained by "A Band of Skilled Musicians from the New England Conservatory of Music."[88] Americans, this literature assured its readers, would feel right at home.

There were any number of reasons that tourism was so strongly associated with the United States. It was far and away the dominant tourist market given its proximity to Canada, had ten times the population, was more prosperous, and had a better-developed vacationing tradition. Steamship and then rail connections along the US's eastern seaboard transported the first tourists to the province, and those transportation links followed well-travelled trade and migration links between the two regions. Seaside holiday destinations spread northward along the eastern United States into Canada. The bulk of relevant travel writing – particularly that available to Islanders – was written by Americans, who quite naturally paid more attention to their brethren than to travellers from elsewhere. And, of course, many of the tourists *were* American.

But many of them were not. The Seaside Hotel's guest register offers some insight as to where late nineteenth-century tourists were coming from. The register was used every year the resort was in operation except 1890 and 1893, and visitors' place of origin was quite consistent across time. In all, 1,064 Americans are listed in the register, far more than the seventy-eight from the United Kingdom, the thirty-four from other countries, or even the 518 who came from New Brunswick and Nova Scotia. Of these Americans, 433 (41 per cent) were from Massachusetts, 262 (25 per cent) from New York, 73 (7 per cent) from Pennsylvania, with the remainder sprinkled from throughout the Union. This confirms the importance of the United States market to this style of tourism, at least.[89]

However, the register also has signatures by 620 Quebec travellers and another 608 from Ontario, meaning that the Seaside registered more guests from Central Canada than from the United States. That seems to have been representative of early Island tourism generally: although Americans got the bulk of the attention, just as many or more visitors came from Ontario and Quebec. It would take a Canadian writing in the *Canadian Courier* early in the new century to suggest that PEI was "a summer resort both for Canadians from the other provinces and for the people of the United States … But it is fairly safe to venture an opinion that people from Montreal and Toronto outnumber all other summer residents."[90] No other contemporary writer voiced this opinion, however. American tourists' significance was out of proportion to their numbers, whereas the most prominent feature of the connection between Central Canada and the Island was its near total invisibility.

Muddying the waters further, some of those who signed the Seaside register as coming from away were undoubtedly returning expatriate Islanders. A major result and cause of the Island's economic hardship in the late nineteenth century, brought on by a limited resource base set against a healthy birthrate, was the exodus of its citizens. The population rose from 81,000 in 1861 to 109,000 in 1881 before stalling, and then began to drop steadily, so that by 1931 there were only 88,000 living on the Island.[91] These numbers actually underplay the scale of emigration, since they are offset by a measure of immigration and by a birth rate that exceeded the death rate. The net loss by migration was 7,000 in the 1870s, 12,000 in the 1880s, and 14,000 in the 1890s; essentially, within a generation, about one-third of Islanders moved away.[92] While some located across Canada, more than three-quarters ended up in the United States, the majority of those in New England, the majority of *those* in Massachusetts.[93] Easily accessible and with a long history of connections, "Boston is the promised land of Canadians in general, and Prince Edward Islanders in particular," in the words of one expatriate.[94] Or as a Boston journalist wrote in a travel account about the province, the name "Prince Edward Island is likely to suggest potatoes, horses, and capable and good-looking servant girls."[95]

Islanders living away retained strong ties to the home place. This can be seen most clearly in the pages of *The Maple Leaf* magazine, a California-based monthly that began publication in 1907. *The Maple Leaf* was written for, by, and about ex-Maritimers, but because it was created and edited by the Island-born journalist Michael A. McInnis, it had an inordinate amount of PEI content and consequently a strong PEI readership.[96] The magazine makes plain that many expatriates were not just remembering their roots, they were returning to them, making pilgrimages back in the summertime. There are countless articles from contributors detailing return visits to the Island, describing the tranquility and "evidence of prosperity" (a recurring phrase) that they found, and listing the many folks they saw – all of whom, it would seem, remembered them fondly and vividly.[97] Since *The Maple Leaf* relied on contributors and subscribers who had particularly strong ties to home, it can hardly be called representative of the expatriate experience. Nonetheless, it documents the existence of a community of Islanders who were not only ambassadors for the province throughout North American but also themselves summer visitors to it.

But returning Islanders were often not considered *real* tourists – and likely would not want to be considered such. When an 1885 writer described a ride on the PEI Railway filled with "tourists, and many natives coming home to visit," he was making a common distinction.[98] The expatriates were visitors and they mattered to the summer trade, but their reasons for coming were more familial than touristic. The irony is that although expatriates helped kick-start the budding Island tourist trade, that very fact would for decades keep many Islanders from taking the trade seriously.[99] Expatriates were advertising in two directions: the mere fact that ex-Islanders were not returning to PEI for good highlighted that they were ambassadors for their new homes as well as their old. Expatriate tourism likely encouraged the creation of more expatriates, weakening the Island's economy and society further, even while simultaneously strengthening it.

Canadian tourists to PEI may have been undervalued compared to Americans, and expatriates compared to first-time visitors, but at least they were seen as *having* value. Not so Prince Edward Islanders, whose participation as vacationers and recreationists was likely critical to the first tourism establishments getting off the ground but was utterly taken for granted. Whereas 1,064 Americans and 1,228 Central Canadians show up in the Seaside Hotel's guest register, 3,366 Prince Edward Islanders appear – more than from everywhere else put together. In some cases, these were well-off Charlottetonians and Summersiders who summered there. In others, they were likely local overnighters enjoying what we would now call a staycation and helping to support the hotel's occupancy rate in the process. In still other cases, they were out for a Sunday afternoon drive, enjoying a bite to eat at the Seaside's dining room along the way, and so diversifying the hotel's revenue. Since travel writers were from away and Island boosters sought visitors from away, evidence of such tourism rarely exists in the archival record, but many Prince Edward Islanders undoubtedly gained their formative experiences of tourism while still on the Island, acting not as hosts but as guests.

Consider the presumably satirical "Diary of a Young Charlottetonian" published in the *Weekly Examiner* in 1881. Its chronicle of dissolute youth begins, "Sunday – Got up at 11:15 a.m., and had breakfast. Started at 12 with Harry and Jim for Beach Hotel. Arrived at 3 and had a fine swim in the surf. Played wist [*sic*] till tea time, with a Jew agent who is stopping at hotel as fourth hand … Set out for home at seven o'clock, and reached town at 10. I think Jim took too much refreshments at the hotel as he didn't drive very steady." The week ends much as it began: "Saturday – … Me and Jim and Harry hired a horse and buggy and started off to Beach Hotel, where we will stop over Sunday for a good time. There are some nice looking girls there, but they are too stiff for me, they ain't like town girls."[100] Just a decade after the first beach resort had sprung up, tourism was already associated with – depending on your point of view – debauchery or fun, to be experienced as much by Islanders as by visitors from away.

The "Young Charlottetonian" may have been drawn to the seashore by another characteristic of early tourism's demography: the majority of travellers

Figure 1.9 ▪ These snapshots at Mutch's Hotel (1897) and nearby Cliff Hotel (1896), both in Stanhope, remind us that the majority of early tourists to PEI were women: travelling with female friends or relatives, or taking the children while husbands stayed at work.

were women. Beach tourism such as PEI offered was associated with repose, convalescence, and childcare, which were all associated with women's sphere. (And since "mixed swimming" was denounced in the nineteenth century, the separate spheres persisted right down to the shore.) Some women came to the seaside with female friends or relatives, while others took the children to the seaside as husbands stayed at work. Some travellers brought female help; the twentieth century Keppoch Beach Hotel is remembered for having tiny adjoining bedrooms for nannies. The Seaside guest register does contain more male than female names, because many male heads-of-household signed on behalf of their family, but it is striking just how many hundreds of "Miss" and "Mrs" – and, in a few cases, "nurse" – there are.[101] It may well be that the majority of Islanders vacationing was also female. An American writer told of visiting the Lorne Hotel in Tracadie Bay in 1885, for example, and finding the house "pretty well filled with about sixty guests, mostly ladies, many from Charlottetown."[102] But if women made up the majority of tourists in the nineteenth century, they were never – not once – singled out by travel writers or later promotional literature. The couple and the family were assumed to be the standard units of travel.

Tourism slowly gained a foothold in Prince Edward Island life. By the mid-1880s, it was already something of a tradition for Charlottetown newspapers to run an end-of-summer debriefing on the tourist season – reporting one good season after another, yet still finding sufficient novelty in the trade to keep treating its existence as newsworthy.[103] Increased knowledge of the Island via travel writing was one reason for the rise in tourist numbers. Another was that seaside resorts in the Maritimes were much cheaper than American ones – "very much less than half," in the words of a Canadian magazine in 1894.[104] Improved transportation to and within the Island was yet another. A steamer had made the first direct runs between Boston and Charlottetown in 1865.[105] The travel time between Halifax and Charlottetown shrank to twelve hours and then eight.[106] And although Confederation-era Premier James C. Pope's confident prediction that the new railway across the province would increase American tourist traffic by £300,000 each year had most certainly not come to pass, travellers' ability to explore the whole Island was easier and faster than ever before.[107]

Nevertheless, tourism's arrival was so quiet and gradual that some of the best evidence of its early existence occurs in discussion of the province's unpreparedness for it. A writer in the Charlottetown *Herald*, for example, looking back on the 1885 summer, began by stating that "a large number of strangers have paid us a visit and left a considerable amount of money among us," before dedicating the remainder of the article to Charlottetown's need for a first-class hotel.[108] Whether because Charlottetown hotels were expected to be of a higher standard than their country counterparts or because they were in fact objectively worse, complaints about them were relentless. One reason was that they were always over full in summer (a clear case of "nobody goes there anymore, it's too crowded"). Though writers constantly railed against the congestion of Charlottetown hotels even as they commended the steady rise in tourism numbers, they never connected the two. Where writers did see improved accommodations was throughout the countryside. As early as 1875, the Toronto *Globe*'s PEI correspondent reported many more tourists than ever before thanks to improved accommodations all over, as manifest not only in the "larger hotels, with their usual attractions" and the "smaller hotels, where there is less ceremony and more quietness," but also the "many well-to-do farmers who sometimes take two or three persons, or a small family, for a short time." Tourists suddenly had a number of options for staying in the country or at the beach, at inexpensive rates of $2.50–$10.50 per week.[109] But those living in the capital fumed that they were not yet making the most of this new business. "We want these persons to come to the Island – we are willing that they should go to the seaside," wrote the editor of the Charlottetown *Herald*, "but we want to keep them for some time in Charlottetown, where they can enjoy themselves very well."[110]

Underlying such civic fretting was the growing belief that tourism could be a good thing for the Island. In 1887, the *Examiner* encouraged Islanders to see how mutually beneficial the travel trade was. "To the wealthy people of the continent the island has afforded a cool and quiet refuge from the intense heat and the heavy cares of business. To the thriving people of the Island their visitors have brought cash and good ideas." But, the editor noted, while "Nature had done much for us, we so far have done very little." Townspeople should be planting trees and flowers, country folk applying paint and whitewash. If spruced up, "the Island would be incalculably benefited in the elevation of the good taste of the people themselves and also in the attraction of wealthy and tasteful summer tourists."[111] Towards the end of the century some Prince Edward Islanders began to regard tourism as not merely a viable trade but a highly appealing one, promoting both economic and social goods – "cash and good ideas" – without apparently depleting the Island whatsoever. It looked to be endlessly sustainable. As a result, more Islanders became drawn into the trade and took greater charge of it. And in the act of promoting the Island to tourists, they further promoted tourism to Islanders.

Ironically, though, just as tourism was being recognized as a potentially lucrative industry for Prince Edward Island, the travel-writing genre that had brought attention to the province as a destination went into decline.[112] Magazine and newspaper writers continued to pronounce their opinions, but their accounts were increasingly overshadowed by promotional literature. By the 1890s, steamship and railroad companies that brought visitors to the Island were regularly publishing guidebooks with sections devoted to the Island. One would only expect these books to be more boostering than travel writing was, and they were, but there was more honest appraisal than one might expect, perhaps because the companies were not affiliated with a single locale. The Intercolonial and PEI Railway's 1892 *Forest, Stream and Seashore* opened its Island section with British writer William Cobbett's line about "a rascally heap of sand, rock, and swamp, called Prince Edward Island, in the horrible Gulf of St. Lawrence."[113] The guidebook then worked diligently to counter this judgment. Still, it may have been such editorial decisions that spurred private and then public efforts to produce homegrown promotional material. In 1893 the Acadia Hotel in Grand Tracadie, for instance, created a tourist guidebook for all of PEI that even included ads for other hotels.[114] And in 1899, the provincial government published its first official handbook, *Prince Edward Island, Garden Province of Canada*, written by court stenographer and legislative librarian W.H. Crosskill. Since advertising was understood to have wide-ranging benefits, the guide was designed to attract tourists, immigrants, and business investors simultaneously.[115]

Having the Island promoted by Islanders changed what was written for tourists but not nearly as much as one might think. Whether early travel writers had been particularly astute, or Islanders absorbed what they had learned tourists expected of them, or both, prevailing opinions hardened rather than changed dramatically. Crosskill even repeated the "rascally heap of sand, rock, and swamp" line, although he did call Cobbett "a prejudiced English writer."[116]

Figure 1.10 ▪ The ten PEI-related playing cards in the Intercolonial and PEI Railway souvenir deck, circa 1910. It is likely that some, and perhaps all, of the photographs are by W.S. Louson. Pastoral and sylvan scenes predominate, with the beach appearing in just one photo. This speaks to the railway's desire to showcase the landscape that tourists would see as their train traversed the Island's interior, but it also indicates what tourists of the day sought, expected, and found on the Island.

Take how Islanders themselves were depicted. Given early travel writers' willingness to associate the province with a bygone world and a bygone time, it is surprising how seldom Islanders themselves had been defined in such fashion. Examples do exist: John Rowan saw the Island's unchanging nature as linked to its people's cultural backgrounds – and as a problem.[117] But it would not be until the promotional material of the 1890s that the Island's Acadians, Scots, Irish, and Mi'kmaq were regularly described in detail and their retention of the old folkways and languages treated as of potential interest to the tourist. The Acadia Hotel booklet of 1893 opens with an essay on the Island's history. Or, more specifically, how Islanders have escaped history. Acadians, we learn, were "peaceful, economical, industrious, in a way belonging to a past age." The Mi'kmaq, "a remnant of the once powerful tribe," "still haunt the northern harbors and to some extent retain the garb and habits of their warlike ancestors." The Irish "were slow to forget either the language, the religion, the virtues or the prejudices of their ancestors." And, of the Scots, "For nearly one hundred years … the Gaelic tongue has been spoken, and the relics and legends, traditions, sayings and family pride … handed down from father to son."[118] A subsequent 1905 Acadia Hotel pamphlet differed only in more directly nudging tourists to visit these people of the past. Readers were assured that "the country people" were hospitable, that Acadian villages were well worth a day's excursion, and that the Mi'kmaq – "once the strongest, fiercest and handsomest of the Abenaquis" – visited Grand Tracadie each summer, and "their camps, canoes, and basket, porcupine quill, bead, birch bark and wood work are well worthy of notice and patronage."[119] These anthropological sketches were produced not by travel writers from away but by Islanders; such characterizations would flourish in the twentieth century. Earlier travel writers had defined PEI's landscape and its citizens' way of life in terms of the past, but it was Islanders themselves who refined the idea and perhaps internalized it.

Rather than portray the Island as a vibrant, living community, homegrown promotional literature stressed how quiet it was – above all, how unscathed it was by tourist hordes. The idea was most fully articulated in the 1897 *Prince Edward Island Illustrated*'s description of the North Shore:

> The solitude of the place is almost complete. The silence is broken only by the murmur of the unceasing sea. On the land the heated air may shimmer and tremble, but on the shore is a refreshing coolness … All the noisy notes of birds and insects, mellowed by distance, affect one slumberously. To lie down, stretched out luxuriously on the side of the sand-bank and to gaze idly over the dancing waters of the Gulf of St. Lawrence, is to be insensibly drifted into a state of contented rest. There

are no brass bands, no side-shows, no screeching steamboats, loaded with objectionable excursionists, to come and picnic under one's own nose; no tramps – the genus is unknown; no foul odors, nor beer saloons, nor gambling-houses; none of the annoyances of a modern seaside resort … Verily this is the place for weary men and women to come to build up worn out tissue, to rest the mind, to banish weariness.[120]

There were no visitor surveys in this era, so it is difficult to know the degree to which tourists were drawn by the Island's promise of a quiet, relaxing vacation, let alone the degree to which they felt the Island delivered. All we have is anecdotal satisfaction. For example, American lawyer Jesse T. Lazear was a guest at the Acadia in 1901 when he wrote home, proclaiming, "Poor father, had extolled the beauties of this place all the years that when things do not go well he feels the responsibility of a landlord and has an explanation for every defect. On the whole we are delighted with the place, principally as the air is so pure & the location healthful, as a nerve restorer it is about the best, as there is nothing exciting; even the appearance of a white starched shirt creates comment."[121]

"The greatest charm of all," according to another guide, "seems to be the fact that the Island is only being 'discovered.'"[122] All the more reason to visit immediately because the inference was that PEI would soon be like everywhere else: "In a few years, Prince Edward Island will have many more hotels, and will be thronged with tourists, but the 'bloom of the peach' is to be the prize of those who first break into this attractive and suggestive territory, so long overlooked by the great world."[123] Tourism promoters assumed that more tourism was inevitable – and promoted the idea. In 1902, a writer in the *Examiner* boasted, "Our destiny is to have our Island shores one long street of summer hotels."[124] No one asked what this might do to tourism or to the Island in general.

A survey of the *Prince Edward Island Magazine*, published from 1899 to 1905, suggests that some expected the explosion would happen the moment that Islanders took tourism seriously. Publisher Archibald Irwin, like a number of contributors, was greatly frustrated with his fellow citizens. "The scenery of Prince Edward Island is like so much capital lying idle," he wrote. "It seems like shouting down a wall to try and impress upon the general public the importance of advertising the natural charms and attractions of our Province … There can be little doubt that the number of tourists annually visiting our shores could be increased even a hundredfold if the shrugging of shoulders, and the making of excuses were to give way to energetic action."[125] That tourism was wholly beneficial was apparently self-evident, since Irwin did not even bother telling his readers why they should encourage it; Islanders were expected to have seen firsthand how valuable tourism could be. But even as the *Magazine* derided PEI for not paying attention to tourism, its own pages showed that attention was being paid. Summer issues were crafted as much for visitors as locals, with typical July articles on "How to 'Hunt' Clams," "The Scenery of Prince Edward Island," and "Sand Dunes." Summer advertising was likewise directed at tourists. In the July 1900 issue, twelve of the twenty-six ads explicitly call out travellers ("Tourists Tourists Tourists," "Tourists! Strangers!" "Tourists Islanders Abroad Everybody"), selling everything from "sand shoes" to souvenir spoons.[126]

More Islanders were also engaged in accommodating tourists. It was still a common refrain that in quality the existing hotels did not meet tourism's requirements and that in quantity they did not meet tourism's potential. Charlottetown businessmen were accused of waiting for one of the steamships companies to build a first-class hotel rather than build one themselves – which was not unreasonable, given the size of the investment, the short tourist season, and the companies' potential for commercial integration. But if they were waiting, it never happened.[127] Instead, smaller, more modest hotels opened up for the summer season throughout the Island: a rare inventory of them in 1899 lists the Seaforth in Alberton, the Port Hill House in Port Hill, the North Shore and Hodgson House in Malpeque, the Seaside in Rustico, Shaw's in Brackley Beach, the Cliff and Mutch's in Stanhope, the Acadia in Grand Tracadie, the Pleasant View in Hampton, the Lansdowne in Cape Traverse, and the Florida in Pownal.[128] The story of the Smiths in Hampton may be representative. They were drawn into the tourist trade gradually, first taking summer boarders on their farm and soon running a seasonal hotel, the Pleasant View. Daughter Edna later recalled, "Guests came from Charlottetown, naturally, but also from Montreal, Toronto, North Bay, Halifax and other Canadian cities, as well as Boston, New York, South Carolina, etc." At age nine, she was given the job of taking the horse and carriage to pick up guests at the Breadalbane train station, twenty kilometres away. And when the Charlottetown steamer sailed by their hotel on its way to Victoria, the boat would blow its whistle if hotel guests were aboard, the hotel would dip its flag in acknowledgment, and Edna would hitch up the horse and go collect them. And their trunks; many guests stayed for the full season. The hotel's mainstay became the clientele that returned year after year: "They were more like members of the family than guests."[129]

Dun and Bradstreet's annual credit assessment books show a steady rise in the number of hotel owners on Prince Edward Island across the late nineteenth century, from twenty-one in 1875 to forty-eight in 1905, a 130 per cent climb compared to 80 per cent across all businesses. The credit books also reveal that many of these new innkeepers used the summer trade to supplement their income, their occupations listed as "tanner, hotel," "saloon, hotel," "gunsmith, hotel" – even "undertaker, hotel." But though the number of hotels rose, their credit ratings did not. Dun and Bradstreet invariably considered Island hotels bad risks. Using a four-point scale in which companies were ranked as worthy of "limited" to "high" credit, not a single hotel on the Island after 1880 earned even a rating of "fair."[130] Travel writers rated them no better. "The hotels of Charlottetown," wrote Moses Sweetser, "are only boarding-houses of average grade, and will hardly satisfy American gentlemen."[131]

But where city hotels were criticized for being modest, life among the country folk was commended for the same thing. The tourism sections of the 1883 and 1888 editions of the province's official handbook are identical, except that in the latter, after "Hotel accommodation has improved vastly of late," the author also recommends "the numerous comfortable farm houses" that take in guests.[132] More were doing so all the time. One early twentieth century railway timetable listed twenty-one boarding houses where small numbers could be accommodated for a few weeks in summer; notably, nine of the twenty-one had female proprietors.[133] Staying with an Island family became so appealing that overzealous boosters felt free to open all Islanders' doors to tourists. An 1890 promotional booklet promised that "Hospitality reigns supreme, and upon any part of the island the belated traveller is assured a welcome, with excellent bed and board until the morrow, with hosts who feel aggrieved by proffered pay."[134] Such blanket invitations would abound in tourist literature for the next fifty years.

The accommodations situation was still not fully resolved by the very end of the century. Around the time he became premier of Prince Edward Island in 1897, A.B. Warburton wrote two letters to William Owen, son of a premier from the 1870s, encouraging him to move back from Minnesota and open a hotel. Neither man had experience in that line of work, but Warburton knew that Owen owned land in Keppoch, across the harbour from Charlottetown, and believed it to be prime location for tourism. "It would not only take the over-flow from the town hotels," he wrote, "but would bring numbers of people who want a nice, quiet cool place to spend some time in summer. Now scores of would-be visitors came down here and finding no place to stay in, go away in the steamer in which they came." The Plant Line steamships alone would provide a good hotel with 200 to 300 guests a night during July and August and half that in June and September. Moreover, while "the number of Americans spending the summer at the North Side is yearly increasing," Warburton thought that "the south shore is sure some day to be a big and profitable business." He encouraged Owen to study how hotels amuse their guests but felt that with Keppoch's "salt-water bathing, boating, stretch of clean sandy beach, mackerel, etc. etc." there should be no difficulty. Owen could over time build up a splendid resort that besides bringing in direct returns would offer an on-the-spot market for farm produce. "Think this over carefully. There is money in it if properly managed."[135] The situation Warburton was describing was, in one sense, the same as it had been for decades: a shortage of tourist accommodation. What was new was a recognition of the situation, a plan to resolve it, and a sense of urgency to do so.

The Seaside Hotel welcomed the twentieth century, but it was showing perceptible signs of decline. Whereas almost 1,300 people had signed the guest register in its first three years in the 1870s, from the 1900 through 1902 seasons fewer than 600 did.[136] It was not that the number of tourists to Prince Edward Island was decreasing — there is no sign of that and every sign of just the opposite — but rather that there were more places for them to stay. And more *ways*. Travel writing and then promotional literature imagined all Island tourists as first-timers peripatetically accumulating impressions for a short while and then leaving, but different kinds of travel were taking place. For example, some travellers were buying or building cottages of their own. The most famous and lasting of such summer homes has been Dalvay-by-the-Sea, built by Standard Oil president Alexander MacDonald in 1896 after having visited the Island the year earlier.[137] As early as 1883, travel writer Anna L. Ward advised her readers outright that, if they were considering building a summer home on PEI, the North Shore was the most desirable spot.[138] The *Globe* reported in a 1901 article on PEI tourism, "Not only has the transient business assumed large proportions, and shows a continual increase, but the number of those who have spied out the 'tight little island's' beauty spots, and who are now making one or more of them summer homes, has been greatly augmented this season." Moreover, the newspaper believed that such affluent cottage owners, by advertising the Island to their friends and neighbours back home, helped rather than hurt the local resort trade.[139] Tourists encouraged more tourists and sometimes in quite direct fashion. Broadway actor Charles Francis Coghlan fell in love with Bay Fortune after a visit in the 1880s and, improbably, established a theatre colony there. New York– and Boston-based actors were soon summering in Bay Fortune — some even retired there. Actor C.P. Flockton not only brought his "Flockton Comedy Company" to the Island in 1894, performing shows in Souris and Charlottetown, but also opened a tourist cottage business of his own.[140]

Tourist travel was also becoming available to more people. Rather than being the sole purview of the upper class who had been the mainstay of the Seaside for so long, it was opening up to the masses. The editor of the *Guardian* argued in 1901 that while the province must still work to accommodate (literally)

Figure 1.11 ▪ The Cape House, C.P. Flockton's summer home in Bay Fortune. Flockton had come to the Island as part of fellow Broadway actor Charles Coghlan's theatre colony and stayed – performing plays and setting up tourist accommodations of his own.

the upper class, it needed to do more to meet the needs of the increasing middle-class traffic. "This class of tourists do not expect to pay fancy prices," he wrote. "They want quiet, rest, the cool, free country air, good, plain, well cooked country food, and fair sleeping accommodations. The seashore, the grove, the bicycle, the fishing rod and the camera supply employment. For this class of summer visitors we have scarcely at all catered."[141] To develop what was showing signs of becoming a more complex industry, the editor called for the creation of a tourist association like those that existed in some other provinces and states.

It was Summerside rather than the province, however, which in 1903 created an Improvement and Tourist Association, headed by councillor J.E. Lefurgey and other leading town figures. The name of the association indicates just how directly tourism was associated with civic progress in this era. So does the preamble to the resolution that established the group:

> Whereas the town of Summerside lacks the spirit which tends to make towns progressive; and Whereas the town is suffering seriously because of the gradual loss of outside trade and the departure of many of its younger citizens; and Whereas, in our opinion, sufficient effort is not being used towards improving the town to attract visitors; and Whereas we believe that much could be accomplished by the rising generation in arousing citizens to the fact that we are moving too slowly to hold our own against rivals …[142]

It might seem from both this preamble and the group's name that tourism was a secondary interest but in fact tourism was believed to be the only industry capable of turning such a depressed place around, enriching its people's spirit and pocketbook simultaneously. The association's first major act – arguably its only one – was to announce that Summerside would host an Old Home Week in July 1904.

New England had introduced the first Old Home Weeks and Homecomings at the very end of the nineteenth century. Experiencing much the same outmigration and related economic distress as had Prince Edward Island, communities there invited expatriates back *en masse* in hopes of reaping social and economic benefits. The events had proven so successful that they swiftly became a summertime tradition.[143] There had been calls on the Island for an Old Home Week prior to the new association's announcement, but Summerside was the first place in the entire Maritimes to pull one off.[144] The Summerside association advertised across the Northeast, negotiated a special excursion rate for those travelling by rail or steam from Boston, and put together what grew into a two-week program of yacht races, horse races, church services, parades, prominent speakers, and theme days devoted to England, Ireland, Scotland, the United States, and "Canadians and P.E. Islanders 'at home.'"[145] Eight hundred visitors arrived in the first three days, and the Summerside homecoming was deemed a great success.[146]

While plans for the 1904 Homecoming were still underway, a Charlottetown Development and Tourist Association was formed along the same lines as the Summerside association. At its founding the organizers, headed by Liberal MLA George Hughes, stated that what was really needed was a provincial association, but it did not wish to interfere with the Summerside group.[147] Nevertheless, within a year it had swapped out "Charlottetown" in its title for "Prince Edward Island" without absorbing any of the Summerside executive.[148] It also announced an Old Home Week for Charlottetown in July 1905.[149] Association secretary and *Prince Edward Island Magazine* publisher Archibald Irwin spent two weeks in New England that spring advertising the event. Five thousand copies of a guidebook for tourists were printed. Reduced rates were arranged for travel from New England and Central Canada.[150] And in an important precedent, the association asked for and received government funding to hold the event – $500 from the province and $300 from Charlottetown, as well as $965 from citizens.[151]

That July, an estimated 3,000 tourists arrived for an Old Home Week full of "Sports, Entertainments and Amusements, Horse Races, Yacht Races, Athletic Sports, Naval, Military, and Society Parades, Firemen's Electric Light Sports, Gathering of the Clans, Immense Farmers Markets, Operative and Dramatic Entertainments, Water Fetes, etc."[152] Charlottetown saw enough of a jump in business to be convinced that tourists, even expatriates, were well worth attracting. (Indeed, one furniture company understood that expatriates generated unique consumer needs, and so advertised to Islanders "Beds of Comfort for the 'Old Home Comers.'"[153]) Overall, the year ended up seeing more tourists come to PEI than ever before.[154]

But it was not sheer numbers alone that made 1905 a turning point in Prince Edward Island tourism. Nor was it that the new provincial tourist association – formally incorporated that year as well[155] – had held what was, in effect, an Island-wide Old Home Week with the aid of private and public funding. The sea change, rather, was the growing and widespread acceptance of the assumptions that underlay these ventures. That tourism could be both economically and socially useful to PEI. That it was a trade that did not just happen but required organization, promotion, strategy, and support. That it was an activity not necessarily exclusive to the rich, Bostonians, or rich Bostonians but one that could and did involve people of more modest means, Central Canadians and Maritimers, and ex-Islanders – maybe even Islanders themselves.

As if to punctuate that the first phase of Prince Edward Island tourism was over, three of the beach resorts that had defined that phase were destroyed by fire within a short period. The long-closed Island Park Hotel, now a 125-room cottage for the Holman family, burned down in December 1904. The Seaside Hotel in Rustico went up in flames on a night in January 1906, the cause unknown. And the Acadia Hotel in Grand Tracadie caught fire one evening that August after a smoldering cigar fell through the veranda floor.[156] The three resorts had been instrumental in giving birth to and defining PEI tourism in its early years, but all physical evidence of their existence was gone.

The Seaside Hotel did live on in one fashion, however. The same month that it burned, L.M. Montgomery completed her novel *Anne of Green Gables*, which would have so great an effect on Prince Edward Island and tourism to it forever after. In the book, set on the Island in the late nineteenth century, there is a North Shore seaside resort called the White Sands Hotel that is modelled on the Seaside.[157] Near the book's end, young Anne performs in a concert there and is at first struck with stage fright. "Everything was so strange, so brilliant, so bewildering – the rows of ladies in evening dress, the critical faces, the whole atmosphere of wealth and culture about her. Very different this from the plain benches at the Debating Club, filled with the homely, sympathetic faces of friends and neighbors." But she overcomes her fear and does splendidly – even earning the praise of the wife of an American millionaire. On leaving, Anne's friend Jane sighs, "I just wish I was a rich American and could spend my summer at a hotel and wear jewels and low-necked dresses and have ice cream and chicken salad every blessed day." A page later, Jane returns to her theme: "Wouldn't you love to be rich, girls?"

But Anne answers, "We *are* rich" – in youth, imagination, and access to the beauty of Prince Edward Island. Anne was certain that none of them would trade places with one of those rich tourists if given the chance. "You *know* you wouldn't, Jane Andrews!"

"'I *don't* know – exactly,' said Jane unconvinced."[158]

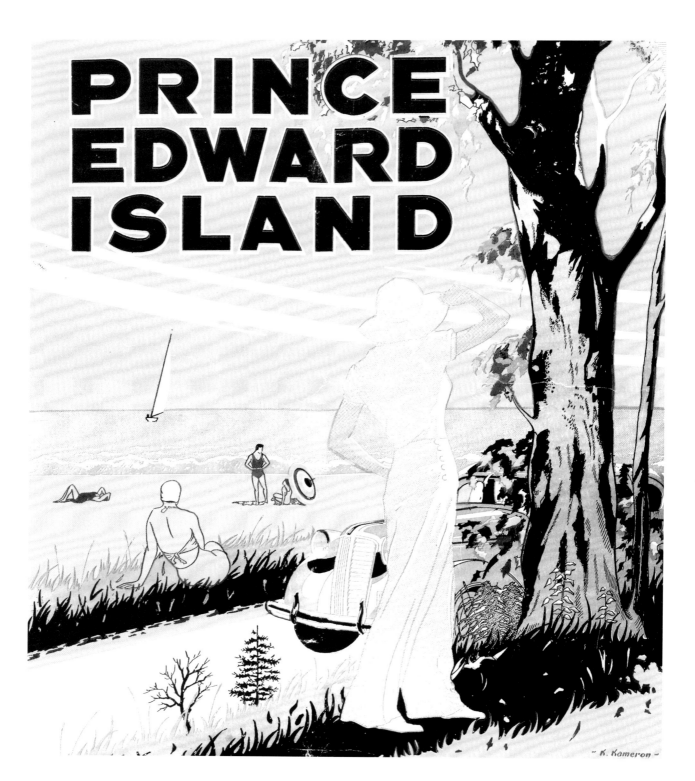

CHAPTER 2

Of Boosters and Knockers

1905–40

On a winter's evening in 1908, the Prince Edward Island legislature debated a private member's bill to ban automobiles from Island roads. Although there were only seven car owners in the province at the time, stories already swirled of accidents and near-accidents involving spooked horses.[1] Church attendance was reportedly down, as were sales at farmers' markets: horse owners were said to be virtually housebound for fear of meeting the mechanical dragons on the road. George Hughes, member for 2nd Queens, rose to speak to the bill. Since Hughes was the founding president of the Prince Edward Island Development and Tourist Association, one might expect him to defend the automobile as a technology that would bring more tourists and their money to the Island. Instead, Hughes not only moved that the resolution be amended, he argued that the proposed prohibition of cars on "roads" should be expanded to take in also "the streets of any city, town or village" – that is, everywhere. His amendment was seconded by Matthew Smith, who besides being member for 1st Queens was owner of the Pleasant View summer hotel in Hampton. As amended, the bill that had been introduced by John Agnew, also a founding member of the Development and Tourist Association, passed unanimously. Under the new Act, anyone caught driving an automobile would be subject to a $500 fine or six months in jail.[2]

That men who were invested in the promotion of tourism were also instrumental in banning the automobile says much about their vision of tourism. George Hughes – an avid horse breeder, by the way – explained his thinking on the ban a few years later: "The argument is advanced that the tourist trade demands the Auto. What was our experience, under the previous Act? Only a certain class came with autos, and ran them in a most reckless manner. The other class will not visit us as it is well known to them our roads are not

Figure 2.0 (facing) ▪ The cover of the provincial Travel Bureau's 1937 *Prince Edward Island: Visit Canada's Garden Province.*

suitable for Autos, and they also understand the feelings of any [many] people."[3] The Development and Tourist Association president's argument was not, as one might expect, that banning autos would keep the Island rustic and pure in a way that would appeal to tourists – the reason Bermuda banned cars the very same year.[4] Rather, it was that good tourists are those who already know us and our roads better than to wish to drive here and so will travel here as they always have. Bad tourists we can do without. Hughes's support for the ban signals that even those promoting tourism at the beginning of the century assumed the trade was an entirely passive one, having no effect on Islanders' existing way of life. Tourism would not require Prince Edward Island to change and would not change it.

But the first decades of the new century would prove this assumption wrong. This chapter traces a period in which tourism slowly infiltrated Islanders' everyday existence, bringing change that some appreciated and others resented. To tourism boosters, the trade was more than just a way to bring revenue to the Island, it was a way to connect meaningfully and reciprocally with the outside world. Provincial handbooks targeting settlers and investors thus also targeted tourists because the goal was the same: to make the Island better known. Yet throughout these decades there remained a disconnect between the boosters' idealistic goals and their means to achieve them because they almost never thought beyond getting the tourist here. Put another way, to boosters tourism *was* publicity – both in the sense that increasing publicity was the only way they knew to develop tourism and that tourism had as its broader goal publicizing the Island. Such an outward-looking focus was bound to alienate some citizens, who did not appreciate how the Island was portrayed in tourist literature or that the trade was being developed without their say. Those who doubted tourism's value or potential – "knockers," as boosters called them – were never very open or organized so it is difficult to gauge how prevalent their opinions were, but it is clear that there developed on Prince Edward Island an undercurrent of antipathy toward tourists and tourism. (And towards tourism boosters. Knockers knocked boosters just as boosters knocked knockers.) As tourism became more important to the economy during the Depression, tensions grew between those who saw it as interfering with the Island way of life and those who saw it as enriching it. The 1936 creation of Prince Edward Island National Park stands as both the first time that tourism on the Island transcended boosting – that it produced a focus, a genuine attraction – and that complaints about tourism came directly into the open.

The establishment of the Summerside Improvement and Tourist Association in 1903 and the Charlottetown – subsequently, provincial – Development and Tourist Association a year later had swiftly led to the hosting of two successful Old Home Weeks and made 1905 the Island's best tourism year ever. Organization had made things happen. But then activity ground to a halt. The difficulty of running volunteer organizations without any dedicated staff or physical infrastructure, whose signature act was the hosting of poorly funded, continentally advertised, weeklong events, was undoubtedly one reason. The members' limited personal stake in tourism's growth was likely another. Almost half of the men who made up the provincial association were merchants, while others were in the media (*PEI Magazine* publisher Archibald Irwin, *Patriot* editor Frederick Nash, and *Examiner* and *Guardian* business managers Robert Cotton and John Hood), and there was a banker, a physician, and a barrister. But how much extra business from tourism would association president George Hughes, a druggist by trade, expect to see? Or J.E. Lefurgey, president of the Summerside association, in his farm produce store?[5] In any case, there was a loss of all momentum after 1905, to the point that within two years the provincial association was left lamely defending the "quiet but effective" advertising it had undertaken in the interim.[6]

But as one group promoting the Island was losing its way, another arose. The "200,000 Club" had as its primary goal the doubling of the province's population to two hundred thousand. Promotional 100,000 and 200,000 Clubs were sweeping across North America at the time; if the former reached its goal, it typically just renamed itself the latter and kept working. The Island branch was spearheaded by the dashing young Reverend Edwin Smith of Cardigan. (Smith would later grow close to L.M. Montgomery, a kindred booster of PEI. She eventually gave him the typewriter on which she had written *Anne of Green Gables*.[7]) The Island's new 200,000 Club proposed at its founding "to appoint a permanent secretary who will look after tourist traffic, advertising our attractions as a summer resort, and among other things seek to develop a spirit of optimism among the people."[8] Encouraged by Reverend Smith's energy, and likely worried about a duplication of effort, the tourist association sponsored him to give a lecture and slideshow tour across New England in the winter of 1907.[9] That summer the association merged with the service group, and the awkwardly named "Prince Edward Island Tourist and 200,000 Club" was born, with George Hughes its president.[10] Reverend Smith gave a follow-up tour of nine New England cities and towns the following winter, "in many cases to crowded houses."[11] But at that point the amalgamated club simply disappeared from the public record and with it any interest in organizing to develop tourism.[12] There would be no tourist associations and no Old Home Weeks on Prince Edward Island for the next fifteen years. In the early 1920s, the *Guardian* vaguely recalled a time when tourist associations had existed in both Charlottetown and Summerside, but "although they both did much effective work and sowed seeds, a small harvest from which is being reaped today, they both died a natural death – from starvation."[13]

It is strange to hear death by starvation described as natural, but that suggests how tourism was widely regarded in the first decades of the century. People saw tourism as something that largely just happened: tourists either came or they didn't. If Prince Edward Island was to become a popular tourism retreat (a future not universally anticipated or desired), it was expected to do so on its own, without support. That helps explain why the provincial government – and, for that matter, the federal one – had so little to do with tourism in this era. Even in the provincial government's 1899 entrée into tourism promotion, legislative librarian W.H. Crosskill's *Prince Edward Island, Garden Province of Canada: Its History, Interests, and Resources, with Information for Tourists, etc.*, the "etc." loomed large. While the handbook covered summer accommodations and attractions, its largest chapter was on agriculture, and a section on the province "As a Field for the Farmer Emigrant" showed that tourists were only one sort of people from away being sought.[14] Beyond providing the provincial tourist association with small grants for three years of its short existence, the Island government did not concern itself with the burgeoning trade whatsoever.

What rare calls there were for state support of PEI tourism tended to be directed at the federal rather than provincial government, usually by the Island's federal representatives. Not surprisingly, they focused on a matter of national responsibility: improving rail and steam transportation to and on the Island. For instance, Conservative East Prince MP Alfred Lefurgey – whose brother headed the short-lived Summerside tourist association – appealed to the Laurier government repeatedly to improve the Island's rail and boat service on behalf of tourists as much as Islanders. Repairs were needed to the dilapidated Kensington train station, he argued in 1903, citing a local businessman who complained that although it was a tourist hub, "wealthy, refined Americans and other tourists down to Indians and drunken toughs" were forced to congregate together.[15] Island politicians also complained about the decrepit cars on the train line that carried tourists east to Pointe-du-Chêne, New Brunswick; the need to double the number of steamship crossings of the Northumberland Strait in summertime; the poor lighting on the PEI Railway.[16] These appeals were always framed in terms of developing the tourism industry – now that the Island, as one member put it, was fast becoming "perhaps the best summer resort in Canada"[17] – but it was surely not incidental that improvements to transportation would directly help Island constituents, too.

There was by comparison so little expectation that the provincial government would engage tourism in this era that we have found only one instance of it being criticized for not doing so – and that from an outsider. Early in the century the editor of *The Canadian Courier* magazine, John A. Cooper, grew obsessed with Prince Edward Island's, and in particular Charlottetown's, lack of large summer hotels and blamed the provincial government repeatedly for not building one. "If you want to rusticate on the Island you have to board with a farmer," he wrote. "The millionaire from Pittsburgh does not take the simple life so seriously as to do that ... His class are inclined to pass by Prince Edward Island."[18] In point of fact, there were summer hotels throughout the Island, of course, as the *Courier* itself noted in a 1907 article on Canadian resorts. The magazine listed five – the Victoria in Charlottetown, the Queen in Summerside, the Cliff (eventually the Stanhope Beach Inn) in Stanhope, the North Shore in Princetown, and the Acadia in Grand Tracadie (the magazine not aware it had burned down the summer before) – which meant the Island was reasonably well-represented against the seven listed for Nova Scotia and eleven for New Brunswick.[19] But Cooper was right that the Island's decades-long struggle for sufficient tourist accommodation lingered. Although he blamed the province for not stimulating hotel development, he recognized that governments in the Maritime provinces were wary of getting into the hotel business because the railroads were so decisive in determining the flow of traffic. The state could not, Cooper noted, "multiply its function like a private road [i.e., railroad] can." Of course, in the coming decades the state did multiply its function, including into tourism.

One of the few bright spots in terms of PEI tourism promotion in this era was the work of prolific amateur photographer W.S. Louson.[20] While working as a travelling sales representative throughout the Island early in the century, Louson captured landscape scenes that reinforced its reputation as a picturesque, peaceful respite. Louson's photos largely continued the tradition of representing Island landscape as it had been in late nineteenth-century travel literature, focusing on pastoral scenes vaguely reminiscent of Great Britain and cliffs along the coast; beaches were still most notable by their absence. What set his work apart was his single-minded devotion to landscape (at the expense of photographs of great men and great buildings), the resultant sheer number of more than 500 high-quality landscape images he produced, and the array of means that the early twentieth century allowed him to distribute them. Louson showcased his work in Charlottetown store windows, lantern slide presentations, and publications such as *The Prince*

Figure 2.1 ▪ Photographer W.S. Louson's "Evening Shadows," from the early 1900s. In books, lantern slides, and above all postcards, Louson's more than 500 published images did much to visually define the Island for tourism in the twentieth century.

Edward Island Magazine and two photo albums produced in Michigan for Charlottetown stationers Carter & Co. But it was in postcards, in this their golden age, that hundreds of his photos received the broadest currency.[21] What's more, the photographer was an inveterate booster of the province – he served on the executive of both the provincial tourist association and the 200,000 Club – and allowed his images to be reproduced freely by any North American media covering the Island. Louson's photographs became the visual representation and the public face of Prince Edward Island in the first decades of the century.

But support for tourism and its promotion was irregular, when it existed at all. In 1912, *Guardian* editor J.E.B. McCready wrote of the need to advertise the province more widely abroad. "[W]e should learn a lesson from our cousins in the Northwest," he wrote, "who employ publicity agents at liberal salaries and spend money with a lavish hand in printer's ink."[22] As editor of a Conservative newspaper with a new Conservative government in power – and one that had just received from the federal Conservative government the windfall of a $100,000 per year boost to the Island's annual subsidy – he might expect

Figure 2.2 ▪ In the first half of the twentieth century, the Mi'kmaq First Nation received only passing mention in tourism promotional literature, where their principal role was to supply a romantic prehistory and a poetical name for the province: Abegweit, "Cradled on the Waves." However, they did feature occasionally on postcards. In this one, a Mi'kmaw family is shown with three common handicraft items: a basket (in progress), an oar, and a blanket.

his advice to be heeded. And it was. Within two months, the seventy-four-year-old McCready retired from the newspaper to become the province's first publicity agent. On a liberal salary.[23] The job looked very much like a political sinecure, and McCready was soon accused on the front page of his old newspaper of having been given "a Government job with $2,000 for doing nothing."[24] But Premier J.A. Mathieson was a progressivist, confident about the Island's future, and McCready was fully expected to publicize the province. The premier directed McCready, while on a trip to the northeastern US, to take the "opportunity of promoting the summer tourist traffic for next season and of ascertaining what steps would be most effective for re-patrioting [sic] some of our people who have settled there and who might improve their condition by a return to this Province."[25] McCready accomplished little, however. Content to write a few articles and promotional brochures that borrowed heavily from Crosskill's earlier handbook and other sources, he was allowed to retain his monopoly on state-sanctioned boosterism well into his nineties.

All in all, the only significant tourism-related action taken by a provincial administration in this era was the 1908 banning of the automobile – significant because of its direct effect on tourists' ability to travel on the Island and because of the opinions it brought to light about the trade. It was "autoists" rather than tourists per se who were being targeted, but as George Hughes's defence of the ban indicates, tourist drivers were singled out as the principal offenders, even though complaints about cars were also made well outside the tourist season. The Toronto *Globe* likewise traced the issue on PEI to "several American tourists" who had taken advantage of the province's unpreparedness for cars: "'Hooray!' yelled the motorists, 'no licenses, no numbers, no restrictions. This is the country for me. Open her up there, Steve!'"[26] (We have looked for such a defining incident in the Island newspapers and have found no record of it, Steve or otherwise.) The subsequent debate surrounding the ban devolved at its worst into a caricatured clash of wealthy, pleasure-seeking, urban autoists against ordinary, hardworking, rural anti-autoists; in a society dominated by agriculture it was obvious which was the more politically savvy side to take.

But the reaction to the automobile ban demonstrated that some Islanders of all stripes understood that if the province wanted tourism, it must be accepting of tourists. "Farmer" wrote in a letter to the editor of the *Patriot* asking, "Will wealthy tourists come here if they are obliged to leave their autos behind? And will the hotels and merchants thus not be injured?"[27] A car advocate from Kings County minced no words: "We have Souris, Georgetown, Montague, Murray River and Murray Harbour, some of the prettiest spots in North America for summer resorts and what we want is summer hotels, tourists and automobiles. What few we had last summer left their dollars at every stop they made."[28] And at a meeting of the PEI Canadian Club, Andrew Macphail, the expatriate author teaching at McGill University, gently suggested that the Island must come to terms with the outside world. "Yet there are many good men who ride in automobiles and take a glass of wine at dinner," he said, connecting the auto ban to the Island's embrace of Prohibition. "Possibly you are better without such persons. That is for you to decide. Yet a thousand tourists means $100,000."[29]

Despite such arguments, the auto ban endured from 1908 to 1913, while the Island weathered a degree of national ridicule over it.[30] Tourism apparently dipped shortly after the ban was instituted. ("Apparently" because no figures were being compiled, so the year-by-year state of tourism was purely anecdotal.) Although the decline was in fact said to be occurring across Canada, on the Island it increased pressure to reinstate cars.[31] At the same time, the automobile was rapidly integrating into North American society. Mass assembly techniques were bringing down the price of cars and making them more commonplace, even as a popular "See America First" movement encouraged Americans to limit their travel to their own country and, in an unlikely act of inclusion, Canada.[32] And on Prince Edward Island, there was something of an economic boom, helped along by a frenzy of speculation in silver fox farming. More Islanders could afford automobiles, and more wanted them.[33] In 1912, the Conservative organ the *Guardian* ran a two-thirds-page advertisement opposing the Automobile Act, complete with a postcard to be cut out and sent to the new Conservative government. In a section of the ad devoted to "What We Lose by Upholding the Act," tourism revenue was the first item mentioned: "The pocket books of Provincial people has suffered to the extent of not less than $250,000 a year by the decrease of tourist traffic."[34] The Mathieson government took no action at that point, but in April 1913 a large delegation of businessmen gathered at the legislature and called for the Automobile Act's repeal. Their foremost argument once more was that "there was no better way to advertise the beauties and attractions of the Island" than to let automobiles back in.[35]

The Mathieson government's compromise was to introduce a new Automobile Act in 1913 but announce that it would not be passed into law until a plebiscite on the issue was held that summer. Although the official results of that plebiscite were suppressed, it is clear that rural communities voted overwhelmingly against repeal. With the wisdom of Solomon, or something, the government declared that individual communities would hold their own votes, and those in which 75 per cent were in favour could open to cars three days a week.[36] In the years that followed, rural Islanders relented bit by bit, the restrictions gradually eased, and following a 1919 Order-in-Council, cars could be driven anytime anywhere. The ban's repeal received less press than its introduction, however, so it is quite likely that some potential tourists believed it remained in effect, thus dampening tourism numbers for a while. As late as 1930, a Quebec member of the House of Commons spoke of there being a prohibition against cars on Prince Edward Island.[37]

The automobile ban had been a case of Islanders' resistance to modernity but not necessarily to modern technology. After all, at the very same time many rural Islanders resisted cars with gasoline engines, a subset of them, lobster fishermen, were busily installing gasoline engines on their boats.[38] Also, once the ban was repealed, car registration jumped immediately, from twenty-six in 1913 to 303 in 1917 to 1,419 in 1920.[39] The automobile debate was more a debate on the degree to which the Island could hope to exist independent of the outside world. Tourism was an important feature of that debate. While pro-autoists spoke of how much money was being lost in discouraging tourism, anti-autoists argued that the ban was fully in keeping with the Island's reputation as a peaceful destination and so would help tourism. As Charlottetown insurance agent F.W. Hyndman wrote in a letter to the editor, "For the one or two tourists who may bring their automobiles, and disturb the whole community, there are thousands of tourists who come here for rest and quiet that will be thankful for its prohibition."[40] (Yet just a few years later, Hyndman's firm seems to have been the first on the Island to sell car insurance.[41]) Other anti-autoists argued that there was no real money in tourism anyway.[42] "I venture to assert," one ventured to assert, "that about two-thirds of tourists who visit our Island every summer are Islanders returning home for a visit ... But if the tourist question is worth considering, are we for the sake of a few paltry dollars (gained by a few) going to sacrifice the comfort and happiness of our people?"

When the ban was lifted, one of the first countryside roads the government opened to the automobile was the Union Road, the primary route between Charlottetown and the beaches of the North Shore.[43] *The Maple Leaf* magazine reported shortly after that "the Charlottetown owners of cars gave the farmers of Union Road an outing trip on the north shore and a dinner at the Cliff Hotel at Covehead."[44] It was a lovely gesture and, although this was presumably not the car owners' intention, it suggested a lesson learned from the automobile debate. Advocates for tourism, besides selling Prince Edward Island to tourists, would have to sell tourism to Prince Edward Islanders.

There was an immediate opportunity to do so, with 1914 marking the fiftieth anniversary of the Charlottetown Conference. The last-minute way in which the province handled this event demonstrates the impromptu nature of its tourism promotion in the era. In 1864, delegates from PEI, New Brunswick, Nova Scotia, and the United Province of Canada had gathered in Charlottetown and agreed in principle to a union of the colonies. The meeting had led to another in Quebec City a month later and ultimately to Confederation in 1867. For decades Prince Edward Island made little of the fact it had hosted the initial meeting – perhaps because it did not join Canada itself until 1873 – but toward the turn of the century a few Islanders began referring to the capital, or the whole province, as the "Cradle of Confederation."[45] Still, the conference's approaching golden anniversary was not even on the Island's radar until Montreal's *La Presse* newspaper suggested in December 1913 that Montreal host a national exhibition the next fall to commemorate the two Confederation conferences.[46] With some indignation, Island newspapers argued that since Charlottetown had hosted the first meeting, any commemoration must surely take place there. The rest of Canada could organize its own celebration for Confederation's fiftieth anniversary in 1917, the *Guardian* editor noted, "But the coming year is OUR OPPORTUNITY and it is our business to make the most of it."[47]

And so on the penultimate day of 1913, fifty of the Island's leading figures met to discuss whether the province would celebrate 1914. Everyone in attendance, from the premier on down, agreed a golden jubilee should be held. They debated whether a monument or a brass tablet was more appropriate. They bandied about the notion of having ninety-three-year-old Charles Tupper, the last surviving Father of Confederation, brought from England by warship to attend. The sheer number of details to be worked out, and on short notice, threatened to overwhelm the meeting. But Charlottetown soldier and commercial agent Major A.A. Bartlett insisted that all that was needed at this stage was optimism: "They did not want any knockers in this matter." In what could be the slogan for early twentieth-century PEI tourism promotion,

Bartlett stated, "Let us get the people here and if we get them here we will know what to do with them."[48]

By early January a committee of the Island's political elite was struck to organize an anniversary celebration.[49] The early planning is notable for its focus on publicizing the Island generally more than tourism per se. (It is therefore also notable that the province's publicity agent, J.E.B. McCready, was in no way involved.) Just a few years earlier, there had been some on the Island arguing for secession from Canada, but having just negotiated the $100,000 increase in annual subsidy from the federal government, the Island now wanted the event to showcase its happy place in Confederation – and give it an opportunity to ask for more. Member of Parliament A.A. MacLean, for example, framed the celebration as an occasion to show "the people of Canada that we are still as strong and as important as in 1864 when we were in the van of Confederation. If we represented that properly to the people of Canada and to the Parliament of Canada, Parliament would give us the thing we should have today, proper representation in Parliament."[50]

Tourism was not the initial rationale for the jubilee, but committee members quickly came to realize its tourism potential, and Provincial Secretary Arthur Newbery worked tirelessly in directing the celebration toward it. The organizers moved the three-day event from the actual September anniversary to a more tourist-friendly mid-August. They created an Accommodations Bureau to help visitors find lodgings and arranged for 400 more rooms in the homes of Islanders if there was an overflow.[51] They arranged coinciding events: the Canadian Track and Field Championships, plus a huge military parade that would bring in 2,000 men from units throughout the Maritimes.[52] And they convinced the federal government to contribute $20,000, by far the largest state support for a tourism-related event in the province to that point.[53] In fact, the organizers prepared for everything.

Short of war.

On 3 August 1914, with conflict in Europe imminent, it was decided there was no alternative but to postpone the celebration. The following day, Great Britain – and so Canada – declared war on Germany, and the day after that the first military contingent shipped off Prince Edward Island.[54] The celebration was never rescheduled. The planned 1914 event had opened the door to the Island honouring its place in Confederation, but its only tangible legacy was an already-commissioned bronze tablet in Province House by sculptor Hamilton McCarthy, commemorating the Charlottetown Conference of fifty years earlier. No tourist came for the anniversary, and all the Island got was this lousy plaque.[55]

But tourism would not stop just for a global conflict. Indeed, with Europe essentially closed during the First World War, many American travellers turned

Figure 2.3 ▪ During a 1917 stay, artist Robert Harris made this sketch of Sheepcote Cottage in Holland Cove, just across the harbour from Charlottetown and so a popular summer retreat for Islanders and tourists alike. Such rustic cabins could be rented from Charlottetown Summer Resorts for as little as $60 per season.

their gaze northward, and tourism in Canada held relatively steady, at least until the US joined the war in 1917. Numbers would have been higher but for the rumours persisting in the States that wartime Canada did not want visitors, that tourists must register at post offices, that they might be conscripted, that passports were required, and, strangest of all, that women would not be allowed to return home.[56] Wartime seems to have been the death knell of PEI's grand seaside resort tradition, with more hotels closing. The only success story during this era was the 1913 establishment of the Charlottetown Summer Resorts in Holland Cove, Rocky Point, by a Charlottetown consortium. At incorporation, the Resorts was capitalized at $290,000 and empowered to do everything from "carry on the business of hotel-keeping, inn-keeping, summer resorts, and seaside hotels" to run a fishing operation, farm, stone quarry, and brickworks. The Resorts ended up being more modest, a collection of forty separate cottages rented for as little as $60 per season, and sharing a central dining hall, tennis court, and pier. The Holland Cove development was probably patronized more by Charlottetonians than come-from-aways, but the initiative encouraged the growth of summer rental accommodations throughout the Island.[57]

In general, it is difficult to determine the state of Prince Edward Island tourism during the war, in part because there were no official numbers and in part because newspapers had more pressing matters to write about. That the war drove tourism from Islanders' concerns is hardly surprising; that the end of the war did not herald a renewal of interest is more so. In a keyword search of the *Guardian* on islandnewspapers.ca, variants of "tourist" or "tourism" appear 1,581 times between 1905 and 1914 but only 895 times between 1915 and 1924. (For purposes of foreshadowing, there would be 2,716 occurrences between 1925 and 1934.)[58] The steady rise of autotourism meant that tourists dispersed throughout the Island more, filling farmers' boarding houses at the expense of larger beach resorts. Smaller operators made for a seemingly smaller, and certainly quieter, summer trade.[59] There was no boosting because there was no tourist organization. And there was no knocking because the reinstatement of the automobile meant there was no galvanizing anti-tourist issue. The First World War initiated a decade-long tourist doldrums on Prince Edward Island. And with the Confederation jubilee cancelled, the Island did not host a single tourist-related event between 1905 and 1924.

"I have never met a tourist who came to the Island who did not complain," said J.O. Hyndman, president of the PEI Associated Boards of Trade, in 1926.[60] And with good reason, he might have added. That Prince Edward Island tourism came into its own in the mid-1920s and grew strongly and steadily for the next decade and a half – increasing visitors, improving organization, even developing its first attraction – was amazing enough. But it was especially amazing considering everything that worked against it. The greatest, never-ending complaint was that travel to the Island was time-consuming, unpredictable, and expensive. The SS *Prince Edward Island*, the first car ferry between Cape Tormentine, New Brunswick, and Borden, PEI, only entered service in 1917, and even then "car" meant "railcar." Automobiles rode as freight: they were driven onto a flatbed railcar, the railcar driven onto the ferry, and the process reversed on the far shore. (Towards the end of the First World War, in fact, touring autos were refused entry to the Island outright to ease handling of freight.[61]) Things did not improve when the visitor arrived. Although the Island invested heavily in roadwork in the 1920s, it focused on building up the substructure of roads rather than paving their surface, so drives remained alternately dusty and muddy affairs. Accommodations were still insufficient and there was not enough for the tourist to do. Pretty much everything was closed on Sundays, including restaurants.[62] After 1930, Prince Edward Island was the only province that still prohibited alcohol. And dogs: fear of a rabies epidemic within the province's fox population led to a ban on off-Island dogs from 1928 to 1936. Toto-toting tourists discovered they would have to leave their best friend with someone in Tormentine if they chose to visit. Most chose not to.[63]

Weighed against all these disadvantages was the one thing Prince Edward Island had that nowhere else outside Sweden had: a fictional red-headed, pig-tailed girl. For anyone who needs reminding, *Anne of Green Gables* is Lucy

Figure 2.4 ▪ Although the crossing from Tormentine to Borden was only fourteen kilometres, the Island's first car ferry, the ss *Prince Edward Island*, had interior furnishings that recalled a transatlantic passenger liner. Here, the ladies room and dining room are shown.

Figure 2.5 ▪ Even after Prince Edward Island fully repealed its ban of cars in 1919, would-be autotourists still faced logistical issues. Until the ss *Prince Edward Island* was renovated to create an automobile deck, the only way to get a car to the Island was on a railway flatcar.

Maud Montgomery's 1908 children's novel set in the fictional PEI village of Avonlea. It tells the story of how Anne Shirley, a spunky orphan adopted by an elderly brother and sister, becomes part of their family and community. Anne falls in love with the Island, which all but plays a character in the novel, and so *Anne* not only captivated readers around the world, it enticed them to PEI. They wanted to visit the landscape Anne rhapsodizes about and to seek out Avonlea. Almost immediately upon the book's publication in 1908, Prince Edward Island began to reap the tourism benefit of being thought of as a real fictional place. In 1911, *Saturday Night* magazine ran an imagined interview with Montgomery that includes the following exchange:

> "Do you know, that charming island province ought to erect a monument in your honor? You have done it more good than all the railroad circulars ever written."
>
> "You are entirely mistaken," [Montgomery] said with quiet hauteur, "Prince Edward Island has no desire to be exploited, and is no paradise for the common or garden variety of tourist."
>
> "Then you shouldn't make it so attractive. Why, one of the midsummer dreams of the Canadian traveller is to find Green Gables and catch a glimpse of Anne."[64]

Even readers who could better differentiate fact from fiction were drawn to visit places from Montgomery's childhood, particularly her birthplace in

Figure 2.6 ▪ Within years of the 1908 publication of L.M. Montgomery's Anne of Green Gables, literary pilgrims were seeking sites associated with the book and its author. This photo from a tourist's album of their stay on the Island sometime in the 1910s is labelled "Green Gables, Cavendish" and shows the now-abandoned Macneill homestead where Montgomery had been raised. Montgomery's uncle grew so tired of trespassers that he tore the house down in 1920, allowing Myrtle and Ernest Webb's nearby Cavendish home to become the unrivalled "Green Gables."

New London and the house in Cavendish that had inspired Green Gables and became known by that name. By the mid-1920s there were enough annual pilgrims to Green Gables that the editor of the *Guardian* argued for monetizing the "P.E. Island Shrine." "Why not capitalize it?" he wrote. "Not alone for mercenary ends or for moneymaking but to add to the pleasure of our visitors and ourselves." Blurring the lines of reality, he noted, "Green Gables is still in existence, the Lake of Shiny [sic] Waters still glimmers in the sun as Anne saw it … Avonlea could, with a little enterprise, be converted into a shrine which thousands of tourists would visit."[65] The editor seemed unaware that capitalizing on Green Gables' fame was already underway: the owners of the house, Myrtle and Ernest Webb, began taking in guests in the early to mid-1920s. Jeremiah Simpson and Katherine Wyand both also operated tourist accommodations in Cavendish, and Wyand soon opened an accompanying Avonlea Restaurant, a lunch counter right at the beach.[66]

Author L.M. Montgomery was at first simply proud of the attention she had given the Island's North Shore, but by the late 1920s it somewhat appalled her. "You ask in your letter if 'Cavendish has become a place of pilgrimage for my admirers?'" she wrote a friend. "Alas, yes. And the chagrin expressed in that alas is not an affectation at all but a genuine regret and annoyance. Cavendish

Figure 2.7 ▪ While government and business attempted to organize tourism in the interwar period, individual Islanders were developing the trade on their own. Making the most of Cavendish's association with the fictional community of Avonlea, Katherine Wyand opened a summer restaurant at the shore and Avonlea Cottages shortly thereafter.

Avonlea Restaurant

At Cavendish Beach, a lunch counter is opened, where luncheon, ice-cream and cake, soft drinks and fruit will be served to the public on Wednesday, Saturday and Sundays and all holidays until further notice.

is being over-run and exploited and spoiled by mobs of tourists."[67] The dignified, well-kept farming community she remembered had, in her eyes, grown shabby. Montgomery's distress seems positively quaint now, since Cavendish became so much busier a tourist spot in the decades that followed. But her shock at what she and Anne had wrought was understandable. In little more than a decade, Cavendish had gone from a place unnoticed by tourists to one in which a hundred cars parked *on the beach* on weekend days in the summer.

As important as *Anne of Green Gables* was to tourism's rise, the automobile revolution was even more so. It took some time after the automobile ban was lifted for the Island to experience the full force of the autotourism boom already starting to sweep the rest of the continent.[68] But in the mid-1920s the number of cars ferried to the Island rose swiftly and steadily, despite the inconvenience of the crossing: from 800 in 1923 to 1,400 the next year to more than 2,100 the next. The Island even elected to switch to driving on the right-hand side in 1924 in deference to American tourists. By the end of the decade, traffic on the ss *Prince Edward Island* was increasing by 1,000 cars per year. A crude automobile deck was installed, but there were calls for an additional ferry to handle the increasing traffic.[69] The effect of the automobile – and, for that matter, the *Anne of Green Gables* literary phenomenon – in increasing visitation to the Island is a valuable reminder that, of all industries, tourism cannot be understood solely in terms of "supply," the destination. It is always tied to "demand," the circumstances and desires of people from away.

Likewise, the Island tourism industry did not mature in a vacuum but alongside other locales also struggling to improve their economy, and which were seeing tourism as one means of doing so. As on PEI, New Brunswick had a privately run provincial tourist association (operated by the Saint John Board of Trade) that prospered for a few years at the beginning of the century and ran at least one Old Home Week. It went into hibernation in the 1910s before awakening around 1920 following a merger with the All-New Brunswick Fish, Game, and Resource League.[70] Similarly, a private tourist association was established in Nova Scotia in 1897 then died out in the new century, until it was resurrected as a semipublic body by the provincial government in summer 1923.[71] Prince Edward Island experienced many of the same economic problems (depression, debt, outmigration) and many of the tourism challenges (inaccessibility, a short season, lack of infrastructure) as its neighbour provinces, and it was well aware of how these provinces were starting to organize for tourism. The early 1920s saw the rise of a Maritime Rights Movement that in the face of economic and political stagnation sought better treatment for the Maritime region within Canada. The movement was spearheaded by boards of trade and journalists in concert with politicians – the same informal alliance that had been promoting tourism in each province – and when the movement failed, the provincial alliances seized on tourism as an economic lever of unrealized potential.[72] The decision by a group of prominent Charlottetown and Summerside businessmen in late 1923 to form a Prince Edward Island Tourist Association was in part imitation of what was going on elsewhere and in part simply a sign that the whole Maritimes were experiencing the same cultural and economic situations.[73]

The new provincial Tourist Association at first radiated some of the same overenthusiasm as earlier tourism boosters had. It initially planned to make 1924 an "Old Home Summer" but eventually scaled this down to a low-key Old Home Week. It then had nothing to do with an Old Home Week that Charlottetown hosted the following year and let the would-be tradition peter out altogether in 1926.[74] And yet, the Tourist Association quickly developed into a stable organization in a way previous such organizations had not. Highly visible and active leadership was a primary reason. The association's president was Aubin E. Arsenault, an ex-premier and a sitting judge of the provincial Supreme Court. Arsenault might well have been expected to serve as figurehead, particularly since his term as premier had demonstrated no interest in tourism whatsoever. Instead, he proved himself an indefatigable tourism booster, was often in the news on tourism matters, and remained the association president for almost twenty years. He even stayed on while serving as the first president of the Canadian Association of Tourist and Publicity Bureaux from 1929 to 1931.[75]

After a short term with Reigh Tinney as manager, the day-to-day running of the Tourist Association was placed in the hands of M.K. "Minnie" MacFadyen, who rose from "secretary" to "manager" to "director." MacFadyen

Figure 2.8 ▪ Judge Aubin E. Arsenault, the former premier of PEI (and the first Acadian premier in Canada), became the province's principal tourism booster in the interwar period. He was the first and long-time president of the PEI Tourist Association and later the first president of the Canadian Association of Tourist and Publicity Bureaux. M.K. "Minnie" MacFadyen did the actual day-to-day running of the provincial association throughout the 1920s and '30s, while she and husband Jim MacFadyen operated the Stanhope Beach Inn.

oversaw the Association's Queen Street office in Charlottetown and set up a second office in Summerside in 1931. She also answered the growing number of off-season enquiries; in 1933, she told of receiving 848 in a single month and making sure they all received personal replies.[76] Arsenault wrote that it was largely due to MacFadyen's "enthusiasm and energy that the tourist business in this Province was placed on a sound and permanent basis. During the tourist months, MacFadyen stayed on the job from early morning until late at night and, with only one assistant, did the work of three or four persons."[77]

The Tourist Association toyed with its name constantly in its first few years, becoming by turns the Publicity Association, the Tourist Publicity Association, and the Tourist and Publicity Association. It reverted to being the Tourist Association in 1930 because "It was pointed out that the word publicity smacks of propaganda whereas a tourist association is thought of as a service organization."[78] The association positioned itself as more a service club than an interest group for a fledgling industry. It insisted on the volunteer nature of its efforts: "not one of the officers ... will receive any salary, all the funds going directly to the main purpose, which is to advertise Prince Edward Island as a summer resort."[79] (Minnie MacFadyen did, in fact, eventually receive an annual salary.) The association in its early years also obtained most of its funding from private contributions. In 1928, for example, it received $2,931 from subscriptions, more than the $2,850 from the province and the towns of Charlottetown and Summerside combined.[80]

The association's determination to appear as something of a charity demonstrates that tourism was treated – as it still so often is – as a financial exchange that must be veiled as a social exchange, for the sake of propriety or self-respect. And such delicacy was not just good taste; it was good business. In the 1927 election campaign, the provincial Conservatives ran a remarkable advertisement showing how much more generous the sitting Conservative government was on social issues than the previous Liberal one had been. It compared grants on eight items: seven of them health and social services such as hospitals and orphanages, and the eighth the Tourist Association.[81] That promotion of tourism could be lumped in with support for a school for the blind – and that it was assumed Island readers would accept the comparison – suggests the degree to which the association was successful in preaching tourism as a social good.

Yet those who advocated for tourism did so primarily in financial terms. At the founding of the Tourist Association, the *Guardian* published an editorial entitled "Found Money." "The revenue from the tourist business is 'found money,'" it said. "It is money from outside, money added to the ordinary resources of the country … [M]oney is circulated and everybody is benefited."[82] The association's first manager, Reigh Tinney, told Islanders, "The territory from which we can draw results is large, the ground is fertile; your support and our endeavour are the seeds and with this material the crop is sure, the land cannot be depleted and the result is bound to be a golden harvest for Prince Edward Island."[83] Such an agricultural metaphor was well suited to a province that still saw itself as a fundamentally agricultural one (even if Tinney was unaware that in tourism, as in agriculture, the land *can* be depleted). In general, this association devoted much more energy than its predecessors had to promoting tourism to Islanders. It relied heavily on statistics to do so. "For every dollar expended by the association in summer advertising it is reasonable to expect five dollars in return," the PEI group claimed at one point.[84] At another, the approximately 11,000 tourists who arrived on the Island in 1925 were estimated to have spent $825,000 in the province.[85] The Old Home Week that year was projected to cost just $10,000 but bring in $150–$200,000.[86] Such statements were, it must be said, ordinary or even modest by tourist association standards: in the same period, the publicity bureau in Victoria, British Columbia was promising a one hundred to one return on tourism investment.[87] It hardly mattered that the figures and the multiplier effects the PEI Tourist Association bandied about were opaque, to say the least: they gave the summer trade a tangible value it had never enjoyed. In its first year the organization received a $1,000 grant from the province – the government's first support of tourism in a decade and a half, and support it would never again relinquish.[88]

The Tourist Association divided itself into "Publicity," "Housing," and "Attractions" departments, suggesting it had a more holistic view of the industry's needs than previous boosters. Early in its existence it organized two special events, a Maritime Step Dancing and Fiddling Contest that was praised for rejuvenating dying traditions and a weeklong retreat for high-ranking railway executives from across the Northeast.[89] But such initiatives soon fell away, and the association devoted most of its efforts to publicizing the province, since this both distributed benefits to everyone equally and did not compete with existing business interests. In its first year, it spent almost $2,500 in advertisements but only $66 in aid of housing and attractions.[90] It sent out letters of invitation to all 9,000 car owners in Nova Scotia, a tactic thought so successful it did the same for New Brunswick drivers the following year.[91] Fifteen thousand guidebooks were also printed and circulated in 1925, as were 10,000 broadsides ("Summer Paradise"), 2,000 folders ("Where to Play on P.E.I."), and 5,000 maps.[92] By 1929, 29,000 guidebooks were being distributed; by 1930, 35,000.[93] The blizzard of guidebooks, published lectures, and media interviews that the association was putting out tacitly promoted not just Prince Edward Island as a destination but the idea of tourism itself.

The relentless optimism of this output, particularly in an era in which tourism really was on the rise, makes it all the more difficult to determine what Islanders actually thought of the blossoming industry. But that not everyone was sold on tourism is clear. Some Islanders disapproved of the money spent on the boosting. In 1933, for example, Charlottetown mayor William Stewart objected to the city's practice of contributing a few hundred dollars annually to the Tourist Association, not because the Island was in the depths of the Great Depression but because there was no proof the support brought more tourists to PEI – and because perhaps it did. To his mind the association's work was "a humbug and an imposition on the people."[94] Yet the city continued to contribute to the association throughout Stewart's term.

Others disapproved of tourists and tourism directly. A farmer running for the provincial legislature as a Liberal in 1926 earned considerable press for his repeated claims that tourists were more a nuisance than a benefit and that they corrupted the morals of the people. How exactly they did so was not said but it was presumably by exposing Islanders to alcohol.[95] Liberal leader A.C.

Saunders felt obliged to tell the House that he was protourism, although he realized not everyone shared his view.[96] Even some in the tourism industry treated tourists worse than they did Islanders, regularly gouging visitors from away. Travel writer G.N. Tricoche warned, "I know for instance a place which is no more than a very ordinary inn, ill-kept, and gives out its rates as sixteen dollars a week; now, the highest regular price for room and board is ten, and 'local people' are charged six to eight."[97]

It is easy enough to shrug off such cases of "hospitility" against tourists and tourism as unrepresentative. Or to explain it away as typical of an island society's clannishness or xenophobia.[98] Or to justify it as a natural dynamic of the tourism trade, given the tourists' inevitably inferior understanding of the place they visit. And all of these were likely in play. But it is also sensible to see such resentment as the culmination of the specific way Island tourism had been presented to locals to date. Though the new Tourist Association was assuring Islanders that everyone would gain materially from tourism's success, nothing was being done to make sure that happened. Tourism was still focused on promotion, and promotion on tourists, not Islanders, so it distanced guests from hosts.

The roots of this distancing are evident in the promotional literature of the first decades of the century. Having largely replaced the critical output of freelance travel writers from away, the new guidebooks and articles were written for the province and often anonymously. One might think that using Island writers would make the material more informed. But because the literature had official government endorsement, everything said had to be laudatory, so the image of Prince Edward Island grew if anything more homogeneous. Nowhere was this more evident than in descriptions of scenery. In the previous century, writers had captured the Island's landscape in diverse ways: from Charles Dudley Warner's "flat from end to end as a floor" to Reverend R. Murray's "gently undulating, like a sea which has sobbed itself to rest." Twentieth century promotional writers, by comparison, pored over their thesauruses to create a single image that became more rigid as it became more refined. Whereas Murray's reference in the 1882 *Picturesque Canada* to PEI's "gently undulating" landscape was reproduced by promotional writers Crosskill in the 1900s and McCready in the 1910s,[99] they ignored his subsequent reference to the "bracing breath" of the sea air. Ozone was out of favour now as a therapeutic. It had been decided that the Island was picturesque, and there was no need, as there had been in the nineteenth century, to make pretensions to sublimity. The writing could still be affected, however. McCready rhapsodized that "Fields of feathery oats alternate with acres of dark green root-crops or windswayed wheat, while verdant meadows dotted with drowsy cattle make this 'a land where it seems always afternoon.' From every hilltop the wayfarer marks the course of rippling river or purling brook winding like silver ribbons athwart the sunlit landscape."[100]

More than ever, the image of PEI became that of a place of soothing serenity. It is entirely appropriate that Crosskill's claim in 1904 that "The majority of tourists, however, go to the North Shore … to revel in the surf and strong air of that famous region" was retouched by his successor McCready in 1912 as "to revel in the surf and calm air."[101] Strong was fine for other places but calm was what tourists to the Island presumably wanted, so calm was what they got. Such marketing grew even more pronounced in the 1920s. The new Tourist Association's publicity described how the Island's scenery, climate, and people worked together to create a distinctly peaceful lifestyle; the group's first publication was entitled *Restful Summer*. "All combine," according to another guide, "to make Prince Edward Island a recreational land in the real sense of the word, where tired bodies, languid spirits and weary minds may be again built up."[102] The simplicity of the Island did not need excusing; on the contrary, it was its primary grounds for being a destination. By 1939, the province concluded its *Vacationland of Heart's Content* guidebook stating,

> Here you will find sun and surf and wholesome food, and all the simple enjoyments that afford complete relaxation from the geared-up turmoil of modern life in the great cities. Here you will find an old-fashioned spirit of hospitality and a sincere welcome among a sturdy, friendly folk unspoiled by present-day hurry and rush.
>
> This booklet is your invitation and your passport to carefree days. Come to "the Island" this year – and *rest!*[103]

It is not that this increasingly standardized image was "untrue": Prince Edward Island could certainly be restful. The point is that it was only one of many possible ways of representing one's experience of the province. It was a choice, and a far from arbitrary one, to present Prince Edward Island as a traditional culture rooted in a pastoral landscape – each helping to shape the other. If tourists to Quebec in the interwar period were meant to discover the peasant stock of Old Quebec, visitors to the Island would find the simpler landscapes of a simpler time.[104] In that sense, it actually helped that the Island's economy had not kept pace with that of the rest of Canada for decades. It suffered low wages, lack of industry, and severe outmigration. When around the turn of the century tourist literature had accompanied general booster literature that also sought to attract immigrants and investment, it was natural to describe the province as a bustling place with a promising future. But when tourism literature began to be written on its own, there was not the same need. Instead, promoting Prince Edward Island in terms of its unchanging serenity, as a respite from modern life, allowed the province's failure to industrialize to be cast as a virtue. It was not involuntarily premodern but rather, with a degree of intentionality, antimodern. If it had somewhat fewer modern amenities, if it was a little poorer, then that was how it wished to be, how it was meant to be. (That tourism offered a means to reclaim outmigrants, if only for a week or two each summer, was a psychological and financial bonus.) Historian Ian McKay's exploration of how antimodernism transformed Nova Scotia's identity in the interwar years has been profoundly influential in the Canadian history field; the story he tells is recognizable on the other side of the Northumberland Strait, too.[105]

Although the provincial government was making a concerted effort in the 1920s to attract more immigrants, trends in tourism promotion generally, partnered with the Island's specific focus on getting away from it all, meant that promotional literature offered less and less of a sense of the Island as a living, breathing society. Descriptions and images of prominent churches and public buildings – staples of earlier accounts and turn-of-the-century postcards – disappeared. As a writer to the *Guardian* said, "There is an impression abroad that Americans come to the Island to look at the Cameron Block. That's sheer nonsense. Most of them would have to hunt in their own towns to find anything poorer. They come to live in the country, to enjoy its grassy lanes, its streams, and woods, and sea-sides, its fresh fish and pure meats, and its unsophisticated men and women."[106] Larger and more numerous photographs pushed text devoted to Island life right off the page. For example, the Intercolonial and PEI Railway's guides to the Island, after many editions, in 1913 doubled the number of photographs at the expense of a section on farming.[107] Promoters were calculating that the tourist was more interested in what they would see at a potential destination than in how their hosts lived – to some degree, surely a self-fulfilling prophecy.

How Prince Edward Island's history was presented also changed, becoming less tied to past residents' lived experiences. Through the late century, some American travel writers had been intrigued with "the land question," Islanders' long struggle with absentee British land barons. But it left twentieth-century promoters cold: they could not relate it to Canadian history, it was not personally relatable, and, perhaps worst of all, it did not direct visitors to a specific destination. Surprisingly, it was not until 1930 – a full decade and a half after the cancelled Confederation Conference jubilee – that the province began presenting Province House, where the conference had met, as an attraction. It apparently worked: Tourist Association President Aubin Arsenault claimed that the number of visitors to Province House jumped from 100 in 1930 to 4,000 in 1937.[108]

History was its most marketable when it was tangible, but even the shadow of history could be made to work. Rocky Point was introduced as worth visiting because of its "historic old French fort" – more accurately, the outline of the earthworks of the British fort built at the same location as an earlier French one. Relics had been found there, readers were told, and more importantly, "The air of romance still lingers."[109] No one said why, until the French fort was described in 1939 as "the scene of an expulsion of Acadians less well known but even more pitiful than that from Grand Pré, in Nova Scotia, told by Longfellow in the poem 'Evangeline.'"[110] There was nothing to see – but it was well worth seeing.

That an air of history might attract tourists, or at least focus them, influenced D.C. Harvey's work with Canada's Historic Sites and Monuments Board. Although most of his working life was spent as provincial archivist of Nova Scotia and professor at Dalhousie University, Harvey was a loyal Prince Edward Islander, and he was even willing to compromise his classical liberalism in his efforts to garner his native province as many HSMB plaques as conscience – and history – would allow in order to promote Island tourism.[111] Meanwhile, travel writers toyed with pushing back the European discovery of Prince Edward Island, not in hopes of drawing tourists to a landing spot but because a longer European heritage would presumably make the Island more historically significant. French explorer Jacques Cartier's 1534 blurb of the Island as "the fairest land 'tis possible to see" ensured he was a good starting point for promotional purposes. On very slim evidence John Cabot, earlier and English (or at least as English as anyone born Giovanni Caboto could be), was occasionally said to have visited the province in 1497.[112] But a still earlier candidate was found. The 1939 guidebook *Vacationland of Heart's Content* featured a cartoon map of the province, complete with a Viking ship sailing toward the north shore, and told the reader, "Possibly visited by Leif Ericson on his Vineland expedition."[113]

Islanders may have bristled at the ways in which their province's scenery, way of life, and history were being presented for tourists. But it was more likely the changing nature of actual interactions with tourists – and how boosters sought to direct such interactions – that soured some Islanders against tourism and its promotion. The Island had a half-century experience with tourists by the 1920s, but that decade saw fundamental changes in how the trade took place. That outmigration was peaking just then meant there were more returning expatriates than ever, but there were also more "real" tourists unfamiliar with the Island and themselves unfamiliar to Islanders. What's more, the geography of tourism was evolving. The automobile distributed tourists into every corner of the province, pulling rural constituencies into the trade whether they wanted to be or not.[114]

This was especially so because of the popularity of autocamping: living, as much as possible, out of one's car while touring, often camping beside the road. The PEI Tourist Association encouraged autocamping, in part because it offered farmers the chance to sell food to tourists from their doorstep.[115] Unfortunately, promoters sometimes promised tourists more than this. Islander Lucy Gertrude Clarkin assured readers, for example, "And it is not always necessary for a hungry motoring party to return to their hotel to satisfy their appetites. The people of Prince Edward Island are noted for their hospitality, and there are few householders in this land of plenty who cannot supply a dainty lunch on short notice."[116] There is no evidence that unsuspecting citizens were subsequently swamped by demanding, ravenous hordes, but such images of the Islander as ever-gracious, ever-subservient host must have rankled. The 1926 edition of one guide announced, "At most of the farm houses throughout the island meals or lodging can be secured when necessary at reasonable rates." The 1927 edition of the same guide is absolutely identical except for a single word: "most" farmhouses had become "many."[117] When the Tourist Association, composed almost entirely of Charlottetown and Summerside businessmen, complained that "the outside districts did practically nothing to assist in our work,"[118] it is tempting to ask whether rural Islanders were disproportionally opposed to tourism, as they had been to the automobile – and whether the association's own make-up was one reason why.

One reason the Tourist Association endorsed autocamping was the perceived lack of alternatives: even more so than in the late nineteenth century, Prince Edward Island was short of hotels. At the association's annual meeting in 1929, it was noted that while tourism numbers were on the rise, the number of hotel rooms had dropped 20 per cent since 1922 … and the very next day, the Island's largest hotel, the Victoria in Charlottetown, burned to the ground. The association as a result discussed halting its activities altogether for the 1929 season, since PEI might not be able to accommodate tourists who did arrive.[119] Association President Aubin Arsenault headed a delegation of leading citizens not to the provincial government but to Canadian National Railways, asking that its hotel division build a replacement for the Victoria. Company president Sir Henry Thornton agreed to sink $1 million in the project, and the new Charlottetown Hotel opened in 1931, twice as large as any hotel in the province.[120] Promotional brochures advertised it as indicative of the type of accommodations available on the Island, and that year's speech from the throne predicted that the new hotel would singlehandedly expand the Island's tourist traffic.

Perhaps it did, but while the Tourist Association was seeking accommodation salvation in grand hotels, Islanders were quietly opening their homes to tourists. They simply posted a "tourists accommodated" sign at the lane

and charged visitors $1 per night. To middle-class tourists with not a lot of money, this was a viable middle ground between autocamping and staying at a hotel.[121] Association manager Minnie MacFadyen estimated that some farm homes were getting upward of sixty tourists per summer, some staying for weeks ("and I am not speaking of 'home comers' but real tourists").[122] Though the number of hotelkeepers in the province declined from thirty-eight to thirty-four between 1921 and 1931, the number of lodging and boarding housekeepers jumped from thirty-eight to 105. Notably, 101 of those were women; tourism was expanding an occupation within the boundaries of what was traditionally the women's sphere.[123] Association president Arsenault stated, "Our work is to bring people here, to receive them, to inform them, but we are not in the hotel business, that is the part our citizens must attend to."[124] Citizens were in fact attending to it, but the Tourist Association, busy lobbying for upscale accommodations, hardly took notice. With the arrival of the Great Depression making money much tighter, private subscriptions to the organization dried up, both in real terms and as a percentage of its budget. The Tourist Association more and more took on the mantle of a private

Figure 2.9 ▪ A postcard image of the Victoria Hotel, on the corner of Water and Great George Streets in Charlottetown. It was the Island's finest hotel in the early twentieth century, until destroyed by fire in 1929. A local lobbying effort convinced Canadian National Railways to construct its own hotel, the Charlottetown, in 1931.

sector trade organization; its pretence of being a service club grew less and less convincing.[125]

Any dissatisfaction with how tourism was being organized in this era only once came close to becoming a public issue. In 1935, the *Guardian* published a remarkable "open letter" from Aubin Arsenault to R.H. Sterns, owner of the Beach Grove Inn (and past owner of the destroyed Victoria Hotel), calling for a "show down" about unstated accusations Sterns had made at the two most recent annual meetings of the Tourist Association. Sterns replied with an open letter of his own. In it he charged the association's Minnie MacFadyen and her husband, who together managed the Stanhope Beach Inn, with funnelling visitors to their inn rather than his. Cryptically, he also called Arsenault "ill-advised, to become interested financially or otherwise in any hotel" while president of the association. Sterns reproached Arsenault generally for being obsessed with the building of new hotels and not supporting ones that already existed: "Until the summer 1933 we had not registered one guest that we could trace to have come to us through the Tourist Association."[126] We might have learned more about tourism in this era had Arsenault or the MacFadyens responded, but this very public feud died abruptly because Sterns himself died abruptly, the very day that his letter appeared in print.[127]

If some Islanders were grumbling about tourism, this was despite – but also, likely, because of – the fact that it was becoming an indisputable, even indispensable part of the Island economy. Not even the Great Depression could stop it. Prince Edward Island had not experienced a Roaring '20s, but it nevertheless felt the Dirty '30s as much as the rest of the Western world did. Income from agriculture and fisheries plummeted. But tourism shone like a beacon. While tourism revenue across Canada dropped from more than $300 million in 1929 to less than $120 million four years later, PEI's numbers essentially held firm. Helped along by the SS *Charlottetown*, a new, larger, and slightly faster ferry carrying not just railcars but fifty automobiles, the Tormentine–Borden crossing saw traffic rise from 4,500 automobiles in the 1930 tourist season to 4,700 in 1931, before dipping to just over 3,900 each of the next two years. It then climbed to 5,500 cars by 1935.[128] Higher visitation from Ontario and Quebec compensated for lower American numbers, and if, as was believed, tourists were not staying so long or spending quite so much, at least they were still coming.[129] An industry that even during a global economic downturn pumped money into the province without taking anything away was sure to attract government attention. Although austerity was the order of the day, the provincial government's annual grant to the Tourist Association actually increased from $2,000 to $3,000 in 1931 and continued at that rate through 1936.[130] (In that year, the new Liberal government under Thane Campbell raised the grant to $3,500 and within two years to $10,000.)

82

The Summer Trade

Figure 2.10 ▪ In rallying tourism against the tide of the Great Depression, the PEI Tourist Association convinced Canadian National Railways to lower the fare on its Borden–Tormentine run to $3 return.

The Canadian state was also awakening to the value of tourism. The sharp decline in traffic from the US during the Depression brought with it the realization that a *laissez faire* policy with respect to the trade was inadequate. As a first step towards a more hands-on tourism strategy, Canada in 1934 established a Senate Committee on Tourist Traffic to determine what the industry needed. The committee was chaired by Senator W.H. Dennis, the long-time publisher of the Halifax *Herald*, who had a wealth of experience in promoting the Maritimes for tourism. The six-member committee also included senators Creelman MacArthur of Prince Edward Island and W.E. Forster of New Brunswick, ensuring the Maritimes an inordinate amount of influence. Prince Edward Island had almost not been represented at all. When Senator Arthur Meighen had first proposed and named a committee and it was noted that he had not included a delegate from the Island, he had shrugged, "It is not necessary to encourage traffic there."[131] It was, in its way, a high compliment to how much tourism promotion on the Island had already achieved.

A Canadian Travel Bureau was born out of the Senate committee's work, and in apparent homage, the PEI Tourist Association renamed itself the PEI Travel Bureau early in 1935.[132] It also felt encouraged to speak with a stronger voice in government affairs. It joined Senator MacArthur in lobbying the federal government relentlessly to have ferry rates reduced for the tourist season, arguing that the Island suffered by being the only province one had to pay to visit. Amazingly, they were successful, and the return fare was lowered from $7 to $5 in 1933 and then to $3 a year later.[133] That, and the fact that the provincial government had, with matching federal funds, launched a make-work project paving Island highways, meant that in the heart of the Great Depression Prince Edward Island was suddenly better able to welcome tourists than ever before. A decade earlier Board of Trade president J.O. Hyndman had said he had never known a tourist to the Island not to complain. Now, in 1935, he was quoted as saying "it was really the first time he could give his wholehearted support to the tourist business. Some years ago, 75 per cent of the people who came here went away knockers, because of the roads or the boat service. Now since the new ferry and the completion of the paved road, all that has been changed."[134]

Prince Edward Island tourism had indeed matured in the previous decade. And yet. Annual passenger traffic was still estimated to be less than 25,000.[135] The Tourist Association turned Travel Bureau was thriving thanks largely to an active, well-known president and a hustling manager, but it was running on less than $5,000 per year, which was somewhat less than before the Depression. The province was demonstrating its commitment to the industry with a small annual expenditure, but this paled against what other provinces, also recognizing tourism's value, were doing. British Columbia, Ontario, New Brunswick, and Nova Scotia had already established far better funded government tourist bureaus, and Quebec was spending $250,000 each year in promotion.[136] The Prince Edward Island tourism industry was such small beans that it didn't even recognize that it was. It would take the Island's first tourist attraction to make both boosters and knockers see how much bigger that industry could become.

A principal recommendation of the Senate's 1934 Special Committee on Tourist Traffic was that the national park system be truly nationalized, with each province given at least one park.[137] Canada had spent more than $22 million on national parks over the previous half-century, but almost all of that money had gone to the West, which possessed the mountain scenery with which parks had become associated. There was no national park east of Ontario. But the Great Depression had made both tourism and government investment more desirable than ever, and the Maritime-heavy representation on the committee ensured the region would be heard.

Figure 2.11 ▪ Dalvay-by-the-Sea in Grand Tracadie had been built in the 1890s as the summer home of a president of Standard Oil. When a site was being sought for a national park for Prince Edward Island in the mid-1930s, Dalvay was thought the logical choice to attract well-off people of leisure. It did become part of the park but was balanced by the more mass appeal of Cavendish and Green Gables. The owner in 1931 was swashbuckling rumrunner Captain Edward Dicks, who reputedly used it as a cover for smuggling liquor ashore.

Premier Thane Campbell, whose Liberals had just swept to power winning every seat in the provincial legislature, returned from a federal–provincial conference noting that "the national park idea at Ottawa seems to be directed, to a large extent, to the promotion of the tourism industry."[138] Although the Liberals' election campaign had said nothing of a national park, early in 1936 Campbell's administration asked the Canadian government to establish one. Campbell clearly conceived of the park not strictly in terms of tourism – and certainly not environmental protection – so much as federal funding generally and road-building specifically. His first letter to the federal government about a national park was directed to the minister of transportation, C.D. Howe, stating that since any site chosen would likely be distant from a paved highway on the Island, the province would be requesting funds to pave to it.[139] At such an early stage, Campbell could not possibly know that the park would be a distance from existing highways unless he was determined to make sure it was.

The 1936 diary of Island businessman Harry T. Holman reveals the intense lobbying that took place behind the scenes to secure a national park location. In late February, well before the provincial government had declared officially any interest in a park to either its citizens or the feds, Holman wrote of Lieutenant Governor "DeBlois trying to interest them in Dalvay," with senior political figures backing the plan. DeBlois's involvement with Dalvay-by-the-Sea is curious, to say the least. The stately Victorian summer home had switched hands a number of times over the years, until in the early 1930s rumrunner Captain Edward Dicks opened it as a summer hotel, with accompanying nine-hole golf course. But he went bankrupt, and DeBlois, one of his creditors, bought it in late 1935 or early 1936. It is entirely unclear whether the lieutenant governor, in pushing to have Dalvay become part of a national park, was principally motivated by a desire to preserve it or to flip it for a quick buck; he would end up achieving both.[140]

Holman for his part led a group that favoured first a Dunk River location and then Holman's Island, where his great-uncle had opened the doomed Island Park Hotel decades earlier. But most of this faction's energy seems to have been devoted to denigrating "the utter foolishness of Dalvay as a park."[141] Having ignited this squabble, Premier Campbell was loath to choose one location over another, so in April he announced that the National Parks Branch (the precursor to Parks Canada) would choose the site and the province would buy it. Privately, the two levels of government agreed that, as minister in charge of national parks T.A. Crerar said, sight unseen, "this Dalvay by the Sea premises will probably be the most acceptable."[142]

But Prince Edward Islanders did not know this, so the two Charlottetown newspapers, the *Patriot* and *Guardian*, were filled that spring with letters to the editor debating the relative merits of locales throughout the province: whose streams were clearest, whose air freshest, whose grass greenest. Many writers believed the planned park was not really for them anyway; it was for tourists. And to those Islanders clutching desperately to retain Prohibition, tourism – any foreign influence – meant iniquity. "Pro Bono Publico," for example, excoriated the government for spending money to "provide a playground, or perhaps something less innocent for tourists."[143] Alex McDonald, on the other hand, did not believe a park would increase tourism anyway, since PEI had a reputation as "a poor place for sport as it is too much Christianised."[144] Rumours swirled that the debate was pointless, that Dalvay had already been chosen. On the eve of the arrival of inspectors from the National Parks Branch in mid-June 1936, Holman wrote in his diary, "Will be very glad when it is over as it has entailed a lot of work and worry."[145]

It must have been a strange experience for the two senior Parks Branch staffers, Frank H.H. Williamson and W.D. Cromarty, to inspect the by that time twenty-two sites – often with the premier and a string of local politicians in tow.[146] After all, two existing national parks, Banff and Jasper, were larger than the entire *province*. It was political exigency that was forcing the Parks Branch to establish national parks in the East, and there is no evidence among staff of enthusiasm for nationalizing the system. Williamson was deputy chief of the parks service, and chief by the time the PEI park was actually established, so his opinion of the Island mattered. Months before visiting the Island, he wrote that it would be impossible to apply existing national park standards there: it was simply too small and lacking in scenic grandeur and wildlife. So it called for a new kind of national park. "Naturally its development should centre around its principal feature – its extensive beaches with warm sea bathing," Williamson wrote. The goal should not be "attracting only hundreds of tourists but many thousands a year. I see no reason why we cannot expect a quarter of a million visitors a year in a few years … It seems to me the best contribution the park can make in the interests of Prince Edward Island and the country generally is to develop it as a typical seaside resort, sans the obnoxious amusements."[147]

The irony is that whereas the Parks Branch envisioned a Prince Edward Island national park as encouraging a more inclusive tourism, on the Island it was championed as encouraging a more exclusive one. An editorial in the *Guardian* supported Dalvay as the park site, stating, "What is a National Park for but to draw tourists to a province? What better have we to offer tourists than our magnificent sandy beaches and surf bathing? What better place for these than Grand Tracadie? What more commodious sea shore hotel accommodation than at Dalvay? The thing is self-evident." To the newspaper, the ultimate proof of Dalvay's suitability was that it was the site chosen and built on by American millionaire Alexander MacDonald and thus fit "our purpose – the development of our tourist traffic asset through attracting wealthy people of leisure of the type of the MACDONALDS to spend their summer and money on our shores."[148] The Parks Branch's and *Guardian*'s point of agreement was that the goal was a park that appealed to "mass" even as the park imprimatur assured it "class."

When Williamson and Cromarty inspected Dalvay, they agreed with the provincial government's recommendation of it, believing it would fit well into the tradition of majestic park hotels. (Or so they told themselves. A decade later a senior parks staffer admitted, "we knew that we were acquiring a white elephant."[149]) But they were also won over by Cavendish because of its beach and its association with *Anne of Green Gables* – an association they apparently first learned about by way of a large signboard the PEI Travel Bureau had erected in the district.[150] Whereas Williamson had called Dalvay "principally for elderly people," Cavendish could appeal "both to those who appreciate beauty and to the younger element who desire variety in their holiday entertainment."[151] Williamson in time listed some of the ways the Parks Branch might develop Cavendish:

(… "Green Gables" stream reserved for young children's fishing and the woods for children's village, picnicing etc; toy yachting on "Lake of Shining Waters," children's canoeing, paddle boating etc.) "Green Gables" might be a children's rest house with museum, aquarium etc. … [Need for] bowling greens and buildings for same; dancing, roller skating and carnival arena, etc. Concessions may be rented for bungalow camps, hotels, boarding houses, restaurants, soft drinks and ice cream, boats, canoes, wheeled bathing houses; beach donkies and ponies; beach ... minstrels; bands; moving picture theatres and other shows.[152]

In later decades, the parks agency would join Islanders and tourists in decrying the intense commercialization of Cavendish, on the doorstep of the national park, but at the outset such commercialization had been part of the plan for the park itself.

In late July 1936 the inspectors submitted their report to Ottawa, recommending a site along the north shore from Dalvay westward, through Stanhope, Brackley, Rustico, and Cavendish beaches all the way to New London. This was a surprise to the provincial government. It had quietly supported Dalvay under the assumption that it was the only place sublime and stately enough to meet national park standards; it was on this basis that the province was willing to pay DeBlois's $15,000 asking price. But now it seemed that the Parks Branch appreciated the seaside scenery of the North Shore generally and was willing to develop it heavily. So the province publicly announced it was accepting the report "insofar as the same recommends" a new park from Brackley to New London – Dalvay was to be excluded.[153] The Parks Branch reacted with alarm. Williamson warned his superiors that a park of "constricted size will not permit of accommodating a large number of visitors which is the only justification for the establishment of a National park on the north shore of the Island."[154] The concern was not that overcrowding would damage the site's natural environment but that the park might become so popular it would change how people thought of Canadian national parks in general. Dalvay was needed as a runoff, a quiet place where a more subdued vision of parks could live on. Cromarty was rushed to Prince Edward Island with an ultimatum: no Dalvay, no park. The Campbell government reinstated it at once.

Now that the site had been finalized, it was up to the provincial government to acquire the strip of land forty kilometres long and a couple of hundred metres wide. Close to one hundred properties were involved. Many were farm families, some would have their homes displaced, and virtually all would be losing the most valuable part of their land, the seaside frontage. With no Opposition in the legislature, the Campbell administration devised a process alternately neglectful and ham-handed to execute the expropriation.[155] It took over the land and transferred it to Canada in the spring of 1937 before it had ever notified the vast majority of owners their land was needed, let alone what price the province would be offering. Only that summer did the province finally move forward on settling claims, and only that autumn did a

The Summer Trade

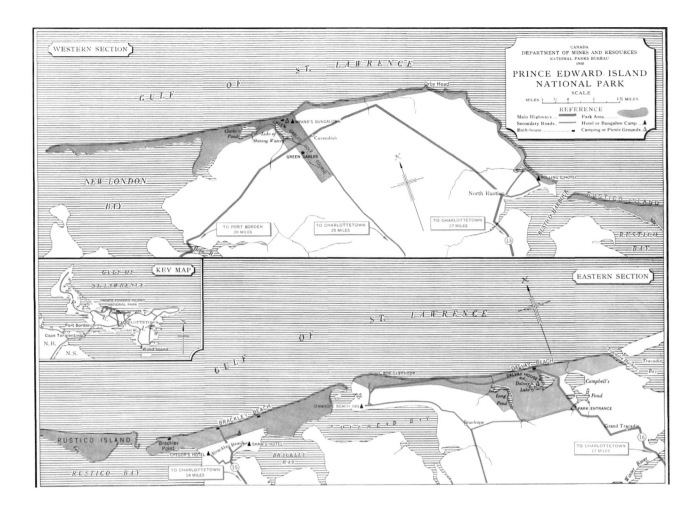

"Committee of Dispossessed Landowners" emerge to oppose the park and the settlements. But the sale of the two prize properties, Green Gables and Dalvay, had been resolved a full year earlier, as soon as the park's site was determined.

On learning in September 1936 of three Cavendish farms that would be purchased, including Ernest and Myrtle Webb's "Green Gables," author L.M. Montgomery despaired of the part she had played in all this. "I feel dreadfully," she told her journal. "Where will the Webbs go? ... Everything changed. I understand these farms were chosen because of *Anne of Green Gables*. It's a compliment I well could spare." The woods and lanes she had walked "will be open to the public – desecrated by hordes of sightseers and by pleasure hunters. It is a bitter thought to me."[156]

Montgomery's lament, delivered with the emotion one might expect of her most famous character, concerned the passing of one way of life for another: agriculture for tourism, a production economy for a service economy, the

Figure 2.12 ▪ Created in 1936 by expropriating the province's most popular tourist area, Prince Edward Island National Park was Canada's smallest national park and, following the interruption of the Second World War, one of its most visited.

secluded for the connected, the premodern for the modern. And Prince Edward Island National Park signalled by its birth, and would help facilitate by its life, all of these transitions. But simply dichotomizing the history of Prince Edward Island tourism as pre- and post-park misses that some of those whose properties would be expropriated were already engaged in the tourism field. The Webbs themselves, after first opening Green Gables to boarders in the 1920s, were giving tours and selling souvenirs, and had built two cottages to accommodate more guests. In other words, they had continued the process that L.M. Montgomery had only begun, of making Green Gables a tourist attraction. And the fact that Green Gables was already an attraction was what made it attractive to the Parks Branch: they could readily envision its potential.

The Webbs resigned themselves to the power of the state and settled quickly, selling Green Gables for $6,500 and the promise of a $50 per month job for Ernest as caretaker in the new park.[157] But other landowners who were engaged in the tourism industry raised their voices against expropriation. Jeremiah and Christianna Simpson, who lived two farms west of the Webbs and whose land sloped attractively down to the shore, had in 1921 been the first in Cavendish to take in tourists as a sideline.[158] Herbert McCallum had been so bullish about the future of the tourism trade that in constructing McCallum's Hotel (Brackley Beach Lodge) he ensured it was sufficiently reinforced so that extra storeys could be added when needed. And Percy MacAusland had bought half of Robinsons Island in 1926 with the intention of eventually buying the rest and developing it as a tourist resort.[159] When the Committee of Dispossessed Landowners formed, many of its members were farmers, and much of their rhetoric was framed in terms of the loss of farms and farmland.[160] But it is telling that tourism operators, and aspiring ones such as MacAusland, became the most vocal of all landowners in their opposition to expropriation. They understood the economic potential of tourism in the land they would be losing and saw the government not as a neutral party but as a rival business enacting a hostile takeover.

The experience of Katherine Wyand is emblematic. She had entered the summer trade in the mid-1920s by opening a food and drink booth on Cavendish Beach on weekends. By the end of the decade she had built Avonlea Cottages there, renting out cabins by the night or week. The Parks Branch tentatively offered to let her continue her business but rescinded the offer after deciding her cottages were not well made or attractive enough to meet park standards. Wyand refused to move and took to writing long letters to the editor of the *Guardian* documenting her struggle with the two levels of government. She protested the governments' argument that she could simply move her business outside the park boundaries. "Utter nonsense," she argued: her present location was ideal, so if she moved it would necessarily be to an inferior one, and she would be facing the "keen competition" of the Canadian government. What's more, she would pay dearly for the privilege, since land prices just outside the park had skyrocketed with word of the park's creation – to $500 per acre, she claimed, about ten times what the province was giving property owners for land inside.[161] Wyand's feud peaked with a front-page, above-the-fold "Open Letter to Members of the Legislature" in the *Guardian* which began, "The challenge which you have issued to Democracy must be taken up, even if it is taken by a woman."[162]

But with the province having expropriated the land and turned it over to Canada in April 1937, the new national park began to gain legitimacy by virtue of its existence. It was given a name, Prince Edward Island National Park.[163] Its boundaries were set out and a fence built around it. It received media attention. (A *Globe and Mail* headline identified it as heralding a new national park aesthetic: "Prince Edward Island Park is Held Unique: Called Only One in Level Country."[164]) And as early as summer 1937, tourists arrived, proclaiming their own brand of squatters' rights by driving down lanes, picking cranberries, and tearing down fences that belonged to landowners who were only just starting to get offers from the province, let alone settlements.[165]

The federal and provincial governments also worked together to justify the park's existence by developing infrastructure for tourism. Prince Edward Island received $40,000 from Canada's "Tourist Roads Programme" to build and gravel roads leading to the park. Another $100,000 of federal funds went to park construction, including a special work relief grant in aid of park construction. Beach and kitchen shelters were built, Dalvay and Green Gables were beautified and shaped up, while buildings associated with other human occupation were torn down or moved away. Premier Campbell crowed in 1938 that while federal–provincial cost-sharing was typically a 50:50 matter, he had gotten Canada to pay a disproportionate part of the park's creation.[166]

A new golf course was seen as crucial in making the park credible as a cultured destination. Canada's leading golf architect, Stanley Thompson, had become the darling of the park system over the previous decade, having built deluxe courses at Jasper and Banff – the latter believed to be, at the time, the most expensive one ever built.[167] Now he was brought in to design an eighteen-hole course in Cavendish with Green Gables its centrepiece. As director R.A. Gibson stated, while the branch would be "glad to have the local people use [it] … the golf course would be justified almost wholly on the ground that it would provide an attraction for tourists."[168] Thompson oversaw a crew of forty men in 1938, more than the number working on the rest of the park combined. They landscaped enthusiastically, nowhere more so than around Green Gables house, where they levelled off a little rise that would serve as the eighteenth green. The house itself was to be a tearoom for golfers, the

Figure 2.13 • Myrtle and Ernest Webb's farmhouse, "Green Gables," in a Parks Canada photograph taken shortly after the farm was bought to be part of the new Prince Edward Island National Park in 1936. The photo is labelled "No.18 green from 225 yd mark."

Webbs' barn the clubhouse.[169] Costs for the golf course ballooned to a reported $18,000 per hole.[170] In the winter of 1939, the *Montreal Star* slammed the golf course for destroying Green Gables's natural beauty, but Premier Campbell defended the development as necessary for protecting "the natural amenities, woods, and the streams, and such-like" from the tourists who were sure to come.[171]

But where would these tourists stay? The national park's creation had eliminated almost all the rented cottages and rooms for tourists between New London and Grand Tracadie – that is, it had upended the tourism trade that had been building over the previous half-century. Apart from Shaw's and Gregor's-by-the-Sea in Brackley, the North Shore was virtually without accommodations for a time. It turned out that Dalvay would need extensive repairs – more than half its purchase price in 1939 alone – just to maintain the illusion that it could be the high-end park hotel the branch had originally envisioned.[172] Moreover, when the Parks Branch put out tenders for cottage concessions, Islanders did not submit bids; perhaps they knew they could not meet the branch's exacting standards. So the Parks Branch approached tourism operators who had just been expropriated. Responses varied. For example, Parks Controller Williamson wrote Percy MacAusland, who had dreamed of building a resort on Robinsons Island, explaining, "we are anxious that private enterprise undertake certain tourist developments … but we have been disappointed that some of these tourist propositions had not already been taken up." MacAusland not only did not take the Parks Branch up on its offer, a generation later he was still writing letters to prime ministers comparing the expropriation process to communism.[173] But Katherine Wyand, who had criticized the park so outspokenly in the press, accepted the branch's invitation to reopen her cottages in the park, once they were moved further off the beach, cleaned up, and painted. She held the concession for more than a decade.[174] Wyand's cottages alone could not resolve the park's lodgings issue, however, and by 1940 the PEI Travel Bureau's annual report warned that in Cavendish accommodation was "BADLY NEEDED IMMEDIATELY."[175]

Accommodations were needed because tourists were coming. Attendance at Prince Edward Island National Park jumped from 2,500 in 1937 to 35,000 two years later. It was almost immediately, and then consistently, one of the most visited parks in Canada.[176] The park was well on its way to accomplishing its mission of being the focus of tourism for the province. Even L.M. Montgomery, who had initially been so distraught to hear about the park, stated that she grew "reconciled" to it when Premier Campbell assured her that Ernest Webb would be staying on as caretaker at Green Gables and that "the woods and paths and dykes would be kept just as they were etc. So I began to feel that it was all for the best because those places will never be desecrated now."[177] Green Gables was almost better than ever – or at least more the idyllic place of Montgomery's imagination. Parks Branch workers tamed wild bushes, and planted trees and flowers. They rerouted what had been the straight laneway, typical of Island farms, so that it wound along the stream in more picturesque fashion.[178] And they painted the house. For what was apparently the first time ever, Green Gables had green gables.[179]

All in all, the establishment of Prince Edward Island National Park happened quite quickly and smoothly. It is remarkable to think that the provincial government acquired roughly one hundred parcels, comprising what was, even at the time, some of the most valuable property on the Island, for little more than $100,000 – about $1,600,000 today, when adjusted for inflation.[180] The Great Depression was one reason; the economic conditions that had made the Island a candidate for a national park also helped it secure one cheaply. Prevailing Canadian expropriation law, which heavily favoured the state, was another. Related to this, the fact that citizens of the day were largely resigned to the notion that governments could do as they pleased was another. The Committee of Dispossessed Landowners withered away in 1938, as those facing expropriation watched more and more of their neighbours receive settlements and felt increasing pressure to sell. Jeremiah Simpson was one of the few who continued to resist. His farm had been in his family for a century and a half, and since they had begun renting rooms to tourists in the 1920s, it was more valuable than ever; "I would not sell it to my best friend," he said.[181] So when almost half of Simpson's farm was taken for the park, he simply ignored the order and kept farming it. He plowed, seeded, and harvested fields next to the Lake of Shining Waters for seven more years, before the park superintendent finally convinced him to relent. But he never accepted the money waiting for him in the Court of Chancery.

Landowners who had been dispossessed to make way for the national park resented bitterly that the state had been so parsimonious in terms of both money and consideration. And yet the irony is that total spending on land, roads, the golf course, and other developments related to the park absolutely dwarfed all previous provincial and federal government investment in tourism put together. Prince Edward Island National Park raised tourism in the province to a new level. It pooled the Island's historical resort area, its new literary mecca, and some of its best beaches, and ensured that the resultant jurisdiction would be designed, protected, and marketed as one, forever. It was the headliner, the tent pole, the anchor that the Island tourism industry hadn't even known it needed. The park's establishment, then, can be interpreted as the culminating victory of tourist boosterism in the early twentieth century. Boosters had promoted the Island's suitability as a tourism destination and the value to the Island of making itself one; the park validated both arguments. It confirmed the summer trade as having become an important, even indispensable, part of PEI society and economy and helped ensure it would continue to be. What's more, tourism was accepted as something that should not be left to chance but, rather, required direction.

Specifically, government direction. Although individual tourism operations were sprouting up throughout the Island in the 1920s and '30s, and although the industry had matured to the point that a provincial association had become well entrenched, the provincial and federal governments' first major foray into Prince Edward Island tourism paid these no attention. In fact, establishing the national park meant not merely ignoring the private developments already underway along the North Shore but sweeping them out of existence. The new park thus reads as both confidence in the Island tourism's future and impatience that Islanders were not engaging in the industry quickly enough or in the right way. It was a validation of tourism boosting that implicitly knocked all that had come before.

In 1936, the MacCallum family of Moncton, New Brunswick were planning a vacation to Prince Edward Island and placed an advertisement in an Island newspaper seeking a place to stay. Forty-two tourist operators – forty-two! – wrote them back. Betty MacCallum recalled her family being especially impressed by the letter from Mrs Leo Murphy of St Peter's, who rented cottages. Murphy described in great detail the newly built cottages, the fine mattresses, the trout pond out back, the swimming nearby. The MacCallums reserved a cottage with the Murphys and found it, in Betty's words, "just about the best place we'd ever been." Betty met her future husband there that summer and lived in St Peter's Bay the remainder of her long life.[182] We sometimes say that people and events are "lost to history" but of the forty-two tourist operators who wrote in hopes of getting the MacCallums' business it would be more appropriate to say they are "lost from history" – they have left so little imprint that they are even lost from a history of Prince Edward Island tourism to which they deserve to belong. Yet these individual, independent businesses were every bit as much a part of this history as was the national park. What those individuals engaged in the summer trade at that moment did not know was that, for good and for ill, government would play a much greater role in their industry in the years ahead.

CHAPTER 3

Escape Velocity
1940−60

Dolph Fleming and his wife Bertha were like most Islanders of the late 1930s. Though the term had yet to be invented, they relied on occupational pluralism to coax a living out of their small mixed farm. They grew potatoes, of course, and marketed their cream to the local co-op, but they also dabbled in fox farming, and they made a few extra dollars by marketing produce to the fishermen just down the road in North Rustico. When conditions were right, they hauled dulse off the shore – soon it would be Irish moss – and they periodically culled their woodlot for pulpwood. Every election, federal and provincial, Bertha worked as a poll clerk, and the family got its share of the little plums – working on the roads, repairing the wharf – that periodically fell from the patronage tree.[1]

The Flemings had a hundred acres on the road that led from North Rustico west towards Cavendish. But they also owned twenty-five acres along the shore at Cape Turner – at least, they did until the property was expropriated in 1937 to become part of the Prince Edward Island National Park. Dolph did not go gentle into that good night. As the details of the expropriations settled in and the incontestable property values were assessed, Fleming joined the groundswell of local protest. "Hot & dry," Fleming told his diary on 28 August. "I to Chtown with Roy Toombs. A big delegation to wate on the government."[2] That fall, Dolph and his son Cornelius tore down a stretch of fence that had been erected to mark the boundary of the new park and stubbornly ploughed their fields down at the Capes.[3]

Civil disobedience notwithstanding, the new park piqued Dolph's curiosity. "We had our first drive on the Park," he recorded that November. The next summer he and Bertha went Sunday driving to Stanhope Beach and Dalvay at the opposite end of the park with his brother.[4] A few months later, their son Cornelius got a job working in Cavendish on construction of the Stanley Thompson-designed golf course intended to lure tourists to the national

Figure 3.0 (facing) ▪ Women were typecast on the cover of the provincial Travel Bureau's 1942 guide. Literally. The cover also demonstrated promoters' short-lived fascination with birch trees when depicting the Island landscape.

park. And when the park officially opened on 19 July 1939, Dolph was part of the crowd. "Big day," he wrote. "Greg & I to opening of Golf course. 3 big plains flew around."[5] Like many other Islanders, he was slowly learning to live with tourism. Over the course of the next two decades, as the tourist *trade* gradually developed into a tourist *industry*, he would even get to like it.

Although Dolph Fleming did not bother to record it, the highlight of the grand opening of the Prince Edward Island National Park was a friendly "match of the century" between the federal minister responsible for the National Parks Branch, Thomas Crerar, and his cabinet colleague, Minister of Transport C.D. Howe. The occasion had been shrewdly co-opted to bulk up the program of a much larger event centred in Charlottetown.[6] Its dazzling success would add another key asset to Prince Edward Island's tourism portfolio. After a number of false starts, the province was finally ready to claim its place as the "Cradle of Confederation."

Ever since the outbreak of the Great War in 1914 preempted Prince Edward Island's celebration of the Golden Jubilee of the Charlottetown Conference, tourism boosters had tinkered with the Island's role in the making of Confederation.[7] "Cradle of Confederation" gave a title to some of the earliest film footage of the province, shot in 1925, and little by little the phrase crept into popular parlance.[8] As late as 1938, not much had yet been done to exploit its status as the nation's birthplace, but seventy-five was a promising number for celebratory purposes and by early 1939 the growing rapport between Thane Campbell's Liberal government and the PEI Travel Bureau had spawned a Confederation Celebration Committee. It was headed by the premier himself, with opposition leader W.J.P. MacMillan as vice-chair and the association's president, Judge Arsenault, as convenor (and thus, responsible for much of the actual planning).[9] The committee's goal was an expanded version of 1914: a weeklong national celebration, beginning 16 July 1939, that would bring thousands of visitors to Prince Edward Island at the height of the tourist season.

As historian Matthew McRae relates, the committee, abetted by the province, had embarked on a process of "site sacralization." It would stage a national celebration of the seventy-fifth anniversary of the Charlottetown Conference because Charlottetown was the Cradle of Confederation; at the same time Charlottetown would be sanctified as the Cradle of Confederation *because* it had hosted this national celebration. To that end the legislative council room, once slated for office space, was now rebranded as a national shrine, the "Confederation Chamber," the place where the

Dominion of Canada was born.[10] That the phrase might be contested – the British North America Act was, after all, drafted largely in Quebec and legislated in London – was hardly an impediment.[11] Money was, though, and even before the committee first met in January 1939 Premier Campbell had written Prime Minister Mackenzie King to solicit federal money to help fund the week-long festival.

There was precedent for federal funding: Ottawa had pledged $20,000 to the abortive Golden Jubilee celebrations in 1914.[12] Just the same, it was unlikely that the federal government would subsidize a local tourist event, and so, its promoters sold the upcoming festival as an exercise in nation building for a Canada battered by Depression and shadowed by the threat of a new war.[13] Not quite convinced, the federal cabinet initially promised only $15,000, and it took a pilgrimage to Ottawa, some furious lobbying, and increasingly frantic exchanges with various officials before an extra $5,000 was squeezed out of federal coffers on the very eve of the event.[14] As with so many Island appeals to Ottawa, the federal response steered clear of principles and precedents and glossed its investment in national rather than provincial terms. The Privy Council minute approving the $20,000 grant noted the celebration's "historical significance and interest, not only to the residents of the Province of Prince Edward Island, but to the people of the dominion as a whole, as well as to the former residents of Canada." And since the celebration would highlight "the tourist possibilities of Canada as a whole" and since any tourists heading to Prince Edward Island would necessarily pass through other provinces on the way, Privy Council found it "expedient" to subsidize "necessary special publicity and advertising."[15]

The grant was funnelled to Arsenault through D. Leo Dolan, director of the Canadian Travel Bureau (CTB). Established in 1934 chiefly to promote American travel to Canada, the CTB had a national, but also a nationalist, agenda that played well to the festival's theme.[16] While Island politicians and promoters frequently complained that their little province got scant shrift in the CTB's imaging of Canada, Arsenault had come to rely on his contacts there, and it was to Dolan that he had turned in the last-ditch appeal for additional federal funds.[17]

Ottawa's money had symbolic as well as practical value. It endorsed the Celebration Committee's claim that its festival was a national, not local, event. For the same reason, organizers were anxious that as many dignitaries as possible attend, including the prime minister, his cabinet, the governor general, and the other eight premiers. In the end, Arsenault had to settle for five cabinet ministers, four premiers, a couple of provincial representatives and assorted MPs and senators.[18] Together they provided sufficient gravitas to elevate the various proceedings to "national" stature.

Figure 3.1 ▪ In 1939, on the eve of another world war, Prince Edward Island sought to cement its claim to the title Birthplace of Confederation with a seventy-fifth-anniversary celebration of the Charlottetown Conference. "The Romance of Canada" historical pageant highlighted the festivities. The PEI float shown here featured Jacques Cartier, the Island's European "discoverer," meeting nobly posed Mi'kmaq – in reality, white Islanders in brownface. Actual Mi'kmaq were almost entirely absent from PEI tourism promotion during the twentieth century.

The essential ingredient for a national celebration was celebrants. Here again, the Confederation anniversary was deemed a success. The Confederation Celebration Committee evidently spent much of its money on advertising and promotion. Fifty thousand tourist folders were distributed within Canada, and the province even staffed a booth at the World's Fair in New York where it passed out 100,000 more. Souvenir booklets were printed and a special Confederation edition of *The Maritime Advocate and Busy East* magazine was distributed across the region. There were newspaper ads across northeastern America, a moving picture, *P.E. Island on Parade,* and even auto and luggage labels emblazoned "Guest of Prince Edward Island."[19]

According to newspaper reports, thousands of spectators attended the various events that highlighted the festivities: parades, church services, athletics, harness-racing, yachting, a musical concert, multiple parades, a military review, a Mardi Gras-style carnival, the official launch of the new Charlottetown Airport. The opening of the PEI National Park drew 500 spectators. The historical highlight came early in the week, on Monday, 17 July. The day began at Province House with the unveiling of Historic Sites and Monuments Board plaques commemorating the Island's seven Fathers of Confederation, each unveiled (where possible) by a descendant as CBC Radio broadcast the ceremonies to the nation. In newsreel footage of the event, the obvious star is ninety-four-year-old Margaret Gray Lord, whose father, Col John Hamilton Gray, had hosted the Charlottetown Conference back in 1864. While other figures grimace uncomfortably at the camera, she poses unselfconsciously for posterity.[20] Afterwards, speeches gave way to spectacle. The afternoon featured a grand historical parade, with floats representing each province and the nation itself. That evening 8,000 people attended the elaborate tableaux of *The Romance of Canada*, a grand, open-air pageant of the country's beginnings staged by nearly 200 local actors and musicians.[21] Everyone (those quoted, at least) agreed that it was spectacular.

There was, of course, no method for measuring the economic impact of the Confederation Celebration or even how many tourists it had attracted. Many of the thousands of spectators were no doubt Islanders, but even the most unobservant would have noticed the number of visitors in their midst.[22] The Travel Bureau reported a 100 per cent increase in inquiries during June 1939, and even with extra crossings, the ferry service at Borden-Tormentine was barely able to cope with the traffic during July.[23] And just as the celebration had exposed many tourists to Prince Edward Island, so it had exposed many Islanders – and their government – to the power of tourism. There was much to crow about.

In terms of site sacralization, the festival was equally successful. In coming years Charlottetown's status as "Cradle of Confederation" gradually became received wisdom. Judge Arsenault must have smiled from his place at the head table in 1956, when Leo Dolan, director of the Canadian Travel Bureau, told delegates at a banquet in Charlottetown, "Here you are – almost I'd like to say, on hallowed ground."[24]

Unlike most of the Island's staple tourist attractions, the Confederation theme put history at the heart of the story. Not just any history, of course. As Ian McKay and Robin Bates have pointed out with respect to Nova Scotia, turning history into a "tourist/history" involves a deliberate process of selection, exclusion, and distortion.[25] The stories that tourist promoters choose to tell must have in mind their audience, and that generally means something unique to the location, safely divorced from present-day controversies, romantic in conception, and broad in appeal. Stories involving class conflict, racism, and violence, such as the deportation of the Island's Acadian population in 1758 or the Island's century-long struggle against leasehold land tenure, remained unpalatable tourist fare. But the voluntary binding together of French and English Canada through the union of disparate colonies, the peaceable founding of a nation: this had national appeal. That Prince Edward Island had stoutly resisted Confederation until 1873 could be glossed over with a smile.

But even the chosen history might need editing in the interests of tourism. The featured speaker at the plaque ceremony was the Island's preeminent historian D.C. Harvey, provincial archivist of Nova Scotia, university professor, and key member of the Historic Sites and Monuments Board.[26] The Confederation festival allowed him to combine his Island patriotism with his liberal Canadian nationalism. But when Harvey reasonably objected that the intended festival date of mid-July was a long way from early September, the actual time of the Charlottetown Conference, Judge Arsenault reasonably countered that all of the province's tourist accommodations would be closed by the end of August.[27] The plaque dedication went forward as scheduled. And Harvey spoke as planned.

It would not be the last time that history and tourism would make uneasy bedfellows. But for now the compromise seemed worth it. In a postmortem published in the *Canadian Geographic Journal*, Harvey termed the Confederation celebration "one of the most significant events in our history."[28] He had in mind the festival as witness to the tenacity of constitutionalism in an anarchic world. But the event was also a tipping point in the role of history in Island tourism. From now on heritage – real and imagined – would merit a prominent place in all of the Island's tourism marketing. And it was strangely congruent with the longstanding image of the province as a pastoral Eden that existed somehow out of time. Both cast the present in terms of the past. The tourism paradigm for Prince Edward Island may have diversified, but it had not essentially changed.

It almost seems as if the planning tightrope of the great Confederation celebrations terminally exhausted the province's private tourist association. Or perhaps the combination of the national park and the hoopla surrounding the seventy-fifth anniversary of the Charlottetown Conference had finally convinced the provincial government that it needed to be more than a silent partner in the developing tourist industry. On 2 January 1940, after a decade and a half as the association's main funder, the province finally took over the Travel Bureau and, for lack of a better option, lodged it under the provincial secretary's office.[29] The association had done good work, Premier Thane Campbell told the Summerside Board of Trade, "but [he] felt the time had come for the government to take the matter up."[30]

Without its physical manifestation, the Tourist Association quietly lapsed. There are no more news reports of its meetings, and during 1940 its office was leased out to the Provincial Boy Scouts Council.[31] The Tourist Association had never been a true grassroots organization. Rather, it represented a narrow, urban base of businessmen, professionals, and newspapermen whose influence arguably was deep but not broad. For them, the Tourist Association had been, perhaps, a flag of convenience, and there were other outlets for their interest, notably the Charlottetown and Summerside Boards of Trade, each of which established tourism subcommittees around this time.[32] Perhaps the Tourist Association felt its work was done now that the government had taken over the Travel Bureau.

Back at the bureau, Minnie MacFadyen continued for a time her largely unsung heroics as general *factotum*, but now there was a new, paid, professional manager, a forty-six-year-old Summerside businessman named B. Graham Rogers. As a token of its earnestness, the government increased his tourist promotion budget to $18,000 for 1940, an 80 per cent increase over 1938 and six times the total for 1936. Still, the enlarged allocation represented less than 1 per cent of the provincial budget.[33]

The bureau's new director was both enterprising and enthusiastic, what his generation might call a "go-getter." For the previous twenty years Rogers had been a successful fox rancher and wholesaler with valuable off-Island connections. He also had impeccable Liberal credentials. His grandfather had been a Liberal lieutenant governor, and until recently Rogers had been president of the East Prince Liberal Association.[34] That did not stop the Conservative *Guardian* from applauding his appointment. "Graham has plenty of energy," it commented, "and is full of ideas for the betterment of our tourist industry. He is an expert on publicity."[35] As the *Guardian*'s own columns would demonstrate, Rogers had a knack for keeping tourism in the news. He regularly addressed service clubs and boards of trade, consulted with his counterparts in other provinces, and fed tourist-friendly stories and traffic statistics to the local press.

While the press of events might defer or delay its implementation, the government clearly had an agenda for tourist development. It is therefore worth examining Rogers's first annual report in some detail.[36] Like any good salesperson, Rogers put the best gloss possible on his inaugural year in office. Anticipating future trends, he was encumbered yet empowered by the vagueness of tourist statistics. There was, after all, no way, short of personally interviewing each new arrival on Prince Edward Island, to count the number of tourists (even if a satisfactory definition of "tourist" could be found). That left two rough measures: the number of automobiles rolling off the ferries with off-Island licence plates and the volume of inquiries handled by the Travel Bureau. Sampling and survey techniques would become more sophisticated over time, but tourist estimating would always remain an inexact science.

Amid the statistical fog, Rogers took comfort in traffic numbers, the only hard data at his disposal. Relying on figures supplied by Canadian National Railways, he reported that 12,826 automobiles had used the ferry to come to Prince Edward Island in 1940, 658 more than the previous year. Of these, 9,888 had mainland licence plates. Admittedly, the majority of them, 5,723 cars, were from Nova Scotia and New Brunswick, but 2,488 vehicles (25 per cent) sported American plates (half of those from Massachusetts). Combining rail and auto traffic, Rogers estimated that 62,420 people had crossed to the Island, up 20 per cent from 1939. At a conservative estimate, he guessed that 42,000 of these arrivals were tourists. Some hopeful math translated that number into a guesstimate of tourist-related revenue: $40,000 in gasoline taxes alone and, at $12 per head, $509,040 in additional spending.

All Islanders, he reminded readers, benefited from tourism, not just those directly involved in the industry. Tourists ate and drank (well, their drinking habits were a sensitive topic in a province steeped in temperance), and that meant markets for Island farmers and fishers. They bought gas and purchased souvenirs and consumed the available attractions. Tourism, then, should be everyone's business; the rising tide floated all boats.[37]

Given tourism's wide impact, more had been done to attract visitors, particularly Americans. The province dispatched two representatives to the World's Fair in New York, and a Talk segment on NBC Radio about the Island had generated 882 inquiries. "The three chief demands for information, of course, concern our tourist attractions, our products and industries and our historical points of interest." Islanders had their own role to play in attracting visitors. Rogers encouraged them to write their expatriate friends and relatives and urge them to vacation back home. Nor did he forget the province's newest tourist attraction: "Our Historic Confederation Chamber ... is becoming more and more an added attraction ... Every citizen of Prince Edward Island should visit this beautiful Chamber and should make a special effort to urge all of their friends and tourists with whom they may come in contact to do likewise." (In truth, the Chamber was an empty room with a table and chairs around it, and visitors' imaginations were expected to do the heavy lifting of imbuing it with historical, national import.) Beyond convincing tourists to visit the province, Rogers worked to expedite their ability to do so. Judging from his report and newspaper accounts of his activities, a fair amount of Rogers's time was spent lobbying for improved bus and rail connections to make it more convenient for people to reach the Island. Meanwhile, he called for more pavement within the province, particularly on tourist routes.

If transportation was one fixation, accommodation was another. Rogers had revived the bureau's annual, informal registry of tourist accommodations, but quality was as much an issue as quantity. "There is an urgent need for more good accommodation," Rogers wrote. In this era "good accommodation" meant flush toilets, running water in rooms, electricity, good mattresses, freshly painted or whitewashed buildings, wholesome food, and clean, neat, attractive surroundings. Modern travellers required modern amenities if the province hoped to make them repeat customers. Transportation and accommodation had always been the two main concerns of tourism boosters. Now they would be the government's tourism priorities. And the same watchwords would apply to both: modernity, efficiency, consistency.

Although it may not have seemed so at the time, the province's takeover of the Travel Bureau represented another subtle but seismic shift in the development of Island tourism. From now on the state, rather than a private organization, would steer the industry and shape its image. Admittedly, the steering was a little wobbly. Between 1940 and 1960 the provincial government tinkered fitfully with its promotional apparatus. From the Provincial Secretary's Office, tourism migrated to the newly formed Department of Industry and Natural Resources in 1949, and the Travel Bureau was absorbed into a "Tourist and Information Branch," which then became the "Tourist and Information Bureau." Periodic adjustment of names and titles had minimal effect on staffing. The number of seasonal employees might vary from year to year but all through the 1950s the permanent staff never exceeded six people. For much of that period the province continued its longstanding tendency to conflate tourism marketing with general promotion of the province. Only gradually did tourism's profile begin to catch up with the ritual iterations of its importance in annual speeches from the throne.

Graham Rogers ended his 1940 report where he might have begun it, with a mission statement. When he was hired, he wrote, he had been given three instructions: "(1) To conduct the Travel Bureau without fear or favour to anyone, and to remember that Prince Edward Island is Prince Edward Island from North Cape to East Point; (2) To try and make our people tourist-conscious; (3) To bring as many people as possible to Prince Edward Island and build a permanent Tourist business." Read with the benefit of hindsight, his bold framing of priorities takes on a timeless quality. They would be restated many times from many different mouths. For now the industry remained in its infancy. Thursday's child had far to go.

Even before Rogers took up his duties, the ground had shifted under the Island's tourism industry. Less than two months after the public relations triumph of the Confederation celebration, in September 1939, Canada was drawn into the Second World War. In an odd inversion of expected trends, the outbreak of war initially boosted tourism to Prince Edward Island.[38] Even as Canadian society set aside leisure pursuits and geared up for the war effort,

Figure 3.2 ▪ Although some previous travel writers had compared the Island's pastoral landscape with southern England, the comparison became the province's prime tourism pitch to the still neutral United States in 1941. With Europe at war and the Atlantic Ocean infested with German U-boats, the Travel Bureau offered a closer and safer alternative: *Prince Edward Island: The England of Canada*. The next year, America was at war and Island tourism was reduced to off-duty servicemen and their families. This guide's bathing beauties were the sporty daughters of the local Charlottetown elite.

American tourists, still officially neutral in the world conflict, looked for safe havens. War-torn Europe was out of reach, while rumours of lurking German U-boats curbed sea travel to places such as the West Indies and Bermuda. That left intracontinental travel, and after an initial slowdown American travellers increasingly looked north. Since American tourists meant American dollars to offset the heavy trade imbalance precipitated by Canadian war purchases, Rogers could even promote tourism as "a war measure." Playing to tourists unable to access the British Isles, the Travel Bureau's 1941 tourism booklet offered a reasonable facsimile, *Prince Edward Island: The England of Canada*.

In her study of the Canadian Travel Bureau, Alisa Apostle identifies three stages in wartime Canadian tourism. From 1939 until late 1941, while the United States remained at peace, tourism was actively encouraged and efforts were made to assuage American tourists' concerns about passports, shortages, rationing, wage and price controls, currency controls, and

Figure 3.3 ▪ Beginning in 1938, New Brunswick and Prince Edward Island shared a tourist information booth at Aulac, New Brunswick — where drivers travelling east decided whether to head to Nova Scotia or the Island. By 1957, the booth had been replaced by an eye-catching A-frame.

wartime conditions. Tourism marketing became a species of propaganda. For a time the CTB's budgets even increased. But the war ultimately hampered the free flow of people, goods, and services that is essential to tourism, and after the United States entered the conflict in December 1941, tourism faltered. The federal government came to regard leisure travel as a luxury, and from a high of $500,000 a year in 1940–42, the CTB's budget was slashed to barely $50,000 for 1942–43. Only in the last years of the war, with victory in sight, did tourism begin to figure in the planning for peace.[39]

The Island's tourist trade followed a similar trajectory. At first, it was business as usual, and tourism budgets rose rather than fell. In 1941, the government's tourist promotion spending jumped to $25,608.[40] There were now satellite offices at Summerside as well as Aulac, New Brunswick (which the bureau operated in partnership with that province) with provision for information booths at the Island's two ferry terminals.[41] But gasoline rationing (only twenty gallons per American tourist car per visit, with a maximum of four visits per year, later slashed to twelve gallons per year per tourist car), tire shortages, a plethora of controls and restrictions, and the general climate of war gradually took their toll.[42] Although tourist promotion spending held more or less steady in 1942, visitor numbers were clearly down, and in 1943, the budget was nearly halved to just over $12,000.[43] Nevertheless, the speech from the throne for 1944 claimed "a notable increase" in tourist traffic in 1943 over 1942.[44] Certainly, traffic had increased, but it would have been difficult to distinguish among tourists, war workers, and soldiers who were coming from, or going on, leave.

Besides, the line between the three frequently blurred. Consider, for example, Gary Aitken of Montreal, who spent six weeks with his mother at Shaw's Hotel in Brackley in the summer of 1944. They were to all appearances genteel tourists of the preferred stripe. And the little boy did what tourists do: played on the beach, went trout fishing, explored the Shaws' farm, and wolfed down blueberry pie and strawberry shortcake. Yet in a sense he was merely coming home; his father Gordon was a born-and-bred Islander – and Gary and his mother were on Prince Edward Island chiefly because Gordon was serving overseas with the Royal Canadian Army Service Corps. His death in combat in August 1944 abruptly ended their summer idyll.[45]

Most wartime Island vacations had happier endings. Periodic news bites about *bona fide* tourists who had visited the Travel Bureau in Charlottetown – the more distant or distinguished their origin the better – were used as markers for the health of the tourist trade as a whole. The handful of names gave little sense of overall numbers and arguably were not representative of the "average" traveller, but, as intended, they put a brave face on the tourist industry.

The war's actual impact on Island tourism is neatly encapsulated in the fate of the government's first purpose-made promotional film. In 1941, with encouragement from the CTB, the province sponsored the creation of a colour film – complete with musical score – that showcased various Island scenes from Souris to Tignish: "shots of the fishing industry, scenes that attract tourists, interesting pictures of fox ranching, etc." It was filmed by Harley H. Bixler of the Amateur Cinema League of America in cooperation with the National Film Board of Canada and was coordinated by the Travel Bureau's own B. Graham Rogers.[46] Rogers had great plans for the film, which would win third place (General Class) in December 1942 at the Amateur Cinema League's annual awards ceremonies in New York.[47] It was shown in Quebec and the Maritimes, and the league had distribution arrangements with more than 200 American cinemas. But for the moment its impact was entirely local. In the fall of 1942 the Travel Bureau partnered with the National War Finance Committee to show the film in twenty towns and villages across the province as a war bonds fundraiser.[48]

Figure 3.4 ▪ Old Home Week racing at the Charlottetown Driving Park. Staged only three times between 1904 and 1939, Old Home Week came to stay in 1940 when war-related budget cuts temporarily cancelled the funding for the Provincial Agricultural Exhibition. The new Old Home Week fused the two events. By the time the prestigious Gold Cup and Saucer Race was added in 1960, quickly followed by an annual parade and quasi beauty pageant, most Islanders had forgotten that Old Home Week as they knew it was not all that old. The state-fair-like agricultural dimension appealed to tourists looking for rural culture, but, in truth, the annual gathering was as important to Islanders as to visitors.

For the rest of the war, Rogers would spend more time doing patriotic war work than overt tourist promotion. His office continued to press transportation issues and schedules but now the emphasis was on the convenience of soldiers' families and war workers rather than traditional tourists.[49] Although talk of tourism's promise continued, the time frame was now generally *après la guerre*. After nailing a tourism development plank to his election platform in the fall of 1943, the new Liberal premier, J. Walter Jones, announced at the next sitting of the legislature that "It was not proposed to do anything other than 'mark time' at present in connection with the tourist trade."[50]

Despite war and time marking, tourism persisted. "It is needless to say," the *Guardian* nevertheless said, as the war wound down in the summer of 1945, "that nearly every nook-and-cranny where one might sleep and eat has been secured for this and next week by former residents and newcomers to our shores."[51] The editorial squib was careful not to use the word tourist, but the promise was plain. "What a wealth there is," it continued, in a familiar refrain, "in the development of this Island as a tourist and health resort, if only some wise man or men would devote time and energy to its development, providing suitable hotel and other accommodation for our visitors." For the moment such wisdom was at a premium.

Figure 3.5 ▪ In 1941, Northumberland Ferries Ltd began a ferry service connecting Wood Islands with Caribou, Nova Scotia. Neither new nor very modern, the tiny MV *Prince Nova* took its name from the two provinces it linked.

Aside from the government's takeover of the Prince Edward Island Travel Bureau, the most significant tourist developments during the Second World War involved transportation. Back in 1937 the coordinated lobby of the province's Tourist Association, various boards of trade, and its provincial government had persuaded Ottawa to construct docking facilities for a new, privately owned ferry service that would shuttle between Wood Islands, in southeastern Queens County, and Caribou, Nova Scotia, during navigation season (roughly May to December).[52] Northumberland Ferries Ltd, an Island-owned company headed by a grocery wholesaler named R.E. Mutch, eventually won the contract to operate the service and the $28,000 federal subsidy that went with it. War played havoc with its efforts to acquire a vessel, but at last on 28 June 1941, the company launched its service in a makeshift little boat, rechristened the MV *Prince Nova*.[53] Although the carrying capacity of the Wood Islands ferry was miniscule, it managed to move 25,000 people and 7,200 vehicles during its first, truncated season.[54] By 1946, those figures had doubled, straining capacity to the limit, and creating purgatorial delays for travellers.[55] Instead of solving the transportation bottleneck, the new ferry service had acquired its own freight of expectation, frustration, and possibility.

The prospects at the western end of the Northumberland Strait were equally fraught. Only a week before Northumberland Ferries began service, the CNR's SS *Charlottetown* was wrecked on the south shore of Nova Scotia on her way to Saint John for refit, throwing the Borden–Tormentine crossing into turmoil and forcing the now venerable *Prince Edward Island* out of genteel semiretirement to become once again the principal carrier on that crossing.[56] The public, private, and political outcry for a new all-season car ferry echoed across the war years, but military priorities consistently trumped civilian needs. By 1945, the design of a new ferry was taking shape, "the best that science could produce."[57] For those predicting a postwar tourist boom, the new boat could not come too soon.

The same year that gave the tourist trade a new ferry service and hobbled its old one also launched a third way for visitors to reach the island province. In December 1941 Charlottetown businessman and pilot Carl Burke launched Maritime Central Airways, its three secondhand planes linking Charlottetown, Summerside, Saint John, and Moncton in a single twice-daily route.[58] Four years later, MCA was the biggest airline in the Maritimes – no great achievement perhaps, but by the mid-1950s it would be the third largest in the country. As a tourist carrier it would always take second place, figuratively and imaginatively, to the ferry service. Capacity was initially limited – MCA's two principal planes could together carry only eighteen passengers.[59] And for many years, air travel remained exotic. And expensive: the inaugural return fare for the short flight from Charlottetown to Moncton was a formidable $11.70, in an era when the ferry cost $2.00.[60] Thus, while the airline brought 13,041 passengers to Prince Edward Island in 1947, proportionately few of them probably qualified as tourists. Five years later, the number had risen by only 10 per cent, to 14,420.[61] Nevertheless, the air link with the outside world theoretically brought Prince Edward Island within the "orbit" of a much larger proportion of the globe.[62] And it provided local tourism boosters with another token of modernity to dangle before potential visitors. It went well with the shiny new ferry on the ways at Quebec, and the plucky little fleet toiling to and from Nova Scotia on the Wood Islands run. The aerial perspective also provided travel writers with a new, satisfyingly homey sobriquet for the Garden Province. By the early 1950s, as more and more travellers viewed the Island from the air, they would begin describing it as a "patchwork quilt."[63]

"The 1946 season promises to the biggest one for tourists ever experienced on the Island," the Travel Bureau exclaimed in its annual appeal to Islanders to register potential tourist accommodations with it.[64] There was, no doubt, an element of hype in that prediction, but it was also based on the volume of inquiries received from intending travellers. And the Travel Bureau was right. So far as its imperfect instruments of measurement would allow, 1946 would indeed prove to be a record year for tourism. So would the next year. And the next. The Island's tourist industry was about to shift into another gear.

Living up on the threshold of Cavendish, Dolph Fleming could notice the changes. "A lot of tourists in Church," he recorded in his diary entry for 20 July 1952.[65] What he was seeing was local evidence of a much larger trend. The postwar democratization of tourism in the Western world has been well documented. A generation of sustained economic prosperity put spending money in North Americans' pockets and gasoline in the tanks of the burgeoning number of North American cars. And even as North American governments were investing billions of dollars in improving road systems for those cars, paid vacations increasingly became the norm for middle- and working-class families.[66] As John Fisher, director of the Canadian Tourism Association, reminded his Island counterparts in 1958, "Nearly every worker gets an annual holiday with pay, and that holiday period is stretching from one week to two weeks to three weeks – not to mention all the special holidays in between."[67] The tourist equation was simple but powerful: money + time + mobility = travel. More and more, boosters, developers, and bureaucrats sought to apply that formula to Prince Edward Island.

In his study of postwar Island tourism, historian Matthew McRae writes of an "accidental tourism industry" that developed during the 1950s despite public apathy and government underfunding. Tourism's growth over the course of the decade continued to be demand-driven.[68] Budget figures tend to support McRae's contention. After investing only $12,772 of its $2.17 million budget in tourist promotion during 1944–45, the province doubled its spending to $25,122 in the first full year of peace. By 1960, the promotional budget had grown to $117,835, a ninefold increase over 1945. But when viewed in the context of the state's phenomenal postwar growth overall, the blossoming of tourist budgets looks much less impressive. In 1960, tourist promotion accounted for 0.8 per cent of the province's total ordinary expenditures, exactly the same percentage as in 1940.[69] Over the entire course of the 1950s, the province spent less than $700,000 on tourist promotion.

And yet, those underwhelming balance sheets tell only part of the story. Government's attitude towards tourism had come a long way since the war. There were "limits in this Province to most everything he could think of,"

Figure 3.6 ▪ When the provincial government took charge of the Travel Bureau in 1940, the private tourist association that maintained it dissolved. But in 1946 an Innkeepers Association, its lantern logo symbolizing hospitality, was founded and soon served as the province's de facto tourist association. It renamed itself the PEI Tourist Association in 1958 and in 1980 became TIAPEI, the Tourism Industry Association of PEI.

remarked Eugene Cullen, provincial minister of industry and natural resources in 1954, "– except the future of our Tourist Industry."[70] The perceived problem was less how to attract tourists than what to do with them. When the Island's "Farmer Premier," J. Walter Jones, complained in 1944 that the Island had as many tourists as it possibly could handle, he was not dismissing the industry so much as recognizing the limitations of the province's tourism infrastructure.[71] And that was precisely where he felt his government could act.

After setting up a one-man Department of Reconstruction with himself as minister, Premier Jones had commissioned an economic survey of Prince Edward Island late in 1944 from Dr J.E. Lattimer, professor of agricultural science at Macdonald College in Quebec.[72] Not surprisingly, Lattimer focused mainly on agriculture, but the last of his fourteen recommendations urged the province to "Capitalize on the natural advantages for the tourist trade by providing communications, better roads and better accommodation."[73] Primed with his report, the government appointed a twenty-five-member Advisory Reconstruction Committee of leading citizens. Among its eight "technical" subcommittees was one dealing with tourism and transportation. In the end, tourism merited a report of its own. It echoed Lattimer. "Our tourist attractions are permanent and always with us," the committee asserted (a little complacently). The key to unlocking their potential was better accommodations and, especially, transportation. If these could be addressed, the committee was confident that tourism would soon become the province's number two industry.[74]

When it came to accommodations, the Jones government adopted a carrot-and-stick approach. The Innkeepers' Regulations Act of 1947 licensed inns, tourist homes, and restaurants and provided for periodic sanitary inspections.[75] At the same time the government set aside $100,000 in the estimates for "Tourist Cabin Loans."[76] Both initiatives played well to the newly formed Prince Edward Island Innkeepers Association. Founded in 1946, it counted fifty members by the time it held its first annual meeting in June 1947.[77] From the beginning, tourism dominated the association's deliberations,[78] and it gradually morphed into a de facto tourist association. It was more broadly based than its predecessor, more alert to tourism trends, more open to women (several of whom served in executive positions during the first decade), and more apt to collaborate with government.[79] In its own crusade to professionalize the hospitality industry, the association consistently endorsed government efforts to regulate, expand, and improve the province's accommodations infrastructure. As Matthew McRae observes, "On Prince Edward Island, shrewd tourism operators knew that although affluent tourists were visiting the province to experience its 19th century rural charm, they still wanted the toilets to flush."[80]

Despite the Innkeepers' support, neither the government's carrot nor stick worked out quite as anticipated. Although a Division of Sanitary Engineering was launched in May 1948 with a survey of tourist accommodations,[81] the Island's bureaucracy soon proved too small (or, perhaps, unwilling) to enforce the Innkeepers' Regulations Act. When the Department of Health finally decided to enforce the Act in 1954, only twenty-nine of the seventy premises that were visited passed inspection. The Division of Sanitary Engineering cited an array of unsanitary conditions, including unsafe well installations, inadequate sewage methods, improper food handling, and substandard toilet facilities.[82] Yet, three years later, inspections had to be "greatly curtailed" due to lack of staff.[83]

The Tourist Accommodations Loan program was also dogged by dysfunction. It began well enough. In its first year, 1947–48, $76,600 of the $100,000 allotment was disbursed, and a further $72,825 went out in loans the following year. Encouraged, the Government budgeted an additional $50,000 for 1949–50.[84] But only $19,500 of that sum was used, and in 1950–51, net loans amounted to only $630.[85] There was another troubling trend, the high rate of delinquency in loan repayment. By 1952, it had become a political football and Premier Jones uncharacteristically agreed with the leader of the opposition that perhaps not all of the loans had been wise. But after all, Jones argued, "The loans were amortized and repayment in five or 10 years could not be expected 'because if there were that much profit in the tourist industry we would all be in it.'"[86] Pressed in the house, the government released cumulative figures for the Tourist Accommodations Loan program. Of thirty-six loans totalling $196,693, fifteen were in arrears to the amount of $27,279.[87]

The loan program was intended to function as a revolving fund, but by 1954, with repayments now $34,000 in arrears, the Liberal government admitted that there was no more money left in the pot.[88] At that point it changed tack. "I believe the future of the tourist industry lies in the motel line not in the construction of cabins as has been the custom during the past five years," proclaimed Jones's successor as premier, Alex W. Matheson. He continued, "The North Shore area serves the tourist trade from the first ten days of July to the last of August and no one living can make a go of such business which lasts less than two months … We need accommodations that will provide a certain amount of heat and the answer lies in motels not cabins."[89]

The shift in emphasis from cabins to motels also argued a shift in scale. Under the old program, loans had been capped at $5,000; the new ceiling was $40,000.[90] Rather than simply setting money aside in the estimates for tourist accommodation loans, the government now committed the program to the closer strictures of legislation. The Tourist Accommodation Loans Act authorized a revolving fund of $300,000 "for the purpose of assisting in the establishment of tourist cabins, tourist hotels, or other tourist accommodations."[91] One hundred thousand dollars was committed for the first year of the new program.[92] There was, Premier Matheson contended, lots of demand for the new line of credit. And he was right. Nearly the entire sum, $99,000, was lent in 1954, $40,000 of it to Wally and Sally Rodd of Highfield, whose family already operated a string of tourist cabins. That year, they built the province's first full-service motel, a sixteen-unit complex in Winsloe, partway between Charlottetown and the North Shore beaches.[93] Others quickly followed. "Motel" was shorthand for "motor hotel," and the name spoke volumes. Long and low, with parking right outside the door and kitchenettes inside, motels were essentially one-night stands for families on the move. The new generation of tourist was not the sort to arrive by ship or train and then settle for weeks at some Victorian-era seaside resort.

While opposition critics might howl about favouritism and mismanagement in the workings of the loans program, the principle of government support for upgrading tourist accommodations was now well established. When the Progressive Conservatives took office in 1959, they aggressively expanded the loans program instead of reversing it. That November, the new provincial secretary, J. David Stewart, vowed to grow the revolving fund from $300,000 to $2 million, "so that the Tourist Industry can become the Island's first Industry and as it can yet lead the Province out of its present Economic difficulties."[94] The fund ceiling was duly amended, and the next year's budget set aside $350,000 for Tourist Accommodation Loans.[95] In 1960–61, the Conservatives' first full year in office, $249,000 was loaned, more in one budget year than during the seven years of the pioneer program.[96] When surveyed the following year, the Island's accommodations sector counted 236 resorts, hotels, motels, cottages, lodges, and cabins, a total of 2,179 units.[97] The days of informally canvassing Islanders each spring to see who might take in visitors were clearly long past.

Although lack of resources continually hampered its campaign to modernize tourist accommodations, the provincial government could at least feel a degree of agency in addressing that need. In the matter of transportation to and from the Island, it continued to be reliant on the unpredictable largesse of the federal government and conflicting interpretations of Ottawa's constitutional pledge to provide "continuous steam communication" with the mainland. During the first decades of Confederation, the principal concern for Islanders had been how to get goods to and from Prince Edward Island, especially in winter.[98] In the new postwar dispensation, tourism increasingly became the driver for the Island's assertion of its "rights of passage." Although postwar lobbies and briefs continued to bemoan seasonal bottlenecks in shipping potatoes to market and the truck-carrying incapacity of the tiny ferries on the Wood Islands–Caribou run, little by little the needs of tourism came to dominate the discourse with federal officials. Mass tourism is impossible if access to an island is difficult or inconvenient. And, of course, mass tourism is just what Island tourism promoters had in mind.

As he had a decade earlier, Charlottetown businessman J.O. Hyndman framed the problem in a 1939 address to the Charlottetown Board of Trade. A "tremendous increase in the number of tourists" was coming, he predicted, but "Tourists [travelling] by automobiles will not submit to delays at the ferry coming to and going from the Island." They would go away "as knockers." That was not the way to promote the tourist trade, he warned.[99] What was true before the war was doubly true afterwards, and the government, the Innkeepers Association, and the Island's several boards of trade all hammered away at the theme in the first years of peace. Graham Rogers was only echoing Hyndman and many others when he used his penchant for all-caps to warn that "TRANSPORTATION is the link which provides access to the multitude of attractions we can offer to literally hundreds of thousands of people who first must be provided with easy, frequent, and attractive ways to get on and off this summer paridise [sic]."[100]

He might well have added that getting them around *within* the Island was important, too. An early connection had been made between pavement and

Figure 3.7 • Perhaps the most beloved of the Island's car ferries, the MV *Abegweit* began service in 1947 amid much hoopla. The *Abby* even made it onto an expensive-for-the-time 1946 postage stamp.

tourist development, and in the postwar era, the provincial government spent much of its available capital on paving rural roads.[101] In 1941, the Island boasted only 206 miles of asphalt; by 1960, the figure was 825.5 miles, 40 per cent of them in Queens County.[102] The convenience of rural Islanders was the principal consideration in road paving – except when it served politicians to emphasize tourism. When the Diefenbaker government launched its "Roads to Resources" program in 1958, principally to open up the natural resources of the Canadian North, the Island government shrewdly identified its particular "resource" as tourism and the whole province as the destination. The resulting federal–provincial agreement eventually produced a series of paved loops to direct sightseers (and Islanders) around the perimeter of the province's three counties.[103]

Pavement, which banished dust and mud – if not potholes – was no doubt important if tourists were to get around the Island, but it paled in significance to the critical issue of accessing the province. On 8 August 1947, six years after the loss of the SS *Charlottetown*, the Island finally welcomed Canadian National Railway's new all-season ferry, the MV *Abegweit* – at the time, the largest, most powerful ice-breaking ferry in the world. Its arrival in Hillsborough Bay merited a whole special section of the Charlottetown *Guardian*. "The new Ferry will attract thousands of visitors," predicted Premier Walter Jones in his own congratulatory message, "especially from the United States ... In so doing these visitors will want to enjoy a sail on the 'Abegweit' and hence will visit our communities in increasing numbers."[104] Whether or not visitors would actually be drawn by a ferry, locals certainly were. When the *Abegweit* held an open house at Charlottetown that Sunday, an estimated 15,000–20,000 Islanders showed up to tour the vessel.[105] Transportation, it was clear, had become the key to Prince Edward Island's postwar reconstruction.

That was certainly the message of the Island briefs to the federal Turgeon Commission when it convened in Charlottetown in July 1949 as part of its investigation of inequities in Canada's transportation system.[106] Only two years after the *Abegweit* had begun service, the province was already pressing for a second, "auxiliary ferry" at Borden to supplement the *Abegweit* in summer. It was, the Boards of Trade asserted, "essential to the satisfactory development of all our industries, particularly the tourist industry." Delays or, just as problematic, the expectation of delays was bad for business. Yet the province's islandness was also a potential tourism asset: "our very isolation, which is such a handicap to us in the development of other industries, can become an asset in relation to the tourist business."[107] The Island must be sanctuary, not prison, though; the journey there a mild adventure, not an ordeal. In a telling departure from previous demands, the Boards of Trade specified that the proposed new summer ferry need not carry railcars.

Over the next decade, the struggle for convenience in the crossing to Prince Edward Island continued at both ends of the Northumberland Strait. Northumberland Ferries pressed for new boats and fended off real and imagined threats of a takeover by Canadian National Railways.[108] After years of Island complaint, the federal government at last financed a new, sixty-car ferry, the *Lord Selkirk*, which entered service in May 1958. Despite Premier Matheson's private assertion that the Wood Islands service was only "supplementary," there was no new ferry for the Borden–Tormentine run during the 1950s, perhaps because the service continued to ring up massive yearly deficits.[109]

Meanwhile, the Island's over-dependence on its sea links had been graphically exposed by a crippling CN rail strike in August 1950, which shut down the Island's principal ferry service in the heart of the tourist season. The abrupt closure provoked a provincial crisis. While auto traffic piled up at Wood Islands, the premier called an emergency sitting of the provincial legislature to demand federal action. In private, there were tense exchanges with Ottawa; in public, howls of constitutional outrage.[110] In the new dispensation isolation was no longer an option.

Even without such labour pains the province's transportation infrastructure could not keep up with the exponential increase in tourist traffic across the Northumberland Strait. In 1941, 182,619 passengers and 31,620 vehicles travelled by ferry to and from Prince Edward Island. By 1950, the figures were 292,595 and 88,747, respectively. Over the course of the next decade the numbers continued to soar, largely without the benefit of additional ferries. In 1955, the figures tabled by the province's Transportation director were 426,434 passengers and 151,792 vehicles. In 1960, they were 467,400 and 226,996, respectively, a 255 per cent increase in passenger traffic over twenty years and a whopping 717 per cent increase in vehicular traffic. At Borden alone in 1960, 86,284 vehicles of all description rolled off the ferries along with an estimated 208,890 passengers.[111]

At last, after years of pressure, the federal government committed to a new summer ferry for the Borden–Tormentine run. It belatedly entered service in 1962. Designed with the summer bulge in tourist visitation in mind, the MV *Confederation* resembled a floating bridge. It was a "ro-ro" ferry (that is, roll-on/roll-off): automobiles drove on one end and drove off the other. It was not equipped to operate in ice and it did not take railcars.[112] In other words, it was essentially geared to tourism.

Extrapolating tourism statistics from ferry traffic was, as always, much more difficult than simply counting cars with off-Island plates, and over time several different formulas were used, based on "average" tourist parties and conjectures about per capita spending. By those rough measures, it seems that the tourist industry achieved a sort of lift-off somewhere around mid-decade. The number of tourists for 1951 was calculated as 35,000. They spent, depending on the guesser, between $2.5 million and $4.2 million.[113] By 1954, visitor numbers had jumped to 92,000. In 1960, by the Travel Bureau's reckoning, precisely 208,507 visitors descended on the Island. According to a Toronto-based consulting firm, the average size of a tourist party was 3.5 people and the average stay was 5.59 days – presumably including time spent in ferry lineups – with an average expenditure of $120 per party. Applying this law of averages yielded an industry value of $7.8 million dollars.[114] Such numbers must always be taken with a grain of sea salt, but the trend was unmistakable. Over the course of the decade, visitor numbers had roughly doubled every five years. That sort of exponential increase was phenomenal if scarcely repeatable.

In some ways 1956 was a pivotal year. That winter the Innkeepers Association elicited 282 entries when it ran a contest to come up with a new tourist slogan for Prince Edward Island. Fifteen-year-old Avonna MacAusland of New Glasgow won the $50 first prize with "Holiday Island."[115] The contest and award ceremony were sandwiched around a telling exchange between Mrs A.B. LePage, a Cavendish-area tourist operator, and Conservative MLA George Dewar. Speaking in the legislature, Dewar, who was a family physician, had worried about the health of farmwives plagued by too many tourists

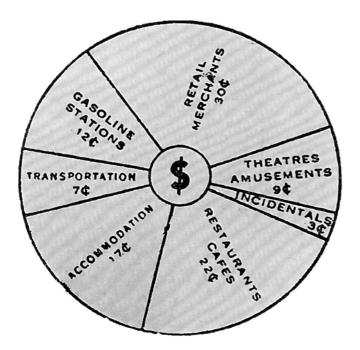

Figure 3.8 • "Where Your Tourist Dollars Go." This 1951 pie chart from the PEI Innkeepers Association promotional booklet was aimed at Islanders themselves, showing how tourist spending rippled out through many sectors of the provincial economy.

and questioned the actual net income from tourism. "I would not trade 100 industrious farmers," he declared, "for all the tourists that come here during the summer."[116] Mrs LePage's rebuttal in a letter to the *Guardian* feigned incredulity. "I find it hard to believe that an educated man would make such a confusing statement," she wrote. It was not a question of choosing between farming and tourism. "Let us have both." And the days of a tourist industry defined by urban expatriates sponging off their country cousins were long gone. "This is a thing of the past while the 'tourist industry' is a thing of the present and the future."[117] In another sign of the times, the provincial secretary, Earle MacDonald, wrote that summer to Inspector Martin of the local RCMP detachment to urge the Mounties to go easy on tourist drivers unless the infractions were "aggravated" or "flagrant," since "harsh justice dealt to a departing visitor is most unlikely to encourage his return."[118]

A few months later, in September 1956, Prince Edward Island hosted the annual convention of the Canadian Tourist Association. The event showcased the province as a tourist destination. You've only just begun, Leo Dolan of the Canadian Travel Bureau told Island banqueters, boosting the boosters: "God has been so good to you – He's given you so many of the tools to work with that I think that within ten or fifteen years, if the investment is made that should be made here, you'll outstrip any part of the Maritime Provinces for the people who desire lovely bathing and who desire all those delightful things which come in a rural atmosphere such as you have."[119]

That December the Innkeepers Association overhauled its bylaws and adopted a mission statement that put tourism front and centre: "To promote and advance the Tourist Industry of Prince Edward Island; To strive for the continued development of tourist facilities offered to the Public by members of this Association; To create a wider interest in the tourist industry among the general public of Prince Edward Island."[120] At the same time it launched a review of its membership categories with a view to expanding its base to include all tourist operators, not just those involved in the accommodation or restaurant business, and began the legislative process of changing its name.[121] Finally, in 1958, the organization was officially relaunched as … the Prince Edward Island Tourist Association.[122]

The new title merely confirmed what the association had already become. In the interval since its namesake's quiet demise in 1940, tourism's grassroots had rediscovered the need for an industry organization. From its inception the Innkeepers Association had preoccupied itself with tourist matters: improved signage, road paving, improved ferry service, better and more standardized accommodations, improved sanitation, and, of course, the weighty matter of advertising its members to visitors.[123] It even joined the Travel Bureau's quixotic campaign to eradicate ragweed from the province in order to attract hay-fevered tourists.[124] (The weeds won, and the Island's "ragweed free" boast had to be modified, then quietly abandoned.[125]) By 1959, the association could count 159 members. Gradually, it had become the chief point of contact between the government and private tourist operators. They would be allies, if not always partners, in developing the hospitality business.

While the Tourist Association's regular forays into tourist promotion concentrated on marketing the province's tourist attractions and accommodations – that is, association members – to visitors once they had arrived, it left the task of drawing tourists to the Island largely to the government's Tourist and Information Bureau. Since it became a government operation in 1940, the bureau had gone through several leaders. Given his fixation with ferry traffic, it was perhaps no surprise that Graham Rogers had traded his position as supervisor of the Travel Bureau (the exact job title varied from year to year in government reports) for a job as the province's director of transportation. His place was taken in 1946 by W.W. Reid, a returned war hero with no particular attachment to tourism.[126] When Reid was named acting director of the Civil Service Board in January 1951, George V. Fraser, the province's newly appointed public relations officer, took his place as director of the Tourist and

Figure 3.9 ▪ George V. Fraser, long-time director of the Island's Travel Bureau and first deputy minister of tourism. Fraser's twenty-year career with the Island government spanned tourism's transformation from cottage industry to key economic sector.

Information Branch.[127] With one brief interregnum, he would be the face of Island tourism for the next two decades.

An Island expatriate with an impressive journalistic pedigree, Fraser had a fertile brain, a facile pen, and an obvious enthusiasm for his job.[128] "I want to tell you that in other parts of Canada he is greatly beloved," Leo Dolan of the CTB assured Islanders in a 1956 speech.[129] He was much esteemed by the provincial Tourist Association as well, perhaps because he was himself a tourist operator, who for a time operated a Highland Summer School at Rustico, featuring his bagpiper son and Highland-dancing daughters.[130] Fraser was clearly good at his job: "one of the best tourist men on the North American Continent," according to the provincial secretary.[131]

The 1950s was the last decade on Prince Edward Island when a single person might dictate the Island's tourist message, and Fraser was often credited with the remarkable boom in tourist numbers during that decade. Admittedly, Fraser was uniquely placed to shape the Island's tourist marketing campaign. He wrote, rewrote, produced, or coordinated most of the promotional copy that came out of the Travel Bureau.[132] In the past the bureau had often been content to pay for offprints of flattering, informative profiles of the province and its charms.[133] But beginning in 1950s, the province began producing its own yearly visitors guide, and most of its budget went into various forms of advertising.[134]

Figure 3.10 • Promotional images of the 1950s and early '60s revelled in social settings. Here, a woman gazes appreciatively over a busy beach, not solitary nature.

The *Guardian* had high praise for Fraser's 1953 guide: "It is beautifully illustrated, beautifully printed, and beautifully written." Fraser's "informal, chatty" text "was nowhere overdone but always in good taste." The accompanying illustrations, "some of them in gorgeous colouring," showed the expected Prince Edward Island panoply of landscape scenes: "churches, villages, racetracks, golf courses, fishing craft, farm scenes, sweeps of wonderful shoreline." But it all looked somehow more modern. "Old pictures for the most part have been dispensed with, along with the old descriptive clichés that have done service far too long."[135] Perhaps it did not matter that the glossy new Prince Edward Island looked pretty much like the old one, merely substituting fresh pictures of familiar touristic tropes.

Yet, in subtle ways, the image projected in the visitors guides *was* different. For one thing, the number of illustrations had risen sharply. And in contrast to the static images and fashionable lassitude of older brochures, there is a great deal of activity in the promotional material of the 1950s. Families, couples, and friends are swimming, golfing, lawn bowling, picnicking, shopping, fishing, horseback riding, sunbathing. Meanwhile locals are pictured going about their business – loading hay, picking potatoes and strawberries, hauling lobster traps, tonging oysters – in distinctly separate sections. In the pages of the visitors guides, it seems, tourists play the province while Islanders work it, and there is little sense of it being shared space.

Besides the beehive of activity, one notices the sheer number of people. In one photo montage from 1951 – arranged like a set of snapshots, which itself suggests that taking pictures is now a standard vacation activity – people seem quite content to camp just five metres apart and children line up to use a playground slide. In the clichéd pose of a woman looking out over the dunes in the 1952 version of the guide, she is not contemplating solitary nature but rather a beach full of people. Recreational democracy meant there were more people vacationing, and the baby boom meant there was simply more people. It was important, then, for Prince Edward Island to advertise itself as a kid-friendly destination, where families would have plenty to do. Indeed, one of the preoccupations of the 1950s-era tourist association was the need to create more attractions for visitors to consume.

Even as Fraser polished up the Island's venerable image for a new generation of tourists, he tried to ensure that his division's contacts with prospective visitors were more systematic and regularized. In his 1958 annual report, Fraser described that process. About 500,000 pieces of travel literature had been sent out that year, he boasted. A typical package included an illustrated booklet, a highway map, an accommodations booklet, a ragweed folder, a Prince Edward Island folder, and a ferry schedule. Many written inquiries received by the bureau included coupons clipped from advertisements that the bureau had placed in various magazines and newspapers. These "are keyed in such a way that we know the papers from which they come. This helps us determine the selection of our best advertising media."[136]

The Travel Bureau's marketing efforts – and its budget – got a considerable boost after mid-decade by sharing in larger marketing campaigns. In yet another manifestation of the postwar expansion of the state in Canada, as well as the amount of federal–provincial collaboration, the Island's Travel and Information Bureau signed on to $300,000 publicity campaign, funded by the CTB, that would promote the Atlantic region to tourist markets in the northeastern United States in the spring of 1957. The funding program placed ads in twenty-five newspapers across seventeen American states and in five national magazines, reaching a combined audience of 160 million readers. The media blitz was expected to prompt 100,000 inquiries.[137] It got 64,000, enough to encourage the CTB to repeat the experiment in 1958. That year, George Fraser reported, his office was involved in three marketing campaigns: the Atlantic Provinces Advertising Campaign; the Maritimes Co-operative Campaign, which targeted central Canada through *Maclean's Magazine* and major newspapers in Ontario (seven) and Quebec (five); and the usual provincial effort spread over selected outlets in Canada and the northeastern United States.[138] By the 1960s, cooperative marketing had become a regular feature of the Island's tourism promotion strategy, a dollar multiplier that extended the Island's modest reach.[139]

In the end, it is impossible to measure the impact of Fraser's efforts. Like watching someone walking a large and energetic dog, it was hard to tell who was leading whom when it comes to 1950s tourism. It would be easy to argue that the tens, then hundreds of thousands of tourists were pushed not pulled to Prince Edward Island, prodded by social, economic, and demographic forces that had nothing to do with visitors guides or tourist associations. Yet it is difficult to imagine visitors finding the province by accident. For the most part, advertising played a key role in priming the pump of the tourist industry. After all, North Americans had to become aware of Prince Edward Island before they could decide to go there. The reach of advertising was important, then, but so was its message. What was it that Prince Edward Island was selling that North Americans were buying? Why did they come?

"Give the tourist what he wants, not what we want to give him," the principal of Prince of Wales College Frank MacKinnon admonished the Innkeepers Association in 1950.[140] To find out what that was the Travel Bureau initiated a tourism survey, the first in the province's history, which canvassed 7,600 visitors in the summer of 1952.[141] The traffic breakdown from the ferries for that year suggests from whom the survey sample was drawn. While tourist marketing remained obsessed with the huge central Canadian and American markets, the bulk of the summer tourist traffic – just under half – continued to originate from the adjacent, largely unsolicited provinces of Nova Scotia and New Brunswick. Quebec and Ontario accounted for about 15 per cent of the vehicles and the much coveted American market supplied just under 30 per cent, over half of them from Massachusetts with New York a distant second. By comparison only sixty-five cars had made the transcontinental trek from California and there was one brave soul from Alaska.[142] Pollsters did not explore whether any of the visitors were expatriates coming to stay with relatives, but they were asked to estimate length of stay and expenditure.

The survey also sampled tourists' perceptions. Not surprisingly, since they were probably interviewed in ferry lineups, they emphasized the need for better tourist infrastructure, especially when it came to crossing the strait. But they also prized the Island's unspoiled landscape and people.[143] Precisely what "unspoiled" meant went undefined, although it involved not gouging tourists and avoiding commercialization. It also played well against the

Island's existing tourist tropes: cool sea breezes to take the edge off summer, uncrowded beaches, and a pastoral people rooted in a pastoral landscape. As it had for decades already, the Prince Edward Island of the postwar era promised an antimodern antidote to urban industrial angst. Indeed there has always been a peculiar consistency in the image that the Island projects of itself to prospective visitors over time. This sample of Fraser's ad copy from 1956 is typical. "Going to Prince Edward Island offers a complete, restful, memorable change," he wrote in "Picture Yourself in P.E.I." It was "the Eden spot, the unspoiled, idyllic Island."[144] What appetite did such depictions satisfy? As Ian McKay has postulated, antimodernism promised for tourists a recovery of "innocence."[145] That childlike, childhood state of certainty and simplicity was a near cousin to the search for "authenticity" – as opposed to "artificiality" – that Dean MacCannell has posited as a key tourist motivator.[146]

Both sensibilities, innocence and authenticity, were hard to define with any degree of precision. Nevertheless, many visitors seemed to perceive the Island in those terms. When Douglas Roche profiled the province for the Roman Catholic biweekly *The Ensign* (which George Fraser of the Travel Bureau had once edited), he was pleased enough with the result to forward a copy of the article to the Island's premier. Roche's Prince Edward Island was the same antimodern paradise of earlier tourist promotion. "Hardly a visitor to the Island fails to come away entranced at the sereneness, the gaiety and quite often the wisdom of the Islanders," he wrote. "Some nervous progress of today's society has by-passed Prince Edward Island, just as it has much of the Maritimes. But the difference between the Island and the other Atlantic provinces is that PEI doesn't seem particularly worried." It wasn't that the Islanders distrusted progress, he continued, "It's merely that the people are reticent about rushing into something that could upset their placid routine … Distractions and the frantic pace of the big city are clearly not for Prince Edward Island." There was money in that mindset, he thought: "The government has lately become aware that by capitalizing on the province's peace and quiet, many thousands of tourists can be attracted each summer."[147] There was apparently no concern that "many thousands of tourists" might destroy that "peace and quiet."

A year earlier Islander David Macdonald of Toronto gave Islanders' serenity a metaphysical dimension. Returning to his native province after an absence of thirty-four years, he was delighted to find that so little had changed in "Canada's 'Garden of Eden,'" which continued to be "'in the world but not of it.'" The reason, he felt, was its islandness: "Indeed, the Strait of Northumberland, like a mighty moat, has rendered the red shores of P.E.I. inassailable [*sic*] to the pernicious forces that have so easily rendered so much of the 'outside world' to the debris of inhuman automatism and loss of human dignity and respect for the individual as a person."[148]

From this perspective, a virtuous insularity was reinforced by islandness, and the literary conceit of island as refuge played well to tourist promotion. "One of the greatest motivating forces in travel is the desire to see and experience something different," explained Alan Field, the new head of the Canadian Travel Bureau, in a speech to Island tourist operators. In the case of their province, he argued, that "something" was the distinctive character that came from being an island.[149]

And how did the visitor craving difference know they had reached the self-contained world of an island? They crossed over water. That crossing announced to the traveller that they had arrived someplace definitively "elsewhere." As geographer John Towner points out, "the journey itself becomes not only a matter of distance, time and cost, but a critical experience for those at leisure."[150] That was especially the case in crossing to an island. According to John Jakle, the voyage itself "could also amplify the sense of being in a unique environment, and of being on a unique adventure."[151] In that process, the ferry was part conveyance, part pleasure boat – and part time machine that transported its passengers to a place out of mind. Coming to the Island, claimed George Fraser, was "almost like going to a different world."[152]

So it was that during the postwar era the "rite of passage" began to seep into the tourist marketing of Prince Edward Island. While promotional literature tendered practical advice about how to reach PEI, blithely minimizing the distances involved and tactfully ignoring the traffic bottlenecks on both sides of the strait, the postwar era's promotional films made more of the journey itself – the short, safe voyage across the strait on an ocean-sized vessel – as part of the tourist experience.

Sometimes the sense of island arrival was implicit, as in *Seaside Holiday: Prince Edward Island National Park* (NFB, 1948) or *Holiday Island* (PEI Department of Tourist Development, 1967), with their lingering shots of approaching ferries (usually the queen of the fleet, the *Abegweit*), which disgorge carloads of eager tourists. And sometimes it was overt. In 1953's *Abegweit*, produced specially for the Prince Edward Island Travel Bureau, an "Island holiday" actually starts as the ferry leaves Cape Tormentine: "The crossing of the Northumberland Strait takes less than an hour," its narrator reassured prospective travellers, "and as the ship leaves the Mainland the feel of the warm sea breezes and the sound of the gulls circling overhead is for many the moment when an Island holiday really begins."[153] The child narrator of Canadian National Railway's *Memo to Mom* (c. 1963) is similarly rhapsodic: "From Montreal we took the Ocean Limited and our train went straight on board the *Abegweit*. Daddy says it's one of the biggest ferries. It's only nine miles across the Strait of Northumberland, but it's a real sea voyage, gulls and everything!"[154] The delicate, Goldilocks-like balance of experience is unmistakable: the Island is near and yet far; tinged with romance, yet prosaic; an adventure, but convenient.[155]

Such films projected the image of Prince Edward Island across tourist markets in central Canada and the northeastern United States. By the mid-1960s, tourism officials would claim that some nine million Americans (and an unknown number of Canadians) had seen *Abegweit*, the Travel Bureau's 1953 effort.[156] If tourism was an "invisible export," as the 1955 report of the provincial Trade Division put it, promotional films were the local tourist products that actually travelled.[157] In the beginning travelogue films featuring Prince Edward Island had publicized the province generally, highlighting its industries as well as its attractions, but as the 1950s rolled over in the '60s, generic promotion had largely given way to a much narrower audience: not potential settlers or investors, but tourists.

Figure 3.11 ▪ In the postwar era, cookie-cutter rental cottages and camping supplanted the summer resort as the most favoured tourist accommodations. Green Gables Bungalow Court inside PEI National Park – in fact, just 200 metres from Green Gables house itself – was designed and built by the federal parks agency. It was intended to provide affordable family accommodations for park visitors, but also to serve as a model for private enterprise.

If the medium was evolving, it was partly because the audience was, too. Baby boomers enjoying recreational democracy might have rising incomes and paid vacations, but they also had growing families and modest travel budgets. A generation earlier, tourists with limited means had camped out in their motorcars. By the late '50s low-income travellers had found another alternative. "This year, for the first time in two decades of tourist travel, a

Figure 3.12 ▪ A postcard of Stanhope Campground. Camping might bring urbanites close to nature, but it was also an affordable way for baby boom families to vacation in the 1960s and '70s.

new and definite trend is noticeable here," went one press report. "A large number of vehicles this season either travelled with house trailers or lived in tents when they arrived."[158] Actually, the Prince Edward Island National Park had already accommodated the trend, building campgrounds and preparing campsites. Its small-scale luxury hotel at Dalvay had failed to attract a wealthy clientele, and even its Cavendish bungalow court, constructed in 1949–50 and geared to middle-class tourists, lost up to $2,000 a year before it was finally sold to its lessee, R.S. Humphrey, for a fraction of its assessed value.[159] Instead, people were choosing to camp. Even the premier noticed. "I visited the National Park area the other day and saw the number of tents that were erected therein," he wrote Summerside businessman Charles Linkletter, who was trying to finance a motel project in that town. "It is becoming increasingly evident that people will not pay the high price that tourist resorts demand, but are prepared to set up their own tents and live for a few days of their vacations along the various shores. If this is a continuing trend, I am sure the Government will hesitate before setting aside additional money for the erection of tourist establishments."[160]

Instead, Matheson was moving in a different direction. As early as 1953, George Fraser had called for the creation of one or more provincial parks.[161] But good ideas were more convincing when they came with money. In January 1956, Robert Cotton, a wealthy real estate developer – who, decades earlier, had founded Charlottetown Summer Resorts – approached the premier about establishing a number of provincial parks in various parts of the province. The object, Cotton stated, was to provide "picnic and recreation grounds for summer visitors as well as for local motorists, providing something more desirable than the roadside tables in other provinces and states where distances between stops are so much greater. Also increasing the number of objectives for local motorists where they may enjoy the shore and woods without trespassing, and making more places of interest available to visiting motorists who might thereby be encouraged to remain longer within the Province, and stimulating an increased use of gasoline as well as other products."[162] With that in mind Cotton had purchased three farm properties totalling 151 acres: one at Strathgartney along the TransCanada Highway in the rolling hill country of central Queens County; another fronting on the Brudenell River, midway along the eastern coast of Kings County; and a third at Belfast Cove in Eldon, not far from the ferry terminal at Wood Islands. He now gifted them to the province, with a tentative offer to endow their development and upkeep, though he (wrongly) believed that they might become largely self-sufficient. A fourth park should be added in Prince County, he noted, and he would be happy to subsidize the acquisition of some forest parks of 1,000 acres or more.[163]

Strathgartney became the Island's first provincial park when it opened in the summer of 1959. It was an immediate hit with both locals and visitors. Some merely picnicked there; others happily pitched their tents. Nature may have called to campers, but cost was one of the major attractions. Provincial parks did not even begin to charge patrons until 1964. Even then, the fees were negligible: seventy-five cents per night for tenters, a dollar for trailers. "Camping is the new force in the economy," parks supervisor Wendell Profitt argued, "and its full impact will be felt more and more as time goes on. Camping activity should climb more than 50 percent in the next ten years."[164] All through the 1960s, the provincial government continued to expand its parks system. By the end of the decade, the provincial government would be operating (but not profiting from) forty campgrounds and picnic sites scattered across the Island where baby boom families could experience a modest version of the great outdoors.[165] The nature that they encountered was not very wild, but it was cheap.

Nova Scotian Will R. Bird was not one of those campers. The region's most famous travel writer was gathering material for a new book when he drove over to the Island one summer in the late 1950s. The author of *This Is Nova Scotia* was busy working up *These Are the Maritimes*. Bird's approach was essentially to cast himself as a local trying to see his region through tourist eyes. As always, he was seeking local colour – local characters, local stories – to entertain his readers. His travel writing extolled the Maritimes' exceptionalism, and for Bird that resided in the peculiar past of each place he visited.

Bird was not, of course, an entirely reliable narrator. Historians Ian McKay and Robin Bates have parsed his deceptively simple prose to depict an "anti-intellectual intellectual," who employed history and anecdote to subtly exalt his liberal notion of the individual, often at the expense of a more complex or ambiguous truth.[166] "In fact," they write, "Bird's imagined Nova Scotia does not really have a history. There are only events, one after the other."[167] Bird's journey across Prince Edward Island seems similarly random, a series of encounters linked only by the author's whimsy. At the same time, read cautiously, his account suggests how the province might have appeared to travellers of the period.

"Now that they're getting fine paved roads over on the Island, everybody wants to go there," a storekeeper at Port Elgin, New Brunswick, assures Bird. Just squeezing onto the *Abegweit*, Bird and his family have the requisite sense of arrival at Borden as a pastoral vista of low red cliffs and green fields unfolds before the incoming ship. And there is the requisite nod to the self-sufficient, insular pride of an islanded people: "nowhere on earth are there good folk who can compare with the Islanders for clannishness and an attitude in general that almost makes them a race apart." It was as if, he writes, "in their heart of hearts they feel sorry for your hard luck in not being born on the Island."[168] Bird's Islanders are unconcernedly old-fashioned and unhurried, self-absorbed, slightly suspicious of "foreigners" – that is, anyone not from the Island – parochial, resentful of their neglect under Confederation.[169] They would be quaint were Bird a little more condescending. Instead, they are *sui generis.* The Island is "a valentine," one of Bird's characters brags, "No fence, building, no stone, no tree or blade of grass is out of place. Best of all – that is the Island's true secret – no human being is out of place either."[170]

Their first night the Birds find, without much looking (for that, too, would be negative publicity), lodgings in the brand new wing of a modern motel in Summerside. Already, by the 1950s, the Innkeepers Association had begun to fret about the clustering of tourists around the North Shore, particularly the PEI National Park, and Charlottetown.[171] But Bird is no average tourist, and he makes a leisurely progress around the province, travelling from west to east in a series of looping day trips, all the while collecting little nuggets of local history and homespun wisdom. Just as Islanders are part of the landscape, the Island landscape is one of the book's characters. "It was fine scenery as we drove along," Bird records of the drive from Bedeque to Charlottetown, "fine views to right and left, the sea, the rolling hills, the pretty settings." And

Figure 3.13 ▪ Woodleigh Replicas, Lt Col Ernest Johnstone's painstaking, scaled recreations of iconic British landmarks, became a poster child for tourism marketing after it opened in 1957 on a thirty-acre site in Burlington. It featured in most promotional films and print literature for decades to come.

so are the tourists: "In fact the Island seemed to become more beautiful with every mile and it was easy to understand why cars with American number plates were driving along at twenty miles an hour. They didn't want to miss the scenery. Here and there a car would be stopped and men and women with colour cameras were in fields, on fences, perched hither and yon, trying to get the most effective colour shot."[172]

The ritual visit to the Confederation Chamber in Charlottetown prompts a passing reflection about what the fathers might think of how their union has worked out, but, otherwise, present concerns seldom intrude into Bird's narrative. At Cavendish he adopts the conceit that Anne of Green Gables is real and sees the house "as Anne saw it during her first years there." "It is no use trying to tell a person what Cavendish is like," he writes coyly. "You must go and see for yourself, come under the spell."[173] Travelling west, Bird highlights one of the new generation of postwar tourist attractions. Woodleigh Replicas, featuring miniature recreations of famous Old World

The Summer Trade

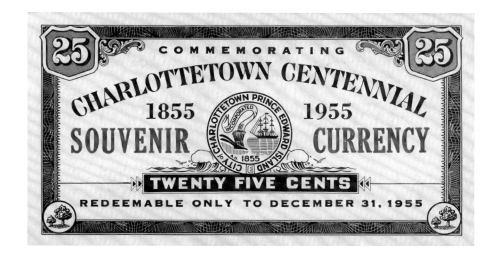

Figure 3.14 ▪ The provincial capital launched an era of centennials – and centennial souvenirs – with the 1955 anniversary of its civic incorporation. This one could be redeemed locally for merchandise during the year.

buildings, had been created by Lt Col Ernest W. Johnstone and earns Bird's plaudits for tasteful display.[174]

Not all of Bird's stops are little treasures awaiting discovery. West of Miscouche there is scrub brush and poverty. Mount Stewart is infested with skunks. The farms back of Morell are growing back to forest. Souris is deserted in the heat. Georgetown has grown shabby and discouraged: blank shopfronts, empty houses, uncut grass "strangling the flowers." Montague on the other hand bustles, sporting the homey new Garden of the Gulf Museum – the Island's first.[175] The Birds' departure via Wood Islands on the *Lord Selkirk* – the brand-new ferry, of course – is wait-free, untroubled, and beautiful. Where they had peered ahead expectantly from the deck of the *Abegweit* as the Island drew near a few days before, now they gaze wistfully backwards through their binoculars as the landscape recedes.

Had he travelled the route a few years earlier, Bird might have encountered eight-year-old Hope McBride of Halifax looking sadly back from the rail of the Wood Islands ferry. In the early '50s, her family – "Dad and Mum," Hope, and three younger siblings – spent three consecutive summers vacationing at Prouds's Parkhill Cottages at Stanhope Beach. Her nostalgia-sweetened memories of those "red-soil summers" offer another glimpse at the '50s tourist experience.

Prouds's five tiny rental cottages (strategically located near their house/store) were primitive, cobbled together from leftover lumber and clad in green, asphalt shingles. Inside there were no ceilings, just the pitched roof, and no insulation. The furnishings were homemade or secondhand. The cooking was done on a woodstove, the washing in the McBrides' own portable electric washing machine. For playground there was a homemade teeter-totter and a set of swings. Little Hope didn't care. For most of the time she lived at the beach (the Prouds had thoughtfully built a stile so that their guests could climb over the national park's boundary fence to reach the shore). There were few dark clouds to spoil her summer idyll – except perhaps her visit to Green Gables: "We followed each other from room to room, upstairs and down, looking and looking. Gradually it dawned on me. What's all this old stuff? Where's Anne? Where are Matthew and Marilla? 'Let's go,' I moaned."[176]

To judge from McBride and Bird, the Prince Edward Island that beckoned across the blue waters of the Northumberland Strait remained "unspoiled." The feature writer for a 1957 article in the *Monetary Times* agreed: "One of the delightful things about the Island is the absence of commercialization."[177] But as tourism numbers began to boom, as the hospitality business sought to professionalize – as the Island itself quickened the pace of its modernization – could that quality be preserved? And how self-conscious could it be before it became artificial, disconnected from a living reality? Matthew McRae captures the ripening dilemma of the postwar tourist trade: "tourism became the central feature of the plan to modernize Prince Edward Island, but at the same time required the Island to retain its underdeveloped rural character. Tourism was simultaneously weaving and unravelling the garden myth it depended upon for its success."[178] For now, at least, the contradiction could be ignored.

Although he did not meet them, Will Bird would probably have taken to Dolph and Bertha Fleming. As the rising tide of tourism washed Island shores, Dolph and Bertha had decided to take the plunge. After all, they were located in prime tourist country, on one of the main approaches to the Cavendish end of the Prince Edward Island National Park. In December 1953, they had a furnace installed in their old farmhouse, and the next February they invested in a proper bathroom with a flush toilet. That May they added a refrigerator to their little mound of debt.[179] On 20 July, there was one last, practical yet symbolic chore before all was ready: "Cleaned out stables & shifted pigs." That evening, "2 Tourist here = 6.00 overnight."[180] The family had added yet another seasonal occupation to their repertoire: tourist operators.

To judge from Dolph's diary, he and Bertha Fleming took to the tourist business. It seemed to go hand in hand with the trappings of modernity. In 1955, Dolph built a garage and soon enough he had a car to put in it. While he was getting his driver's licence, Bertha was earning her first aid certificate – just in case, presumably.[181] By the late '50s, their summer trade was booming. In Dolph's diary, their brand of tourism reads more like a variation on an ancient tradition of hospitality, which welcomed guests rather than customers. It was just as tourist promoters might have imagined. The names of various visitors now found their way into Fleming's diary beside his neighbours and kin, people such as the Kohrs, who paid $100 for four weeks' room and board; Mr and Mrs John Molloy and their son Jack, who stayed for two weeks; or the George Edwards of "Alexander, Virginia"; or "Margret and her girl friend Bessie."[182] After the Flemings welcomed another party from Virginia in July 1959, Dolph reported to his diary, "Intertained and Fed the … People & don the chors."[183] He does not mention how exactly he "entertained" them. He took another group, the Ness family from Utah, out clamming, and brought seven other visitors to the local lobster supper.[184] On another occasion, somewhat to his annoyance, he had to stay home while Bertha went off to bingo, waiting for three expected tourists: *"Arrived overnight,"* he emphasized in his diary.[185]

The Flemings even played tourist themselves. When their daughter, Gertrude Skinner, came home from Halifax with her family, she took Dolph and Bertha Sunday driving on the roads that the government had spent the past decade improving. One such outing, on 23 August 1959, conjures images of a Norman Rockwell painting:[186] "Skinners B. & I started out on a trip to South Rustico for Mass then to Brackley Dalvie Morel[l] to Father Robins [their former pastor] & Souris. Home by Wilfred Moonies Iona & Aunt Mary Mooney had tea. Then home = 193 miles."

Beside and around the periodic references in Fleming's diary to tourists and their stays, the same familiar mantra recurs: "Don the chors." In a sense, the Flemings had merely grafted tourism onto their existing way of life. There was little that was professional and much that was homely about their tourist business: an aging couple welcoming strangers into their house and their lives.

After Dolph died in October 1962, observers might have expected Bertha to abandon the summer trade.[187] Her children already scattered, she soon moved to Charlottetown. For the rest of her working life, she would find winter employment in an old folks home, catering now to a different sort of sojourner.[188] But every summer, like the tourists themselves, she came back to North Rustico where her grandson helped her reopen the tourist home that had become part of her life. When she died in December 1972, her family found the house all set up for another season.[189]

And so, the family that once defiantly farmed the fields taken from them for tourist development ended by accommodating tourism into the rhythms of their lives. It would be reading too much into their experience to say that Dolph and Bertha's story is the story of Island tourism writ small. No microcosm is truly microcosmic, after all. And yet, their adventures in tourism are in some measure representative of the postwar period. There was something wholesomely authentic about the Flemings' farm home.

While the voice in the diary is Dolph's, the entries unintentionally emphasize the crucial role that women played in this sort of tourism industry. Dolph "don the chors" out in the barn, but Bertha did the bulk of the hosting, catering to her guests' needs. One has only to look at the membership rolls for the Prince Edward Island Tourist Association to see further evidence of this projection of an accepted female role. In 1950, almost half of its members – twenty-eight of fifty-eight – were women, even if convention often dictated that they be listed by their husband's names (for example, "Mrs John Burns"). In 1960–61, the membership rolls included forty-nine women among the ninety-seven members, forty-two listed individually and seven recorded with their husbands. Even though the association's leadership during this period remained overwhelmingly (though not exclusively) male, the hospitality industry became a wedge, affording women easier entry into the masculine world of business.

The Flemings' embrace of tourism was arguably emblematic of the industry's progression. For Dolph and Bertha, coming to grips with modernity at midcentury, the tourist trade was more than a hobby but less than an occupation. They never bothered to become members of the Tourist Industry Association nor were party to its growing ambitions. They had simply recognized opportunity when it came knocking on their North Rustico door. Yet, it was in just that fashion that tourism had gathered momentum over the previous twenty years. Whether sought or seeking, visitors had come, and now, increasing numbers of ordinary Islanders, not just well-heeled entrepreneurs and boards of trade, were being drawn into the summer trade. It was becoming more professional and more calculating, had acquired more of the trappings of a formal industry. By 1960 that industry was reckoned the second most valuable in the short list that comprised the provincial economy, surpassed only by agriculture.

Tourist Association members had for some time felt that their industry's rapid growth warranted a cabinet portfolio of its own, but Premier Matheson had not been convinced. He "could see no reasons generally for such a move," he responded to association overtures in 1956, but if the association had any "special arguments supporting such he would be happy to receive and consider them."[190] Less than four years later the association would have a different answer to its lobby. By the time the Progressive Conservatives swept to power in the fall of 1959, ending twenty-four years of Liberal rule, tourism's continuing growth had driven it well up the provincial agenda. The minister responsible for tourism was the provincial secretary, J. David Stewart, the second most powerful person in Cabinet after Premier Walter Shaw. Stewart had big plans for the tourist industry. It "might well become our number one industry in this Province," he told the Charlottetown Board of Trade in November 1959. His one ambition, he stated tongue-in-cheek, "was to have all Islanders catering to the Tourist Industry six months a year under D.S.T. [i.e. Daylight Savings Time] and an enlightened Liquor Law, and then become Tourists ourselves for the other six months of the Year."[191]

At the next session of the legislature, twenty years after it had formally taken responsibility for tourist promotion, the province at last created a separate Department of Tourist Development. Stewart became minister responsible, George Fraser his deputy. It was a momentous, if largely symbolic, decision. For almost a century tourism had grown up largely untended by the side of the road and along the Island shore. It was now deemed too potentially lucrative to allow it to develop on its own any longer. From income supplement and cottage industry, tourism had suddenly become the fastest growing sector of the provincial economy. Something that important merited closer attention and better management. From now on government would deliberately shape the tourist industry. Everything from physical infrastructure to marketing strategy would be closely measured, managed, and monitored. Future tourism would be far more intentional than ever before. The age of expectation had arrived.

Prince Edward Island
CANADA

CHAPTER 4

Great Expectations
1960–80

All through the long, hot summer of 1965, pollsters fanned out across the ferry lineups at Wood Islands and Borden, clipboards in hand, to talk to tourists waiting to leave the province. They canvassed every tenth car sporting off-Island licence plates; 3,910 "tourist parties" in all.[1] It was a measure of the length of the ferry lineups that the waiting motorists had enough time to answer no less than ninety-four questions about their visit to Prince Edward Island.

The survey teams were working for Acres Research and Planning, Ltd, a Toronto-based consulting firm. And Acres was working for the province of Prince Edward Island – though the money was coming from Ottawa. The Island government wanted baseline data about the province's tourist industry to help it decide how and where to spend its promotional dollars. As the deputy minister of tourist development, George Fraser, explained, "The aim was to find out what type of tourist comes to the Island, where he comes from, what he spends his money on and how much money he leaves on the Island."[2] The following summer, Acres would attack the supply side of the equation, working up an inventory of the province's "recreation-tourism" complex – restaurants, roads, accommodations, attractions – and mapping its "recreation-tourism capability." By 1967, after months of collating and analysis, the two-volume report was at last forwarded to a government hungry for knowledge.

The Acres Report is a benchmark document in the history of Prince Edward Island tourism. The most comprehensive and accurate research conducted to that date into the industry, its statistical mosaic captured an image of Island tourism at the end of its adolescence. But it also suggested what tourism could look like if the state took care to develop it rationally and efficiently, addressing its shortcomings and maximizing its potential. Framed with all the postwar era's faith in the transformative power of evidence-based

Figure 4.0 (facing) ▪ The baby boom created customers for the kind of family-friendly holidays that the Island could deliver. Children were more prominent in tourism promotion in the late 1950s through the mid-1960s than ever before – or since.

planning, the study transcended the fate of most consultants' reports. Instead of gathering dust, it became the template for future tourist development. For as Judith Adler has persuasively argued, by the mid-1960s the state had decided that tourism was too important to let it develop on its own. It must be managed.[3] And effective management required detailed knowledge.

The tourism report was actually just one of four major sectoral studies commissioned from Acres by the provincial government of Walter Shaw as it gingerly grasped the nettle of state-driven economic development. By the time it was released in 1967, Acres' prescription for a healthy tourist industry would be caught up in a far more ambitious campaign to modernize the entire Island and rationalize its economy, the "Comprehensive Development Plan." The future of Island tourism would play out within the vaster matrix of its programs, principles, and assumptions.

At the beginning of the 1960s, promoters and administrators were still referring to "tourist development." By the early 1970s, as the Development Plan gathered momentum, the term "tourism" had supplanted "tourist." The person had been displaced by the thing. It was a subtle yet significant shift in nomenclature, and it did not go unnoticed by critics of untrammelled tourism. It was tempting to see behind the smiling mask of period tourism the assembly of a soulless, indifferent marketing machine. But that gives tourist developers both too much credit, in the sense of control over the evolving industry, and too little, since most tourist promoters and developers harboured no designs to subvert the society to which they belonged. For despite the level of intentionality that characterized Island tourism during the 1960s and '70s, the outcomes, both economic and cultural, were often unforeseen. Even with mountains of data to inform strategic thinking and unprecedented investment to transform thought into action, the era's planners discovered that tourism, like the tourist trailers waiting for "the boat," was a difficult beast to steer, and almost impossible to back up.

In touristic terms, the '60s started much as the '50s had ended. Tourism numbers continued to grow by leaps and bounds, 10–20 per cent per year, straining both accommodation and transportation infrastructure at the height of the tourist season.[4] The annual increase masked a growing sense of how competitive the tourist trade had become. It was no longer enough for marketers simply to make travellers aware of Prince Edward Island and its virtues as a destination. Potential visitors had too many options for promoters to be complacent. Today's tourist, the de facto deputy minister George Fraser warned in his 1964 report, was "a more restless type." Clearly, the days of long, leisurely sojourns in the same destination year after year were gone, but the postwar tourist also had grown fickle. As John Jakle points out, the automobile had not only transformed tourist travel, it transformed the tourist mentality. The "diligent tourist," Jakle writes, "mixed pleasure with learning to grow and mature." In contrast, "The irresponsible tourist did not grow, but only pleasured, often learning little and keeping prejudices firmly intact." Moreover, automobile touring, with its relentless succession of landscapes and sensations, ultimately dulled the senses. By obscuring the value of responsible travel, the automobile "encouraged irresponsibility."[5]

To attract those restless, irresponsible tourists to Prince Edward Island and prolong their stays meant countering the auto-enabled notion that the journey itself was the destination. And that required, wrote Fraser, "an up-to-date library of promotional and informational tourist books, guides and maps."[6] Two years later, he returned to his theme. "The competition is keen," he boasted, "but Prince Edward Island is in the forefront with its literature. It compares with the finest in Canada and has the proud distinction of being better than most."[7]

Promotion, as opposed to planning or analysis, continued to be the prime activity of Fraser's tiny department, and promotional budgets kept pace with the rapid rise in visitor numbers during the '60s. By 1965, the year of the Acres surveys, the budget for the Department of Tourist Development topped $363,000. Its share of the province's total ordinary expenditures was now 1.3 per cent, an increase of more than 60 per cent in only five years. Nearly half of the departmental budget, $185,655, was devoted to promotion and advertising. In gross terms, the amount was unimpressive; among Canada's provinces, only Saskatchewan spent less. And yet, in proportion to population – $1.71 per capita – no one spent more.[8]

For much of the decade, the Island's tourism literature followed its instincts as much as its ideas. As in the past, it avoided favouring specific attractions by sticking mainly with generalities; one of its favourite adjectives was "typical." But if the overall marketing message remained consistent in successive editions of *Come to Prince Edward Island, Canada*, their superficial sameness is deceptive. Text was constantly updated, presumably in response to perceived trends.

As often as the text changed, the images changed faster. Once, the same pictures might serve for decades; now they were rearranged for every edition and quite often replaced. This suggests that photographs had become the key discourse in tourism promotion. The "restless" tourist needed visuals. They also craved colour. By the mid-1960s, the province's principal visitors guide had abandoned black and white photographs. The content of the

Figure 4.1 • With new visitors guides being produced each year by the 1960s, it becomes easier to notice incremental changes in the Island's image for tourism. The opening of the 1960 beach section stresses what we would expect during the baby boom: families, children, and activity. But by 1968, promoters had decided that what tourists really wanted to do on holiday was get away from it all – including from each other.

images changed, too. Compositions grew more formal, more geometric – and soon, even psychedelic. Even more noticeable was that the pictorial landscapes were emptying out. Where visitors guides in the '50s had filled their photographs with cheerful tourists, the tourism industry was now discovering that even baby boom families wanted to get away from it all, including other people, when on vacation.[9]

Tourism promotion also recognized that different visitors might want to do different things. The cover of the 1962 guide displays a happy family dreaming of their gender-appropriate vacation on Prince Edward Island: son playing at the beach, Dad showing off his prowess at fishing, and Mom shopping, of course. Canadian National Railway's promotional film, *Memo to Mom*, keeps its motherless family together but hints at the same variations in taste. After a brief pan of various historical sites, the film's child narrator confides, "We had to humour Dad about churches and history things."[10] Such distinctions marked the beginning of a market segmentation that would only increase over time.

One of the Travel Bureau's priorities in the '60s was to update the province's mishmash of promotional films, most of them made by other organizations for their own purposes. In mid-decade the department's Travel Bureau was still relying on old faithfuls, such as its own *Abegweit*, which dated from 1953.[11] It was supplemented by newer films, such as *My Island Home* (1961), a National Film Board production; Canadian National's *Memo to Mom* (c. 1963); and a costume re-creation of the Charlottetown Conference called *Room of Destiny*, but also a *This World of Ours* feature on Prince Edward

Island (c. 1952); and even *Holiday Island*, which dated from back in 1948.[12] A new promotional film, also called *Holiday Island*, finally appeared in 1967, just in time for Canada's centennial. Like its title, the new production was essentially an update of older promotional films. It was light on narration and heavy on Island landscapes (especially beaches), where relaxed tourists swam, clammed, fished, ate seafood, rode, golfed, and gawked. A few popular tourist attractions were profiled, but most of the sights and activities were generic. Unlike their real-life counterparts, the visitors to *Holiday Island* had no trouble getting on or off the Island, and the Travel Bureau's innovative new two-way radio system made booking travel and accommodations as easy as saying, "over and out."[13]

While it gave a modern gloss to the Island's charms, *Holiday Island*'s marketing message remained familiar. "Prince Edward Island," the narrator intones, "has succeeded in preserving something that is rare in North America: a way of life that is calm and unhurried, with its own relaxed tempo." That familiar trope, of the untroubled, wholesome heartland, no doubt struck a chord with many North Americans. Scholars have tried to capture the *zeitgeist* of postwar America and the yearnings of its citizens. In their reading, rapid change in the 1950s further dislocated North Americans, leaving them more mobile physically and economically but feeling less grounded and less secure. It was, perhaps, a familiar refrain but more widely felt. According to historian William Chafe, Americans were wrestling with "the existentialist dilemma of finding a way to create meaning in the face of forces over which one had no control."[14] The result in many cases was to hearken North Americans back towards the imagined certainties of an imagined past, their nations', but also, their own.

It was just this longing that Walt Disney appealed to in many of his films and that he tried to conjure in the artful *faux* world of his postwar theme parks, with their idealization of small town America, their carefully crafted sense of community, and childlike, happy-ending adventures. Looking back, Disney would recall the mood he was trying to recreate in the pastorale section of his 1940 animated film *Fantasia*: "That's what it is – a feeling of freedom with the animals and characters that live out there. That is what you experience when you go into the country. You escape the everyday world – the strife and struggle. You get out where everything is free and beautiful."[15] The sentiment is not so distant from the note of longing that suffuses the much quoted passage from L.M. Montgomery's 1939 essay on her native province:

> Peace! You never know what peace is until you walk on the shores or in the fields or along the winding red roads of Abegweit on a summer twilight when the dew is falling and the old old stars are peeping out and

the sea keeps it nightly tryst with the little land it loves. You find your soul then ... you realize that youth is not a vanished thing but something that dwells forever in the heart.[16]

For Montgomery, as for her characters, the Island provided a physical and emotional haven. The same, arguably, was true for the postwar tourists drawn to the province.

If Disney offered escapists a theme park, Prince Edward Island posed as the real thing (albeit without the rides or the gadgets or the futuristic displays). The Acres report likened the province to one big park with entry points at Borden and Wood Islands.[17] The marketers' job was to mediate between supply and demand, desire and delivery. What the Acres report taught bureaucrats and boosters was to approach that task in a much more calculated way. Public statements and promotional literature continued to use the polite language of hospitality, referring to "visitors" and "guests," but planners increasingly thought in baldly capitalist terms of "clients," "customers," and "resources."[18]

One characteristic that the Island's promotional literature and films shared was the uniformly white skin of the people who populated the tourist landscape. That the imagined tourist was a Caucasian (the same as their hosts) did not necessarily mean that people of other races and skin colours were unwelcome on Prince Edward Island, but it certainly did suggest certain reflexive assumptions about who was wanted.[19] It also hinted at something more culpable.

In September 1962, a Montreal doctor named James A. Phills complained to the Island press that he and his wife, a trained social worker, had been refused accommodations at Gregor's-by-the-Sea, a tourist resort near Brackley on the Island's North Shore, because of the colour of their skin.[20] The Phillses were African Canadian. When the press approached Gregor's owner Jack Cameron he freely admitted the incident: "While he was sorry to do such a thing," he told the *Guardian*, "previous experience has shown that admission of Negroes into his resort causes other guests to move out. He added that he was in a difficult business where it was hard enough to make a profit without giving cause for his guests to leave."[21]

The real bombshell came three days later, when the Charlottetown *Evening Patriot,* citing an "informed source," alleged that race discrimination was "general throughout the North Shore and extends not only to Negroes but also to Jewish and French Canadian families."[22] Reaction was swift.

Plate 1 ▪ Robert Harris had become one of Canada's leading artists by the time he painted these oil sketches. An Island expatriate living in Montreal, he regularly vacationed on PEI, where he created visions of the Island in tune with those being extolled by the embryonic tourism industry. The untitled landscape at bottom presents farm field, woodlot, and water, such as those that charmed turn-of-the-century visitors. In *Brackley Beach* (top) he captured another of the Island's signature attractions, its healthy "ozone" (i.e., sea air) and therapeutic saltwater. In keeping with the day, the women and children shown are bathing, not swimming.

"SEASIDE HOTEL" RUSTICO BEACH, P.E.I.
ADDRESS, J. NEWSON & CO. CHARLOTTETOWN, P.E.I.

LORNE HOTEL
SUMMER RESORT, TRACADIE BEACH, LOT 35, P.E.I.

Plate 2 ▪ By the time *Meacham's Atlas* was published in 1880, tourism was gravitating to a stretch of coastline from Malpeque Bay to Tracadie Bay known as the North Shore. The Seaside Hotel typified a late nineteenth-century beach resort. Here, bathers brave the modest surf and boaters take to the water, while landlubbers play a genteel game of croquet or take carriage rides into the countryside. The Lorne Hotel at Tracadie Beach adds hunting, fishing, and archery to its illustrated list of tourist pastimes. In the ad for the Point Pleasant Hotel, which would later become the Stanhope Beach Lodge, cows illustrate the bucolic nature of the setting, while inset images highlight the seaside activities. Other tourist accommodations, such as Glencourse at Stanhope, offered what were essentially farm-stay vacations, demonstrating that early tourism was often a side gig for Islanders in their straitened post-Confederation economy.

Plate 3 ▪ Already by the turn of the nineteenth century, Island newspapers were advertising souvenirs for sale. Many were generic chinaware stamped with Island images or town names, such as the ones shown here proffering memories of Montague, North Rustico, Tignish, and Alberton, each hoping for its share of tourist traffic. Others were Island-crafted. Artist Helen Haszard (1890–1970) specialized in portable Island landscapes for the summer trade, such as this clamshell painting of fields and dunes. In 1933 she was advertising "souvenir sketches of 'Island' colorful scenery in hand water colors" through the Tourist Association. Centennials inspired their own ephemera, such as this 1964 commemorative token featuring the new Fathers of Confederation Memorial Building. The ubiquitous "Smiling Father" mascot of the 1973 centennial of PEI's entry into Confederation here sports a removable hat, revealing the souvenir to be a whisky decanter.

Plate 4 ▪ L.M. Montgomery's first and most famous novel, *Anne of Green Gables* (1908), made Prince Edward Island a literary pilgrimage site. Not only did the book promote the Island's pastoral landscape worldwide as an attraction worth visiting generally, it gave the province its first specific tourist destination: "Green Gables" house in Cavendish. The sacralization of Green Gables was made complete when it was included in the new Prince Edward Island National Park in 1936. Or near complete; as this 1940 postcard of the house shows, the Stanley Thompson–designed park golf course was built perilously close to it. Foreign language editions, such as the Polish one shown, have nourished Anne's international reputation, but it was the book's translation into Japanese that, by the 1980s, led to a bloom of wedding packages and tour groups intent on seeing the home of "Akage no An" – "Red-Haired Anne."

Summerside Tourist Bureau, Summerside, P.E.I.-44.

Plate 5 ▪ Tourist information booths, invariably open for only a few months of the year, had to be simultaneously inexpensive and eye catching. The first tourist bureau at Read's Corner assisted travellers on their way into and out of Summerside. In June 1949, Mae Dewar was hired at $100 per month for three months to operate the bureau, which was located next to her husband Robert's service station. Their young daughter Katherine whiled away the days napping on the boxes of brochures. A-frame constructions became a staple architectural form for such booths in the '60s and '70s, including the new Summerside bureau shown, bottom right. But the province chose a lighthouse design for its 1963 booth in Albany, catching travellers just outside Borden where roads branched off east and west. The building was meant to be noticed by tourists, but it may also have confused some.

Plate 6 ▪ Rising incomes, paid vacations, and the growing ubiquity of the automobile meant that the North America of the late 1940s and the 1950s was thrown open for tourism like never before. A number of federal bodies, including the Canadian Travel Bureau, the National Film Board, and the National Parks Branch, worked to promote Canada for tourism, often together. One of the places they repeatedly favoured with their gaze in this era was Cavendish Beach: it offered a distinctive, scenic landscape, was next door to Green Gables and part of a national park, and its PEI location assisted with the goal of distributing tourism – and the agencies' spending – across the country. Promotional stills of the day show young (white) people cavorting in the dunes and graphically demonstrating PEI's claim to have the "warmest seawater north of Florida." Even the cyclists are navigating a countryside that is steering them towards the national park.

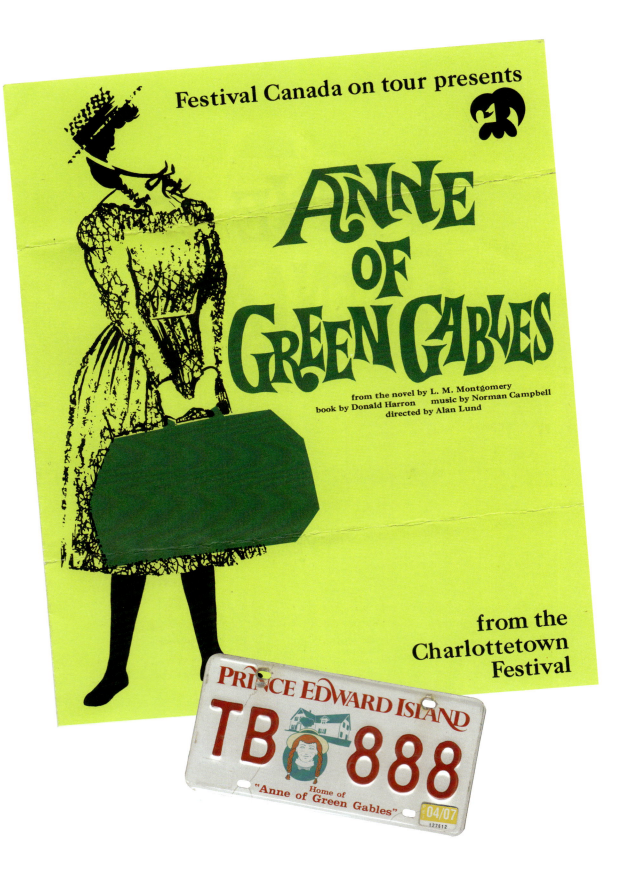

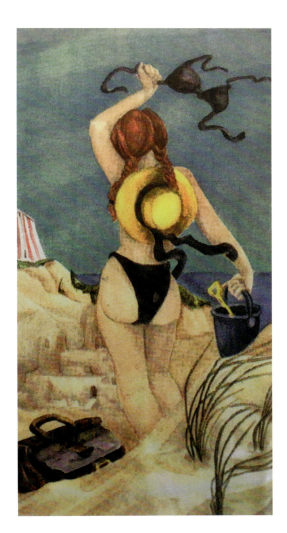 

Plate 7 ▪ As much as *Anne of Green Gables* has given definition to PEI's tourism image, it has also been subject to cultural reinterpretation. Premiering in 1965, the musical adaptation of L.M. Montgomery's novel became the mainstay of the Confederation Centre of the Arts Summer Festival, not to mention the longest running musical in stage history. But not all reinterpretations have found favour. A vocal minority of Islanders avoided getting the "Anne licence plate" adopted by the province in the 1990s either on aesthetic terms or because they considered it Anne overkill. Artist Dale McNevin's 1995 "Topless Anne" T-shirt design ran afoul of the Anne of Green Gables Licensing Authority, which protects the trademark and deems what are appropriate depictions of the literary icon. The creators of the 1990s sketch comedy *Annekenstein* rather hoped to be sued by the Licensing Authority, but satire fell outside the right to legal sanction.

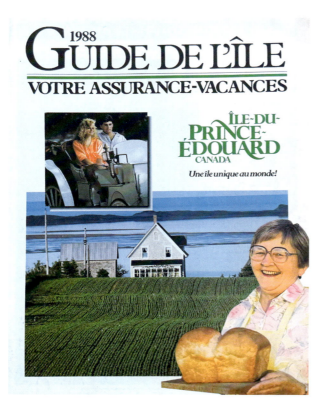

Who among us does not have a happy memory of a family day at the beach, when the atmosphere was so relaxed that we didn't even notice the sand in the hot dogs? Or the days when the excitement of piling into the car in the grey light of dawn for a family road trip was well worth the boredom that developed miles later.

Whose family photo album doesn't have at least one happy goofy "here we are on vacation" shot, where the composition may be off and the kodachrome is faded, but the mood is unmistakably relaxed? And of course, who wouldn't want to re-live those moments in the company of our own children? Prince Edward Island seems to provide just the magical mix of nostalgia and fun, with an ease of access and minimum hassle. An Island family vacation is designed to be as wholesome and uncomplicated as an ice-cream cone on a summer afternoon.

Maybe it's waking up in a tent pitched near the ocean, or a lobster boil on the deck of a cottage. Maybe it's as simple as early morning beach walks, or as exciting (and affordable) as tickets to a full-scale production of *Anne of Green Gables - The Musical™*.

How about a day spent visiting kid-sized theme parks with plenty of green space, or a bicycle excursion on a trail with no hills or car traffic. The Island is all this and more. We promise your Island holiday will become part of those legendary "remember when" family moments.

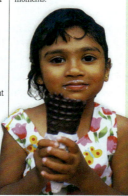

the vacation include at least one theme park visit, don't limit your vacation to fun parks; take a look at these suggestions:
✧ Take a ride on the mini-train at Elmira.
✧ Learn all about windmills at North Cape.
✧ Take a walk with an interpreter in PEI National Park.
✧ Enjoy free Charlottetown Festival outdoor theatre at lunch time.
✧ Play one of our great nine-hole courses, or try mini golf.
✧ Take a boat tour (kayaking, seal watching, deep-sea fishing, harbour tour...)
✧ Enjoy the traditional sport of harness racing.
✧ Climb to the top of a lighthouse.
✧ Eat ice cream!
Looking for more ideas on creating your own family memories? Visit our website **www.peiplay.com/fun** for plenty more fun.

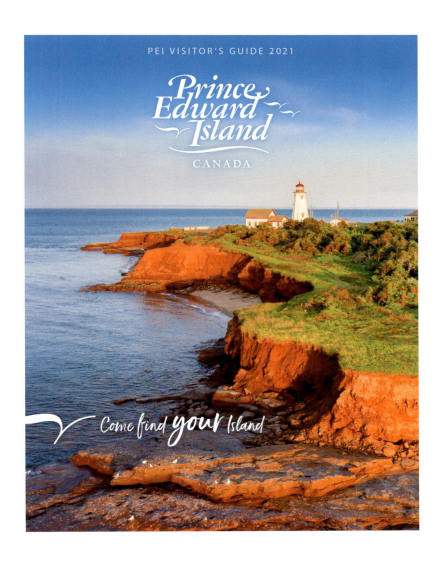

Plate 8 ▪ Since 1982, the province has published an annual *Visitors Guide* – or, as of 2010, a *Visitor's Guide*, shifting the emphasis from the masses to the individual. The guides allow one to trace the incremental changes in how the Island has presented itself for tourism: the rise and fall of golf, the rise and rise of culinary tourism, etc. The demographics of people shown, guest and host alike, have changed to some degree, particularly in terms of age: with a more mobile, affluent, empty-nest population, there is more grey hair to be seen. But the vast majority of images have been, and still are, of nondisabled, white, heterosexual couples and their families. With the exception of a very occasional Mi'kmaw, the first appearance of a visible minority person in the *Guide* seems to have been this girl with apparent South Asian features in 2005. This is remarkably late, especially given that by then the Island had been marketing heavily for Japanese tourism for a generation. Slowly, slowly diversity is coming to the pages (if not yet the cover) of the annual Guide – a recognition of the changing demographics both of potential visitors and of the Island's own population. Cover of French-language edition, 1988. Tourism PEI/ Barrett & MacKay (couple in buggy), John Sylvester (field), Gordon Johnston (woman). / Cover of English-language edition, 2010. Tourism PEI/ Russell Monk. / Child with ice cream cone, from 2006 edition. Tourism PEI/John Sylvester. / Cover of English-language edition, 2021. Tourism PEI/Sander Meurs.

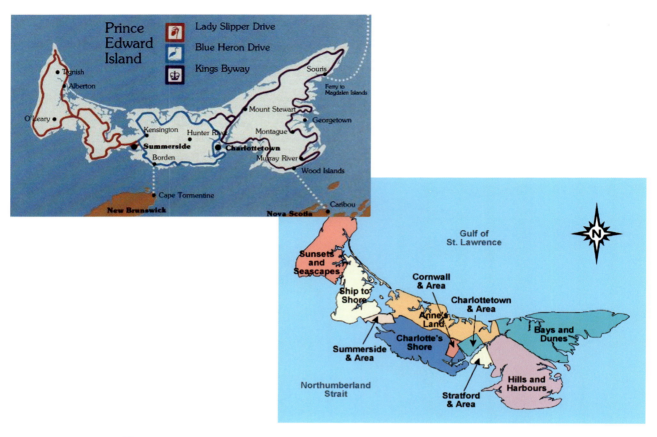

Plate 9 • The spatial distribution of tourists across the Island's landscape has long been a tourism marketing priority. In the 1970s, tourism maps featured three coastal loops roughly based on the province's three counties. By the 1990s, these were supplemented with creatively named tourist "regions," meant to organize day-trips or overnight stays. By the 2010s, coastal loops were back with new, nondescript names. Tourism PEI.

The Tourist Association's president (Cameron's neighbour) declined comment, but its secretary predicted that the subject would be aired at the upcoming annual meeting, and the acting premier Andrew MacRae promised a thorough investigation.[23] Meanwhile, the Canadian Press picked up the story and quickly retailed it to a much larger audience already schooled in the rhetoric of the civil rights struggle in the American South.[24]

Everyone (except, perhaps, Cameron) seemed to agree that discrimination was unacceptable and uncharacteristic. "We like to think," the *Guardian* editorialized,

> in this Cradle of Confederation, that we are as free from prejudice of this kind as any part of the continent. But this is an idle boast when we fall back on the excuse of having to cater to the prejudices of others. The few tourists who expect us to toady to them in this matter are asking too much. We value their patronage, but not at the expense of humiliating other people just as good as ourselves.[25]

When someone complained to the *Evening Patriot* that its public airing of the allegations was bad for business, it retorted that the appearance of doing nothing about them would be worse:

> Certainly, though, if there is damage to the tourist industry through the reporting of such incidents, the fault lies with those who perpetuate them and not in the reporting. The shame lies in racial discrimination, and in tacitly encouraging it by keeping silent about it, but not in facing it as a social weakness which requires correction.[26]

The "thorough investigation" took less than a week and concluded that the incident at Gregor's was an anomaly. There was, stated Minister of Tourist Development J. David Stewart, no systemic racial discrimination among Island tourist operators, and he blasted an "irresponsible" Island press for claiming there was. As if to belie his own findings, Stewart also released the text of a circular that he was sending out to members of the PEI Tourist Association. It read in part, "This province has always had the reputation of being discrimination free, insofar as people of other races or colours is concerned, and the Government of this Province is insistent that this reputation be maintained." For now, the Phillses had been sent an apology on behalf of Islanders and Gregor's-by-the-Sea had been sent "a letter of admonition." But if there were any further incidents of this nature, it "will force the Government to bring in [anti-discrimination] legislation."[27] Clean up your act, the government seemed to be saying, or we'll clean it up for you.

The *Guardian* and the *Evening Patriot* were publicly unrepentant about their reporting and denied spreading the story, but they pulled in their horns.[28] Their coverage of the Tourist Association's annual meeting the next month meekly omitted the heated discussion that took place about "last summer's unfortunate Racial Discrimination incident at Brackley Beach."[29] When Minister Stewart suggested that the "informed source" who had spoken to the press was none other than association secretary Walthen Gaudet, "This was immediately and emphatically denied as a Dam [*sic*] Lie." Association member A.H. Holman then invited Stewart to pass antidiscrimination legislation so that future offenders could have their licences suspended, but Stewart preferred that the association discipline its own members in future (Jack Cameron among them). In the end, the meeting passed a motion "that our PEI Tourist Association go on record as opposed to discrimination in any form, against anybody."[30] And there the matter ended.

Such pious pronouncements about racial tolerance knowingly struck a politically correct pose, but they were not necessarily insincere. True, a reputation for discrimination might be bad for business, but one suspects that Islanders in the early 1960s did not perceive themselves as racist, at least not in the way that racism was understood at the time. The province had no Jim Crow laws, no segregation, no Ku Klux Klan, no racially explicit social conventions. In that sense it was, indeed, as "free from prejudice as any other part of the continent." That claim rang hollow, of course, since no part of the continent was free from prejudice, and as Jim Hornby has demonstrated, Prince Edward Island had a long history of racial and ethnic intolerance.[31]

Nor was the Phills incident quite as isolated as advertised. It is hard to imagine that Raoul Reymond, who in 1962 managed both Stanhope Beach Inn and Dalvay-by-the-Sea, was not being disingenuous when he asserted in a letter to the editor that there had never been any incidents of racial discrimination during all of his time at those establishments.[32] In 1948, the same year that Reymond took over the Stanhope Beach Inn, the new concessionaire at nearby Dalvay was reprimanded by his landlord, the National Parks Branch, for a brochure advertising "restricted clientele" – code for "no Jews" – at his resort. He was ordered to remove the offending phrase, but the next year, much to the chagrin of parks officials, the same brochure was still in circulation since, the concessionaire protested, he had to use up his existing stock. This time Ottawa ordered the brochures destroyed.[33]

Similarly, when the Charlottetown *Guardian* defended its decision to report the allegations of racism within the tourism industry by righteously observing that "a malignant growth of this kind flourishes best in an atmosphere of secrecy," it chose to forget a widely known yet unreported incident from only four years earlier involving no less a celebrity than African-

146

The Summer Trade

Figure 4.2 ▪ Martin Mitchell, custodian and interpreter at Micmac Indian Village. Around 1960, Charlottetown businessman Earle Taylor created the attraction near the Mi'kmaw reserve at Rocky Point. It claimed to offer "an authentic recreation" of Mi'kmaw life in the sixteenth century, prior to sustained European contact, through a blend of artifacts, exhibits, demonstrations, reconstructions, and handicrafts. The artifacts were real, the reconstructions somewhat fanciful. By the twenty-first century, the Mi'kmaq of PEI had reappropriated their heritage and asserted more agency in how Indigenous culture was portrayed and interpreted for the tourist gaze.

American jazz trumpeter Louis "Satchmo" Armstrong. In July 1958 Armstrong and his All-Star Band, "The Greatest Musical Show that ever hit P.E.I.," played at the Sports Palace in Charlottetown before nearly 2,000 appreciative fans.[34] Afterwards, though, they were asked (or offered – accounts differ) to give up their booking at Canadian National Railways' Charlottetown Hotel when, according to local lore, a busload of tourists from the American south objected to sharing the hotel with "Coloureds." The story had an upbeat ending. After a quick consultation with her employers, Dr Joe and Eileen McMillan, the manager of the Dundee Apartment Motel, Loretta Perry, took Armstrong's party in. Early next morning, Perry's birthday, Satchmo and his band memorably serenaded her with a rendition of "Happy Birthday" and presented her with a signed birthday card.[35]

A common thread in these incidents was the tendency to explain – and so excuse – discrimination as a response to the expectations of racist visitors. In this reading, Islanders were more sinned against than sinning. The truth is certainly more complicated and more contingent. The Phills incident was a flare that briefly illuminated a hidden terrain on Prince Edward Island.

Afterwards, the shadows returned. It would be decades before racial diversity seeped into the Island's tourism marketing. In fact, *no* person of colour is shown touristing in Prince Edward Island promotional material until the new millennium (and this despite the fact that, as will be discussed later, Japanese tourism became an important niche market in the 1980s). Likewise, only the extremely rare appearance of a Mi'kmaw in the guidebooks suggested the existence of Islander people of colour. It would be even longer before there was any public discourse about the industry's attitude towards the LGBTQ community. For now, tourism promotion lapsed back into a colour-blind complacency – it saw only white. The Travel Bureau's only concession to diversity was to begin publishing French-language versions of its visitors guides.

While the tourism sector struggled with its image, the Island government grappled with how to manage the province's future. Anticipating funding opportunities afforded by the federal government's Agricultural Rehabilitation and Development Act (ARDA), legislated in 1961, the provincial Department of Industry and Natural Resources established a "Research Division," headed by Premier Walter Shaw's development guru, Hartwell Daley, to position the Island to take full advantage of potential ARDA funding. An "exhaustive" study of community and area development models in North America soon informed its "Resources Development Program." Meanwhile, a "Provincial Planning Division" would advise about where to create new parks and recreation areas. And overseeing it all was a new Cabinet "development committee," comprising Premier Walter Shaw, Minister of Agriculture Andrew MacRae, Minister of Industry Leo Rossiter, and J. David Stewart, doubling as provincial secretary and minister of tourist development.[36]

Government's approach to development was necessarily piecemeal since it relied heavily on fitting the Island's foot into the tight shoe of available federal funding. As might be expected, the province fixated on rural life and the sorts of manufacturing that might be grafted onto it. In that effort tourism was not so much inconsequential as tangential. Nevertheless, it would benefit from the larger romance between the Canadian state and the experimental field of regional development planning.

In terms of tourism development, the two most important federal programs were ARDA, which preserved its acronym when the program was broadened into the Agricultural and Rural Development Act in 1965, and, in 1966, FRED, the Fund for Rural Economic Development. FRED ultimately focused on five discrete regions of Canada plagued by unemployment and economic deficiencies, including one province: Prince Edward Island.[37] The objective was to cure regional disparity by building human, fiscal, and infrastructural capacity. The prescription involved large doses of federal dollars, intelligently delivered. As a result, by the mid-60s the Shaw government wallowed in a wash of surveys and studies that it had initiated, either independently or in tandem with ARDA. There had already been eight of them by the time the province signed a five-year planning agreement with the federal government in 1965.[38] This was the context for the tourism study commissioned in 1965 from Acres Research and Planning.

In a story headlined with the agricultural metaphor "Heavy Crop," a local reporter marvelled in 1965 at the latest tourism numbers for Prince Edward Island, a suspiciously specific 377,606 visitors spending $14,207,510. Of course, the writer added, the estimated average spending, put at $40 per head (four times the 1961 estimate), "would be much more impressive if there was a way to winnow out the homecoming sons and daughters and grand-children of Islanders taking an inexpensive vacation at the family home and the incoming tide of freeloading relatives with moths hibernating in their pocketbooks."[39] That was just the sort of detail government hoped that its new survey would supply. According to the Department of Tourist Development, the Acres study would help it decide where in North America its promotional dollars should be spent.[40] Acres' conception of the work was far more expansive: to determine the scale and characteristics of the industry, to determine the nature and magnitude of its economic impact, to evaluate expected future changes, to maximize the range of recreational value, and to maximize the development impact on the provincial economy.

After the first summer of data collection, representatives from Acres addressed the Tourist Association's annual meeting, and the following year many of its members were interviewed as the consultants set out to map the Island's "tourist plant" – that is, its attractions and accommodations.[41] But when Acres' findings finally became available, the association found them unpalatable. Instead of the $40 per person per stay that the Department of Tourist Development used as its base for tourist spending estimates, Acres estimated that in 1965 the average tourist spent only $24 on the Island. It also low-balled the number of visitors.[42] Thus, instead of an industry worth more than $14 million, Acres found that tourism contributed only $5.8 million in direct spending to the provincial economy. No wonder, wrote Hartwell Daley in his newspaper column "Capital Beat," that the government seemed reluctant to release Acres' tourism numbers.[43] At the Tourist Association's annual meeting that November, there was "a grand old discourse on the Acres Tourism Report, how really accurate its figures and conclusions are, and its value to the Industry."[44]

Of course, there was always room for scepticism when it came to tourist estimates; they had all the precision of a Second World War bombing raid. Still, Acres' survey sample was bigger than anything previous, and there was also far more to its findings than the bottom-line numbers that obsessed the Tourist Association. The report offered an unprecedentedly detailed profile of both visitors and their hosts. It was divided into four sections: Physical Capability (an assessment of the Island's land and water base for potential tourist use), Demand Study (information on the origins, spending patterns, preferences, and recreational habits of visitors), Supply Study (an inventory of the quantity, quality, and economic characteristics of the existing tourism infrastructure), and Plan (the way forward).[45]

Though train, bus, and airplane accounted for some thousands, Acres confirmed that the vast majority of tourists still arrived by car. Distance from the Island also continued to be a key determinant. The largest group of tourists, nearly 40 per cent, came from next door, Nova Scotia and New Brunswick. And most of *those* lived within 200 miles of Prince Edward Island. Another 28 per cent hailed from central Canada (twice as many from Ontario as from Quebec). The United States accounted for about 30 per cent of tourists, nearly half of them from the region closest and with the most expatriate Islanders, New England.[46]

While the breakdown of visitor origins merely confirmed conventional wisdom, other data broke new ground. For instance, Acres also sorted tourists according to length of stay. There were "summer residents," who spent two weeks or more in a seasonal dwelling of some sort; "overnight visitors," who stayed up to two weeks; and "day-trippers (about 12% of the total)." Their characteristics played to logical assumptions. Maritimers were the most likely to return, but they also came for the shortest time. Vacation cottagers stayed the longest, an average of 13.3 days, followed by people visiting with friends or relatives. The latter constituted nearly 20 per cent of the sample. The bigger the travelling family, the more likely they were to choose the cheapest form of accommodation – or to bring their own, that is, either tents or trailers. Eighty-seven per cent of those arriving by car reported that they were visiting the Island for pleasure. Just over half of them were coming for the first time.[47]

The longer the tourist stay the greater the likelihood that Prince Edward Island was the chosen destination rather than a pit stop. But when one subtracted the Maritimers, the expatriates, and the people visiting friends from the total, the visitor sample grew much smaller. The remaining tourists came largely from central Canada and the eastern seaboard of the United States, and they arrived on Prince Edward Island as part of a more extensive tour of eastern Canada or the Maritimes. According to Acres, "the pattern of travel through the Maritime Provinces is ... a grand circular tour during which

150

The Summer Trade

each of these parties spends one to four nights in each of the Maritime Provinces. During the time the tourists are in each province they attempt to see as much of the area close at hand in the province and participate in as many activities as their time schedule will permit." They travelled light and fast, and they had little room in their travel plans for time-consuming activities such as golf. But they did crave a slice of Maritime life, seeking regional cuisine and "characteristic regional wares."[48]

Tourist income levels were comparatively high: 44 per cent of drivers in the survey sample reported occupations within the categories of "owner and managerial" or "professional and technical." Less remarkable, given baby boom demographics, 44 per cent of the tourist parties included children. The most commonly reported activity while in the province (85 per cent of respondents) was also the most popular (for 21 per cent) and the most passive: touring. But 68 per cent of visitors also shopped, and 52 per cent of them sought out historic sites (though a disappointing 3 per cent listed that as their preferred pastime). Although swimming ranked only fifth among the most reported activities (sunbathing was not listed), it was the second most favourite. The same percentage of visitors spent time with friends or relatives. A surprisingly small proportion of tourists, given longstanding promotional tropes, took up traditional visitor pastimes such as fishing, boating, golfing, or harness racing.[49]

To some extent, the types of tourist activities reflected available choice as well as preference. The same might be said for where they stayed. Ever since the creation of the Prince Edward Island National Park furnished the industry with a physical and thematic locus, tourism had developed mainly within the "golden triangle," anchored by Borden and Summerside in the west, following along the newly finished TransCanada Highway eastwards to Charlottetown, and running northwards to the narrow strip of the North Shore stretching from Cavendish to Dalvay that comprised the national park. Accommodations and attractions had located in the places where tourists went. Fresh boatloads of tourists then went where the accommodations and attractions were in a sort of touristic ouroboros, a self-perpetuating circle of demand and supply. Only the private and provincial campgrounds provided any sort of pan-Island coverage.[50]

Thus, by 1965, nearly half of all visitors found accommodations either around the national park (25 per cent) or in Charlottetown (24 per cent). Another 30 per cent stayed either in Summerside or on the road to Charlottetown. Only 6 per cent overnighted west of Summerside. Over a quarter of tourist parties found rooms in one of the Island's characteristically small motels. Another quarter (23.4 per cent) sought out campgrounds and trailer parks.[51] Since the bulk of tourist expenditures fell within a few sectors of the

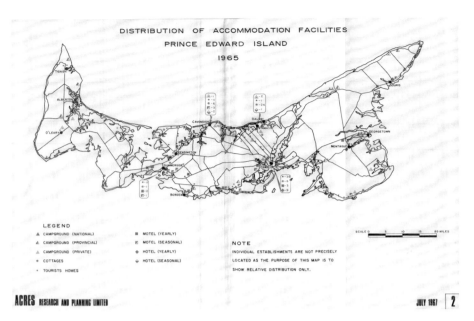

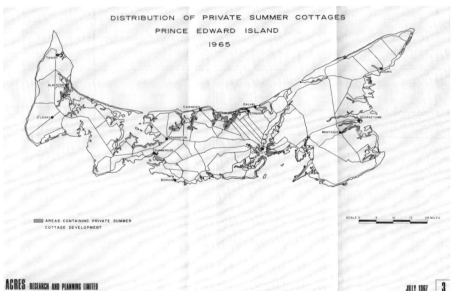

Figure 4.3 ▪ As part of its investigation of the Island's tourism industry, Acres Research and Planning produced these maps showing the concentration of accommodation facilities and summer cottages. Both were clustered in central PEI, especially around Charlottetown and the North Shore. A half-century later, accommodation facilities were even more centralized, whereas the entire coastline of the Island was girdled with a band of private and commercial cottages.

economy (food, lodging, and transportation services), the herding of tourists into the "golden triangle" also concentrated their economic impact there.[52]

The concentration of tourist activity in central PEI posed a particular challenge, since Acres' employers, the Island government, was anxious for both practical and political reasons to spread the benefits of tourism across the province. And so, Acres set about mapping the Island's "recreation–tourism capability." The results were encouraging. "It is quite likely," Acres enthused, "that Prince Edward Island has the highest proportion of good quality, usable shoreline, to unusable shoreline, of any province or region in Canada." Moreover, the unique conjunction of ubiquitous water, red soil, and rolling, garden-like farmscape – "the pattern of cultural development over a period of 300 years" – had fostered "a unique environment in terms of scenic quality and restful atmosphere."[53] Better still, the bulk of the land rated as either Class 1, "very high," or Class 2, "high," was located in tourism's two outliers, Kings and Prince Counties. Of the Island's 1.4 million acres, 22,600 were deemed Class 1 land for recreation/tourism. If one included the first three categories, ranging from "very high" to "good," the total jumped to 151,500 acres, 60,000 of them in Kings County.[54] In planning terms, it was as if rich seams of gold or silver had been discovered in the most underdeveloped and economically challenged parts of the province.

If expanding tourism's geographic reach was one goal, lengthening the frustratingly brief tourist year was another. As with so many destinations in Canada, high summer was high season for tourism, partly because July and August were school vacation months for baby boom families and partly because that was the traditional holiday time for North American families. It was also the period on the Island when the weather became reliably hot and the inshore waters at last reached the encouraging "it's-nice-once-you're-in" level. But pushing the rising tide of tourists through the bottleneck of July and August was causing serious problems by the mid-1960s. Besides long waits at the ferry terminals, there was too often no room at the inn. "There were instances in July 1966," Acres reported, "where tourist parties could not find overnight accommodations and were faced with leaving the province or sleeping in cars."[55] Yet, the high level of seasonality discouraged new investment in lodgings, since the limited returns on the short peak season did not justify it. Like many observers before and since, Acres was encouraged by signs that tourism was beginning to increase in June and September.[56] In the end, such reports of shoulder season growth were like Sasquatch sightings, insistent but never substantiated.

Given the short season, it was no surprise to find that tourism's labour force was largely seasonal, part-time, and unskilled. Acres estimated that tourism directly employed about 2,500 people, about 4 per cent of the provincial workforce, but only 535 of them were full-time. The workforce was dominated by women and students, many of them blood relations of their employers. Their earnings rippled through the local economy, but, "*In the final analysis*," and here Acres emphasized the statement, "*very few employees are able to make a living directly from recreation.*"[57]

Acres also provided a snapshot of the industry's physical plant. The capital investment in accommodations and restaurants topped $10.5 million, with nearly a third of that value added during the previous five years. There were sixty-three year-round restaurants and 2,454 units of accommodation scattered across sixteen hotels, forty-six motels, 106 cottage and cabin businesses, and 185 tourist homes. Of the 353 accommodations, no less than 277 were summer operations. Most were small. The motels averaged only twelve units each and the number of cabin/cottage rentals averaged only about seven per operator.[58]

That Island tourism remained a mom-and-pop operation might be considered attractive in an inauthentic age, but Acres did not see it that way. Very few tourist operators, it found, enjoyed high returns. Many of them thought and behaved like part-timers. Some did not even keep proper books.[59] In Acres' estimation, though, quality of services was no more important than "the quality of the whole environment." In that sense, the landscapes and seascapes mattered more than the people who had shaped them. "People surveyed repeatedly stressed these assets as the greatest attraction of Prince Edward Island."[60]

Such "assets" were vital if the Island hoped to lure its share visitors. For, as Acres warned, just because tourist demand was destined to rise that did not mean all tourist destinations would benefit equally.[61] Prince Edward Island was a long way from eastern North America's major population centres, after all, and "visitor rates are highly sensitive to distance."[62] Nevertheless, Acres forecast continued growth. Since 1960 the average annual increase in Atlantic region tourism had been 10–15 per cent per year. Prince Edward Island, Acres predicted, would enjoy a 7–10 per cent yearly increase over the next decade, with 650,000 visitors by 1976. "The challenge is not whether to accept or reject this change, but to focus on the nature of change and how best to preserve and enhance the values held by islanders."[63]

Acres' eighteen recommendations ranged from the proscriptive to prescriptive and the sweeping to the specific. In the consultants' opinion, for example, public campgrounds, which operated below cost, should stop competing with private operators. Instead, provincial parks should be "reorganized and re-oriented" towards natural and cultural heritage. The province should create at least three scenic loop drives that would "pass through the most pleasant routes and connect scenic overlooks, scenic areas, campgrounds, and sites for interpreting natural and cultural features of the province."[64] Abandoned farmhouses should be converted into summer homes. Concise information about attractions and accommodations should be communicated more efficiently to visitors. At the same time, the Travel Bureau should devote more time to data collection and analysis. Coordination of the industry's various levers should be delegated to some central agency.

The last point highlighted the central thrust of the recommendations, a call for greater professionalism and closer management of the tourism industry. Deputy Minister Fraser may have felt that the chief purpose of Acres' research was to help the Island find its tourism market, but its most sweeping recommendations homed in on the tourist product that visitors would encounter once they arrived. "Indirectly," Acres argued,

> it is the naturally-evolved combination of open field with bordering woodlot which is the basis for the numerous tourist comments concerning the "charm" and "tranquility." It is in the best interest of the recreation–tourism business to maintain to the maximum extent possible the present relationship of crop land, pasture, and woodlot. Unspoiled agrarian landscapes such as are found on Prince Edward Island may be as important, or more important, than the untrammeled forest wilderness so popular in today's conservation literature.[65]

To maintain the Island's "park-like atmosphere," Acres advised that the whole countryside be subject to "new and imaginative land-use controls and planning devices." It recommended similar protection and land-use restrictions for the province's other great landscape asset, its shoreline. Thus, in the well-ordered universe of the planner, the tourist landscape — nature itself — would become consistent, controlled, rational. Essentially, Acres was demanding that Island tourism become more professional (that is, modern) so that it could present a more authentic (read premodern) face to visitors. At the time, this paradox was largely ignored, yet it lay at the heart of the Island's summer trade.

The Acres report was prescient. While its recommendations and stratagems were generally adapted rather than adopted, almost every topic raised in its pages would find its way into public discourse over the next decade. On only one count did Acres prove a false prophet. "In the main," it argued, "the problems of the Prince Edward Island recreation-tourism industry can be resolved through organization and planning, rather than by additional massive inputs of public funds."[66]

By the time that Acres was ready to table its tourism report in 1967, the Island had a new government. The previous summer, the Liberals under Alex Campbell — son of 1930s premier Thane Campbell — had narrowly defeated the Shaw Conservatives. The incoming regime inherited a massive public debt (in relative terms) but also the federal-provincial planning process that dated from 1965. Acres' sectoral studies now provided the statistical baseline for a new, more sophisticated, more coordinated approach to economic planning. That process was entrusted to the Economic Improvement Corporation, a Crown agency headed by economist Del Gallagher. It began working with federal planners to translate Acres' wealth of data into an economic blueprint for Prince Edward Island.

When Acres' inventory of tourist resources emphasized the asset embodied in a pastoral landscape shaped by "300 years" of cultural development, it conveniently overlooked the 10,000 years of cultural development that came before. Just as tourism was achieving lift-off in the 1950s, the Mi'kmaq First Nation was increasingly pushed into the province's four reserves, their seasonal migrations actively discouraged and their dependency on meagre federal handouts progressively strengthened. Without easy access to materials and markets, traditional Mi'kmaw handicrafts – baskets, axe handles, paddles – languished.[67] As they disappeared from the physical landscape, it became easier for the Mi'kmaq of the present to fade into the Mi'kmaq of a reimagined past. It was the vision of an ancient, self-sufficient existence that informed the incorporation of the Micmac Indian Village Encampment and Crafts, Ltd, in 1960.[68]

The one-of-a-kind tourist attraction was the brainchild of Charlottetown jeweller Earle Taylor, an entrepreneurial antiquarian, past president of the PEI Historical Society, and former member of the Historic Sites and Monuments Board of Canada.[69] His chosen site was at Rocky Point, across the harbour from Charlottetown, a stone's throw from the old Charlottetown Summer Resorts development at Holland Cove, not far from the earthenwork remains of Fort Amherst (today, Skmaqn-Port LaJoye-Fort Amherst National Historic Site), and adjacent to a small Mi'kmaw reserve established in 1913. The "Micmac" (as 1960s usage spelled it) that Taylor had in mind were not the marginalized, demoralized population of recent decades or even the actual nearby reserve; rather, they were an idealized First Nation living in communion with nature on the cusp of European contact in the sixteenth century.

Site interpretation at the Micmac Indian Village was usefully informed by a gifted amateur archaeologist, medical doctor John Maloney,[70] as well as the site's manager and principal interpreter, Martin Mitchell, an off-reservation Mi'kmaw and grandson of Chief Jim Louis Mitchell. In the letters patent for the new company, "Martin Mitchell, carpenter, Rocky Point" was listed among the five principals.[71] Colourfully attired in "traditional" Mi'kmaw costume, Mitchell figured largely in postcards promoting the site, where he was most often identified as "custodian." *Holiday Island*, the Department of Tourist Development's 1967 promotional film, likewise featured footage of Mitchell animating the site for visiting children. We have no way of knowing Mitchell's personal views on the Indian Village and the part he played at it; his part in the business might reasonably be

156

The Summer Trade

dismissed as either exploitation or co-option. Equally, its positive imaging might be taken as a sign of agency in how the Island's First Nations were portrayed – and portrayed themselves.

The Indian Village was a striking outlier among the era's tourist attractions, both in portraying Indigenous heritage and in its outdoors museum setting. Period brochures promoting the Island's "Big Five" attractions – no doubt selected by those featured – regularly included the site. But tourism's spatial development left it off the beaten track, it gradually dwindled in prominence, and by the end of the century quietly ceased operations.[72]

Agency was clearer when the Lennox Island Band took steps to market its heritage in the early 1970s. For generations, Lennox Island had experienced tourism essentially one day each year: on St Anne's Sunday in late July, when fishermen ferried visitors from the PEI mainland across for a religious service, chicken dinners, handicraft booths, and, in later years, carnival rides and a community baseball game. Crowds bloomed to five or six thousand each St Anne's day in the 1950s, to the point that the RCMP had to step in and require the boats be equipped to transport passengers.[73] Numbers dropped thereafter. But in July 1973, with a new causeway now providing easy access to the island reserve, the Band launched a handicrafts centre in a small A-frame just off the causeway, with Irene Labobe as manager. Almost half of the items on sale were wood carvings, bark work, headdresses, necklaces, and leatherwork that had been fashioned by Band members. Newspaper reports did not distinguish between traditional Mi'kmaw designs and generic tourist objects, but the following year a federal Manpower grant funded a winter works program to train local craftspeople. Two Indigenous teachers were brought in: Margaret Johnson to instruct female students in leather- and beadwork and John Bernard to teach woodworking to the men. As Bernard told reporters, "There is a growing market for authentic quality Indian handicrafts." Supplying it meant "rekindling old skills."[74]

By 1983, there was an ad hoc museum in the former parochial house on Lennox Island, which doubled as a crafts workshop in the off-season.[75] Working through the Island's technical school, Holland College, Mi'kmaw artisan Peter Thomas offered a winter-long course on basket making. Tourism was now an explicit focus of the handicraft centre. There was a "great market" for handmade baskets, Thomas reported, "especially during tourist season."[76] The repurposing of heritage for tourist markets is often artificial, but in this instance, using traditional techniques to produce tourist souvenirs represented an assertion of dignity as well as identity. And there was no inherent contradiction in the commercial applications of reclaiming one's heritage.

In its inventory of tourist resources, Acres had focused almost entirely on what it considered the Island's principal assets, the countryside and the seashore, within a year-in, year-out tourism industry. Yet, the most successful promotion to date in the province's tourist history had just capitalized on a completely different attraction, Charlottetown's self-proclaimed status as "Cradle of Confederation." As the next decade would demonstrate, Islanders seemed to find such splashy, "one-off" commemorations easier to embrace than the routine tourist round.

Ever since the Confederation celebrations of 1939, tourism promotion had invariably highlighted the "room of destiny," where the Fathers of Confederation had dreamed a nation back in September 1864. The de facto guide to the building in the '50s was a Scottish-born commissionaire named Robert Craig. He became a fixture at Province House, showing up in both promotional films and print media. "Thousands have visited the historic Chamber this month alone," the *Guardian* exclaimed back in August 1953, "and Commissioner [sic] Robert Craig, the genial guide, has told the story of the room to so many people he has long since lost track of the number."[77]

The branding campaign gained even more significance as the centennial of Confederation drew nearer. As one historian of the period writes, "In the mid-1960s, a nation in search of a nationalism contracted a case of centennialitis. The contagion eventually infected all parts of the country, even Quebec. Symptoms included a mild euphoria with a marked tendency toward nostalgia. The condition was not terminal, though it lasted for nearly a decade, and it came in distinct waves, cresting in 1967."[78] The epidemic began and ended on PEI with further outbreaks at suitably round-numbered intervals thereafter. That Charlottetown had been touting its Confederation credentials for decades – and had just celebrated its own civic centennial in 1955 – gave it an indispensable head start in the race for national recognition and centennial funding. By January 1959, even as Prime Minister John Diefenbaker was canvassing his cabinet for ideas about how to celebrate Canada's one-hundredth birthday, the PEI provincial government was organizing a Centennial Planning Committee of its own.[79]

Frank MacKinnon, the principal of Prince of Wales College in Charlottetown, was the logical choice to chair the committee's board of directors, which was at length appointed in March 1962. A political scientist-cum-historian and son of a former lieutenant governor, MacKinnon had built a national reputation; his 1951 *The Government of Prince Edward Island* won the Governor General's Award for Non-Fiction, and he was a founding member of the Canada Council. He cast a long shadow locally as well. He had been an active member of the local Board of Trade and was heavily involved in the '50s with the Atlantic Provinces Economic Council. He was tireless, wilful, and visionary. When Charlottetown celebrated its civic centennial in 1955, MacKinnon had served on the planning committee and supplied the historical essay for its anniversary booklet. His mayor at the time, J. David Stewart, was minister of tourist development in 1962, when preparations for the 1964 centennial began in earnest.

By then MacKinnon was knee-deep in another, even more ambitious centennial project, the Fathers of Confederation Memorial Building.[80] In 1958–59, local citizens and municipal officials had begun mobilizing support for a modern cultural complex that would house a civic auditorium, a museum and archives, a library, an art gallery, and offices for various local services, including a tourist bureau and a bus terminal. MacKinnon took up the prevailing notion that the building should commemorate Charlottetown's role in Confederation, and when his colleague on the Canada Council, Calgary oilman and philanthropist Eric Harvie, seized on the idea, they together turned an entirely local project serving entirely local needs into a national campaign to construct in Charlottetown Canada's first (and, to date, only) national memorial to the Fathers of Confederation. The proposed building would house a cultural centre, but it was sold as a shrine.

With MacKinnon as principal pitchman, backed by Harvie's seed money and personal connections, they recruited a prestigious national board for their Fathers of Confederation Memorial Buildings Citizens' Trust and skilfully courted Canada's first ministers to fund their dream. Improbably, they succeeded. The funding formula was settled early in 1962 when Prime Minister Diefenbaker pledged that Ottawa would contribute one-half of the cost of construction, up to $2.8 million, on the basis of 15 cents per capita – if MacKinnon and company could raise the balance. Armed with that commitment, the fundraisers went back to the premiers to convert their apple-pie endorsements of the project into hard cash. Each conditional promise ("I will if the others will") was used as leverage to convince the undecided. One by one the provinces anteed up, although the last commitments came only weeks before the project was due to break ground in the winter of 1963.[81]

MacKinnon and Harvie's visionary concept of a "living memorial" to the fathers – a tagline that was popularized after the fact – was no doubt attractive to Canada's politicians. But convincing nine premiers to contribute to an arts centre located in another province was a prodigious accomplishment even in a Dominion feeling the first symptoms of centennialitis.[82] Undoubtedly, it helped that MacKinnon and Harvie were first in the field in terms of centennial projects – indeed, theirs would have to be grandfathered into the

Figure 4.4 ▪ The design of the Confederation Centre of the Arts, Canada's only "living memorial" to the Fathers of Confederation, was careful not to overwhelm adjacent Province House – and used the same stone for its exterior cladding. When it opened in 1964, the complex housed a theatre, an art gallery, a library, and the provincial archives. When the theatre began staging *Anne of Green Gables – The Musical* in 1965, the centre became the only site in the province to bring together under one roof two of the Island's most durable tourism tropes, Confederation and Anne.

federal funding programs that were eventually established. The project must also be understood in its political context, the birth of equalization payments that redistributed federal tax revenues from "have" to "have-not" provinces and its cultural milieu, the Massey Commission's impassioned argument for public investment in the arts. But placing the memorial in Charlottetown was also proof that most Canadians had come to accept the Island's claim that it was, indeed, the birthplace of the nation, so much so that Island politicians were able to convince Ottawa that Canada's centennial should actually begin on Prince Edward Island … in 1964.[83]

The $5.6 million "Confederation Centre of the Arts" opened on time (barely – workers were laying carpet half an hour before its first scheduled event) and on budget (technically – there would be tens of thousands of dollars spent on touch-ups over the next several years) in a commanding location on Queen Square, next door to the Confederation Chamber. At completion it housed a state-of-the-art theatre, the largest art gallery east of Montreal, a public library, and, almost as an afterthought, a tiny provincial archives. Canada's gift to Prince Edward Island became the centrepiece of the centennial celebrations, capped by its formal opening by Queen Elizabeth II in October. A month earlier, amid solemn reenactments and patriotic effusions, Prime Minister Lester B. Pearson presided over the self-conscious symbolism of a Dominion–Provincial meeting at the site of the Charlottetown Conference.

Provincial librarian Dorothy Cullen captured the sense of occasion in her diary. "The big day is here. Great crowds on the streets. Laura and I saw the parade and I took several pictures. The crowd was equal to anything I've ever seen here."[84] Inside the Confederation Chamber, Premier Shaw reminded his fellow first ministers, "We, too, are the Fathers of Confederation."[85]

The Confederation Festival in 1939 had lasted a week and been financed almost entirely with a $20,000 federal grant. The 1964 celebrations spanned the entire calendar year and cost more than half a million dollars, $420,000 from the province supplemented by a $100,000 grant from Canada's Centennial Commission.[86] The size of the provincial grant (compared to the moneyless moral support of 1939) reflected how far the tourism industry had advanced in the government's estimation. The 1964 centennial would be "our Province's 'Shining Hour,'" Tourist Development Minister David Stewart predicted to the Tourist Association's annual meeting in 1962, where he stressed "the tremendous Tourist potential of that year."[87] To make sure the hour shone, the province's Travel Bureau and the Planning Committee embarked on an unprecedented publicity blitz, portraying the Island as, in Matthew McRae's words, "the wellspring of Canada's past, a place where the nation could go for spiritual healing."[88]

Whereas 1939 had essentially been a Charlottetown event, now the entire province was treated as the Cradle of Confederation. Every community was encouraged (and subsidized) to celebrate with "Centennial Days," although many did not quite know how.[89] Across the Island there were special parades and pageants, sports days, midways, picnics, concerts. There were province-wide promotions as well: a special centennial logo, "Century Farm" plaques, a history-themed essay contest, costume balls and heritage fashion shows, commemorative coins showing both Province House and the Confederation Centre, even a souvenir "Cradle of Confederation" licence plate – the whole gamut of what soon would be standard centennial fare in other parts of Canada. The season of celebration attracted the notice of the National Film Board, which sent a crew down to the Island to shoot footage for the Canadian Centenary Committee's use as a springboard to 1967. *The Hundredth Summer* followed three small communities, North Rustico, Miscouche, and Victoria-by-the-Sea, as they celebrated the 1964 centennial.[90]

The Centennial Planning Committee's program divided the calendar year into two unequal parts: a glut of tourist-friendly events timed for the summer season and for the balance of the year events aimed mainly at Islanders.[91] While much of the centennial program was ephemeral, even frivolous, the significance of the celebrations went well beyond bricks and mortar. As publicist Dennis L. Clarke admonished centennial planner William Hayward, "We must not think of this publicity project in relation to promoting a one year centennial, but in terms of its long range effect on every area of Prince Edward Island's economic future." In other words, they were not just promoting a centennial; they were promoting PEI. It was impossible to overestimate the importance of the publicity that the Island gained in 1964, the Centennial Planning Committee asserted in its final report: "the effects … will last for many years and be important to tourism and other industries."[92]

The tourism impact seemed unmistakable. The Travel Bureau reported yet another record year, an estimated 333,951 tourists (up 20 per cent) spending nearly $12.7 million (up 22 per cent). Given postwar trends (and setting aside the gnarly issue of accuracy), it might be expected that tourism numbers would have risen even without the draw of a centennial, though 20 per cent was admittedly a remarkable rate of increase. According to department officials the smorgasbord of centennial events in spring and fall had also extended the tourist season, and almost certainly the extra promotional push was responsible for an unprecedented number of conferences (104, more than twice the previous high) as well as bus tours.[93] Over at the PEI Tourist Association, President Gordon Shaw echoed the department's sentiments: "The year 1964 will probably go down in history as one of the most interesting and in many ways the most exciting in the 20th Century on Prince Edward Island."[94]

Of course, Shaw was preaching to the choir. The Centennial Committee's publicists had their sights set on a much larger constituency. Even as they marketed the centennial to mainlanders, they were selling tourism to Islanders. Each exhortation to them to become "absorbed in the 'spirit' of confederation," to "replace small dreams with larger ones," to realize that the centennial could change "the whole future of this province," was, in effect, an appeal for the general populace to buy into the promise of tourism.[95] That struggle for hearts and minds had a long history, and the campaign was far from over, but centennial represented a victory. According to the committee's final report, the year's program of events had spread culture, educated the young, brought communities together, encouraged local improvement, and, most important of all, centennial-related spending had percolated through the provincial economy.[96] As its supporters had always argued, tourism was good for business. That year the Tourist Association's membership rose by 43 per cent.[97]

The most concrete legacy of the 1964 centennial was the brutalist bulk of the Fathers of Confederation Memorial Buildings. They were intended, as Matthew McRae observes, "to be the crown jewel of the centennial," confirming Charlottetown's status as a sacred site but also "an attraction worthy of the tourist's gaze."[98] Local opinion was divided on the aesthetics of Charlottetown's newest tourist attraction. Outside opinion had qualms about touristic Charlottetown. The Island countryside was wonderful, wrote Douglas Ambridge of the Fathers of Confederation Memorial Buildings Citizens Trust, but

Charlottetown … is a mess. Shabby houses with broken windows, broken sidewalks, weeds and general untidiness. I think we should make it known in some way that we take a dim view of having the magnificent memorial buildings surrounded by appalling shabbiness and I think we should seriously urge the city fathers to do something about it.[99]

It was not the sort of opinion that got quoted for promotional purposes.

The Confederation Centre was an artistic triumph – "Something wonderful has happened in Charlottetown," wrote the *Toronto Star*'s theatre critic Nathan Cohen[100] – and the complex attracted lots of visitors (more than 200,000 in 1967),[101] but it threatened to be a financial disaster. Back when the project was little more than a far-fetched notion, the province had unwisely agreed to assume financial responsibility for its operation and maintenance if completed.[102] It took only one season to demonstrate that major cultural complexes do not turn a profit and that the provincial government could not afford to keep its promise.[103] With the Centre only days from an embarrassing bankruptcy in the fall of 1966, Ottawa came to the rescue, reluctantly acknowledging that a national memorial deserved a modicum of national funding.[104] The doors stayed open and the Centre stayed solvent, but in the ensuing decades its staff would get all too used to walking a financial tightrope.

The Confederation Centre was fiscally malnourished, but its financial situation would have been far worse had it not been for the smash hit of the 1965 Summer Festival, *Anne of Green Gables, the Musical*. Next to the beach itself, Anne had long been the major attraction at Prince Edward Island National Park. The decades since L.M. Montgomery's death might have dulled her literary reputation but not the popularity of her novels. The passionate attachment of her readers made many of them pilgrims to the Island's North Shore. The fictional redhead was easily the Island's most famous pseudocitizen. As Gordon Shaw of the Tourist Association mused in 1964,

In my travels outside Canada it has been my observation that we do not perhaps play up enough the fact that Prince Edward Island is the place where the Anne in Anne of Green Gables lived and the story was written. Every year these stories are read by millions and every reader is a potential visitor. Ask an American woman where Prince Edward Island is and she will often be able to tell you only that she read about it in one of the Anne books.

There was money in that, he said: "Let's capitalize on the free selling these books do for us."[105]

Anne's arrival on the Confederation Centre's main stage added another dimension to her appeal. The musical had begun in 1956 as a CBC television production, and by 1964 its creators, Norman and Elaine Campbell and Don Harron, were adapting it for the stage. That October a song from the musical featured in a variety concert performed for Queen Elizabeth II as part of the Confederation Centre's official opening. In the receiving line after the performance, the Queen complimented Norman Campbell on the musical selection.

"That was a wonderful number, Mr Campbell," the Queen said, "but tell me, where is the rest of it?"

"The next time you come, Your Majesty," Campbell replied, "we'll have more."[106]

The full musical debuted in 1965 to large crowds and rapturous reviews. Quickly, it became the staple offering of the Centre's annual Summer Festival and its emotional core, even as the festival became the bellwether of the Centre's fortunes. As of 2014 the play ranked as the world's longest-running annual musical theatre production.[107]

While the musical's cutout sets could not reproduce the Island's pastoral countryside, its nostalgic setting, as well as its tone – pert, poignant, and wholesome – captured something of the culture that had made – and been made by – that landscape. Thus, the Confederation Centre, alone among Island tourist attractions, brought together its two most marketable myths: the innocent, unspoilt garden and the wellspring of Confederation. Of the two, the former was probably more instrumental in convincing visitors to come to the province, while the latter, if nothing else, gave them something to do on the days when it rained.

Of course, neither myth could work its magic if tourists weren't able to get "over to the Island." By the mid-1960s both politicians and promoters alike considered the growing congestion at the Northumberland Strait the single greatest impediment to the growth of Island tourism, and the "transportation issue" had become the longest running soap opera in dominion–provincial relations. Islanders continued to complain about their own inconvenience in crossing the strait, but the meteoric rise in tourist traffic raised the stakes even as it compounded the problem. All through the '50s and '60s, demand and supply played leapfrog at the ferry terminals. Every improvement in transportation facilities encouraged more tourist traffic, creating new bottlenecks and triggering fresh calls for more ferries and more crossings.[108] As

Highway officials grimly noted in 1968, even eight to ten crossings daily did not seem to help with the daunting ferry lineups at Wood Islands–Caribou. This was "consistent with the pattern established by both ferry services over the years, i.e., that each improvement in accommodation or operating schedules generates so much additional traffic that the ferry services appear to be losing ground in their efforts to reduce traffic lines and waiting periods to an acceptable level."[109] And, since the tendency was for tourists to arrive on the Island at Borden and depart via Wood Islands, any improvement at one end of the strait promised to make things worse at the other.

Provincial officials were obsessed with ferry statistics, and it is easy to see why. The numbers were daunting. Back in 1918, a single ferry had made 1,100 crossings to Borden. In 1942, with two ferry crossing points, 3,900 crossings were made. Between 1941 and 1965, passenger traffic on the Borden ferry crossing tripled. On the Wood Islands route, the margin was 807 per cent, with a 1,311 per cent increase in vehicle traffic. In the five years since 1960, alone, passenger traffic at Wood Islands and Borden had gone up by 50 per cent and 55 per cent, respectively.[110] According to one estimate, 80 per cent of the cars disembarking at Borden in 1966 had off-Island licence plates.[111] And there was no end in sight. In the decade after the Acres report, the combined number of round-trip ferry crossings from Borden and Wood Islands would rise another 40 per cent, from 9,500 to 13,000 per year. At Borden–Tormentine alone, annual passenger numbers would increase by 128 per cent between 1965 and 1985 to 1.6 million people.[112]

Roughly half of each year's ferry traffic was crammed into the months of July and August. The results of this crush were entirely predictable. The marine transportation system simply could not keep up. One of the Island's best assets was its wide open beaches, tourist John H. Gill helpfully wrote to the Island's minister of tourist development, "However, when a tourist tries to send a postcard home with this message he is confronted only by a choice of eight or ten pictures of ferries – all of which he is doing his utmost to forget."[113]

Some of those postcards were sent directly to the premier. A visitor from Toronto wrote straight from the ferry lineup at Borden. On the back of a postcard depicting the MV *Abegweit*, he wrote, "We are at this moment 1 car of over 200 bottled up for hours here for no good reason – wasting precious time in an all too short holiday – Surely another ferry or two would help?"[114] Mrs A.M. Faux of Perth, Ontario, vented her "disgust and dismay" from the side of the road about a mile from Wood Islands. After four days camping and touring around Prince Edward Island, her family were three hours into their wait, stranded without access to food, bathrooms, or garbage cans. "We have been told that we may not make it to-day, but if we leave our spot in the line-up, we shall be worse off to-morrow." Before she could finish her tirade, an RCMP car with a loudspeaker drove by, advising motorists that they would not make any of that day's crossings.[115]

Others waited until they got home, but they told similar stories. Mrs B.M. Bayne of Montreal, her husband, and their four children had enjoyed "one of the loveliest holidays of our lives" at Corby Croft near Dalvay Beach. The nightmare came when they tried to go home. They spent hours stuck on the shoulder of the road outside Borden in the blazing sun with hundreds of other hot, hungry, frustrated travellers. "I would suggest that your campaign to bring tourists to your gorgeous Island borders on the immoral when you do not warn people of the horrors of reaching & leaving it." She signed off, "Hoping we have the courage to return to P.E.I. next year."[116]

To his credit, Premier Alex B. Campbell answered each such complaint personally, always within days of receiving them. He was considerate about the travellers' inconvenience and patiently recited the ongoing efforts to improve the ferry service, but he was also careful to point out that transportation across the Northumberland Strait was actually a federal responsibility. The premier reserved his own frustration for frequent and bitter complaints to those responsible in Ottawa.

The passage to Prince Edward Island might indeed be a highlight for visitors, as the Tourist Association claimed in an appeal for more boats and crossings but the traffic jams at the terminals were killing tourism.[117] "There is a great deal of evidence," Premier Campbell wrote in 1968, "that many thousands of persons do not come to Prince Edward Island because they hear at the garages, motels and other information points on the mainland of the difficulties in getting to Prince Edward Island."[118] A period cartoon by Bob Chambers of the Halifax *Chronicle-Herald* suggested the Island premier was right. "For the next two weeks," his caption reads, "I'll either be here" – pointing to a couple sunbathing on a deserted beach signed "PEI" – "or here" – a ferry lineup so long and stationary that his car is festooned in cobwebs.[119]

Given the everyday disparity between ferry traffic and ferry capacity during summer, any straw imperilled the camel's back. For example, the long tense build up to a CNR strike in August 1966 was "crippling" for tourism, since many travellers wrote the province off their itinerary or rushed to get off the Island to avoid being trapped by a work stoppage. The labour dispute essentially brought the tourist season to a premature end and ignited a fresh round of constitutional fireworks between the island province and Ottawa.[120] On the other hand, the following summer was scarcely better for tourists. By mid-July a 20 per cent jump in traffic required "emergency measures." A courtesy van with a two-way radio and loudspeaker was dispatched to Cape Tormentine, "where the situation was critical," to provide "on-the-spot help, assurance, information and advice."[121] It is not clear how

166

—

The Summer Trade

much these were appreciated. The waits at Tormentine and Borden often stretched to seven or eight hours.

That year was perhaps the low point in the postwar instalment of the transportation saga. That fall a new ice-breaking ferry, the MV *John Hamilton Gray*, commissioned back in 1965, at last began service at Borden–Tormentine. With its arrival, the sooty old SS *Scotia II* and the SS *Prince Edward Island*, the latter considered obsolete way back in 1930, were finally retired. As a stopgap measure to relieve congestion, a second-hand ferry, renamed the *L.M. Montgomery*, was acquired in 1969.[122] Meanwhile, CNR began work on vehicle compounds and new terminal facilities at Borden and Tormentine.[123] In 1971, two new roll-on/roll-off ferries, the *Holiday Island* and the *Vacationland*, were added to CN's Northumberland Strait fleet. Their names reflected their purpose: to handle summer tourist traffic.

New vessels helped speed up the flow of traffic and the expanded terminals provided relief for parched throats, empty stomachs, and full bladders, but the transportation bottleneck persisted. In a brief to the federal government late

Figure 4.5 ▪ The Island's ferry traffic bottleneck became notorious, as Bob Chambers's 1966 cartoon in the Halifax *Herald* makes clear. As Mrs B.M. Bayne wrote PEI's premier Alex Campbell in 1968, "I would suggest that your intensive campaign to bring tourists to your gorgeous Island borders on the immoral when you do not warn people of the horrors of reaching and leaving it."

in 1968, the Prince Edward Island government emphasized the hobbling effect on tourism of the inadequate ferry service. Quoting the Tourist Association, it claimed that "The matter of easily accessible and continuous transportation across the Northumberland Strait is the single most important factor in any contemplated expansion of the tourist industry towards its maximum potential." The "maximum potential" now had a number. According to the Stanford Research Institute, the Island could comfortably accommodate 3.6 million tourists per year, about eight times the 1968 figure.[124] How it arrived at this improbably large figure was unclear. How Islanders might react to it went unasked.

Premier Campbell and his cabinet had their own cure for the transportation canker, and until a few months previous, they had believed it was Ottawa's cure, too. In fact, it was the real subject of their brief. They demanded a fixed link that would provide an automobile and rail conduit between New Brunswick and Prince Edward Island.

When Will R. Bird came to Prince Edward Island in the late 1950s to gather material for his next travel book, he passed the time on the ferry from Cape Tormentine by eavesdropping on conversations. "Two men sat near us," he recounted in *These Are the Maritimes*,

and they began to argue rather loudly about the good old days, and the present. One claimed that when fox farming was at its peak the Island had the best times it would ever know. The other declared that when a Causeway was built travel to the Island would double and it would become the greatest vacation land in the east.[125]

The idea of a fixed transportation link was almost as old as the Island's tourist trade. What began as an answer to the mismatch between winter steamers and ice conditions in the Northumberland Strait had been revived around the time of Bird's visit as a response to summer ferry congestion. Although the design concept eventually combined stretches of causeway, bridge, and tunnel (with 60 per cent open water),[126] the proposed crossing was from the beginning dubbed "The Causeway." Canso, linking Cape Breton to the mainland, had one. Why not Prince Edward Island?[127]

After Walter Shaw's Progressive Conservatives campaigned as the "Party of the Causeway" in 1959, federal officials had launched a round of feasibility studies, and by the early 1960s federal political leaders had promised the causeway halfway to reality.[128] First, John Diefenbaker, then Lester B. Pearson pledged himself to its construction. Where the fixed link discourse had once been dominated by the need for a timely flow of goods to and from the Island, now it was as much about the timely movement of tourists. Acres Research

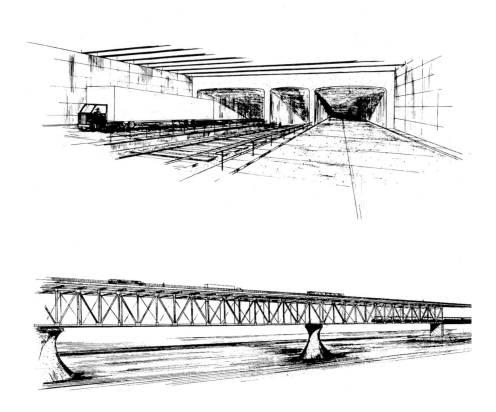

Figure 4.6 ▪ Mid-1960s concept drawings of the proposed PEI Causeway, a combination of bridge, tunnel, and causeway. The Causeway became a panacea for all that ailed the province, including traffic bottlenecks getting on and off the Island.

and Planning predicated its own recommendations for the tourism industry on the completion of the causeway, predicting a 20 per cent spike in traffic in the year following its completion (just in time for the centennial of the Island's entry into Confederation).[129]

After so many years and so much talk, the idea of a fixed crossing – impervious to rafting ice, unshackled from ferry schedules and capacities – had acquired almost messianic potency. It came to embody the 1960s ideal of "progress" and the federal government's obligation to combat regional disparity. In the popular imagination, as with the Islander on Will R. Bird's ferry ride, it was a panacea for all of the province's economic ills and a potent symbol of high modernity. No wonder the Campbell government clung tenaciously to the federal promise of its construction.

In 1965, even as Acres Research and Planning began polling tourists in the summer ferry lineups, the call for tenders went out. While federal officials waited for prices and the provincial government waited impatiently on federal officials, preliminary work began on the approach roads at either end of the proposed crossing. Then the tenders came in. When Prime Minister Diefenbaker had announced in 1962 that the fixed crossing would go ahead, the project was pegged at $105 million. By 1965, when the tenders were called, the rough estimate had risen to $148 million.[130] By 1968, the cost for a stripped-down fixed crossing without any rail link (dropped over the Island government's furious protests) was put at $208 million, with an annual maintenance burden of $800,000.[131]

When federal communiqués dropped any further reference to start times and federal Finance Minister Edgar Benson announced that Ottawa was investigating alternative ways to live up to its obligations to Islanders, the rumour mill began grinding the causeway project into oblivion.[132] Alarmed, Premier Campbell and his cabinet descended en masse on Ottawa in late October, armed with a sixteen-page brief that demanded the federal government keep its promise.[133] To no avail. A few weeks later, in December 1968, Prime Minister Trudeau and his cabinet quietly decided to set aside the causeway in favour of the "Comprehensive Development Plan" for PEI that had slowly been taking shape since 1965. Afterwards, federal officials pressed Premier Campbell to state publicly that his government had chosen one project over the other. When Campbell doggedly refused, the newly formed federal Department of Regional Economic Expansion was forced to choose for him.[134] The causeway was officially abandoned on 5 May 1969. Two days later the new federal–provincial agreement was unveiled. There would be no causeway to lubricate the flow of tourists to the Island. Instead, under the rubric of the Development Plan there would be two new ferries – and much more besides.

The prevailing storyline for twentieth-century Prince Edward Island plays the Comprehensive Development Plan as the watershed moment in the history of the century.[135] In touristic terms, at least, that interpretation represents something of an overstatement. There was considerably more continuity than break in the industry's development during the Development Plan years, that is, 1969–84. What the Development Plan particularly did for Island tourism was to polish its image and concentrate the state's Plan-inflated investment. Above all, as with other parts of the economy, it sought to control and direct tourist growth rather than react to it.

The plan itself, the first comprehensive development planning exercise to encompass an entire province, was worth $725 million, spread out over three discrete five-year phases and across a wide range of cost-shared programs. The agreed funding split was $255 million from the federal government, with the balance raised from provincial coffers. The ratio was much more even in phase one, $118 million in provincial funds against $125 million in federal dollars.[136]

The Development Plan's tourism provisions resided within an ambitious master text. It began with a familiar assumption, that economic growth should be based on the Island's staple industries, then proceeded to a radical hypothesis, that making growth sustainable would require fundamental social change. Each part of the plan was meant to be interlocking, like pieces in a puzzle. Higher incomes for farmers and fishermen would be achieved through better training and greater specialization – and by dividing the returns among fewer operators. The surplus farmers and fishermen would be assisted to acquire modern housing and retrained for employment in other industries. While the adults retrained or upgraded, their children would be socialized for appropriate careers in the new economy within a modernized and reformed education system. On a broader level, investments in health and welfare reform would keep Islanders physically and psychologically fit for progress. To ensure that the Island's principal resource, its land, was used most efficiently, the government would gradually acquire available properties and reallocate their use. Tourism and manufacturing, meanwhile, would be expanded through judicious spending on physical infrastructure and incentives to private business. And, finally, once the expert planners had done their work, the management of change would be confided to a more expert and efficient civil service that had been taught to think strategically.[137] The plan's stated target was a 7 per cent per annum increase in the Island's gross domestic product over the course of the agreement. Its stated goal was to "restore flexibility and capability" to the Island's economy. The unstated objective was to make the province economically self-sufficient.

When it came to tourism, the strategy focused on tourist spending rather than visitor numbers:

> The objective of the program, therefore, is to assist the development that must take place in the face of the pressure of demand and to provide the degree of regulation necessary to optimize the returns to the Island's economy. In particular, through the lengthening of the season, through the development of facilities that will encourage higher per capita spending, and through regulation and control to prevent unsightly development, the objective is to increase total tourist expenditure to $18 million by the tenth year of the Plan.[138]

Given that tourist expenditures supposedly had topped $15.2 in 1968, the objective, an 18.5 per cent increase over ten years, seems rather modest.[139]

One suspects that the Development planners discounted the tourism department's statistics.

If nothing else, the Development Plan was a licence for change. To plot the direction of that change, it leaned heavily on data. Its approach was not inhuman, but it was dispassionate – the plan's favourite word seemed to be "rationalize." It arguably had trouble distinguishing between people and "units of production." So much money and so much ambition made the plan a battleground, and, especially during its initial phase, every step was contested. Optimists maintained that the plan was the Island's last best chance to seize its future by the throat. Pessimists lamented that Islanders had surrendered control of their province to callous outside experts and "Ottawa mandarins." Cynics saw the agreement as a giant funding funnel with the narrow end pointed at Prince Edward Island. In this war of words tourism too often found itself in the crosshairs.

"THE DEVELOPMENT PLAN IS SIGNED!" exclaimed the tourism industry's newsletter, *Tourist Talk*, in 1969. "Great things should happen in the Tourist Industry! Let all of us be open-minded and progressive and help rather than hinder progress."[140] Already by then, a stream of unsolicited overtures was flowing into the premier's office as entrepreneurial Islanders tried to take advantage of the rumoured dollars for tourism. "I have 40 aces of shore farm in Campbellton," wrote Walford MacEwen of Kensington. "Have been told it would make a good trailer park. Could you send out a man from the Tourist Development Department to have a look at the area?"[141] Boyd Bernard of Tignish was even more direct: "In reviewing your statements and by what we read, there is a large sum of money, for the people of this Province and different branches and the main one I'm interested in is for tourist." He went on to outline a proposal for the province to build a dam on the Tignish River and buy his site there to create tourist facilities.[142]

Such letters were typical. There were proposals for government to fund motels, cabins, trailer parks, a mobile canteen, even an art gallery. But one of the Development Plan's imperatives was to bring order out of ad hocery. And so, when such petitioners played the political card, it was politely shuffled to the planners working with the provincial Department of Development. By 1970 the tourism department – like almost every other ministry – also had its own special planning unit.[143]

For their part, bureaucrats and consultants were hard at work devising a strategy for Island tourism. The ends followed on from the Acres Report: more tourists spread out more evenly across the province, spread out more evenly across the seasons, staying longer, and spending more. The means were worked out through a fresh round of studies and surveys. There were more polls, it seemed, than on election day; more maps – of every conceivable sort – than a military campaign. Things were mapped, measured, counted, categorized, analyzed, optimized, potentialized.

West Prince, in particular, was subject to the tourist planner's gaze. It was the least modernized part of the province and the least developed. A special study of the region recommended developing the area around Alberton as a tourism hub to encourage overnight stays rather than just day-trips from Summerside. It even sketched a Potemkin-like "Harbour Village" complex at Alberton Harbour. At the same time, the study urged caution. "The goal of bringing more visitors to stay longer could eventually be self-defeating. The sense of identity with sea and shore which one now feels in many areas in West Prince, and which is attractive to many tourists, may, in the end, be destroyed by the proximity of too many other people."[144] Any tourism strategy for the region, it recommended, should mix new attractions with controls so that "the character of the environment is maintained … not weakened and spoiled." Although West Prince entrepreneurs anxious to cash in on tourist spending might not wish to hear it, the planners had voiced the central dilemma of sustainable tourism: how many tourists can consume an attraction before they fundamentally alter it?

At length, in 1971, the tourism department circulated its blueprint for tourism development. The orderly, interlocking plan would be rolled out in three orderly, overlapping phases. Phase one, "Physical Resource Planning," would stretch from 1971 to 1973; development of the "Tourist Market" would occupy 1972–74; the 1973–75 period would highlight "The Tourist Plant."[145]

The plan's central elements clearly echoed the Acres Report. Essentially, the Island's tourism plant would be upgraded and modernized – rationalized – along carefully determined lines. One goal was to double the length of the tourist season, currently ten weeks, by offering incentives to businesses to stay open and getting the businesses to offer incentives, that is, off-season rates, to visitors. Other objectives focused on the tourist experience. Since first impressions were crucial, work must be done to beautify the "gateways" to the province at Borden and Wood Islands. As the planning document observed, "The boat trip creates a sense of arrival much stronger than merely passing over provincial boundaries. The entrance areas should offer a pleasant atmosphere of beauty and service." The government would encourage (how was not specified) the construction of high quality vacation cottages and condo resorts to provide a "stable base" for the tourism industry. To distribute tourist traffic more generally across the province, the planning document expanded on Acres' idea for loop drives, one for each county, that would take in sites of natural, historical, and cultural significance. The designated routes, which never strayed far from the seacoast, soon had suitably scenic names: Lady Slipper Drive in

Prince County, Blue Heron Drive in Queens, and the eponymous King's Byway in Kings County.

In the perfectable universe of planning, the tourist loops became far more than roads. They were meant to orchestrate the whole tourist experience of the province. As Caroline Spankie of the Tourist Development Planning Unit explained to Premier Campbell, the scenic drives would be the "basic infrastructure for the Island's tourism–recreation program." Each would have a designated theme. Each would primp for the tourist gaze, their "integrity" preserved by regulation of land use and/or the quality of development. There should be land and site planning, control over advertising, careful attention to landscaping, preservation of natural features and heritage sites and buildings, even rules about the design and appearance of structures.[146] Spankie's sweeping proposals represented an unprecedented level of state interference in Islanders' everyday lives. It remained unclear how far government would want to go down *that* road.

The planners' "recreational corridors" would also deliver travellers to a set of "destination attractions."[147] Back in 1967, Acres had flagged a trend towards "more sophisticated and higher quality motel accommodations" and warned that the Island's hospitality industry must respond.[148] Since local entrepreneurs proved cash-poor and risk-averse, the province, flush with Development Plan dollars, decided to step in.[149] To attract the growing market of higher spenders, the government would establish a series of recreation complexes. One of them, Charlottetown, was more or less nominal, but three others would be built along the designated tourism corridors. Brudenell Provincial Park near Georgetown in central Kings County would be one; it was already under expansion anyway.[150] Mill River in western Prince County would be another. The third was intended, somewhat vaguely, for the area around Summerside. Deputy Minister George Fraser had already floated the idea of a major tourist attraction on Holman's Island in Summerside Harbour that would include a zoo, botanical garden or planetarium, the world's largest salt-water swimming pool, an amusement park, a band shell, and a "Seaquarium," built around a replica of the long vanished Island Park Hotel – all reached by hovercraft! It would have been a fascinating full-circle to the Island's tourism history; however, the idea sank without a trace.[151]

Besides making high-end – relatively speaking – accommodations available to visitors, the resort strategy was meant to prime the pump of private investment. Anticipating the "growth pole" strategy later adopted by the federal Department of Regional Industrial Expansion, the resort areas would lure tourists into lightly visited parts of the Island, which, in turn, would encourage entrepreneurs to start up their own businesses nearby, eventually creating a tourism cluster that would stimulate the local economy.[152] That this emphasis on luxury accommodation irked key provincial department officials, who emphasized the pursuit of quantity over quality, is a needful reminder that the shape of Island tourism was contested terrain within government as well as in the larger community.[153] The debate pitting big spenders against the hoi polloi might be cast as a contest between quality and quantity, but it also raises questions about the underlying character – the soul – of Island tourism. Was the province to become an elite resort for the rich or a modestly affordable playground for the type of tourists whose pretensions more closely resembled their hosts?

The new scale of investment in tourism – and the role of the federal government as its principal backer – is exemplified in Brudenell Resort, the first and, for a decade, the only one of the five planned resort complexes to be completed. The original eighty-acre park was acquired by donation from philanthropist Robert Cotton. ARDA funds were used to acquire a further 295 acres in 1963. More ARDA money funded the construction of a golf course, beginning in 1967, and the Atlantic Development Board subsequently financed work on a fifty-unit motel. Development Plan dollars then expanded the motel into a resort populated with peculiar, beehive-shaped chalets. By the time Brudenell Resort officially opened in July 1971, the overall project had cost $1,243,994 with another $531,800 forecast for 1971–72, bringing the grand total to $1,775,794. The federal share of that figure was just over $1.3 million.[154]

Mill River Resort, a postplan creation and the product of much plan-related research and consideration, was slower out of the starting blocks. Only its golf course was ready by 1971 (despite what Acres had said on the subject, planners were certain that the sort of tourist who stayed at high-end resorts was the sort of tourist who had time to golf), but already it had consumed $367,000 in Development Plan funds. As with Brudenell, 75 per cent of that sum came from Ottawa.[155] By 1972 the two resort projects had cost between them over $2 million. They were easily the highest profile tourism initiatives under the Development Plan and so, the most prone to second-guessing. In particular, the Mill River project would soon be overtaken by a public crisis of confidence in the whole growth pole strategy. It would be over a decade before the resort hotel and the nearby Mill River Fun Park opened for business.

There was nothing new in planners' revelation that Prince Edward Island's greatest tourism asset was its landscape. If Islanders didn't know it already, they'd been told as much by observers for decades. Ned Belliveau, whose firm, Tandy Advertising, had the contract for selling Island tourism, was echoing those others when he turned on the charm for members of the Tourist Association in 1971. "You on Prince Edward Island have it all," he told them. Yet, there was an implicit "but" at the end of his praise:

> You are still unspoiled. You still have the peace, the beauty, the unpolluted air and water, the trim fields, the uncrowded roads and pleasant towns … the glorious coastal beaches. You have charm, a special way of living which is more and more the envy of all regions suffering from the blights of modern society. The best thing you can do is *keep it that way*.[156]

What changed in the 1970s was the perception of the landscape's fragility. That is really what lay behind the tourism planners' penchant for regulation and zoning and land use controls.

When the Acres Report had likened Prince Edward Island to one big park, it had in mind a landscape park not an amusement one. So did many visitors, and by the early 1970s what they saw began to worry them. When John and Judy Kirby of Richmond Hill, Ontario, returned to the Island for the first time in five years, they were struck by the proliferation of "tourist traps" on the highway between Summerside and Charlottetown. "Please do not turn P.E.I. into another Niagara Falls," they pleaded in a letter to the premier.[157] Manitoban A.B. Brooks zeroed in on the tourist heartland of Prince Edward Island, the area just outside the boundaries of the national park. Like the Kirbys, he noted a radical change in the landscape between his visits in 1965 and 1969. "The crossroads at Cavendish was now a busy intersection – wax museum on one corner, modernized gas station on another, and stores, restaurants and motels in all directions. I wish they had at least been in good taste, but nothing about their facades impressed me so much as their lack of taste and their dedication to dollars above all."[158]

Brooks's comments came in response to a story by David Cobb published in the *Star Weekly* magazine in 1971 titled "Tourist Traps, Billboards and a Plaster Kangaroo."[159] Cobb's criticisms were the more compromising because more public. His title – and its accompanying photo spread – said it all. When G.O. Best of Toronto saw Cobb's article, he, like the Kirbys, lodged a protest with the premier. "Surely," he wrote, "your Government will not be responsible for the desecration of one of our most inestimable treasures – the purity and rural beauty of Prince Edward Island."[160] Local critics, such as artist-activist-aesthete Marc Gallant of Rustico, entered the fray as well, condemning in Wildean terms the needlessly ugly.[161] According to Cobb, Gallant even received a Canada Council grant to create a documentary record of the tacky tourist landscape. The owners of the attractions that Cobb pilloried – small operators trying to scrape a living out of a short season with limited capital – might well retort that his taste was all in his mouth, but his article was hardly calculated to lure tourists to Prince Edward Island.[162] As Judith Adler points out, cheap facsimiles of Disneyland or Africa only appealed to people who were unlikely ever to visit the originals, that is, low-income travellers from within the Maritimes, not the more distant and affluent travellers that planners felt Prince Edward Island should be courting.

In yet another letter to the premier, Elizabeth T. Greenlee framed the tourist development dilemma. A resident of Cleveland, Ohio, with a summer home at Savage Harbour, Greenlee straddled two worlds, and in her experience they were becoming too much alike. Pretty soon, she wrote the premier,

> we can all stay home in our plastic trash and pretend we went to P.E.I., because there won't be any difference. I am not saying that Prince Edward Island should turn "quaint" and just sit there quietly on view for the nostalgic tourist looking for Ye Olde Islande Waye of Life; but it does seem to me that there is a middle way between stagnation in the one hand and tourism blight on the other.[163]

Like many roads on Prince Edward Island, that middle way proved hard to find.

The same Islanders incensed by a 1967 episode of CBC TV's *Telescope* because it depicted PEI "as a typical back woods community about fifty years behind the times," with its scenes of "horse drawn mail deliveries, run down farms and shacks and general depressed areas,"[164] would be insulted a few years later when the province contracted with Kitten Clubs International to operate its resort at Brudenell. The club's female servers, feline equivalents of Playboy bunnies, all fishnet stockings, cleavage and cat whiskers, were a radical departure from Island tourism's traditional image. At first Premier Campbell was amused, addressing a memo to "Hon. Lorne Bonnell, Pussy-Cat Dept.," and asking, "How much did you pay for this publicity?" But his smile soon faded. In a later memo, following months of snide publicity, the premier warned Bonnell, "It would be a rather major tragedy if the Brudenell Recreational Resort were to become popularly known as the Kitten Club Resort."[165] The contract was not renewed.

While it would be easy to make too much of this handful of complaints, it would be equally wrong to dismiss them as exceptions, the specific masquerading as the general. The letters and clippings were carefully preserved in the premier's files. If nothing else, they remind us that tourism in 1970s PEI was always political. For cabinet, the criticisms underscored the importance of controlling the tourist landscape. At the end of his speech to the Tourist Association, Ned Belliveau had rallied his audience with an appeal to their better instincts:

Figure 4.7 ▪ Patsy Glover, one of the hostesses at the Kitten Club Lounge in the provincially owned Brudenell Resort, in 1971. Sexing up the resort was an attempt to diversify PEI's tourism image, but it was a misguided, front-page disaster. Kitten Clubs International's lease was not renewed for 1972.

Do not allow your beautiful island to be spoiled. Do not tolerate shoddy roadside nuisances ... eyesore billboards ... trash ... poor service, poor food or untidy accommodation. What *you* have ... is what other people are thirsting to have ... and *don't let them spoil it either*. You are the Islanders. It is your home. You make the rules ... and the visitors will obey them.[166]

The greatest threat to Island tourism, he seemed to be saying, was tourism itself.

It was more a semantical than philosophical leap for the tourism sector to move from this concern about tourist "landscape" to talking about "environment." The two words were treated almost as synonyms. The domino effect of Rachel Carson's eco-classic *Silent Spring* may have cracked even Islanders' complacency about the potential effects of pollution on the Island's ecology, but the doors of perception only opened so wide. And so, when Ron Orton urged the Tourist Association's semiannual meeting in 1967 that something be done about "the Pest of all Pests – the Damned Mosquito," the director of Wildlife Services had to remind "all hands that widespread [DDT] spraying is very detrimental to our wildlife."[167] Chastened, perhaps, members left the issue to the discretion of their executive. A larger and more serious concern was the sinking of the 3,700-ton oil barge *Irving Whale* on 7 September 1970 about sixty kilometres northeast of North Cape. Most of its 2,400-ton cargo of bunker "C" oil went down with it (the rest drifted ashore on the Magdalen Islands), but the wreck remained an ecological time bomb left perilously close to the tourist beaches of the Island's North Shore until it was finally salvaged in 1996.[168]

The *Irving Whale* incident may have played into the departmental reorganization that took place the following year. After Lorne Bonnell was appointed to the Canadian Senate in 1971, Robert Schurman became minster of the newly constituted Department of Environment and Tourism. The twinning of portfolios was no marriage of convenience. In the 1972 speech from the throne the government retroactively explained the decision:

> Because of the great role that Tourism, Fish and Wildlife, and Park development play in the shaping of our environment and because of the necessity to co-ordinate our activities in these areas with all other forms of land use, and most importantly, because of the mutual concerns of pollution abatement, my government transformed the Department of Tourist Development into the Department of the Environment and Tourism.[169]

But renaming the ministry did not represent any visionary concept of "environmental tourism." In a literal sense, the commitment to environment was all about appearances.[170] The new department brought together tourist development, land use planning, and environmental control. After rehearsing the usual list of tourist objectives (longer season, longer stays, more spending, better spatial distribution), the speech from the throne added a new plank to the tourism platform: "the protection of an attractive Island environment and the prevention of unsightly developments."[171]

Putting environment first in the department's name was a tacit act of diplomacy for it put Islanders first as well. As the speech declared,

> The accelerating rate of land acquisition by non-residents require that we act promptly to insure public ownership of the outstanding natural landscapes, beaches and recreational resources which are fundamental elements of a quality tourist image, and more importantly, to preserve for all time the distinctive scenic qualities of Prince Edward Island which are the heritage of all Islanders.

Those distinctive qualities might be the heritage of all Islanders, but it seems that the "unsightly" was defined largely from the point of view of the tourist. All through the '70s, the environment branch was preoccupied with landscape aesthetics and visual pollution. In 1973 the government introduced a new signage act that strictly limited the number of promotional signs along the highway and standardized a severely modest design for them.[172] Derelict car legislation followed in 1975 whereby Islanders paid to have more than 17,000 abandoned car bodies removed from view.[173] Another edict banned a prime source of roadside litter, aluminum beverage cans.[174]

The widely perceived subtext for the "can ban," that it also protected the province's handful of pop bottlers from off-Island competition, illustrates that the environmental legislation was sold as benefiting Islanders as much as – or more than – visitors. When it came to visual aesthetics and overt commercialization, one could reasonably argue that tourist and local were singing from the same hymnbook. Both had reason to object to litter in the ditches, billboards crowding the roadside, or plywood Camelots along tacky commercial strips. The same pastoral countryside that charmed tourists was, after all, the natural outgrowth of an agrarian society – as poet Milton Acorn proclaimed at about this time, "The figure in the landscape made the landscape."[175] For Islanders to protect it against adulteration was an assertion of ownership. Each of them then, host and visitor, valued the visual integrity of that landscape, if for different reasons, and each had a stake in its preservation.

It would be a mistake, then, to cast the 1970s as a Manichean struggle between agriculture and tourism for the souls of Islanders. Nevertheless, the tensions were real. As tourism bounded forward, claiming an ever-greater share of publicity and attention, agriculture, the traditional backbone of both the Island's economy and its culture, struggled through some of its worst years in recent memory. And while the Development Plan promised to grow tourism, it threatened to dismantle the traditional family farm in favour of a more efficient, more industrial model built around monoculture. When the National Farmers Union fanned agrarian discontent into open protest in August 1971, it was no accident that the demonstration targeted the tourism industry. The "Great Tractor Blockade" took an endemic tourist annoyance, slow-moving farm tractors, and clogged the highway leading to the ferry terminal at Borden with them.[176] As Matthew McRae reasons, "The fact that the NFU had chosen to protest by interfering with tourism, rather than gathering at the legislature or some other symbol of government authority, indicates that tourism was then perceived as the government's primary concern by the angry farmers."[177] A seed of resentment, long buried, had sprouted in the hothouse climate of the Development Plan. Here was hospitility with a vengeance.

Even the plan's allegedly favoured child, the tourism industry, often rankled at the government's tourism strategy. Sometimes the issue was advertising emphasis. For example, the Kensington and Area Tourist Association

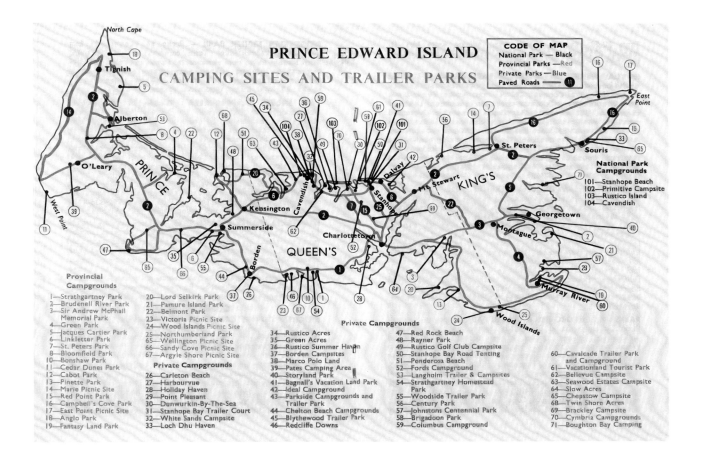

found the 1971 tourist map, with its new loop drives, "discriminatory and highly unacceptable in its present form" because it did not highlight major trunk roads leading to Summerside, Kensington, or the national park areas. "It is therefore with the utmost regret, expecially [sic] in view of the waste of taxpayers [sic] money, that we must insist that the present map be destroyed and replaced in a more acceptable form." The letter finished darkly, "we have a very unhappy feeling that something very ugly is happening within our otherwise beautiful Province."[178]

The most frequent cause of complaint was the unfair competition that resulted from government's hands-on approach to tourism. Insurance executive Keith Jenkins, who owned a campground near Stanhope, hounded the premier for years with complaints that public campgrounds undercut his business by operating below cost, suggesting at one point that the national park campground at Robinsons Island should operate only in the shoulder season. In a 1970 letter, copied to six members of cabinet, Jenkins broadened the scope of his criticism:

Figure 4.8 ▪ This 1971 map shows the proliferation in the era of provincial and private campgrounds, which were especially attractive to budget-conscious families and young adults. That the National Park and the province operated camping facilities was often regarded as unwelcome competition by private operators.

I suggest that this area is where the tourist business was founded in Prince Edward Island by a few people squeezing their savings and doing without in order to begin and hold a cottage or whatever it might be – that this area and the people in it were the "guinea pigs" of the industry and a substantial (very) [source] of the tax dollars that have been keeping PEI as a province and that if we have money and resources to develop other areas in large sums then why not help to hold what we already have in the "father" area.[179]

Jenkins might sound a little like the Prodigal Son's aggrieved elder brother but his exchanges with government offer a revealing glimpse at divisions within the tourism industry. The government's determination to retain control over the levers of tourism through legislation and public ownership protected the industry from dollar imperialism, but it also antagonized the private sector within the province.

As Jenkins's reference to "money and resources to develop other areas" suggests, the government-financed resorts at Brudenell and Mill River were a particular sore point. Kathryn Wood, who operated a guest house in Victoria-by-the-Sea, couched her critique in a general complaint about lack of government support for tourism development on the South Shore: "I should think the Government, instead of competing against us, would be helping to establish the [tourism] industry by encouraging and giving assistance to privately owned enterprises to help keep our people from leaving the Island."[180] The Cavendish Resort Association seconded her objections, finding the government's "entry into commercial tourist operations" an unwarrantable competition with the private sector that would "jeopardize existing tourist operations and discourage private enterprise,"[181] while spreading tourists across the province would only ensure that visitors "will simply pass through their area of concern without stopping."[182]

Dissension within the industry could be soothed with quiet reassurance and half-promises of assistance, and tourism planners no doubt passed them off as growing pains. Certainly, they attracted less publicity than tractor demonstrations. What is revealed in these tensions between rival tourist regions, between public and private sector priorities, between the "mom and pop" past and the high-end future, is the growing complexity of the tourism sector. Its fiercest critics, however, stood outside the industry, where they chose not to look behind its monolithic façade. From that vantage they saw both something objectionable and the symbol of a broader, deeper malaise.

182

The Summer Trade

It had once been enough just to reconcile Islanders to tourism by convincing them of its widespread benefits. The Development Plan's goal was more ambitious. It attempted a sort of social fracking, meant to drive tourism awareness down into the bedrock of the broader community so that every Islander would consciously become a tourist ambassador. In Bermuda, the arbiters of its tourism industry, the Trade Development Board, had, over time, successfully engineered a "seamless integration" of society and tourism. Certain tourist-friendly behaviours – decorousness, politeness, deference – were encouraged and eventually embraced by the community.[183] But Bermuda was a society oriented almost entirely around the hospitality industry. The same message was a much harder sell on Prince Edward Island.

A breaking point of sorts was reached in June 1973 when the Department of Environment and Tourism ran a ham-handed advertisement advising Islanders about how to engage with tourists during "Welcome a Visitor Week."[184] The notice read:

1. Ask if you can give help when a stranger appears lost or hesitant.
2. Take time to give accurate and specific directions.
3. Speak slowly and distinctly (but don't "shout") when assisting a foreign visitor.
4. Walk with him a block, or even more, to point out the way.
5. If he is a photo fan, offer to take a snapshot of him with his camera. Many tourists appreciate this courtesy.
6. Be enthusiastic and well-informed about your local sightseeing attractions.
7. Post this on your office, union, church or synagogue bulletin board.
8. Be friendly. Be helpful. Be hospitable.

Telling Islanders what their shared countryside should look like was one thing, but telling them how to behave around tourists was a whole new level of interference.

The condescending hospitality lesson drew the ire of a loose circle of likeminded critics that had been brainstormed into being by two young historian–activists, David Weale and Harry Baglole, late in 1972. The group named themselves the Brothers and Sisters of Cornelius Howatt after a diehard opponent of the Island's entry into Confederation. Their preferred acronym was "bs-ch" (with the emphasis perhaps on the "bs"). Their preferred weapon was humour. Their logo was a manure spreader *in medias res*, their

Figure 4.9 • The manure spreader logo of the Brothers and Sisters of Cornelius Howatt. Anti-tourism was a major strand of their satirical critique of the Island's 1973 centennial as a Canadian province. Tourism conditioned Islanders, according to cofounder David Weale, "to think of ourselves, not as an independent farming and fishing community, but as a pandering people – a province of flunkies and attendants."

motto, "Spread the Word." The Brothers and Sisters were articulate and funny, but behind the clever facade of their satire, they were angry about where their province was heading in the new dispensation represented by the Development Plan.[185] Taken together the BS-CH positions represent a critique of modernity, although not, as some contemporaries charged, a simple aversion to change. The BS-CH riposte to the official romance with tourism was to invent the Pie-faced Kid, "an Island farm boy turned desperado who bore a terrible and implacable grudge against all tourists and foreigners."[186] The Kid's comic misadventures as a tourism saboteur highlighted the shower of press releases and publicity stunts that pitched cold water at the Island's tourism calendar.

If the larger context for the BS-CH disenchantment was the Development Plan, its catalyst was the self-congratulatory hoopla attending the celebration of yet another centennial, this time the Island's entry into Confederation in 1873. Provincial licence plates might proclaim that PEI was "The Place to Be in '73," but the BS-CH had their doubts. They did not so much challenge the claim to "Cradle of Confederation," as question why the Island's reluctant surrender of its independence to become the smallest, least powerful, and most dependent province in Canada should be so uncritically celebrated. In their view, the centennial was little more than a tourist event that measured their province's worth only according to its cameo appearance in the national story. They preferred other stories, ones that empowered Islanders by demonstrating historic virtues of stubborn self-reliance and singularity. In a symbolic battle of the mascots, the fictional Pie-Faced Kid squared off against the real-life emblem of the 1973 centennial, the "Smiling Father," who employed his notorious "Centennial pin" to wrestle the Kid into temporary submission.[187]

As for tourism, in the BS-CH view, it was a soulless transaction that prostituted the Island's culture, transforming yeoman farmers into servants and particularity into quaintness.[188] The portrayal exaggerated at both ends, but it was a good enough likeness to discomfit many Islanders. The fullest articulation of the BS-CH's antitourism stance came in an op-ed piece from August 1973 titled "Tourism – the Big Sell." In it, Brother Weale accused tourism of corrupting genuine hospitality by crassly professionalizing it. Visitors were "cynically and avariciously regarded in terms of the money they bring," while Islanders were "conditioned to think of ourselves, not as an independent farming and fishing community, but as a pandering people – a province of flunkies and attendants." After "dolling" themselves up for the tourist trade, Islanders would be "in a position to sell our friendship, sell our scenery, sell our hospitality, sell our favours, and even sell our soil to our affluent visitors." Weale ended with an unblushing appeal to abandon tourist promotion altogether: "It should simply be understood that those who want to come to visit the Island of Islanders are welcome, but that the tourist who is seeking a highly developed, honky-tonk, Coney Island environment ought to go elsewhere."[189]

As far as the Brothers and Sisters were concerned, tourism turned all the proper priorities on their head and that put the very nature of Island society at risk. As a contemporary cartoon from Summerside's *Journal-Pioneer* suggested, the "Garden of the Gulf" was turning into "Holiday Island."[190] Or, as Brother Baglole suggested, "the Bermuda of the St. Lawrence."[191] One of Baglole's early mentors, teacher/artist/poet/iconoclast Elaine Harrison, expressed her own anger and anguish in poetic terms:

> And I am an Island that
> dreams and talks in its sleep
> I will soon be only a place
> for tourist dollars and nightmares[192]

The touristic comparison most often referenced by naysayers was not Bermuda, or even Coney Island, but Cape Cod, where summer residents had displaced and essentially disenfranchised the locals. When environmentalist Anne W. Simon was invited to Charlottetown to lecture about the despoliation of Martha's Vineyard, she spoke to a packed house that included the premier.[193] The same risks – dispossession, pollution, unrestrained development – seemed real on Prince Edward Island, where rising tourism and cheap land values in the mid-1960s caused a run on recreational properties.

The startling revelation that 92,000 acres and some seventy-eight miles of shorefront were controlled by nonresidents, including real estate developers, speculators, and promoters, had already triggered a Royal Commission on Land Use and Land Ownership in 1972. Even before it began its deliberations, the province had passed the Real Property Act, which required that all purchases by nonresidents in excess of ten acres or 330 feet – five chains – of shore frontage be approved by the governor-in-council. In practice the legislation served more as a deterrent than a prohibition, since most applications were routinely approved. Nonresident cottage owners were hampered but hardly prevented from acquiring their own (little) piece of paradise.[194]

The principled, sometimes hyperbolic, opposition to tourism from the Brothers and Sisters of Cornelius Howatt formed a philosophical bookend to the practical criticism of tourism policy coming from within the industry. Although the BS-CH had numerous supporters and an unknown number of sympathizers, in the end theirs was a minority report. Yet, it does appear as if their satirical barbs left a permanent scar affecting the rhetoric, at least, of state-sponsored tourism. In his introduction to the Department of Environment and Tourism's annual report for 1973, the new minister, William M. Gallant, emphasized that, while his department aimed at "the greatest economic return to all Islanders," tourism expansion "must not harm the growth and character of our Agricultural Industry and the basic life styles of the Island." Tourism was committed, he continued, "to examine the directions and growth of this industry" and to build it on "quality rather than quantity and unrestrained growth."[195] After two decades of booming visitor numbers, it was a modest but telling admission to acknowledge, not that there *might* be limits to tourism growth but that there *should* be limits. It is hard to believe the Brothers and Sisters of Cornelius Howatt had nothing to do with that realization.

The echo of BS-CH rhetoric could even be heard in the tourism department's new promotional film, *Prince Edward Island: Come in from Away*, launched in 1976. At the beginning, a bearded, "ye olde fisherman" mouths a familiar island conceit: "There are two parts to the world. One part, the Island. The other part, we just call all that Away." From his lips the phrase sounds quaint, but for the BS-CH it was pardonable pride. Amid the usual promotional tropes, there are new nods to environmental awareness – "We used to take our dunes for granted. Now we take care of them" – and to local history – "The Island's people are becoming prouder of their heritage" – before a curious coda: "When it's time for you to go just leave us the way you found us. That's important to all of us."[196] BS-CH and tourism promoters might agree on very little but they both had a stake in preserving the Island's distinctiveness.

186

The Summer Trade

In writing about PEI's 1970s, academics have tended to focus on the anti-tourism critique of the 1973 centennial rather than on the event itself. By most measurements, it was actually a notable success. After three previous celebrations of Confederation, Islanders had clearly gotten the hang of things. Organizers, too. Whereas Canada's centennial in 1967 had been more a national than local phenomenon, 1973 trained the tourist spotlight back on the nation's smallest province.[197] The year-long, Island-wide, event-heavy approach that had worked so well in 1964 provided a convenient template for the 1973 celebrations, which brought the country's centennial decade to a close. If the blueprint was the same, the bankroll was much bigger: nearly five times the budget for 1964. The federal government provided $1.44 million in centennial funding, calculated on a per capita basis; the province kicked in another $900,000.[198]

Preparations began in earnest in 1969 with the appointment of the 1973 Centennial Commission, followed a year later by the Centennial Celebration Act, which announced the participation of individual Islanders as "the primary single aim of planning." As Matthew McRae records, they did not do badly. Although visible minorities were largely invisible among the organizers, the centennial team had geographic, demographic, institutional, ethnic, and religious breadth. It included twenty-one commissioners (with an eight-person executive committee), twenty-five honorary directors, a thirty-six-person executive staff, 200 members on twenty-two provincial committees, 1,500 citizens participating in approximately one hundred community committees, and an uncounted army of volunteers.[199] With so many planners, pundits might be forgiven for wondering whether there would be any Islanders left over to attend the nearly 400 special events that were scheduled. There were, of course, along with a record number of tourists.[200]

The lasting legacy of the 1964 centennial had been the Confederation Centre of the Arts, a highbrow cultural complex doubling as a national shrine. What sort of inheritance the 1973 centennial might leave became the subject of prolonged debate among the twenty-one centennial commissioners. After months of argument, the commission decided in the spring of 1972 to invest the bulk of its $1.44 million federal grant in the province's heritage.[201] The decision came as the culmination of at least three trends. One was the backwards perspective engendered by a decade of centennials. Another was an acute sense of loss as antique dealers carted off the Island's material artifacts, accident and intention demolished its built heritage, and rapid modernization undermined its oral culture. The third was a feeling of urgency as the

Figure 4.10 ▪ The 1973 licence plate, with the ubiquitous centennial mascot "the Smiling Father." The rhyming tagline worked well in 1973, less well when retained in subsequent, nonrhyming years.

Development Plan hastened the pace of social and cultural change.[202] Heritage seemed especially relevant precisely because it was endangered; a wave of heritage awareness was the natural consequence.

If the Development Plan harmed the Island's heritage, it was less deliberate act than collateral damage. In fact, the Campbell government intended the past to be part of the Island's future. In November 1969, Premier Campbell gathered together a small group of heritage advocates to discuss the Island's historic resources, and in January 1970 he invited a representative group of heritage-minded individuals from across the province to a follow-up meeting on the subject.[203] That June the PEI Heritage Foundation was formally incorporated, with retired Chief Justice Thane Campbell, the premier's father and an ex-premier himself, as titular chair and heritage activist Catherine Hennessey as executive director.[204] Soon the organization had hundreds of paid-up members. The premier apparently intended it as both sounding board and advisor. As he explained to a colleague in 1972, "There are literally dozens of historical projects being proposed by individuals or groups, to the government for consideration. The central purpose for establishing the Prince Edward Island Heritage Foundation was to bring the heritage interests of our citizens together, in one single organization, and recommend to Government those areas most deserving of public and financial support."[205]

The Heritage Foundation began as a volunteer-based, heritage advocacy group dedicated to preservation, conservation, interpretation, and proselytization. The rush of centennial money put wind in its sails, and soon it was working with provincial officials to develop a series of historic sites scattered across the province. In March 1972 Premier Campbell announced in the legislature that capital funding would be provided for six major heritage projects. Three of them would address traditional Island industries. There would be a shipbuilding museum at Port Hill in western Prince County, a living history museum dedicated to agriculture at Orwell Corner on the road to the Wood Islands ferry, and a fisheries museum on a spectacular beach site at Basin Head in northeastern Kings County. For Summerside there would be an as-yet unspecified museum (eventually the Eptek Exhibition Centre), situated in a new waterfront complex. Money was also earmarked for the historic Townshend Woodlot, a rare stand of old-growth forest near Souris, and for the Heritage Foundation to acquire a headquarters. Its eventual choice was a former shipowner's mansion in Charlottetown's west end, now known as Beaconsfield Historic House.[206] Most of the projects were somehow rushed to completion during centennial year, allowing for a high-profile series of official openings. A decade later the clutch of interpretive sites would provide the basis for the Island's decentralized provincial museum system.

From the beginning the Heritage Foundation intended that the new sites should cater to Islanders, but, inevitably, they were also strategically located tourist attractions. That quickly caused friction with the Department of Environment and Tourism, which naturally expected to control any government-spawned tourist sites. The heritage movement welcomed tourists, but a heritage sector geared to tourists was fundamentally, if subtly, different from one aimed at residents. In December 1976, after a fierce and drawn-out battle between foundation and department, Premier Campbell delegated to the Heritage Foundation the responsibility for developing Island heritage.[207] Even after the foundation was reconstituted as the PEI Museum and Heritage Foundation in 1983 and most of its staff were converted into civil servants, its operations would remain at arm's length – short arms, admittedly – from government.

The Brothers and Sisters of Cornelius Howatt would have applauded the victory,[208] but the organization had already self-destructed (as promised), at midnight, 31 December 1973, after nailing its "Last Will and Testament" to the door of Province House. To the Island's Tourist Association it bequeathed a select list of inappropriate attractions:

> one can of Causeway [the BS-CH was steadfastly opposed], several Fantasylands [that is, low-budget, generic amusement parks], one small herd of buffalo [a questionable centennial gift from the province of Alberta], the Bonshaw 500 [go-cart track], pig races [self-explanatory], the Royal Atlantic Wax Museum [not Tussaud-quality], one rather tattered Smiling Father costume and one slightly-used lobster suit, Marco Polo Land [a campground named for a ship, not the Venetian traveller], several hitherto unexploited Lucy Maud Montgomery relics, plus other bric-a-brac and various assorted articles too numerous to mention.[209]

The choice of location for the Brothers and Sisters' last official act was quite deliberate. Besides the Confederation Chamber, Province House was home to the provincial legislature, the second oldest elected assembly in Canada – in fact, 1973 marked its 200th anniversary. And the government of Prince Edward Island had just tried to give it away.

The Province House pickle is a graphic illustration of the financial pressures facing cash-strapped provincial governments – and the temptations. Blackened by soot, grown shabby inside and out, the Island's 125-year-old legislative building was a source of pride but a financial burden as well. That the Confederation Chamber, the constitutional "holy of holies," had become one of Charlottetown's premiere tourist attractions did not deter the new Liberal government from offering it to the Historic Sites and Monuments Board in September 1966. Indeed, that status justified the overture. "I would appreciate knowing whether the Historic Sites and Monuments Board is interested in taking over the building as an historic monument and assuming the financial responsibility for its maintenance and administration," Premier Campbell wrote HSMB chair C. Bruce Fergusson. "It must be clearly understood, of course, that the Legislative Assembly would at all times be available to the Members of the Assembly, as well as certain adjoining offices for the use of the Leaders of the political parties, officials and servants of the Legislature."[210] In effect, Campbell was proposing that the Island's government become tenants in its own legislature.

Province House quickly got its designation, in October 1966,[211] but the offer of ownership went nowhere in the short term, and the province continued as landlord to the national shrine. Yet when the Liberal government introduced a modest admission fee the following year to help pay for its upkeep, Canadians were mortally offended. The premier's files are well stocked with complaints from tourists upset about being charged admission to visit.[212] Joseph A. Pinto was "so appalled" that he "immediately ushered my wife and daughter from the premises."[213] John E. Proctor felt "shock" to find "a government-sponsored tourist trap involving a national shrine."[214] J.A. Davies was just disappointed – and underwhelmed: "There is very little worth seeing on the inside! The let-down (particularly of tourists from the United States) is patently obvious."[215] Philip Saunders supposed that he spoke for thousands of visitors when he declared, "Canadians should not have to pay to see the Birthplace of Confederation. Free access to the Confederation Room should be the right of us all. A 50¢ charge, while small, is a slap in the face." He added, "It appears to me that [the fee] is a means of pressuring the Federal Government into taking over the whole building."[216] Saunders probably struck close to the mark; each letter of complaint was answered with polite regret that Ottawa had not yet seen fit to help shoulder the burden of maintaining a site of such significance to the nation's story.

190

The Summer Trade

After years of desultory negotiation the Liberal government proudly announced in October 1973 that PEI and Ottawa had signed a memorandum of intention to transfer Province House and its grounds to federal ownership. In return, Ottawa promised to "restore, preserve, interpret, and administer" the building as a National Historic Site while allowing the Island legislature to continue using certain parts of it. Instead of praise for its fiduciary acumen, the Liberal government got protest. The Brothers and Sisters of Cornelius Howatt draped the entrance to Province House in black crepe and nailed a proclamation to the door. What self-respecting province, it asked in an appeal to Islanders' pride, would surrender ownership of its own legislature? It was tantamount to surrendering its sovereignty.[217] Both local and national press quickly chimed in. "We may be poor," the *Journal-Pioneer* editorialized, "but surely we aren't that poor."[218] We weren't. By the next sitting of the legislature the agreement had been amended to replace the embarrassing transfer of title with a long-term lease and shared management. Over the next decade, Parks Canada (the new name for the National Parks Branch) carried out a massive program of repair, restoration, and interpretation that the province could never have afforded. More visitors than ever filed through the restored building. Under the management of Parks Canada, the cradle of Canadian Confederation stopped charging admission.

Figure 4.11 • Red double-decker buses, direct from London, were a familiar if incongruous sight on Island streets and roads for decades. The first was brought for the 1964 Charlottetown Conference centennial, but Conn and Shirley Murphy of Abegweit Sightseeing Tours soon purchased a fleet, which they operated until 2010.

In the summer of 1969 Maj. D.A. Macdonald revived his longstanding campaign to get the Prince Edward Island National Park to absorb his boyhood farm at Wheatley River, four miles outside the current park boundary, and build luxury rental cottages there. "I firmly believe that the salvation of this Island is [as] a Tourist Haven," he wrote Jean Chrétien, the minister of Indian affairs and northern development.[219] Chrétien politely declined. "Your proposal for a Tourist Haven on Prince Edward Island is an interesting one and probably had much to recommend it," he replied. "However, the purpose of National Parks is to preserve the natural landscape of Canada intact and unimpaired. I interpret this purpose not on a tourist promotion programme but rather as a means to display and interpret our natural heritage to people whose visits in Canada may be based on any number of attractions.[220] Chrétien's high-minded refusal to make decisions based on tourist potential is a trifle specious. The National Parks Branch (soon to be Parks Canada) was not interested in Macdonald's 180-acre farmstead, but it was open to expansion. Even as Chrétien was disappointing Major Macdonald, his officials were picking up a dangling conversation with the PEI government about the possibility of creating a second national park in the province.

The discussions, which dated from 1962, represented a rough intersection of cross-purposes: the provincial government wanted more tourist development; the National Parks Branch needed more land.[221] Prince Edward Island National Park had long been a victim of its own success. By the early 1960s, it was crowding more than a million visitors a year into its narrow strip of North Shore coastline. Parks personnel had never really reconciled their wilderness ethos with the mass recreation that dominated the park, and by the late '50s the emergence of a new ecological sensibility helped reassert the old distinction between middle-brow visitor masses and a more intellectual, more environmentally aware elite who could appreciate the sublime beauty of wild nature.[222] At the national park the only real wilderness was the overcrowded beach. That was a problem. Parks officials considered buying up adjacent property to thicken the belt of parkland and screen out with second-growth forest the commercial strip that lined its borders, but North Shore real estate had grown pricey. Then there was always the thorny question of what to do with the existing tourist operations. Hemmed in and overcrowded, PEI National Park was a commercial success but an aesthetic failure. Each half of that statement drove the quest for a second national park, one that would preserve a substantial block of once and future wildland and relieve the growing congestion at the North Shore location.

While the National Parks Branch sought a return to its wilderness model, the government of Prince Edward Island craved the sort of economic development its first national park had generated (and the political dividends that went with it). Preliminary discussions with the Department of Northern Affairs and Natural Resources led to a detailed reconnaissance of potential sites by Parks staff in the summer of 1964. Its report cautioned that "The shoreline is the only outstanding natural feature, unchanged by the works of man, present on the island, and suitable as a base for a national park." Any new park, then, "would … be limited to supplementing the features offered at the original, rather than offering new park values."[223]

So be it. But where along the shoreline should the prospective new park go? Five sites in all were considered. The Shaw government was determined that Ottawa should develop Cedar Dunes Provincial Park near West Point in the economically under-nourished western end of the Island and, when Ottawa objected that the site was too tiny, offered to acquire enough land to bulk it up from one hundred to 2,800 acres. The National Parks Branch was equally adamant that the only suitable location for a new national park was the northeast corner of the province, a blunt wedge of land anchored by East Point at the tip, stretching westwards towards North Lake and south to the area around Basin Head.[224] As Acres Planning and Research discovered in its capability mapping exercise, that end of the Island boasted the greatest acreage of class 1 land for recreation–tourism.[225] It was bordered on two sides by saltwater that washed long stretches – some fifteen miles – of superb beach. The shoreline also possessed a number of unusual, if undramatic, ecological features, especially around Basin Head, that were worth preserving.[226] Just as important for the Parks Branch, the recommended property provided the desired elbowroom to disperse the crush of national park visitors; at between 8,000 and 8,900 acres (suggested boundaries varied), the site was nearly twice the size of the PEI National Park. The relative absence of tourist development in the area was even attractive. Pastoral countryside (if preserved by proper land zoning) would make a much better transition into the proposed wilderness park than the unregulated commercial development that had blighted the landscape on the north shore.[227]

With a provincial election in the offing and no national park deal in sight, Premier Walter Shaw ungraciously bowed to the Parks Branch's insistence on East Point. "In looking over the survey reports," he wrote the federal minister Arthur Laing in February 1966, "I find that the West Prince Area situation is somewhat similar to that of the original National Park on the north side of the central part of the province. But apparently the main characteristics of the area are not sufficiently high enough to pass the criteria which you mention in your letter."[228] The Conservative premier's obvious pique was partly political. He chose to believe that Parks' preference for East Point was based mainly on the Pearson government's desire to benefit the Liberal candidate there in the next federal election.[229]

At this point, in 1966, the grail quest for a second national park seemed tantalizingly close to fulfillment. The federal government, its National Parks Branch, and the provincial government all desired it. They even agreed (more or less) on the location. All that remained was for the province to acquire the land in question and transfer title to Ottawa, while Parks staff worked up a detailed plan for developing the site. Instead, as in Arthurian legend, the trials were just about to begin.

In the beginning the problem was money. By the time the costing of park-suitable properties began, Alex Campbell's new Liberal government (elected, as it turned out, on the strength of two by-election victories in the very area covered by the intended park) had inherited the second park brief. William L. Meggison of the Department of Municipal Affairs provided a preliminary list of property owners and calculated that it would cost $113,854 to buy them out.[230] But as the months passed and park rumours floated, property values crept upwards, even after the provincial government used the Planning Act to place a freeze on development in the region. An undated Parks memo, probably from 1969, upped the purchase estimate to $364,000 for 8,097 acres.[231] By the early '70s provincial officials had raised the ante to a million dollars, maybe four.[232] Even the least of those sums exceeded the disposable income of a provincial government that as recently as 1966 had teetered on the brink of insolvency.[233] In the time-honoured tradition of postwar Atlantic Canadian governments, the province hoped to get a goodly share of the purchase money from Ottawa.[234] In the meantime, it began incrementally buying up relevant properties within the proposed park as opportunity and funds allowed.

The Comprehensive Development Plan, with its growth pole strategy for tourism and loose purse strings, finally jump-started the stalled project by helping address the money issue. After some wrangling, both sides agreed in principle that the province would pay for 25 per cent of the land. The two levels of government would cost-share the remaining 75 per cent on a 50:50 basis.[235] In another concession to the province, Ottawa acquiesced to a phased transfer of the necessary land.[236] Even those conditions failed to clinch a formal agreement. There is a sense of urgency in the memorandum prepared by John I. Nicol, director of the National Parks Branch, in December 1971. "The future value of Prince Edward Island as a tourism-oriented province hinges to a large extent on the establishment of the proposed East Point National Park," he claimed. That overstated the case, but Nicol probably had in mind the direful overcrowding at the Island's existing national

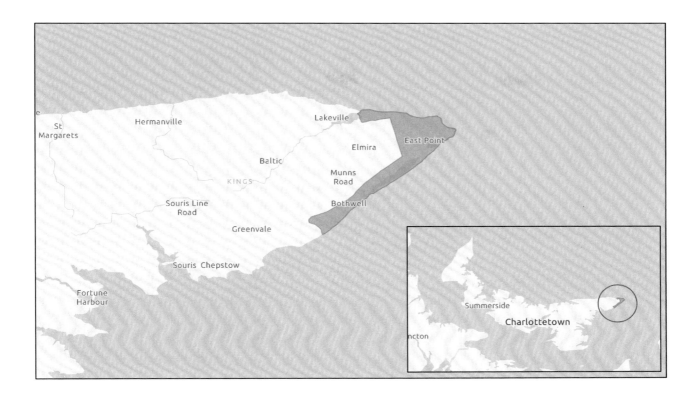

park, where annual attendance now topped two million visitors, more than double the 1960 figure. To break the funding deadlock he now suggested a simple 50:50 funding split for the park property, with the potential of DREE assistance to underwrite the Island government's half.[237] By now land values in the area ranged from $30 an acre for woodlots to $1,000 per acre for waterfront.[238] At those rates, assembling the property for the new park would cost around $2.4 million.

In the end it was not lack of money that killed the East Point National Park but popular protest. It might be thought that a new national park, with its promise of plentiful tourist traffic and new jobs, would appeal to an underpopulated region buffeted by out-migration and economic decline.[239] And it did. At first. In 1965, the year after the initial site reconnaissance and before a park site had officially been chosen, the provincial government received a bundle of petitions in favour of the park bearing the signatures of some 550 area residents.[240] That October a delegation from the Eastern Kings Board of Trade waited on Tourist Development Minister Lloyd Macphail to press their region's case.[241]

The petitioners – like Shaw's government – had imagined the new park would resemble the existing one, a thin strip of beachfront that followed

Figure 4.12 ▪ Proposed East Point National Park map. Eastern Kings residents assumed that the new national park rumoured for the area would cost landowners only a thin strip of their shoreline. When it became apparent in the early 1970s that Parks Canada intended to convert much of the district into parkland and embargo commercial development along park boundaries, interest turned to resistance.

along the coastline. After all, that is what tourists did: go to the beach. When rumours about the actual draft boundaries drifted out into the community, eagerness gave way to unease. Unlike the North Shore farmers of the 1930s, people in Eastern Kings understood that assembling lands for a national park meant the purchase or expropriation of any private property within it. While much of the proposed parkland was either nonagricultural or abandoned farmstead, it also included good farmland and productive farms. Those farms would not just lose their shore fields if the park went ahead as proposed; they would be swallowed up whole.

At a public meeting in Kingsboro in June 1966, East Kings residents opposed what they knew of the park layout and endorsed a counterproposal, which their local board of trade then tabled with the provincial government. Their version of East Point National Park actually increased the amount of beach frontage without displacing anyone who was not already willing to part with their land. At 3,715 acres, roughly the size of the PEI National Park, it was far smaller than the Parks Branch's plan, but it would only cost, its proponents claimed, about $60,000.[242] Their proposal never really stood a chance. The local citizenry did not know or did not understand Parks' appetite for more land. For its part, Parks was slow to grasp the depth of resistance to expropriation in East Kings. What we had here, as a popular movie of the era was wont to observe, was a failure to communicate. That left the prospective expropriator, the provincial government, to mediate between the two opposing camps.

From the beginning the province had been palpably reluctant to force expropriation on Islanders living inside the proposed park. Its reasons were possibly principled, certainly political. At a time when public attention was fixated on the Development Plan's controversial intention to "rationalize" agriculture and reallocate land use where appropriate, expropriation would take viable farms out of production. This contradiction of policy became a formal objection to expropriation. An additional, unstated complication was that one of those productive farms belonged to the Island's popular minister of agriculture, war hero Daniel J. MacDonald.[243] Expropriation would also be accompanied, inevitably, by negative publicity that might well cost the government votes. Premier Campbell was no doubt mindful of the fallout from when his father's government had expropriated the shore fields that became Prince Edward Island National Park back in the 1930s.

When park negotiations between the Province and Ottawa picked up in 1969, the provincial officials proposed that existing residents be allowed to continue living within the park boundaries.[244] Federal officials refused; it was against Parks' longstanding policy, shaped by its wilderness mandate.

196

The Summer Trade

But delivering an uninhabited park site in East Kings to Ottawa would entail dispossessing hundreds, not dozens, of people.[245] The province's stubborn insistence that some sort of accommodation be made for them became, along with the sheer expense of acquiring the land, the principal stumbling block in negotiations.[246] By April 1970 Ottawa had drawn up a draft agreement laying out its position on the new park. A year later, there was still no official counter from the province.[247]

It did not help matters that the Island government seemed unsure of its own mind. As the lurching, on-again, off-again talks dragged on, provincial officials variously suggested considering Malpeque Bay as an alternative site, replacing the second park idea with some sort of joint beach-park development, or simply expanding the existing park inland and/or eastwards along the northern coast all the way from Tracadie Bay to East Point.[248] By March 1972 the former minister of tourism, Senator Lorne Bonnell, was lobbying Minister Chrétien for a shift in park location from East Point to a different stretch of Kings County coastline between Panmure Island and the wonderfully named Poverty Beach.[249] The province's changeable – and multivocal – bargaining stance suggested a lack of conviction.

The way forward became clearer in 1972 when Chrétien conceded that compromise was likely on the residency issue.[250] Embroiled in fierce expropriation controversies at two other ongoing park projects, Kouchibouguac in New Brunswick and Gros Morne in Newfoundland, the Parks Branch was groping towards a new policy. It was now prepared to view local inhabitants carrying on traditional occupations as part of a national park's natural landscape. Parks officials agreed that those sorts of occupants inside East Point National Park should be allowed to lease back their expropriated homesteads, so long as they maintained permanent residence, continued their traditional employments, and allowed Parks to regulate the visual appearance of their properties.[251] They would become, in effect, living exhibits, their daily round put on display for the tourist gaze. But they could stay. With this last issue resolved, the project could proceed. In March 1973, after a decade of back and forth, Ottawa and the province finally agreed on a formal proposal for a national park in northeastern Kings County. At just that point, everything fell apart.

The problem was with those living exhibits. When provincial fieldworkers began a belated round of public consultation with the people of Eastern Kings, they encountered a rising tide of resentment towards the whole project. The locals did not trust the planners, who talked but, they felt, did not listen. They disliked the leasing arrangements, did not care to be displays in a cultural landscape park. They saw little profit in proposed zoning regulations that would maintain a strictly noncommercial green belt along the park's borders. And they expected few jobs in a park design that emphasized campgrounds and beach facilities while excluding resorts or other recreational facilities. They were not rejecting tourism per se, but a tourism that involved burdens without tangible benefits. As the opposition grew more militant, and with the locals corresponding with park opponents in Kouchibouguac and Gros Morne,[252] the provincial government backed away. In a dramatic gesture, Premier Campbell tore up the federal–provincial park agreement during a public meeting at Fairfield on 28 June 1973. There would be no second national park for Prince Edward Island.

The East Point park controversy demonstrated how much tourism was entangled with larger issues during the Development Plan era (and how much the province had changed with respect to tourism since the creation of the national park in the 1930s). It encapsulated Islanders' ambivalent relationship with progress, their frustration with the lack of public input into planning, their annoyance about excessive control over land use, their anger about planners' willingness to move people around like pieces on a chessboard, their fear that tourism might become the tail that wagged the dog in their province. Those feelings lingered long after the torn-up pieces of the park proposal had been swept away.

"Will Success Spoil Prince Edward Island?" journalist Dorothy Eber asked in her 1966 article about the impact of mass tourism on Island culture.[253] A decade later, Islanders were no closer to an answer. To get one, of course, they would have to agree on what might be spoiled, and they would have to define "success." Certainly, the oscillation in the first years of the Development Plan between ovation and outcry in discussing the hospitality industry suggested that there were limits to Islanders' tolerance for unfettered tourism. The balance of the decade showed that there were limits to tourism, too.

Even as it pressed forward with its growth pole strategy to redistribute tourism, the Department of Environment and Tourism got unwelcome news about the prospects for broadening the tourist season's narrow shoulders. According to the government's long-time marketing agency, Tandy Advertising, surveys showed that fall tourism was a nonstarter with North American travellers, who considered the Maritimes in fall "cold, damp and generally unappealing." Even worse, the general perception was that the region was only worth visiting once (in summer), and, for Canadians, at least, it was mostly from a sense of obligation to a part of the country considered "poor and economically depressed." For would-be American visitors, "The prime appeal of the Maritimes … is that it is undiscovered, beautiful and clean, untouched by the American tourist, quaint, relaxing and an opportunity to escape from it all." Psychographic data suggested that people who visited the Maritimes tended to be "much slower paced than average," were not interested in nightlife, and tended to stay in one place. As for Prince Edward Island, it was considered "a place to be visited, but only if time allows because attractions are felt to be limited."[254] A few months after this damning assessment, the province abruptly dropped Tandy as its advertising agency, citing "major shifts in [Tandy's] relationship with other firms and in its personnel makeup."[255]

Mid-decade reports on other aspects of the industry were equally discouraging. When Dymaxion Research Limited examined the employment impact of tourism on the Island economy in 1976, its profile of the tourism sector was eerily similar to the picture painted by Acres Research and Planning back in 1965: small-scale, family operations, mostly employing friends and relatives, especially women and students, on a part-time, seasonal basis. Not only did the sector look much the same, it had not materially reduced the Island's high rate of seasonal unemployment (except by adding a number of civil servants to government's tourism branch). In another report completed at around the same time, ABT Associates found there was still much room for growth before the Island reached tourist saturation point (whatever Islanders' perceptions). In spending terms, it reported, unsurprisingly, that high-income tourists trumped expatriates and both trumped campers, with their canvas tents and shoestring budgets.[256]

ABT also measured opposition to tourism among Islanders. It found that people living in central Prince Edward Island were far more supportive of tourist development in the east and west than people actually living in those regions (70.5 per cent of respondents in Queens County, compared to a diffident 55.2 per cent in Prince and Kings Counties). As Judith Adler speculates, "One can hazard a guess that experience of tourism makes some residents anxious to avoid growth in their region, but receptive to the idea that others should be raised to the level of development from which they suffer."[257] The general consensus among Islanders was that tourism was important but that government should spend less on it and that the province had more than enough tourists, thank you.

They got their wish. Just when it seemed both tourism's boosters and knockers were about to see their expectations realized, the industry faltered. ABT Consultants had predicated "normal" tourist growth at 2.8 per cent per year, far below the bounding increases of the 1960s. Instead, the rate of growth slowed and then stalled. Even allowing for the unreliability of departmental estimates, it is clear that visitor numbers essentially flatlined – and even declined – between the mid-1970s and the mid-1980s.[258] An offsetting increase in tourist spending over the same period was more apparent than real, given the galloping rate of inflation.

The end of the tourism boom was partly, of course, a global phenomenon. As the mid-decade oil crisis pushed up the price of gasoline, auto travel, the packhorse of postwar tourism, became much more expensive. The North American economy limped along as "stagflation" combined high unemployment with double-digit inflation that eroded buying power. Soaring interest rates discouraged travel loans and business mortgages. The international trends were a sobering reminder that local tourism was vulnerable to factors over which it had no control and little influence.[259]

One of those reminded was the government of Prince Edward Island. Ten years into the Comprehensive Development Plan, after millions of dollars and masses of planning, after so much controversy and criticism, government might be excused if, like a disgruntled tourist, it complained that all it had gotten in exchange for the money and abuse was a lousy T-shirt. Yet, behind the disheartening statistics, the tourism sector had evolved significantly since the Acres Report of 1967. Its attitude was more professional and more sophisticated than before. Its messaging was more nuanced as well. And for better – and worse – it had a far greater profile. It had at last penetrated into the consciousness of ordinary Islanders. In token of that maturation, the PEI Tourist Association – once the Innkeepers Association – rebranded itself yet again in 1980, becoming the Tourism Industry Association. The new emphasis on "industry" was a marker of magnitude, a statement about the sector's growing importance and increasing professionalization.

For its part, the provincial tourism department's capacity for planning and data collection had grown exponentially since Acres had criticized it in 1965. And although the results were mixed, government's role in the tourist sector now went well beyond marketer or banker or even watchdog; the state was up to its wallet in the business of tourism. As guide, it had a clear set of objectives and better tools for working towards them – even if it still lacked a lever to tilt the tourist globe its way.

Along with change there was continuity. The province's main appeal as tourist destination remained – for a certain, desirable class of visitor – the unspoilt nature of its landscape and people. The problem that the boom years exposed for this "Island imagined" was that a modern, professional tourism industry demanded from its purveyors a heightened self-consciousness in

200

The Summer Trade

order to ensure a consistent, repeatable experience for visitors. As Adam and Eve had discovered in that other garden of Eden, self-awareness was incompatible with innocence. It remained to be seen whether Prince Edward Island's tourism industry could sustain that sort of paradox.

CHAPTER 5

Laws of Attraction, Rules of Engagement
1980–2000

On a windy March day in 1981, a small group of protestors from the Prince Edward Island Heritage Foundation floated a trial balloon at a building site on Charlottetown's waterfront. They were not testing an idea; they were floating an actual balloon as part of a demonstration. The building site was the prospective location for the most ambitious private construction project in the history of the province, a hotel and convention centre that its advocates believed would become the anchor for downtown tourism. The demonstrators were not protesting tourism per se, just its choices.[1]

Back in 1973, as part of their three-volume blueprint for redeveloping the Island's capital, consultants Stevenson and Kellogg had called for construction of a medium-size (175–200 rooms), high-end hotel and convention centre, franchised to a brand-name chain with promotional reach, on Charlottetown's decaying waterfront "to stimulate development and encourage refurbishment of the Charlottetown area centre-core."[2] Only a largish hotel, the reasoning went, could attract larger conventions, which would, in turn, ripple business out to the other hotels and motels in what casual observers dismissed as a "rainy-day city" for weather-challenged beachgoers.[3]

When local developer Bernie Dale took up the report's recommendation seven years later, he did not follow the blueprint exactly. The number of rooms was similar, and the Hilton International chain was tentatively tabbed as operator, but where Stevenson and Kellogg had postulated a building of between four and seven storeys "in keeping with the existing scale of development," the fourteen storeys of the proposed "Prince Edward Hotel" would tower 150 feet above the waterfront, completely dwarfing the period buildings on either side. Heritage advocates found that scale entirely inappropriate, and

Figure 5.0 (facing page) ▪ The West Point Lighthouse and child actor Martha MacIsaac headlined the 1996 *Visitors Guide*. MacIsaac would soon star in the TV series *Emily of New Moon*. Tourism PEI/ John Sylvester.

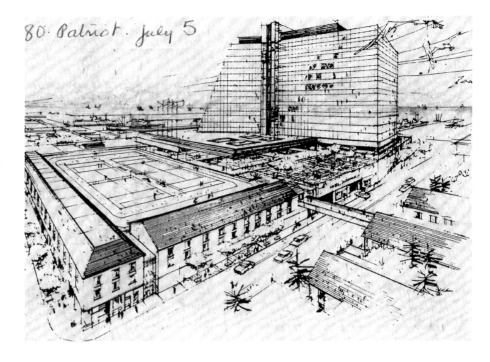

Figure 5.1 • Concept drawing for the Prince Edward Hotel, 1980. Assailed for failing to fit into the heritage streetscape and beset with financial woes, the hotel's eventual design was a bland brick box several stories lower than the original intention.

to illustrate their point, they floated a big yellow weather balloon to the proposed height of the new construction. The balloon was tethered to a pickup truck hung with signs bearing slogans such as "Save our City scale" and "Isn't small still beautiful?"[4]

Stevenson and Kellogg had likewise emphasized that the hotel must be "be of very high quality in terms of concept and design, landscaping, exterior signs, and building materials furnishings, décor, staffing and management." It should be, they continued, "a landmark building of symbolic value which enhances Charlottetown as a special city and as a provincial capital." But the concept drawings for the Prince Edward struck many as painfully generic and incompatible with the surrounding architecture.

The heritage lobby was apparently instrumental in knocking four storeys and forty feet off the initial height.[5] Cost may also have been a factor. Stevenson and Kellogg had thrown out a figure of $3.85 million for the sort of complex they envisaged, with only $15,000 coming from public funds.[6] When it launched the project in April 1980, the Dale Corporation at first projected an outlay of $18 million, although that quickly jumped to $26.8 million, including $3.8 million in public money.[7] By the time the project staggered to completion in 1984, ravaged by economic recession, multiple lawsuits, and runaway interest rates, the actual cost for its ten storeys and 198 rooms had spiralled to $32 million, $23 million of it guaranteed by the federal and provincial governments. Within months of its opening, Hilton was gone, the complex had gone into receivership, and Dale had retired from active business.

To salvage something from its investment, the PEI government purchased the hotel in 1985 for $5.1 million, prompting opposition calls for a royal commission into how construction had been financed.[8] The whole affair reeked of failure: the hotel went through four owners in its first year of existence, the Tory government got a public relations black eye that contributed to its defeat at the next election, and the Prince Edward was widely derided as a white elephant that was costing other accommodations business. Downtown tourism, one might say, had dragged its anchor.

A generation later, Bernie Dale was in the Island's business hall of fame and the Prince Edward had done exactly what Stevenson and Kellogg had predicted it would do, become a four-star mainstay of the downtown's tourist accommodations.[9] The bland, redbrick bulk of the hotel still dominated the waterfront, but even heritage advocates had gotten used to it. Most people had forgotten, or chose to overlook, its controversial beginnings. It had indeed become "a landmark building of symbolic value," though not perhaps in the way that Stevenson and Kellogg imagined. Its origins tied together many of the themes that characterized the post–Development Plan era: its abiding faith in professional expertise; its devotion to brand-new infrastructure; its sense that tourism and heritage had different, if overlapping, agendas; its vexing questions about the proper proportions of public and private investment in tourism development; its dogged pursuit of perpetual growth; and even its jealousies and resentments. Like the Prince Edward Hotel, tourism loomed large on the post-Plan landscape – and Islanders would not always like living in its shadow.

As part of the ritual unveiling of its annual Tourism Marketing Plan in 1979, the Department of Tourism, Parks and Recreation took a moment to glance back over its shoulder. Over the past twenty years, it marvelled, the tourism sector "has grown from a cottage industry to one that reaches and influences the life of every resident of Prince Edward Island." The statement was both boast and burden. The industry that touched everyone was, in turn, touched by everything else. The preamble continued with a more familiar refrain, "Competition for the tourism dollar is becoming more intense as other vacation and travel trade regions are developing strategies to capture larger shares of the travel market and dollar."[10] It was no longer good enough for Island tourism to rely on its good looks and charm in order to court visitors.

Inexpensive air charters, package tours, changing consumer values and attitudes, emerging travel patterns: all challenged the Island's market share. Global tourism was on the rise, but that only overwhelmed travellers with the tyranny of choice. And so, the marketing plan that followed was sprinkled with imperatives, what tourism providers "should" and "must" do to spread out visitors, lengthen the season, change perceptions, improve the tourism product.[11]

The sobering synopsis was defensive in tone partly because the march of tourism on PEI had slowed to a shuffle by the end of the '70s.[12] Tourist spending was up, but inflation accounted for most of that, and the double-digit jumps in annual tourism numbers that had defined the 1960s could no longer be used as a rough and ready yardstick of the industry's vitality. That tourism's expansionary phase ended just as the West's postwar economic boom was petering out only sharpened the implicit sense of closure. Like other extractive industries – fishing, forestry, mining – tourism would in future have to expend ever more effort and continually refine its methods in order to maintain itself.[13]

Peering in the rearview mirror like this did not predict the road ahead (even as it slightly distorted the past), but it did capture how tourism had shouldered its way into the economic and psychological landscape of the province. By the 1980s, the industry had achieved a certain equilibrium. Once mostly potential, then touted as prodigy, tourism had become an accepted part of life in the province.[14] The old summer trade was now entrenched as the second most lucrative industry in the province. In 1985, Hillsborough MP Tom McMillan, Canada's ambitious minister of state for tourism, claimed that tourism currently accounted for 14.8 per cent of the province's gross provincial product. Tourism was more important to the local economy than in any other province, far more than in Nova Scotia (8.2 per cent) and Quebec (4.7 per cent).[15]

Tourism would continue to gain ground over the next two decades but in a frustrating, snakes-and-ladders pattern: bounding forward, then falling back. Visitor numbers dipped towards the half million mark in the recession years of the early 1980s, set new records in 1987 and '88, then shrank to 630,000 in the trough of another economic downturn in 1991, before rebounding by mid-decade.[16] Each increase was interpreted as evidence that the industry was doing something right. Each decline in visitor numbers or spending spread doubt even as tourism spokespeople sought (often with justification) external explanations for the failure to prosper. One seemed to validate, the other exposed, the illusion of control.

No one openly boasted anymore that tourism would soon be the Island's number one industry. If tourism boosters still believed it, they had learned it was better to hold their tongues. The same learned reticence was busy re-branding "tourists" as "visitors" in promotional literature in a semantic effort to sidestep the negative stereotypes often associated with the word "tourist." For depending on one's perspective, the Island's growing reliance on tourism was either promising or ominous.

Tourism might have fallen short of its boosters' expectations but neither had it fulfilled the dark prophecies of the doubters who had proliferated in the hothouse climate of the early Development Plan. Nevertheless, the tourism critique persisted into the 1980s. "Placed in its proper perspective," wrote Bill MacDonald in the left-leaning *New Maritimes*, "tourism is not inherently evil." Yet he made it sound so: "The economics of tourism present a text-book case of dependency in one of its most blatant forms." It served a fickle external demand; it quaintified Islanders, ignoring their real-life struggles and challenges; its jobs were mostly seasonal, as well as "poorly paid, unskilled, unfulfilling and non-unionized"; much of its spending leaked back out of the province to pay for imports of tourist-related goods and services (the official figure was 31 per cent); and instead of being used to complement other rural industries, its profits were either spent on luxuries or reinvested in tourism. The needs of Islanders, not visitors, should come first, he concluded.[17]

Although MacDonald's assessment was forceful, by 1983 it was a minority opinion, the dying fall of the loud criticisms from a decade earlier. Islanders seemed to have made peace with the industry that permeated their society without dominating it. The 1982 annual report of the Department of Tourism and Recreation boasted that a tourism awareness campaign directed at Islanders had resulted in "great public support for the tourism industry." A few years later, in 1988, a residents' survey found that 95 per cent of respondents thought further tourism growth was possible, and 85 per cent considered it desirable (even if many wanted to direct it to the underdeveloped west). Sixty-five per cent of them even felt the summer season could accommodate more visitors.[18]

Although tourism boosters would likely have conceded some of Bill Mac-Donald's points, the glass that he insisted was half empty, they saw as half full. For the industry's practitioners and promoters, the remedy for tourism's inadequacies was more development, not less. And that, they were convinced, should be premised on detailed, accurate research.[19] For the landscape of tourism was not just more cluttered than ever before, it was also more complicated. As the need to know your "market" and your "product" — each now understood as plurals rather than singular — grew ever sharper, the quest for self-knowledge became continuous. In the two decades between 1980 and 2000, outside consultants produced nearly fifty tourism-related studies and surveys (not counting annual exit surveys and other intradepartmental undertakings) for various combinations of federal, provincial, and private sector interests.[20] A cynic might say that more money was spent on studying tourists and tourism than on promoting the summer trade, but, actually, it just seemed that way.

As much as anything, this appetite for research defined the post–Development Plan era in Island tourism. For even if the Development Plan had failed to pitchfork tourism to the top of the economic heap, it left behind a residual faith in expertise. More than ever research was seen as the key to future growth. If knowledge is power, then the industry gradually grew more powerful in the closing decades of the twentieth century as planners, promoters, and practitioners strove to master the laws of attraction. Manipulating them would prove less easy.

Having scaled back its most grandiose ambitions, the fifteen-year Comprehensive Development Plan signed in 1969 died a natural death in 1984. What began as a blueprint for social and economic transformation ended as a convenient mechanism for federal funding. In its place Ottawa and the province negotiated, sector by sector, a series of Economic Regional Development Agreements (ERDAS) for periods of up to five years. The agreement on Tourism Development signed on 30 October 1991 and renewed several times was typical. Its purpose was to promote market- and research-driven entrepreneurship, bolster competitive strengths, explore ways to package and promote, enhance sustainable development, and encourage diversification.[21] In practical terms, this meant a familiar set of preoccupations: new products, site creation and enhancement, quality and human resource development, promotion – all built around market research.

The ERDAS constituted a critical funding supplement for a tourism department that continued to twin with other portfolios in marriages of administrative or ministerial convenience.[22] (For simplicity's sake, we will refer to the "Department of Tourism" and "Tourism" or its assorted divisions.) Within the sometimes odd pairings – such as "Department of Fisheries and Tourism" – the Tourism Division and its Tourism Marketing Branch constituted a necessary island of continuity and access to expertise. For a unit with more profile than finances – annual operating budgets seldom exceeded $10 million – the federal funding helped catalyze tourist development by subsidizing strategic initiatives justified by ongoing research.[23]

Although Ottawa put money on the table, the Department of Tourism's most important partner in the 1980s and '90s was the newly rechristened Tourism Industry Association (TIAPEI). As its membership ballooned from

Table 5.1 ▪ Position of the tourism portfolio within the provincial government, 1940–99

1940–49	Provincial Secretary
1949–60	Department of Industry and Natural Resources
1960–71	Department of Tourist Development
1971–75	Department of Environment and Tourism
1975–80	Department of Tourism, Parks, and Conservation
1980–83	Department of Tourism, Industry, and Energy
1983–86	Department of Finance and Tourism
1986–90	Department of Tourism and Parks
1990–92	Department of Tourism, Parks, and Recreation
1993–97	Department of Economic Development and Tourism
1997–99	Department of Fisheries and Tourism

After being its own department throughout the 1960s, the provincial Department of Tourism was invariably paired with other portfolios. These were often marriages of convenience as much as congruence. The trend continued into the millennium. In 2021, tourism was lodged under the omnibus Department of Economic Growth, Tourism, and Culture.

ninety-seven in 1961 to 650 by 1990, so had its resources. In 1973, the association hired its first full-time general manager and by the mid-1980s it had a small permanent staff, plus an elastic complement of project employees.[24] Its bolstered human and financial resources boosted its credibility as the informed voice of tourism operators, especially after it reconstituted its board to include the presidents of each of the province's dozen or so regional tourism associations.[25] That inelastic but overtly representative governing structure magnified TIAPEI's lobby.

Departmental rhetoric reflected the changed relationship. Its 1981 annual report emphasized efforts "to develop and strengthen" government's relationship with TIAPEI, praising the advantages of cooperation "in a highly competitive market." The following year, TIAPEI was given formal input into the development of the tourism marketing plan. Again, the virtues of partnership were extolled: "The cooperative and mutually productive relationship between the Department and the private sector is vital to the continuing success of Prince Edward Island Tourism."[26] By 1987 TIAPEI's marketing committee was meeting biweekly with the marketing branch for months at a time to settle priorities and objectives.

The official emphasis on private–public partnership was more than boiler-plate or even internal philosophy. It was driven by necessity. As the 1988 marketing plan noted, more emphasis was being placed on the private sector to replace departmental marketing dollars (a reminder that the same economic downturns that reduced visitor numbers also slashed departmental budgets, forcing bureaucrats to do more with less).[27] As a private sector, industry-wide organization, TIAPEI was particularly well positioned to access funding in the new, supply-side dispensation that characterized federal thinking during Brian Mulroney's tenure as prime minister in the 1980s. The shift in regional economic development policy towards fuelling entrepreneurship directly rather than filtering it through provincial bureaucracies (actualized in the creation of the Atlantic Canada Opportunities Agency in 1987) gave TIAPEI a pipeline to programs the provincial Department of Tourism could not access.

For much of the Development Plan era, expertise – and so, power – had resided mainly with governments. Those experts had done things *for* tourism operators; more often now they did things *with* them. From little brother, TIAPEI had been elevated to the status of partner. For its part, the Department of Tourism no doubt preferred to deal with a single entity rather than a multivocal industry that by 1993 counted 5,691 full-time and 8,322 part-time employees.[28]

Whether or not the close relationship between industry and government was unprecedented in Canadian tourism, as Minister Gordon MacInnis claimed in "Partners in Marketing," the three-year media and marketing plan for 1988–90, it did mark an attitudinal sea change in Island tourism. More and more, government's Tourism Division preferred to frame itself as collaborator rather than leader.[29] As Leslie Miller, chairman of TIAPEI's Marketing Committee noted, they had been "consulted on almost every element of the plan's formulation."[30] TIAPEI's status as the voice of "industry" now went unchallenged. It had become, bragged Minister MacInnis, "one of the strongest tourism organizations in Canada."[31]

The new relationship dynamic was exemplified in the adoption in 1988 of "Tourism 2000: A Statement on Tourism Development." A collaboration among the tourism troika of industry, province, and Ottawa, Tourism 2000 aspired to raise tourism numbers to one million visitors annually by the end of the century.[32] Its eight development principles incorporated much of what the industry felt it had learned since the mid-1960s, and its wording was as much political as operational. Tourism development must proceed in concert with other sectors, admonished principle one (a tactful avoidance of inter-departmental jealousies). And – a nod here to the cultural critics of the '70s – it should promote the "lifestyles, values, heritage and cultural traditions while preserving the attributes and attractions unique to the province." Respect for local culture went hand in hand with respect for nature; attractions must be "appropriate to our environment" and "in harmony with the conservation and preservation of that environment," stated principle three. The decades-old mantra about spreading visitors more evenly across time and space was again endorsed but now with a commitment to provide quality product and service "measured against first-class standards of excellence." While principle six might seem self-evident, it underscored the primacy of proper research over politics or patronage: marketing strategies should be based on "potential demand, consumer need, willingness to pay, and the opening of new markets." The last two principles cast government in the role of "support and service" for the private sector and – not surprising in a plan with a twelve-year horizon – committed the partners to "revisit and revise" the strategy as necessary.[33]

For the next several years, references to Tourism 2000 were sprinkled across tourism division annual reports, but the reminders gradually disappeared, overtaken by unplanned events (not least among them a sharp recession), unforeseen opportunities, and fresh planning studies.[34] Even after the references faded, its commonsense principles pervaded tourism thinking. Those principles mattered more in the end than any specific actions, and the principles, in turn, were perhaps less important than the gospel of a collaborative partnership that gave lip-service at least to the idea that the industry, not the state, would drive tourism forward into the new millennium.

By January 1993, when the provincially appointed Task Force on Tourism submitted its report to the province, the division of labour had been further refined to reflect lived experience. Government, the Task Force suggested, should formulate the "vision" for tourism – in consultation with industry – and create the conditions for success, "including planning, research, coordination, regulation, and some product development." The private sector should do what in theory it did best: marketing, development, and quality control.[35] TIAPEI thus had a say, if not always a hand, in most of the major industry initiatives of the 1980s and '90s. Its relationship with government was not without friction. As in any alliance, there was chronic bickering, simmering resentment, conflicting agendas and personalities. Nevertheless, the public face of the partnership was mostly positive.

Relationships within TIAPEI could also be fractious, as individual tourist operators found themselves angrily out of step with the general consensus, while the regional tourist associations, each represented on the TIAPEI board, sought to defend, promote, and enhance their own region's particular interests.

As that era's general managers, Jim Larkin and Don Cudmore, might tactfully admit, steering a coach hauled by a team of twelve or more headstrong horses required diplomacy, a thick skin, and patience. Many of the disagreements were contained within TIAPEI meeting rooms, but occasionally they spilled out into the public sphere, exposing the stress of competing interests that characterize tourism in every constellation of host communities. It is a needful reminder that "tourism" might be monolithic, but any tourism industry hosts a diversity of interests and approaches.

Two flashpoints in particular illuminate the stresses within the tourism sector: marketing levies and ratings. The idea of taxing all members to help finance tourist promotion and marketing found little traction during the post-Development Plan era. The proposal was pushed by municipal governments in Charlottetown and Summerside, two of the Island's most visited locales, and supported by many of the larger tourist operators. Advocates believed it was necessary if the industry was to grow, arguing that a rising tide of tourism would lift all boats. TIAPEI's leadership warmed to the proposal, but smaller operators and outlying tourist regions doubted that the benefits of a marketing levy would be distributed equally across the sector. Rather than see the rich get richer at their expense, opponents of a marketing levy preferred to keep their money in their own wallets.[36]

Members' opposition deterred TIAPEI but not the cash-strapped provincial government. When it unilaterally imposed its own one-dollar-per-room-per-night tax in 1990, a "furious" TIAPEI executive resigned from all joint committees with government. The executive objected less to the "looney tax," which it supported in principle despite fierce internal opposition, than to where the revenues it raised would go: into the province's general revenues instead of directly to TIAPEI for tourism promotion. The minister responsible justified the tax by citing reduced ERDA funding for tourism promotion and vetoed the idea of turning the tax over to TIAPEI since "government does not give money to associations because that would allow willy-nilly marketing schemes."[37] Although the act was quietly repealed the following year, the very public spat temporarily damaged the public–private partnership built up so carefully over the previous decade and did nothing to endear TIAPEI's membership to the idea of marketing levies.[38] The proposal came up again periodically, but it did not fly. In the end, only the Island's two largest municipalities, Charlottetown and Summerside, imposed a marketing levy on local tourism operators.[39]

The TIAPEI-Tourism Division leadership had better success when it came to selling the virtues of ratings systems for attractions and accommodations. Their adoption reflected a commitment to quality that soon found its way into Tourism 2000's statement of principles. The cookie-cutter format of advertising in the *Visitors Guides* of the early 1980s belied the fact that all attractions were not created equal (or aspired to be). For many ratings advocates, it was all about managing expectations.[40] To do that, tourism advocates had to imagine themselves as tourists. And according to the Department of Tourism and TIAPEI's executive, tourists were anxious to know what they were getting for their money if they ventured to Rainbow Valley or Basin Head or the Mill River Fun Park; booked rooms at Brudenell Resort or Cold Comfort Farm B&B or Green Gables Bungalow Court. Both TIAPEI and Tourism had long preached the importance of standards; the existing licensing and inspection regulations were predicated on their necessity. But in the hypercompetitive tourism market of the 1980s, standards also meant standardized, and that meant ratings.

The first and less contentious application was a ratings system for attractions. The 1987 annual report of the Department of Tourism and Parks announced the impending introduction of a ratings system for attractions in concert with Michelin Travel Services, "the oldest and most respected tour guide service in the world," according to the department. Attractions, it continued, would be rated on "the basis of an internationally-accepted set of criteria."[41] The work was done by 1988, and the first ratings were ready in time for the 1989 *Visitors Guide*.

The same year, a tourism operators' survey found that 89 per cent of the 160 operators polled felt that an accommodation grading system would benefit the region, as a way to assure visitors of consistency and as incentive for tourism providers to increase quality.[42] Achieving consensus about rating accommodations was more difficult than grading attractions, in part because there were so many more of them (just more than six hundred establishments in 1981 with 3,900 units; 960 with some 5,446 units by 1989, not including the 4,000 spaces available in private campgrounds).[43] Some operators worried about losing business if they could not match competitors' star rating. Others pointed out that a ratings system scaled according to certain amenities made little allowance for architectural, historical, or proprietorial charm. All wanted proof that the monetary cost involved in grading would be redeemed by the return on investment.

TIAPEI's management and provincial officials worked together on the issue, and gradually the membership came round, co-opted in part by tying the provincial proposal to a regional ratings initiative involving tourist associations in the whole Atlantic region.[44] It was hard to reject accommodation ratings if the neighbours were adopting the idea. The province initially used its own ratings system, but in 1992 the Department of Tourism contracted a private-sector company, Tourism Quality Services, to manage the Canada Select Grading Program, "a rating system that ensures national standards will be met at Island accommodations."⁴⁵ In a manner of speaking, the stars had aligned.

Or not. Disgruntlement at the shift to Tourism Quality Services' higher standards soon spilled into the local press. For one tourist operator, John Brewer, the elaborate requirements to earn a three-star rating were "absolutely absurd." And lumping perfectly respectable midrange cottage accommodations in with the old two-star operations would, he predicted, "send a lot of tourists back home swearing never to return."⁴⁶ The sound and fury of barbed protest eventually faded to echo, although the tale it told signified something about the diversity of opinion and approach within the tourism industry and demonstrated yet again that the critique of tourism's assumptions and priorities came from inside the tent as well as out.

Although managing tourists' expectations might have been the principal motive behind ratings, the implicit assumption among operators that more stars meant more business did encourage improvements to tourism's infrastructure.⁴⁷ At the same time, annual training programs tried to professionalize tourism's work force. The goal again was consistency, but it remained to be seen whether or not standardization would induce homogenization, and if so, whether homogenization might somehow compromise the visitor experience, make it seem more generic, less "real." Addressing such questions about the product involved knowing as much as possible about the customer.

So it was that the conjectured tourist of the late nineteenth century became the much-studied specimen of the late twentieth. Since the 1950s, with varying degrees of sophistication, tourism officials and their consultants had been counting and categorizing visitors to Prince Edward Island. Geographic origins continued to beguile would-be marketers. Over time, they had added statistics about travel and accommodation patterns, modes of transportation, and spending habits. In the 1980s and '90s the counters created even more demographic layers, analyzing family size, income, marital status, age groupings, viewing audiences, reading habits, motivations for travel.⁴⁸ They even grouped tourists by "type": visitors (who came to stay with friends and relatives, and so, spent less); family travellers (who stayed longer and consumed more of the formal tourist infrastructure, such as rental accommodations); adventurers (restless, active explorers, least likely to return); watchers (sedentary creatures of habit, who came back to familiar destinations); entertain me types (passive consumers of packaged activities, rather than self-directed); escapers (seeking alternatives to their familiar domestic landscapes); culture buffs (who spend proportionately more on local heritage, arts, and entertainment).[49] Each desired demographic required its own, seasonally adjusted marketing spin. Tourists had become categories. People had been turned into data.

While surveys dissected the tourism market, other studies carved up the Island's tourism resource according to geography, ethnocultural grouping, day-tour potential, type of attraction/accommodation.[50] These divisions were often governed by the longstanding goal of distributing tourists more evenly across the province's eleven (by the late 1990s) tourism regions.[51] Armed with their studies, tourism marketers continued to be matchmakers, playing consumer desire against available "product."

At one level the promotional literature of the era is too prolific to treat comprehensively. TIAPEI commissioned its own advertising, as did the regional associations, and there were numerous other private sector initiatives. However, the industry's principal publicist and trend-setter remained the provincial government, and it was determined that its material be "on message." The plethora of glossy pamphlets, programs, promotions, guides, brochures, films, ads/advertorials, commercials, and maps generated through the Tourism Marketing Branch painted the Island's attractions in both broad and fine strokes, but each "lure" was meant to share the particular season's over-arching theme. If the 1970s might be remembered as the era of the tourist jingle, the 1980s and early '90s were surely the heyday of the sloganeer. For much of the 1980s a bold invitation to "Discover an island" alternated with "Feel our warmth," with its dual allusion to climate and hospitality. Starting in 1987, active verbs gave way to an appositive boast: "One of the world's great islands." A decade later, the unaffected grin of child actress Martha MacIsaac, star of television's *Emily of New Moon* series, amplified the season's catchphrase, "Come play on our island."[52] The clever phrasings dressed the same old tropes in trendy clothes, promising visitors warmth, welcome, and small "a" adventure. As Tourism's 1998–99 annual report explained, its new TV campaign "featured the Island as a destination where stressed-out, over-worked individuals could forget their worries," while the print message reinforced the return to innocence with its "Forget about your problems/ Remember how to play" theme.[53]

The rhapsodic introduction to the 1987 marketing and media plan might as well have been cribbed from one of the tourist brochures it brandished. It praised the "'special kind of light' that touches the Island, igniting multiple shades of green." It went on:

> The Island's shores are a never-ending surprise of white sand, red sand, sandstone capes … and our rivers delight us, skirting villages which are the lifeblood of our true character … The Island is the end of a journey

and a heartbreaking place to leave. There is, after all, romance amid the dunes and memories of a last glimpse of fields of grain as they wave good-bye in the wind.[54]

L.M. Montgomery would have been proud.

The verbal message of the chosen themes was reinforced by constant repetition. Amid the multiplication of multimedia lures, the annual *Visitors Guide* immediately became the centrepiece of the industry's promotional efforts after it adopted its current format in 1982. The next twenty years were, perhaps, its golden age in terms of scope and importance. Designed with flair, lavishly illustrated, with a print run that regularly approached a quarter million copies, it soon swelled to omnibus dimensions, a compendium of accommodations, attractions, activities, touring routes, and handicrafts, along with thumbnail sketches of the province's human and natural history. In 1982, the English-language edition of the *Guide* totalled sixty-four pages; by the end of the century, it was 200. A surprising number of Islanders even began collecting it, partly for visitors, partly to compare with earlier editions, partly to inform their own, intra-Island tourism, and partly, it seems, as a sort of Island almanac, a way of tracing the seasons in their own lives.

Paradoxically, the burden of being all things to all people at first made the *Visitors Guide* less visually revealing than earlier promotional literature. The political pressure on government to treat all attractions equally meant that the guide went from advertising many specific sites to advertising all of them. By the early '90s, the guide had abandoned this visually uninteresting policy in favour of a return to pictorial archetypes that traded the specific for the universal. Even in a government agency committed to spreading tourism across the province, promotional democracy had its limits.

Over time, the *Visitors Guide* shrank to more modest dimensions as the province deployed other ways and other media to court its clientele. The 2010 edition marked another, subtle change. The title went from the plural to the singular and possessive, "*Visitors*" to "*Visitor's*" guide. Instead of luring the masses, the guide now catered to the individual traveller's experience.

Of course, the *Visitors Guide* mainly influenced travellers who were already planning a vacation on Prince Edward Island. The bigger challenge was convincing them to come in the first place. That continued to mean treating editors, transportation providers, and tour operators to what the industry called "fam" – familiarization – tours and a judicious investment in print, radio, and television ads targeting preferred audiences. In 1992, for example, the Tourism Marketing Branch ran ads or inserts in twenty-nine magazines and twenty newspapers in the United States and eastern Canada with a combined circulation of 9.9 million.[55] As they had since the 1960s, marketers continued to partner with their counterparts in neighbouring provinces through shared promotions. For example, the Island joined the ACOA-sponsored Atlantic Canada Tourism Partnership in a pooling of resources to reach distant markets such as Europe and the Asia Pacific region. It was a shrewd way to stretch limited budgets and also a recognition that for such travellers a visit to the Island was most often part of a larger tour of the region. In 1995, a new era opened when the Tourism Division announced that on a trial basis it had published a version of the *Visitors Guide* on something called the "World Wide Web."[56] Finding one's audience would never be quite the same again.

Who did the marketers' blandishments bring? What did they want to see? Here again apparent continuity with the tourist past masked subtle changes. Pleasure seekers far outnumbered business travellers, usually by about ten to one. Typically about a fifth of visitors came to see friends or relatives.[57] They did not spend as much as other pleasure seekers, but they were more likely to come back. In the 1960s, the majority of the expatriates were apt to be Americans, who did not need to be wooed to come home. Changing patterns of out-migration over many decades had winnowed the American cousins; the expatriates were now more likely to be travelling from Ontario or the Maritimes. From the beginning of tourism on Prince Edward Island, Americans had always been the preferred customers. They still came, and their numbers were on the rise by the end of the century (27 per cent of pleasure visits in 1994), but the lure was less likely Aunt May's strawberry jam than favourable exchange rates and, as researchers determined, the sense that Atlantic Canada offered a "different yet familiar," slower, more "authentic" lifestyle.[58]

The Island's next-door neighbours, New Brunswick and, especially, Nova Scotia, remained its greatest source of tourists, although their share of overall visitation slid over the last decade of the century.[59] Quebec remained a volatile, highly elastic market. Ontario was the marketers' new promised land, the region that combined the most potential for growth with some of the biggest per capita spenders among Canadians.[60] Writing in the 1990s, journalist Calvin Trillin glibly generalized the Island's marketing strategy in this way: "PEI markets relaxation to Ontario, beaches and scenery to Quebec, and history and culture to New England."[61]

The marketing invitation to "come play" might have suggested something entirely different if applied to, say, Las Vegas. But the market here was still mainly families and, more and more as the century waned, the demographic bulge of aging, affluent baby boomers, now "empty nesters" no longer fettered to school vacations when planning travel. Marketing plans tended to lump them in with a slightly broader category: Double Income, No Kids, or DINKs. Money, time, education, and interest made them a much desired market segment. They offered hope for shoulder season expansion and longer stays.[62]

Spreading tourism across the seasons had long been one of Island tourism's ambitions, and all through the 1980s and '90s it was the subject of much speculation and state intervention. Even more than their regional neighbours, Island tourist operators still crammed most of their business into high summer, July and August.[63] No one needed Shakespeare to tell them that summer has all too short a lease. And yet expanding the season required rewriting a Catch-22 scenario: no one comes in the shoulder season because nothing is open, but nothing is open because no one comes. So, as planners wooed the bus tour trade and staged or sponsored special shoulder season festivals and events, grant programs made it worth tourist operators' while to open earlier and close later. For several seasons, Tourism even sponsored the Confederation Centre of the Arts to prolong its Summer Festival into September.[64]

By the mid-1990s, considerable effort had managed a modest bump in fall tourism, especially during early autumn, a generally reliable transition period from sun and heat to blustering cold. But the spring shoulder remained intractable, perhaps because of its notoriously erratic weather. As generations of marketers routinely rediscovered, the shoulder season was a tough sell, especially since any advertising campaign had to promote spring and fall without antagonizing operators by shortchanging the traditional peak season. The larger truth was that the image of Prince Edward Island was fixed in the popular imagination as a summer destination. It would take more than creative scheduling to shift that perception, and so, despite a muscular marketing regimen, the tourist season continued to have discouragingly narrow shoulders.

Those that came continued to come mostly in July and August. When they weren't staying with friends and relatives or in their own cottages, the tourists of the 1980s and '90s preferred hotels and motels, though that percentage was declining, partly because the number and kind of accommodations was on the rise. The era saw a tremendous growth in bed and breakfasts, which soon outnumbered the humble tourist homes of an earlier time. Once towards the lower end of the rental spectrum, B&Bs had reinvented themselves as artful accommodations that often combined heritage charm and upscale amenities. Even provincial campgrounds enjoyed a renaissance after a decade of decline and retrenchment. The young baby boomers of the 1960s, who once had camped by choice and financial necessity, were now returning in middle-age in campers and RVs.[65]

Successive surveys suggested that sightseeing continued to be the most popular pastime (in terms of both intention and actuality).[66] As in the past, the beaches beckoned the young (and the very young's guardians). Some visitors came in order to conspicuously do nothing; most, according to the consultants, craved active experiences, although hunting and fishing, the presumptive pastimes of Victorian males, mattered far less than other forms of outdoors recreation (with the notable exceptions of deep-sea fishing and angling for Bluefin tuna). The bigger spenders were said to crave culture and heritage. As it had in the past, "getting away from it all" meant getting "to" a place that felt different but not intimidatingly strange. Tellingly, travellers spent far more money on places to stay, things to eat, and souvenirs than they did on actual attractions.[67]

Although the tourist plant appears to have upgraded in response to a 1980 study's urgent call to modernize and professionalize, its essential nature continued to illustrate yet another paradox that resided at the heart of Island tourism. For the same study had found that most tourism businesses were profitable mom-and-pop operations that succeeded because of their small scale, low level of financing, occupational plurality, and family labour. In other words, they had thrived for precisely the reasons that were allegedly holding them back.[68] The implicit argument of the tourism plant analysis, then, was that what worked in the past set unacceptable limits on future growth.

In spatial terms, the mass of visitors still flocked to Cavendish and, especially on rainy days, to Charlottetown. A smaller, but significant number frequented the other North Shore beaches and ventured as far west as Summerside. But despite decades of strategic planning and considerable effort, the rest of the province still felt like leftovers. Into the mid-1990s, "Up West" and Kings County continued to receive only a fraction of the visitation to Prince Edward Island, and those who came generally spent less than other tourists. The province's small size encouraged visitors to lodge in a central location and tour the peripheries in a series of day trips.

But was tourism's "golden triangle" – Borden/Summerside, Cavendish/National Park, Charlottetown – the most popular and promoted tourist area because it was central, because it was the most attractive, because it had the most attractions, or simply because that was where public and private money had invested in tourism for the past century? There was a chicken-or-egg quality to this sort of discourse among those who habitually complained about neglect of the extremities that government generally chose to ignore. Instead, during the Development Plan years, it had invested heavily in resort complexes in the east and west to jump-start entrepreneurship in those regions. It had developed (and, predictably, under-funded) its network of provincial parks across the Island to augment recreational opportunities (adding "Parks" to the tourism department's title for a period) and spread a necklace of Visitor Information Centres along the main highways. Meanwhile, the *Visitors Guide* studiously avoided playing favourites, promoting all parts of the province equally.

Yet, in terms of the Island's assets, it was an inescapable fact that not all regions were endowed equally. Of the longstanding tropes associated with

Prince Edward Island in repeated tourist surveys, potatoes and pastoral culture gave no particular advantage to any one area, but beaches, Anne of Green Gables, and Confederation still favoured specific locations. The North Shore had the haunts associated with L.M. Montgomery, and its beaches had lifeguards and other amenities. Charlottetown was – by parliamentary resolution – the "Birthplace of Confederation," and right next door to Province House was *Anne of Green Gables – the Musical*. And so, the conundrum of how to grow tourism equitably across the Island continued. As with the shoulder season strategy, the chosen way forward proved paradoxical: developing new thematic emphases while doubling down on the old ones.

Although the pastoral landscape had long been central to Prince Edward Island's tourist appeal, the environmental turn that characterized the early 1970s had signalled a new variation on the old theme. There was no real "wilderness" in Canada's most anthropogenic province, and its wildlife was mostly found in small town Legions and downtown bars, but given its largely rural terrain of field and woodlot, land and sea, there was lots of what historian Richard Judd calls "second nature," that is, nature mediated by human hands.[69] And it was easy to be out in it. The environmental lobby in the province, a collision of conservationists (mainly hunting and fishing enthusiasts keen to protect habitat and promote their sport) and preservationists (who valued "nature" for its own sake), had grown steadily stronger since the early '60s. In 1979, the Island Nature Trust became Canada's first provincially based nature conservancy, and in 1987, Prince Edward Island became the first province in Canada to produce a provincial conservation strategy.[70]

By then, tourism planners had jumped on the trend. In 1987 the regional director for Parks Canada – since 1973, the new name of the federal parks agency – convened a two-day conference on "Tourism and Nature." One major outcome was the decision to adopt as a promotional theme for 1988 "Touch Nature," which promoted recreational encounters with the Island environment.[71] Soon the Touch Nature logo, featuring the silhouette of a Great Blue Heron in flight, was showing up on a variety of promotional materials that packaged activities such as bird watching and hiking. Although the natural history emphasis was reportedly well received, Touch Nature soon had to yield its place in the sun to other promotional ideas. In any case, according to yet another study, this one exploring the potential for "green tourism," Island operators had been poorly positioned to package attractions for green tourists.[72]

In the context of Prince Edward Island, argued Smith, Green and Associates, "green tourism" in the early '90s really meant "nature tourism," and they defined it in very broad terms as "travel whose primary objective is to enable visitors to experience and enjoy nature first-hand, in an environmentally sensitive way, while respecting local traditions and contributing to the conservation of ecosystems."[73] Their consideration of green tourism activities canvassed both the active and the passive, what was already happening but could be done better, and what might be done if properly encouraged. There were typical ecotourism pastimes, such as whale and seal watching, birding, and nature art, but also a comprehensive range of outdoor recreations: hiking, cycling, horseback riding, beachcombing, skating, skiing, windsurfing, sailing, canoeing, and kayaking. Snorkelling/scuba diving made the list. Swimming (but not sunbathing) found itself rebranded as a form of green tourism, as did fishing – so long as you put the fish back where you got them. Viewing land-, star-, and seascapes rounded out the generously inclusive catalogue of packageable experiences.[74]

How much touching can nature take before it spoils? No one gave it much thought in late twentieth-century Prince Edward Island: the rate of nature consumption was still too modest to place noticeable stress on the natural environment, except perhaps in Cavendish. But that did not mean tourism and environmentalism made comfortable bedfellows. The shallow consensus that nature should be shared proved fragile, and it quickly broke down when ambitious private development proposals clashed with nature advocates' determination to protect sensitive habitat. Caught uncomfortably in the middle of this tension was the provincial government, anxious to facilitate tourism growth and chary of tampering with the rights of private property, yet legislatively empowered to regulate development and morally tasked by many voters with being good stewards of the environment. As the state struggled to reconcile these warring agendas, "touching nature" took on a whole new meaning.

Figure 5.2 • The Touch Nature subtheme for 1988's marketing campaign touched off four consecutive years of special theming. The Festival of the Descendants promoted the 125th anniversary of the Charlottetown Conference, while two heritage-based themes played off the Island's Irish and Scots heritage. Despite considerable promotion, none provided an antidote to the global economic recession that depressed visitation numbers, and the annual special theme experiment was more or less abandoned after 1991. Tourism PEI.

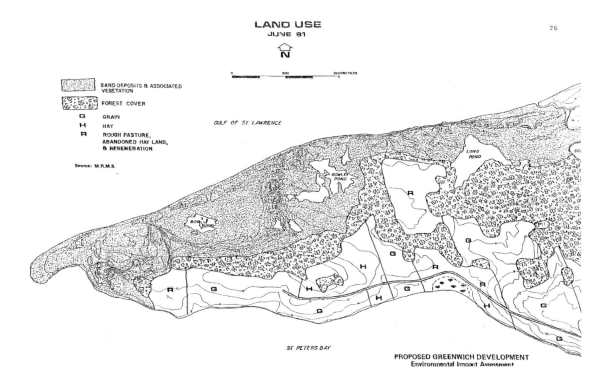

Figure 5.3 • Planned development for the Greenwich peninsula near St Peters represented both threat and opportunity: profit for developers, a piece of paradise for prospective sojourners and property owners, jobs for locals, environmental threat for conservationists, and loss of patrimony for heritage advocates. For Parks Canada, which eventually acquired the site to be an addition to PEI National Park, it represented an opportunity to correct mistakes it felt it had made in overdeveloping the park for tourism.

The frequent antagonist in these highly public disputes was the Island Nature Trust, which acquired a full-time executive director, Diane Griffin, in 1984. Feisty, well informed, and media-savvy, Griffin preferred "good planning to confrontation," as Rosemary Curley observes,[75] but she did not run from a fight. Backed by the vocal minority and bankrolled by their donations, the Nature Trust fought successful battles to thwart resort development schemes at Deroche Pond near Blooming Point and on the abandoned farmlands of Boughton Island at the mouth of Cardigan Bay. But the poster child for the conflict between tourist development and wilderness conservation was the struggle over the Greenwich peninsula, a long finger of land dividing St Peters Bay from the Gulf of St Lawrence on the north side of PEI.[76]

In 1988, the Island Nature Trust spearheaded a controversial campaign to block off-Island developers from building a $40 million, 600-unit resort complex, complete with an eighteen-hole golf course, marina, restaurant, and private air strip, in an ecologically sensitive area near the western tip of the peninsula.[77] The 1,400-acre site included towering parabolic sand dunes, rare wildlife habitat, and the earliest archaeological evidence of human habitation in the province.[78] It also featured superb beaches, a sheltered bay for boating or windsurfing, and stunning vistas.

At that point the question of what development to allow at Greenwich had been simmering for nearly two decades, ever since British Columbian real estate developers H.R. Dickie Ltd had acquired the property at the end of the 1960s. The battle lines were stark and predictable. The private developers dismissed any negative environmental or cultural consequences with talk of buffer zones, (limited) public access, and solemn promises to respect local sensibilities.[79] Cynics distrusted their assurances, and even moderate opinion railed against delivering a valuable part of the province's environmental and cultural heritage into the hands of outside interests. As with Eastern Kings residents in pursuit of a second national park during the mid-1960s, local residents were desperate for jobs and development. They rallied to the prospect of work during construction, service jobs afterwards, rising property values for everyone, and more tourist spending within the region. They rankled at outside interference in what they perceived as a local issue. "It's ironic," commented one resident, "there is so damn much concern about maintaining the national beauty in Greenwich by people who don't live there. They don't have to worry about maintaining their churches, their schools, and educating their children."[80] The provincial government was unavoidably involved; back in 1975, the minister of conservation and tourism, Gilbert Clements, had declared the Greenwich peninsula a special planning and conservation zone.[81] On several occasions already in the early '80s, it had used the special status to delay or defer development proposals.

Years of debate, legal delay, and public confrontation presumably frightened off prospective investors. Finally, in 1995, the province acquired the core of the Greenwich site, some 900 acres in three parcels, from the latest set of developers, George and Phyllis Diercks, by trading adjacent property with them. Three years later, the provincial government gifted the land to Parks Canada to become a detached annex to the PEI National Park.[82] Greenwich had been "saved."

For Parks Canada the addition of a block of environmentally significant habitat represented a belated denouement to the "second national park" saga of the early 1970s. Parks Canada officials had craved more wilderness; now they had it. They had also learned the value of extensive consultation with stakeholders as they felt their way forward with eco-acceptable development of their new acquisition. Early on there were plans to build a forty-bed ecolodge onsite and talk of major tourist development just outside its boundaries, but public pressure soon scotched that idea.[83] The most militant eco-activists demanded that people be entirely barred from the Greenwich annex to the park. Instead, Parks Canada set an annual quota of 100,000 visitors – an estimated 1,000 per summer day – more than it preferred but less than tourism promoters would have wanted. To the relief of environmentalists and

Figure 5.4 • The Confederation Trail's conversion of 435 kilometres of abandoned railbed into a trans-Island hiking, cycling, snowmobiling, and ski trail was a 1990s tourism success story, particularly because it so clearly benefited tourists and Islanders alike. Tourism PEI.

the chagrin of many locals, the expected stampede of tourists to Greenwich did not materialize. The number of visitors never approached the allowable maximum. For better and for worse, Greenwich did not become the next Cavendish. But then, that was never what Parks Canada had intended.

For the little village of St Peters, a few miles from the front gate of Greenwich, having a national park with minimal development did have a positive knock-on effect, even if it fell short of press conference boasting. Park-related spending helped the local economy without sparking a land boom or attracting major outside investment. It might be argued, in fact, that the new row of craft shops on the St Peters causeway got as much business from its location at the eastern end of the most scenic stretch of another major nature tourism investment, the creation of a trans-Island hiking/cycling/snowmobiling trail along the former route of the Prince Edward Island Railway.

Once the principal means for tourists to get to and around the province, the old railway (since 1919 absorbed into Canadian National Railways) had died a slow death through progressive amputation of its unremunerative service. Even before the last train rolled out of the province at the end of 1989, Islanders had begun to discuss what could be made of the 472 km of abandoned rail bed.[84] In 1991, executive council established the Rail Lands Development Corporation with a mandate to develop a master plan for the abandoned rail lands.[85] The Tourism Industry Association knew what should be done. As it told consultants engaged by the Department of Tourism, Parks, and Recreation, "the availability of the rail lands presents a unique and almost unparalleled opportunity to develop a new tourism product in the Province and also to expand tourism into areas of the province in a way hitherto not possible." Converting the rail bed to recreational use would benefit Islanders, of course – and that was a key argument in forging broad consensus – but the advantages for nature tourism were too obvious to ignore. In 1994, with rails and movable property now removed, the province purchased the former rail line from CN's parent, the federal government – then used mostly federal money to develop it.

Over the next four years, "Rails to Trails" incrementally converted the rail bed into a popular, trans-Island recreation corridor.[86] Given the railway's historic role in forcing PEI into political union with Canada, there was a certain irony in naming its replacement the "Confederation Trail." But then, in the 1990s, it seemed that anything not tied to Anne of Green Gables was warped into name-checking the Island's national status as the Birthplace of Confederation. Heritage tourism, especially Confederation-related tourism, had become big business.

By the mid-1980s, the widespread sense of urgency that fired the heritage movement of the 1970s had settled into a genteelly underfunded maturity. The Museum Act of 1983 officially enacted a provincial museum system with a human and natural history mandate, grafting it onto the old Heritage Foundation. The reorganization signalled a subtle shift away from activism towards less strident forms of preservation, conservation, display, and interpretation. With Parks Canada now responsible for the upkeep and interpretation of Province House, and lacking the convenient occasionalism of the centennial era, interest in marketing the Island's status as "Birthplace" also lapsed for a time. All of that changed in the second half of the 1980s when new research told tourism strategists what artists and heritage advocates already believed, that cultural tourists were a highly lucrative – hence desirable – species of visitor.

In the 1980s Western society's search for authentic experience encountered an internally driven, heritage-inspired push for a return to the sort of tourism that emphasized what was distinctive rather than generic about Prince Edward Island. The impulse played to postwar tourists' desire to recover a sense of cultural continuity by visiting more traditional, more deeply rooted ways of being. The desire differed more in degree than kind from the "pastoral people in a pastoral landscape" trope of earlier tourism, except that it now took on a greater specificity. This cult of authenticity, tourism historians argue, bespoke the transience and felt rootlessness of postmodern urban North America.[87]

And so, modern tourism on Prince Edward Island, as elsewhere, once again exposed one of its central contradictions. The tourist experience has to be regarded as genuine rather than ersatz, and it values spontaneity. Yet, at the same time, it must be conveniently consumed and consistently reproduced. However "authenticity" is defined, visitors seldom have time or inclination to discover a culture on their own terms. It needs to be packaged for them. In other words, mass tourism requires commodification. Tourism, after all, is inescapably self-conscious; it is performed under the gimlet-eyed scrutiny of what sociologist John Urry calls the tourist gaze. The calculus of profit dictates that even what is intrinsic to the physical and, especially, cultural landscape becomes to some degree contrived. Tourism operators are entrepreneurs, not philosophers, and it should not be surprising that Island tourism did not directly confront the industry's underlying dilemma. Yet if the tourist experience was to be scripted, its scriptwriters were at least convinced that it should take its stories from real life.

As with so much else in the era, the stepping-stones to the new wave of cultural tourism were a series of consultants' studies. In August 1987, the DPA Group submitted "Opportunities for Development; A Proposal to Commemorate the Birthplace of Canada" to the province's Heritage Resources Steering Committee. Once again it called upon tourism partners to exploit the niche strength represented by the Confederation theme, but this time within the context of the Island's larger history. The more inclusive approach recognized that provincial heritage organizations were now necessary stakeholders, but it likely also reflected the convictions of the report's principal investigator, John Eldon Green, who as deputy minister of social services back in 1973 had the audacity to join the Brothers and Sisters of Cornelius Howatt.[88]

DPA's follow-up study in 1988 argued the economic importance of the Island's cultural industries, especially when it came to tourism.[89] The study covered the literary arts, performing arts, visual arts, arts education, crafts, film and video, sound production, heritage institutions, and festivals. "There is a significant but imprecisely identified linkage between tourism and cultural industries on PEI," it found. Since "culture buffs" spent more than the average tourist, they should be targeted, and cultural agencies had a valuable role to play since they "help present to visitors an understanding of the inner life of the province." Those sectors needed development and encouragement, and government's job was to be catalyst, promoter, regulator, and funder. The cultural industries report was a pivotal study and was often referenced in years to come to provide a hard economic rationale for state investment in arts and heritage. In the 1970s, heritage had been preserved primarily for Islanders, in order to protect their sense of self. Tourism was considered a welcome by-product. Now, heritage would be packaged particularly for tourists with the tacit approval of a heritage sector short of resources and sensitive about its low funding priority.

226

The Summer Trade

The fresh commitment to culture and heritage soon translated into successive marketing initiatives. The "Touch Nature" subtheme developed for 1988 yielded pride of place in 1989 to the Festival of the Descendants, which played off the 125th anniversary of the Charlottetown Conference. The event was modestly successful in drawing heritage-minded tourists, especially the rather narrow cohort of actual descendants of the original Fathers of Confederation. The most visible – and lasting – legacy of the year's special initiatives was the Confederation Players, a troupe of young actors in period costume representing all twenty-three Fathers of Confederation (and several "Mothers"), who made personal appearances and performed skits based on the Charlottetown Conference. A scaled-down version of the program, employing students and editing out most of the original delegates, soon became a permanent fixture of summer in the city, the reenactors soaking their Confederation-era garb with successive generations of historically accurate sweat.

Nineteen-ninety was designated the year of the Irish. The season's new subtheme, "We're Akin to Ireland," played up the province's substantial Irish roots and rolling green countryside in an appeal to Irish Americans, who might not be able to afford Ireland itself but could encounter a reasonable facsimile just a few hundred miles to the north.[90] By the time that 1991's Scottish-themed "Road to the Isle" ran its bag-piped, tartaned course, the enthusiasm for one-off subthemes was clearly waning. After all, Nova Scotia – "New Scotland" – had already cornered the Highland-culture tourist market, even if Prince Edward Island had proportionately far more people of Scottish descent. Meanwhile, tourist operators without any Celtic axe to grind had grumbled at the special treatment afforded those ethnicities. More to the point, the subthemes could not demonstrate success. From 1989 to 1992, tourism numbers were dragged down by a painful round of recession that was evidently impervious to heritage.

The cultural impact of the themed promotions is more difficult to parse. A regional revival of interest in traditional fiddling and its fusion with modern rock music to create a unique "East Coast" music was contemporaneous with, but not a product of, Island tourism's summer romance with cultural heritage. Nor was the College of Piping and Celtic Performing Arts in Summerside, which gathered momentum in the early 1990s and played well to tourists.[91] They were related phenomenon rather than a chain of cause and effect. What tourism's investment in cultural heritage did encourage was the creation of a sort of cultural simulacrum. In the same way that commercial lobster suppers facsimiled "old-fashioned" Island cuisine and state-sponsored training programs had revived "old-fashioned" handicrafts (or, sometimes, coaxed them into existence) to supply the tourist market, institutionalized event attractions such as *ceilidhs* (from the Gaelic word for "visit") recreated "old-fashioned" entertainment for visitors and locals, taking an actual tradition, the community concert, and giving it a faux backstory (a uniquely Gaelic origin) as a way to popularize it. As Cape Breton's experience had already illustrated, the new form of *ceilidh* saved traditional music by moving it from the kitchen to the stage. The same might be said of the culture that had provided the music with its context.

The past is always messier than history pretends in its telling, and not all heritage tourism fits neatly into the linear, cause-and-effect narrative of consultants perceptively encouraging what became trends. Even while the Scots and the Irish were taking their turn in the tourism spotlight, other ethnicities vied for attention and funding as they turned to tourism to bolster self-pride and communal identity alongside economic development.[92] In the francophone Evangeline region west of Summerside, insular pride in *la survivance* morphed into a more robust, tourist-directed display of heritage. In 1971 a winter works project involving local fishermen in Mont Carmel had created the Acadian Pioneer Village, a huddle of log cabins meant to evoke an 1820s Acadian settlement. Traditional Acadian dishes, such as *râpure*, *poutine*, and *fricot*, soon highlighted the menu at the adjacent restaurant, L'Étoile de mer. (La Boeille discotheque, which opened the same year in nearby Abram-Village, was just as historic – if somewhat less historical.)[93] When the restaurant launched an Acadian-themed dinner theatre, Cuisine à Mémé, in 1985, it launched a number of careers as well, including several founding members of Barachois, one of the most successful Island musical acts of the 1990s.[94] Barachois's exuberant blend of cheeky comedy and traditional Acadian music successfully projected Acadian culture to both anglo- and francophone audiences. That was the larger ambition of the cultural complex in Mont Carmel as well. By 1985, regional development funding combined with cooperative principles had helped add a motel, swimming pool, and sixty-seat lounge to the existing site.[95] Despite American visitors' perpetual fascination with Acadians – a likely legacy from Longfellow's famous epic poem, *Evangeline*, and certainly tied up with Acadians' perceived "otherness" – tourism marketing had taken little notice of the province's francophone heritage, aside from ritual references to Jacques Cartier's "discovery" of the Island in 1534. Now, belatedly, it began to take more notice. In 1987, with help from the secretary of state, Tourism hired future MLA Robert Maddix as a development officer to help foster tourism growth in the Evangeline region.[96]

As with tourism's heritage thrust generally, it was difficult to measure success when so many other factors affected statistical indicators. It would take more than Acadian cuisine and a modest pioneer village to break Island tourism out of its well-worn trackways. Nor was the marketable Acadian

Figure 5.5 ▪ Mi'kmaw handicrafts included decorative yet functional baskets such as this one. The art of basket-making was revived in the 1970s and '80s with an eye to the burgeoning tourist market for Indigenous souvenirs.

culture confined to the Evangeline region (or even to francophones).[97] Yet the impact on Acadians' own self-image was considerable. By the 1990s, Evangeline had positioned itself as the heartland of authentic Acadian culture, and its tourism providers felt they were sharing rather than exploiting it.

Tourism and tradition continued to make comfortable bedfellows for the Mi'kmaq First Nation as well. The revival of basket-making techniques in the 1970s extended into the next decade as Band councils cast about for ways to generate income and self-esteem. By 1984 a group of Mi'kmaq had formed the Minegoo Arts and Crafts Society, which focused on basket-making as a way to preserve culture and provide a living for Mi'kmaw craftspeople.[98] The following year, a small basket-making factory went into production in East Royalty. Like most new businesses of the time, it was seeded with federal funding, in this case, from Canada Employment and Immigration, Ottawa's Native Economic Development Program, and the Department of Indian and Northern Affairs. By the time it celebrated its third anniversary in 1988, it had ten full-time employees, annual sales in excess of $120,000, and a comprehensive line of handcrafted Mi'kmaw baskets for "gift shops and market garden trades." Within a year, the venture had folded, done in by over-expansion, high overheads, and a loss of federal funding.[99] The reappropriation of Indigenous traditions was a small triumph, but tourism had not paid the bills.

The next time that the Mi'kmaq ventured into tourism's deep waters, their strategy would weld together one contemporary trend, environmental tourism, with another, cultural tradition: Indigenous peoples' longstanding image as stewards of the environment. In 2004, the Lennox Island First Nation launched an ecotourism complex as the physical centrepiece of its Aboriginal Ecotourism Strategy, an ambitious assemblage of experiential tourist activities that included a hiking trail, kayaking, boat charters, a nature shop, restaurant, and Mi'kmaw cultural centre.[100] Their version of ecotourism was thus grounded in traditional teaching.

Critics have argued that when customary practices become acutely self-conscious, they end up being artificial.[101] Certainly, the "traditional culture" to which tourism promoters and cultural preservers gave a forum was now a recollection of something that had once been spontaneous and natural. And yet, because modernization came to them relatively late, Islanders *were* a great deal closer than many other North Americans to the customs and practices that their tourism commodified. Even within the relentless reductionism that characterizes modern tourism, there was a nearby authenticity, a time within memory, that could inform the stylized version of traditional culture that entertained visitors hungry to connect with an earlier time.[102] Tourism did not generate these cultural trends; it simply capitalized them. In return, its marketing accents and promotional dollars lent them an energy that has long outlasted the special marketing themes.

As the heritage thrust in tourism promotion gradually blunted, defeated by hard times and lack of demonstrable success, Confederation remained. In December 1990, Premier Joe Ghiz appointed the Confederation Birthplace Commission (popularly known as the Birthplace Explored Commission) to produce a plan of action to "develop and present the Charlottetown region as the birthplace of Canada." Ghiz, the first Canadian premier of non-European descent, was a passionate Canadian nationalist caught up in the rolling constitutional crisis that had begun with the repatriation of the Canadian Constitution without Quebec's consent, deepened with the failure of 1989's Meech Lake Accord, and would soon produce the abortive Charlottetown Accord. "If we are to have powerful dreams," Ghiz orated in announcing the commission, "we must first have powerful memories."[103] The Birthplace Explored Commission felt that developing the birthplace theme could "build a bond of understanding and national pride among all Canadians to counter the forces of fragmentation throughout the country."

But it also pointedly emphasized that it would "diversify PEI's [i.e. not just downtown Charlottetown's] base of visitor attractions, drawing more people to the province and holding the promise of substantially increased off-season visitation." Echoing conventional wisdom, its report argued that birthplace-inspired tourism would play to emerging trends: "'short stay' vacations which enrich the visitor through culture, learning, and enjoyment of the environment."[104]

The commission's findings, released in October 1991, set out a template for spreading the benefits of "Birthplace" status across the greater Charlottetown area and the rest of the province, making "the setting worthy of the theme" through a program of heritage preservation and development, and raising awareness through strategic promotions and events. Its principal recommendation was the creation of an administrative agency responsible for those things, a capital commission similar in some respects to the one in Ottawa. The agency was duly legislated, and for the rest of the decade it pursued its work, although its impact outside of the downtown was perhaps questionable. The Capital Commission invented the Festival of the Lights, built around Canada Day, and the Festival of the Fathers. The latter was originally held in early September to coincide with the annual anniversary of the original Charlottetown Conference but was gradually inched back into late August before Labour Day could summon vacationers home for school. Instead of elbowing its way into the shoulder season, the festival was actually pinched by it.

The Capital Commission began well, bolstered by the Charlottetown Area Development Corporation's (CADC) ongoing efforts to rehabilitate the city's deteriorating waterfront. In 1995, the two groups converted an abandoned oil tank farm on the Charlottetown waterfront into a six-acre park.[105]

Figure 5.6 ▪ Whereas Province House offered the Confederation Chamber, and the Confederation Centre honoured the nation's founders through the arts, a new Founders' Hall, completed in 2001, converted the Confederation story into educational entertainment. It never met expectations in terms of visitation and closed in 2016.

The following year, the two rescued an architectural remnant of the old Prince Edward Island Railway dating from 1876, the red sandstone "Brass Shop," from layers of soot and neglect, and turned it into a visitor information centre. Of the two surviving brick sheds on the abandoned railyard next door, one was deemed beyond repair, but the other was creatively repurposed as Founders' Hall, a Confederation-themed tourist attraction adjacent to the visitor portal provided by the nearby cruise ship dock.[106] At around the same time, an extension to the newly built Charlottetown bypass helped convert Water Street from a forgotten back street into a major auto entry into the city.

Gradually, the Capital Commission would stray (or was nudged) from its mission statement. That tourism ultimately took precedence over nation building was symbolized by its merger in 2006 with Meetings PEI to form Tourism Charlottetown.[107] One of the reorganized agency's first decisions was to cancel the Festival of the Fathers because it was "not enough of a tourism draw."[108] Founders' Hall, opened amid much fanfare in 2001, was an artistic success, more or less, but a business failure. Although it saved a valuable piece of architectural heritage, its trendy, high-tech invocation of the Confederation story could not generate enough visitors to pay the rent, even as historians quibbled at its historically selective, celebrationist tone.[109] After years of struggle, it closed in 2016. Three years later, it was reinvented as an urban market.

Could there be too much Confederation? In the 1990s, it waxed ever brighter in PEI tourism strategists' imaginations. The former Brothers and Sisters of Cornelius Howatt must have winced at its overweening shadow. When Parks Canada interpreted Province House, completed in 1847, it was hardly surprising that it would highlight the Confederation era. Yet when extensive restoration work was done on Government House, built in 1834, the restorers chose the 1860s period for its exterior finish. A generation later, the nearby defensive works at Fort Edward were restored to their 1860s appearance. When CADC constructed its waterfront park in 1995, it was dubbed "Confederation Landing." The Rails-to-Trails program produced the "Confederation Trail." The new car ferry on the Wood Islands–Caribou run was christened the MV *Confederation*. Four years later, with a conspicuous air of inevitability, the fixed link to the mainland became the "Confederation Bridge." Finally, in 2017, an act of Parliament formally recognized Charlottetown as "the Birthplace of Confederation." In the burgeoning world of branding, "site sacralization" had patently advanced to a whole new level, even if, as politicians might have warned, Confederation had its limits.[110] The same might be said for another great growth industry, Anne of Green Gables.

It was impossible to escape Anne of Green Gables in late twentieth-century Prince Edward Island. Her stock figure, with its red braids and straw hat, turned up everywhere, it seemed: in print promotions, on stage, at events and attractions. Through much of the 1980s, the province's annual *Visitors Guide* actually avoided giving Anne precedence, presumably to dodge accusations of favouritism from Anne-less tourist sites, but by 1991, Anne was not just featured, she was on the cover. By the end of the decade, she was ubiquitous in tourism promotion.

What had changed? In one sense, nothing. Over decades of tourism evolution, Anne and her Island had been "kindred spirits" in obvious and subtle ways. *Anne of Green Gables* did not create the appeal of the Island's pastoral landscape, but it brilliantly evoked it. As one literary scholar argues, "'The Island' is adolescence. And Adolescence, that time of intense dreaming, of romantic yearning and disturbing hostility, remains as a part of every consciousness."[111] What was new by the 1980s was not so much the nature of Anne's appeal as her reach.

Anne of Green Gables had already been adapted for the screen several times before Kevin Sullivan's two-part, made-for-television movie, starring Megan Follows as Anne Shirley, aired on CBC in December 1985. The ratings were spectacular; it became the most watched television program in Canadian history.[112] Beginning in February 1986, the film aired in the United States on PBS and then the Disney Channel to widespread acclaim. Over the next two decades Sullivan made no fewer than three sequels. Meanwhile, his Montgomery-inspired television series, *Road to Avonlea*, with Sarah Polley as Sara Stanley, had a seven-season, award-winning run on CBC (1990–96) and was syndicated around the world.

Others soon prospected where Sullivan had found gold. A new television series based on a later trilogy of Montgomery novels, *Emily of New Moon*, started shooting on Prince Edward Island in 1996 with funding assistance from Enterprise PEI and Islander Martha MacIsaac cast in the title role of Emily Byrd Starr.[113] Almost as soon as filming got underway, the principal set at Cabot Beach Provincial Park began attracting tourists.[114] In Charlottetown, the Confederation Centre of the Arts mounted a musical adaptation, *Emily*, in 1999. Attendance was sufficiently encouraging to bring it back the following season.[115] These works and others wooed Montgomery fans, but the gold standard in adaptations of her works remained Kevin Sullivan's phenomenally successful Anne franchise.

Save for a handful of long, establishing shots, both the *Anne* movies and *Road to Avonlea* were filmed on location in Ontario. Nevertheless, it was Prince Edward Island that viewers imagined they saw. These two shows in particular had a global distribution, and tourism marketers grasped that the shows' international reach meant international tourism potential. Although *Anne of Green Gables – the Musical* and other local productions might captivate audiences, they seldom drew them to the province. As with Montgomery's books, the Sullivan films created tourists.[116] A few months after Sullivan's *Anne* first aired, a survey of 4,000 first time visitors found that only 219 of them had been directly influenced to come to Prince Edward Island by *Anne of Green Gables*, but of that number, 139 people had been drawn by the new Anne movie, only eighty by the Anne books.[117]

One visitor cohort attracted almost exclusively by Anne of Green Gables were Japanese tourists. They were mostly young women, sometimes with chaperones or male partners in tow, highly visible in the tourist landscape.[118] There has been much speculation about the nature of Japan's fascination with *Anne of Green Gables*. Part of it was simple exposure. The novel was first translated into Japanese in 1952 by Hanako Muraoka, and was widely available in paperback after 1954. Besides being for a time prescribed reading in Japanese schools, it was often used as a text to teach English. By 1991, the novel had sold an estimated 2.5 million copies in that country.[119]

Of course, falling in love with "Red-Haired Anne" involved more than mere opportunity. Like many young Japanese in postwar Japan, Anne is an orphan but undaunted by her circumstances. She is plucky, irrepressible, and emotionally extravagant. Those were seductive traits in a society where, Japanese scholars observe, women were too often expected to conform, conceal, and keep silent. Moreover, Anne's life is embedded in a staid community ruled by convention and custom (as in Japan). Yet, instead of ostracizing Anne for her assertive individualism, the community comes to embrace it. She is not browbeaten into obedience; she is accepted for herself.[120] Other scholars emphasize the novel's love of family and its celebration of friendship, themes that played well to young Japanese readers caught up in what Donald Ritchie has termed "the cult of innocence."[121] The other major character in Montgomery's fiction, the Island's pastoral landscape, also resonated with Japanese society's deep reverence for nature, in this case nature as carefully curated garden.[122]

As exposure and attraction created potential tourists, official policy in Japan propelled them outwards. In the mid-1960s, the Japanese government reversed its previous position and began encouraging its citizens to go out and see the world.[123] Cultural approval combined with rising affluence to generate a highly visible tide of Japanese tourism that eventually washed the shores of Prince Edward Island ten thousand kilometres away. In 1987, the Tourism

Department was persuaded to float a special promotional campaign for the Japanese market, Anne of Green Gables – My Dream.[124] The initiative was periodically renewed in subsequent years. In 1991, about 8,000 Japanese tourists came to PEI as a highlight of their Canadian vacations, usually staying four nights as part of a ten-day tour. The reported number was 12,000 five years later.[125] Those visitors' romance with the land of Anne sometimes played out literally. By the turn of the century, an estimated fifty Japanese couples per year were getting married in package-deal ceremonies where Montgomery herself had chosen to be wed, at the Campbell home at Park Corner.[126] As Island folksinger Lennie Gallant wryly joked, "We put the 'Anne' in 'Japan.'"

The Japanese tourists spent far more than the average tourist, and over time a small tourism subindustry developed around serving their particular needs, such as translation services.[127] Some restaurants even began printing their menus in Japanese, as well as English and French, in a bid to attract their business. The attention the Japanese garnered masked the fact that they actually represented only a small fraction of the annual visitation numbers. But their presence made good copy for the journalists and travel writers that marketers courted each year. Bemused articles about the Japanese tourist phenomenon lucratively showcased Prince Edward Island, though not to the Japanese market; the free publicity really targeted the curiosity of thousands of potential North American visitors. While tourism marketers were willing to play up Japanese visitors to travel writers, they are conspicuously absent from the promotional literature. In the thousands of photographs published in the annual *Visitors Guide* during this period, there is not a single discernibly Asian tourist. The imagined audience remained resolutely Caucasian.

Visitor statistics at Green Gables House in the National Park provide a measure of Anne's burgeoning attraction. In 1983, 150,000 people trooped through the house, peering at "Anne's bedroom" and other entirely imagined recreations that artfully blended historical fact and literary fiction. Four years later, the number had soared to a quarter of a million visitors per year, and by 1995, when Parks Canada began charging a $2.50 admission fee, it topped 320,000 even though the site was open for eleven fewer days than in the previous decade.[128] In 2000, according to one estimate, 43 per cent of tourists to Prince Edward Island made the trek to Green Gables,[129] making it the single most frequented tourist site in the province. Going to Anne-based attractions was the second most common activity for visitors.[130]

A more informal, but no less telling index to the pervasiveness of Anne tourism could be found in the pages of the tourist guides and signed across the Island landscape, especially in the Cavendish Resort Municipality (itself an anomaly, being a rural municipality). Since the early 1920s, well before Green Gables became the lodestone at the heart of the Prince Edward

Island National Park, commercial sites along the North Shore had traded on L.M. Montgomery's works.[131] Decades of Anne tourism had greatly multiplied them by the 1990s. Some were austere and tasteful, even reverential; some less so.

And so, Anne pilgrims could tour the Lucy Maud Montgomery Birthplace, the elegantly understated Macneill Homestead, a schoolhouse museum in Lower Bedeque, a parsonage in Bideford, the Anne of Green Gables Museum at Silver Bush, and her well-groomed burial site in Cavendish – in other words, where she was born, raised, taught, boarded, married, and now is buried. And, of course, there was also Green Gables House itself, said to be the inspiration for Anne's fictional home, not to mention Avonlea Village, a faux hamlet theme park. They could seek out Anne-named landmarks such as the Haunted Wood, Lover's Lane, the Babbling Brook, and the perennially misidentified Lake of Shining Waters. To make sure they found all of the important locations, they could pick up a copy of *The Sacred Sites of L.M. Montgomery*,[132] and to make sure they fit them all in, they could package their explorations with Avonlea Tours.

Once they had finished with the sacred sites, Anne tourists could play golf at Green Gables Golf Course or just play at Rainbow Valley amusement park. When they got sleepy they could bed down at any number of Montgomery-themed accommodations: Green Gables Bungalow Court, Montgomery Tourist Home, the Lake of Shining Waters Lodge, Anne Shirley Motel and Cottages, Anne's Windy Poplars, Anne's Everglade Cottages, Avonlea Cottages, Ingleside Lodge, Rachel's Tourist Home and Cottages, White Sands Cottages and Campground, White Sands Motor Court, Blythewood Trailer Park, Kindred Spirits Country Inn and Cottages, Anne's Whispering Pines RV Park and Campground. When hungry, they could eat at Marilla's Lobster Lunch, relax at the Shining Waters Tea Room, experience fine dining at the Culinary Institute's Lucy Maud Montgomery Dining Room – even sample Marilla's Pizza. Once sated, souvenir hunters could shop at Miss Stacey's and Lady Cordelia's (both selling collectibles) or the Silver Bush Gallery Workshops, where they might purchase Anne Shirley Dolls, or at Cavendish Figurines (specializing in Anne-themed china sculptures) or Green Gables Keepsakes.[133] And if it was Annescape that they loved best, they could always donate to the L.M. Montgomery Land Trust, which was sworn to preserve the pastoral landscapes that the author had cherished.

This catalogue of businesses, attractions, institutions, and products is exhausting but by no means exhaustive – and it barely samples the proliferation of Anne merchandise, everything from red wigs and rag dolls to paintings and posters, from Anne of Green Gables chocolates to (nonalcoholic) raspberry cordial. In 1995 local artist Dale McNevin made her own cheeky contribution to the commodification of Montgomery's redheaded heroine. She created a painting that the buyer, Anne Putnam of Charlottetown's The Island Store, liked so much she turned it into a T-shirt that quickly caused a tempest in an Island teacup. The design was of a bikini-clad young woman on an Island beach, her back to the viewer, with telltale red braids and a straw hat dangling down her back. In one hand she carries a sand pail and plastic shovel. With the other, in a burst of exuberance, she is flinging her bra to the breeze. Although there was no explicit identification, the reference seemed obvious to would-be souvenir buyers. It was also obvious to a newly formed agency called the Anne of Green Gables Licensing Authority. Its representatives were not amused and accused McNevin and Putnam of "trading on the image." Claiming artistic licence, Putnam refused to be cowed, but when her store went out of business later that year, so did the T-shirt.[134] To casual observers, trying to banish the "topless Anne" seemed tantamount to breaking a butterfly upon a wheel, but the new licensing authority was not simply being prudish, it was making a point. Anne was no longer just a literary character, she was an industry, and vested interests were determined to assert their control over it.

Established in 1994, the Anne of Green Gables Licensing Authority (the "Annequisition," as some dubbed it) resolved a custody battle over the red-headed orphan between two parties with a proprietorial stake in how she was raised: the heirs of L.M. Montgomery and the government of Prince Edward Island. The Montgomery heirs wished to share in the considerable income generated by her commercialization; the Province was anxious to nurture the local crafts industry; both wanted to protect Anne's image from cheap or inappropriate exploitation. Well before copyright expired on Montgomery's works (fifty years after her death in 1942), her heirs had sought to trademark them.[135] In a deal that would later be the subject of protracted litigation, they licensed the Sullivan films in 1984 in exchange for a lump sum payment and a share of future profits.[136] Concurrently, the Province of Prince Edward Island declared its own claim to Anne based on the significant part the Island played in Montgomery's novels. When copyright officially expired in 1992, the province moved to trademark Anne's image.[137] The embarrassing legal battle that ensued ended with the former litigants agreeing to share custody within a newly created licensing agency. All of the Anne trademarks were then transferred to the new Licensing Authority and its eight-person board comprised of provincial officials and the Montgomery heirs.[138]

The stated purpose of the Anne Authority was "to protect the integrity of the images of Anne, to preserve and enhance the legacy of L.M. Montgomery and her literary works, and to control the use of Anne of Green Gables and related trademarks and official marks, including Green Gables House ('Anne' trademarks)." The authority required that purveyors obtain a licence from it for any "product, service, or event" employing "images of Anne" (defined as "words and images depicting the fictional characters, places, and events described in Montgomery's novel *Anne of Green Gables* and related novels"). To qualify, the product must be appropriate to the image of Anne, appropriate to the intended use, and of high quality – as determined by the authority.[139] (Topless Annes on T-shirts evidently did not meet the standard.) In deference to provincial wishes, properly licensed local producers were exempt from paying royalties to the Macdonald heirs. Mainland producers were not.[140] Twenty-five years on, scores of products are licensed each year by the Anne of Green Gables Licensing Authority although some legal scholars question the lawfulness of mixing moral protection of a cultural treasure with personal profit.[141] Anne might be an icon but she was also, as one journalist put it, "a cash cow."[142]

For those who feared that Anne hoopla was unhinging Island tourism or found the orphan's saccharine wholesomeness too "Lucy Maudlin," there was always *Annekenstein*. Through much of the '90s, Charlottetown's Off-Stage Theatre Company, masterminded by Rob MacDonald and director David Moses, titillated audiences with sketch comedy that gleefully lampooned "our Island's obsession with and dependence upon a freckled-faced, carrot-topped precocious piece of Edwardian fiction."[143] Sketches included the "World's Fastest Anne" (conveying the essential plot in less than three minutes), a "Win a Waif" contest (pitting Anne against Oliver Twist and Huck Finn to gain a foster home), an Anne-a-holics Anonymous support group for fans convinced Anne was real, and a slow-motion, Martin Scorsese version of the famous slate-breaking scene.[144] Although Off Stage would have welcomed prosecution for the sake of the publicity, they were safe from the Annequisition by reason of satire.[145]

If the Anne Authority played legal guardian, Anne herself had become something of a cultural bully by century's end. She was an industrial-strength monster, her image everywhere. It was perhaps inevitable, then, that at the height of her fame she would wind up on the Prince Edward Island licence plate. The province that had been "The Garden of the Gulf" for many years and "The Place to Be in '73" (and '74 and '75) now became "Home of 'Anne of Green Gables.'" Asked by the Motor Vehicle Branch to work up some ideas for a new Prince Edward Island automobile licence plate in 1992, designer Baxter Ramsay quickly roughed out several proposals, including Anne, Province House, and the Confederation Bridge, which at that point was a work in progress. So was Ramsay's Anne design, but the next time he saw his hasty sketch it was embossed on the 1993 licence plate.[146]

238

The Summer Trade

The choice of Anne to project Prince Edward Island's image (rather than the fact that the rendering looked suspiciously like Alfred E. Newman in a red wig) sparked a telling controversy. In a letter to the editor, Ian Munro complained, "Are we not sufficiently inundated with both the name and visage of this entirely annoying character? Does Prince Edward Island have nothing more to offer than the fact that it is the setting for an utterly beaten-to-death work of questionable literary merit?"[147] While others sprang to her defence – "Anne attracts tourists. It's best to flaunt what you've got," an editorial in the Charlottetown *Guardian* riposted – it was clear that some Islanders, at least, had developed an allergy to "Anne with an E." It was a particularly specific variant of "hospitility."

That tourist operators as well as the host society might be suffering Anne fatigue became public in 2000 when consultants unveiled a new five-year strategic plan for the Tourism Industry Association. Focus groups, it blandly reported, "felt that limits should be placed on further development in relation to the Anne of Green Gables theme which is well-exploited."[148] That year the musical *Emily* ended a modest, two-year run at the Confederation Centre of the Arts, and *Emily of New Moon*, the made-on-PEI television series, was cancelled after three seasons. The Anne wave had crested. And while its proponents might not concede it yet, so had another, Tourism's campaign to brand PEI as the Garden of the Golf.

Perhaps golf was only "a good walk spoiled," but it played particularly well to Prince Edward Island's touristic pretensions. Its measured rhythms paralleled Island society's traditional – and projected – sense of self. Its manicured fairways, water hazards, and contrived vistas were also nature-friendly (if one ignored the chemicals involved and the environmental costs of heavy irrigation).[149] It had the potential to bring more tourists in the shoulder season. And it catered to the tourist demographic that almost every consultant and industry observer of the era doggedly referenced, aging baby boomers with leisure, money, and an appetite for mildly taxing outdoor activity. That the sport was booming all across the Western world merely emphasized that the Island would have competition in its bid to become a golf mecca. As in the Development Plan years, when the government had used golf courses to anchor resort complexes meant to jump-start tourism in eastern and western Prince Edward Island, the state once again took the lead.

The Tourism Branch initially seeded the idea of the Island as a premier golf destination in the late 1980s by annually cosponsoring a Canadian

Professional Golf Association tour stop at provincially owned courses, beginning in 1988 at Brudenell.[150] Over the next decade, other high-profile events, such as exhibition matches and televised Skins Games featuring major PGA and LPGA stars amped up the interest in Island golf. It helped that Canada's top professional golfer, Lorie Kane, was a proud Islander. By the time that the province formed "Golf Island Inc." in 1991 to promote the sport, a new eighteen-hole championship course, designed by renowned architect Tom McBroom, was in the works for Lakeside. Perhaps not accidentally, it was directly across St Peters Bay from the abortive resort/golf course development at Greenwich. When it opened in 1993, The Links at Crowbush Cove quickly became a critical success, consistently ranked (despite its especially voracious mosquitos) as one of the top courses in Canada and reporting an operating surplus.[151]

Management of Crowbush was vested in government's Tourism Development Division, whose mandate was soon amended to include advancement and promotion of "PEI's golf product."[152] To find out how best to do that, it – naturally – hired consultants, in this case, industry giants KPMG Management Consulting. Its "A Golf Strategy for Prince Edward Island" (1994) quickly became the bible for growing the game's tourist potential.[153] KPMG began by reminding Islanders that golf was the fastest growing participation sport in North America, adding a million new golfers each year. Canada alone had 2.2 million golfers, a number that was increasing by 10 per cent annually. To tap into that lucrative market, PEI needed to develop a proper golf infrastructure. In 1994 Canada had 1,400 golf courses with 400 more projected by the end of the century. Prince Edward Island had eleven, only two of them rated as excellent.[154] On the positive side, the "golf impact" averaged $244 per visitor. Logically, then, the Island either needed more of its tourists golfing or more golfing tourists. What was required, the report outlined, was more quality courses, attractive vacation packages, and compelling publicity about "a land made for golf."[155] Its recommendations included the creation of another top-end, eighteen-hole course with ocean views as well as improvements to existing courses. The goal of the expansion was to increase the "round capacity" of the province from 299,000 to 338,000 rounds per year.

The instant celebrity of the new links at Crowbush implicitly endorsed the new marketing direction. In an awkward if telling pun, Tourism PEI titled its 1996–97 marketing plan "Driving Towards a Longer Season." By 1998, its annual report was touting the "dramatic increase" in golf's popularity in the province, citing a 15 per cent increase in the number of rounds played at provincially owned courses.[156] That April a separate body, Golf Links PEI, was incorporated to manage them. A year later, in June 1999, it was lodged under a new Crown corporation, Tourism PEI, created to handle the government's tourism enterprises.[157] Meanwhile, private developers were mobilizing

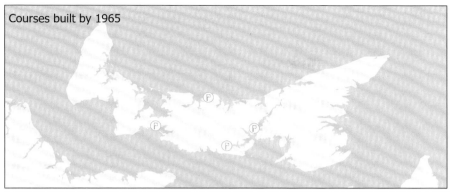
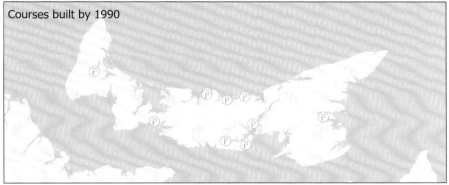
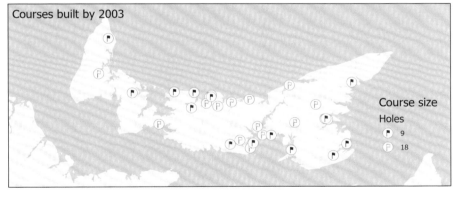

Figure 5.7 ▪ In the mid-1960s, there were only three eighteen-hole golf courses on Prince Edward Island. By 1994, there were eleven. By 2003, twenty-six.

to meet the anticipated tourist demand by constructing new courses at both ends of the quality spectrum. By 2003, when the Island's first golf course, Belvedere, celebrated its centenary, there were thirty-two courses in the province, all of them teeing up golf-bag toting visitors.[158] Tourism and golf had become regular playing partners.

Among KPMG's requirements for capacity building were "high service accommodation arrangements" to complement the challenging new course.[159] Accordingly, the new Conservative government signed a partnership agreement in 1998 with Calgary developer Hal Walker to construct a $10 million, 150-bed resort on provincially owned land adjacent to The Links at Crowbush Cove.[160] The confident drive toward luxury development promptly hooked into the rough. Despite generous promises of government funding, the embryonic project was plagued by lack of investors, environmental concerns over sewage disposal, multiple missed deadlines, unpaid contractors, and labour disruptions. When the resort finally opened in 2002, it was back-page news. Walker was long gone (along with his successor, Strait Crossings Inc.). The expenditure had jumped to $14.2 million, then dwindled to $8 million; the number of rooms from 149 to 118 then forty-eight (with thirty-two cottages); the resort operator had downscaled from an international chain to the eventual developer, Island-based Rodd Resorts;[161] and federal and provincial funding had accounted for all but $3 million of the publicized price tag.[162]

As the struggles at Crowbush uncomfortably demonstrated, golf's high profile was a double-edged sword. It accentuated failures as well as triumphs. That was nowhere better demonstrated than in the Conservative government's ill-starred decision in the late 1990s to follow KPMG's advice and add a fourth "signature" golf course to the three that Golf Links PEI already operated at Brudenell, Mill River, and Crowbush. Almost from the beginning, the Dundarave project, which came with a golf academy and coincided with a major expansion at Brudenell Resort, was dogged by controversy.[163] The site was carved out of Brudenell Provincial Park and handed over to a group of local developers that included several high-profile Conservative supporters, who then leased the finished course back to the province for $675,000 per year.[164] The course was built in record time, but within two years, the government bought it back from the "Group of 10" for $6.95 million, even though its own consultant had recommended a buying price of between $5.7 and $6.4 million.[165] At the same time, the province's technical school, Holland College, paid $3.55 million for the money-losing Golf Academy, which consultants had appraised at between $1.7 and $2.1 million.[166]

Government justified its purchase price for Dundarave on the grounds that the 48,000 rounds of golf projected there for 2000 and 2001 would collectively generate total revenues of $3.48 million. The actual numbers turned out to be 29,500 rounds and $2.45 million. In 2002, even that rate of usage fell, by 1,000 rounds, despite Dundarave's stellar 4.5 star rating from *Golf Digest*, and Golf Links PEI continued to ring up deficits.[167] Instead of driving Island tourism, golf was now defended as its loss leader. The editors of the Charlottetown *Guardian* did not lose faith in golf, but they doubted government's management of it: "Prince Edward Island's golf empire, and especially Dundarave, is built on a foundation of big promises, sweetheart deals and screwy mathematics."[168]

Government shrugged off the accusations of nepotism (easily, since the Opposition had only one seat in the legislature) and stood by its investments: what was an $80,000 deficit for Golf PEI, it sniffed, against the value of an $80 million industry? Nevertheless, Tourism Minister Greg Deighan confided to reporters in 2002 that "future developments in the sport would have to come from the private sector."[169] The next year, still smarting from the auditor general's criticisms, Deighan's successor as minister, Jeff Lantz, confirmed that his government had no plans to construct any additional courses. "We're at a saturation point now," he said.[170] In fact, in the decade after 2003, no new golf courses opened on PEI, while several closed or endured financial troubles.[171] The great golf boom was over.

While the whiff of patronage tarnished the glitter of Prince Edward Island's bold golf venture, larger realities limited the sport's impact on the tourism industry. In a 1999 update on the Island's golfing strategy, KPMG argued that golfing demand still exceeded supply.[172] Perhaps that was true, but by 2003, developers had clearly overbuilt; too many courses were chasing too few players. The lack of business was partly a function of economic cycles but also of the Island's short golf season, its distance from major population centres, and high green fees, which comfortably undercut those in urban Ontario but actively discouraged the local golfers that courses needed to supplement visitor rounds. The costly expansion at Brudenell had been expressly designed to "serve the more sophisticated end of the tourism market,"[173] but the emphasis on high-end courses may actually have discouraged duffers overmatched by the difficult layouts.

Whether government was best cast in the role of golf entrepreneur was also open to debate, some of it ideological in nature, and conclusions tended to be driven by the bottom line. When the province began actively trying to get out of the golf business in 2007, it could not find buyers for its four courses. The following year, it quietly wrote off $10 million in bad debt on Golf Links PEI's books. When the International Association of Golf Operators named Prince Edward Island its "Undiscovered Golf Destination of the Year" in 2010, it was a backhanded compliment, coming after fifteen years of concerted government promotion.[174] In 2015, after another golf season in which nonmember rounds on Island courses had declined, the Atlantic Institute for Market Research published a study of golf's impact on the Island economy. "Given the trends since the turn of the millennium," it reflected, "financial losses, course closures, weak tourism figures, and declining numbers for the amount of golf being played — one might wonder whether the original concept of using golf to lure tourists has been turned on its head so that other means of attracting tourists now are needed to save the golf industry."[175] Island governments had paid dearly to discover that golf is an expensive game.

The whole premise behind the golf strategy, which targeted a "sophisticated," high-end market, hinted at something else. Like the larger courtship of DINKs to bulk up the shoulder seasons, golf promotion privileged class over mass, balancing lower numbers against higher expenditures. There was no official policy change in tourism's annual reports or marketing plans; the summer trade still appealed to its traditional, broad market of family fun seekers. Yet the emphasis in the new initiative suggested a sea change in the nature of Island tourism as the millennium turned.

Hindsight's sharp vision when it came to golf strategy conveniently overlooked the buoyant, blinkered expansionism of the period during which it was framed. That *zeitgeist* owed much to the economic rebound of the mid-1990s but even more to a mega-project that was nearing completion, a fixed crossing that would connect PEI to the mainland. Its opening in the spring of 1997 capped a decade of wrenching debate because, depending on one's perspective, the "fixed link" either promised or threatened to transform Island life.[176] And Island life had long been at the heart of Island tourism.

Transportation bottlenecks at the ferries had continued to vex travellers into the early 1980s; at Borden alone, passenger numbers rose 128 per cent between 1965 and 1985, to 1.6 million people per year.[177] But the slowing in tourism growth and the launch in 1982 of a massive new ferry on Marine Atlantic's Borden–Tormentine run made frustrating waits for "the boat" there a thing of the past. The new *Abegweit*, a 250-car, icebreaking ro-ro ferry, was as elegant as a parking garage – an expensive parking garage, since it cost $50 million, over seven times the price of its midcentury namesake. In May 1988, Ottawa announced that it would also build a new vessel for Northumberland Ferries Limited at the other end of the strait. In between those events, the province marked the centenary of the first campaign to convince Ottawa to construct a fixed crossing to the mainland. As if to mark the occasion, Public Works Canada received no less than three proposals during 1985 from private-sector companies seeking to construct some sort of link across the Northumberland Strait.[178] One of the century's most durable fantasies had been revived. Cynics smiled, but this time was different, for Ottawa, not the Island, was doing the dreaming.

One principal motive was money. The price being bandied about for a fixed crossing, $500–600 million, was only ten times the cost of the new *Abegweit*. As a way to finance that, promoters revived a stratagem that Ottawa had summarily rejected back in 1969: private enterprise would take on the project in exchange for federal loan guarantees and annual subsidies. Discouraged at the escalating expense of new ferries, keen to promote a megaproject in the Atlantic region, and philosophically inclined towards privatization, the federal government of Brian Mulroney made it clear that a fixed crossing would be forthcoming – if Islanders wanted one. Suddenly, "the Fixed Link" became a full-blown public issue once more, engendering passionate debate about the transportational, economic, social, cultural, environmental, aesthetic, even metaphysical merits of fixed crossings versus marine ferries.

What Islanders thought of the renewed agitation was of considerable importance to its outcome. As political commentator David Milne noted at the time, the jurisdiction involved in a fixed crossing was federal, but the crossing's main impact would be provincial.[179] No one was more aware of that than Islanders themselves. A project that had once been pursued as a panacea for the Island's economic ills now encountered a groundswell of criticism. A substantial number of Islanders feared that a fixed link would create more problems than it solved.

There were two phases in the debate that followed: the campaign leading up to a nonbinding provincial plebiscite in 1988 about whether or not to pursue the idea and the trans-Island public hearings held in the late 1980s and early '90s after opponents forced an environmental assessment of the proposal. Like tourism itself, the sometimes-heated dialogue engaged both the real and imagined Prince Edward Island.

The leading anti-link group styled themselves "Friends of the Island," a title that managed to imply that its members were the true guardians of the Island's best interests. The Brothers and Sisters of Cornelius Howatt, whose barbed send-up of the 1973 centennial still lingered in memory, provided the spiritual underpinning and some of the leadership for the group, which formed in November 1987. To their way of thinking, the Northumberland Strait was a moat against cultural and economic imperialism, and an efficient ferry service was as much drawbridge as the Island needed. The Friends' friends included, for example, Local 127 of the Canadian Brotherhood of Railway, Transit and General Workers, the collective bargaining unit for Marine Atlantic ferry workers, whose livelihoods were at stake, along with the mayor of the Town of Borden, where many of the ferry workers lived. The PEI Fishermen's Association feared the disruption of fish habitat in the Northumberland Strait and consequent loss of income for local fishermen. Environmental groups were equally worried about habitats, although for different reasons. These were joined by reflex conservatives suspicious of change, especially change with an external impetus, and artists and intellectuals with metaphysical concerns about the continued erosion of cultural, political, and economic distinctiveness.[180]

245

Laws of Attraction, Rules of Engagement

The chief organization in favour of the link took similar care over naming. By calling themselves "Islanders for a Better Tomorrow," its founders refuted the notion that the fixed link project was being foisted on the province by outsiders and set themselves up as exponents of progress in opposition to those who were mired in the past, afraid of change, or both. The group was a loose alliance of organizations and individuals who either believed a fixed link was essential to future development or who stood to gain from its construction – sometimes both. Its members were confident that they spoke for the silent majority, and they resented their opponents' claim to the moral high ground. Although both sides promoted themselves as advocates rather than opponents, as positive rather than negative, the momentum of debate quickly cast "Friends of the Island" in the role of naysayers.

The fixed link debate unfolded in the media, at public meetings, in submissions and briefs, and in countless private arguments. In reductionist and somewhat moralistic terms, it has been framed as an argument about *quality* of life versus *quantity* of life, as measured in material terms.[181] The exchanges tended to cluster around three general impacts: economic, cultural, and environmental. While both pro- and anti-link campaigners professed to put the province's welfare before their own, sheer pragmatism determined how convictions translated into polemics. Self-interest, cultural philosophy, and gut instinct generally determined positions for or against the fixed link, but expediency shaped the arguments as advocates and opponents employed whatever weapons promised best in battle. Ferry workers destined to lose well-paying jobs developed an appreciation for environmental risk. Construction organizations anxious for work became advocates of the "progress" a fixed link symbolized. Tourism operators argued the merits of modernity in terms of transportation infrastructure even as they busily commodified traditional culture.

The tourism industry, in fact, was one of the principal drivers in the pro-link lobby.[182] Jim Larkin, TIAPEI's general manager, chaired Islanders for a Better Tomorrow. Early in the twentieth century, tourism advocates had favoured keeping cars out of the province. Now their basic argument was simple: all things being equal, the easier it was to drive to Prince Edward Island, the more tourists would come. And, from a business point of view, the more tourists the better. Citing survey statistics, they argued that the ferry ride to the Island was a deterrent for weekend sojourners, who were wary of delays in getting into or out of the province.[183] Moreover, they claimed, a fixed crossing of such extreme length might itself become a tourist attraction, particularly if a bridge were built.[184] They weren't alone. "I think it could be sold as one of the modern wonders of the world," Tom McMillan, Island MP and federal

246
—

The Summer Trade

minister of the environment, told a CBC documentary. "It could enhance the Island's attractiveness as an island and could be a tourist attraction."[185]

Marine Atlantic vigorously disagreed. Citing exit surveys done by the provincial Department of Tourism and Parks, it maintained that 70 per cent of respondents felt the ferry ride was actually one of the Island's attractions.[186] "Our PEI ferries are much more than simply passive vehicles which take tourists from one shore to another," it argued. "The ships themselves and their nine-mile voyage across a body of salt water offer visitors a suitably brief nautical experience – a unique experience for many people – that occupies a prominent place in the total package that makes a vacation in our province so enjoyable."[187] Marine Atlantic's self-interested assessment was shared by others. "Coming to the island by ferry is part of coming to the island," Dorothy Marks of Montague told Summerside's *Journal-Pioneer* in 1987, "and a [fixed] crossing will certainly destroy something unique to the island."[188] The same exit survey that touted the ferry trip found tourists split over their own preferences. Although 51 per cent of those surveyed favoured a fixed link over the ferry, 169,000 visitors said they would not visit more frequently if there was a fixed crossing, compared to 39,000 that would.[189]

The most common anti-link position when it came to tourism was to question whether more was necessarily better. Increased tourist traffic, Friends of the Island claimed, would clog Island roads and hog parking spaces.[190] The predicted congestion also raised doubts about the carrying capacity of the very resource that tourism exploited, the Island's pastoral landscape and traditional culture. Over-crowding and over-packaging might destroy the genuineness and distinctiveness of the experience that tourists sought.[191] That for many Islanders the cultural repercussions of link-fed tourism growth might more than offset its material benefits underscored the existential dimension of the fixed link debate (as well as Islanders' continuing ambivalence about tourism). While it was difficult for many people to articulate, "islandness" was central to their sense of identity. To be less of an island compromised, perhaps fatally, the province's uniqueness.[192] Would the Island still be an island if the Strait were bridged?

Whether or not that might matter to tourists, it mattered to Islanders. A "Resident Tourism Survey" conducted for the Department of Tourism and Parks and the Department of Regional Industrial Expansion in March 1989, before construction was certain, sampled the opinions of 307 Islanders about tourism and the possible impact of a fixed link. Of those polled, 53 per cent felt a fixed crossing would expand the tourism season. Only 9 per cent worried that it would shorten tourist stays, but 27 per cent feared overcrowding. More than half of respondents (54 per cent) thought the Island's way of life would be affected and 11 per cent agreed that it might diminish the province's distinctive identity.[193]

Joe Ghiz's Liberal government had shrewdly chosen a nonbinding plebiscite as its way of gauging Islanders' wishes so that it could abide by them. The ballot posed a simple but ambiguous question: "Are you in favor of a fixed link crossing between Prince Edward Island and New Brunswick?" What sort of link and under what conditions was not stipulated. On 18 January 1988, 59.1 per cent of those casting ballots opted in favour. Only in Kings County, where a fixed crossing would place the future of nearby Northumberland Ferries in jeopardy, did a majority vote against the project. Given the intensity of the campaign, the turnout was much lower than expected, only 65 per cent, meaning that the "yes" vote actually represented a minority of the overall electorate.

As a preliminary to the plebiscite, Premier Ghiz had set ten conditions that any fixed link proposal must meet if it hoped to win provincial support. "Joe's 10 Commandments" were mostly economic, but the main sticking point was the question of environmental soundness. Bowing to public pressure, Public Works at length commissioned an independent Environmental Review and Assessment Panel to examine the only surviving option for the crossing, a bridge. Opponents of the fixed link rejoiced when the panel announced in August 1990 that the generic plan available for consideration posed "unacceptable environmental risks."[194] Public Works Canada merely shrugged its shoulders, declared that it would modify its bridge design, and pressed on.[195]

Assessment by assessment, then span by span, the bridge inched closer to reality. In October 1993, the federal government signed a formal contract with Strait Crossing Incorporated of Calgary, whose design had been chosen over two other competitors. In return for building the bridge, SCI was guaranteed a $42 million annual subsidy for a period of thirty-five years. That sum was equivalent, the federal government alleged, to what it spent each year on the ferry service. (Marine Atlantic estimated its actual subsidy at about half that figure.) The projected construction cost was set at $800 million, including $120 million in financing. The completion date was set for 31 May 1997.

The first of the forty-four bridge piers was poured in July 1994. By the summer of 1995, with construction at its peak, SCI had 2,600 people on its payroll. Subcontractors employed another 500.[196] Exactly as predicted, the local economy boomed. Friends of the Island fought to the last through the courts, then clung, almost to the last, to the belief that either the project or its political support would collapse. It did not. The "longest bridge over ice-covered waters in the world" proceeded on time and pretty much on budget.[197] For three years, passengers riding the pendulum-swing of the ferries gathered at the rail to view the structure taking shape off to the westward.

248

The Summer Trade

At 5 pm on 31 May 1997, the first regular traffic rolled onto the "Confederation Bridge." A mile away, the MV *Abegweit* began her last commercial crossing, filled largely with Marine Atlantic employees and their families. The province was now securely tethered to the mainland. It was left to the purists to argue whether or not it should still be called an island.

Figure 5.8 ▪ The Confederation Bridge opened in the spring of 1997 to much fanfare and discussion about its likely impact. One immediate effect was a huge spike in tourism numbers: from approximately 700,000 in the mid-1990s to more than a million thereafter.

Besides a sudden boom in bridge metaphors, the most immediate impact of the Confederation Bridge was, as predicted, on tourism. The year that the bridge opened, tourism numbers and revenue shot up by nearly 60 per cent. For the first time ever, the number of visitors coming to Prince Edward Island topped one million (officially 1,238,100), three years ahead of the schedule set out in 1988 by the Tourism 2000 strategy. The following year, visitation increased by another 4.4 per cent, and tourist spending rose 9.9 per cent. Afterwards, the numbers dipped, falling below the magic million mark in

2004 amid much intra-industry finger pointing.[198] On any given day during the peak of the tourist season, the Island's population swelled by more than 40 per cent – 50,000–60,000 extra people, most of them crammed into the middle third of the province.[199]

The Confederation Bridge got the credit and, sometimes, the blame for the remarkable surge in tourism. Admittedly, the bridge had nothing to do with the strong North American economy, which gave people the money to travel, or the weak Canadian dollar, which persuaded Canadians to vacation at home and Americans to come to Canada. But curiosity did tend to bring travellers to PEI to see the much-promoted engineering marvel.

The closer the bridge, the stronger its attraction: many of the 1.2 million visitors came from exotic locales such as Halifax, Moncton, and Saint John.[200] While tourism marketing continued to target people who would stay longer, spend more, and break out of Island tourism's "golden triangle," Maritime tourists tended to do just the opposite. For them the bridge made Prince Edward Island easier to get to, but also easier to leave. No one counted the number of day-trippers to the province, although many tourist accommodations complained that their visitors were not staying as long as in other years. For the time being, the increase in volume more than made up for any fall in unit value.

In actuality, tourism was already on the move *before* the fixed link opened, rebounding from the recession of the early '90s. Between 1993 and 1997, tourist spending had risen by 40 per cent. The opening of the bridge, then, accelerated an existing trend. The overall increase in visitor spending between 1993 and 1999 was even more impressive, a whopping 173 per cent. As the millennium approached, tourism, the industry that relied on the kindness of strangers, finally seemed ready to overtake agriculture as the province's economic leader. The cultural history of the twentieth century, lamented fixed link opponent David Weale, "can be summed up in how we've gone from being 'Spud Island' to 'Holiday Island.'"[201] He was not simply being nostalgic, he was making a value judgment: pitting the intrinsic virtue of self-reliant yeoman farmers against a tourism that he felt created a society of servants as the fulcrum for Island culture.

From a distance the Confederation Bridge looks almost delicate, a thin line of symmetrical arches framing miniature views of the Northumberland Strait. Stand closer, under the long shadow of those arches and it becomes massive, a ponderous weight bearing down on nature, on the landscapes of tourism. For the significance of the Confederation Bridge for Island tourism goes well beyond greater accessibility or the remarkable, transient boom its completion energized. It was still possible, after all, to choose the "rite of passage" involved in a marine crossing to the Garden of the Gulf. Northumberland Ferries down at the Wood Islands end of the strait lost traffic in the years after the fixed link opened, but its numbers stabilized and it has survived. And even with the bridge, tourism boomlets still come and go in cycles that neither marketers nor consultants can do much to control, no matter their grasp of the laws of attraction. But the whole fixed link episode represented the last great debate (so far) on the place of tourism in Prince Edward Island culture. In pursuing a false binary of tourism as either blessing or curse, it actually traced a broad spectrum of opinion on tourism's impact and desirability. The discussion also rehearsed what exactly it was that made Prince Edward Island attractive to tourists: its landscape and climate; its uncrowded, unhurried way of life; its sense of being a place apart, an island of difference rather than sameness.

Islanders could feast on the post-bridge tourism statistics, but, as the first come-from-away cars rolled off the bridge past the newly fabricated "Gateway Village" and out into the tourist landscape, the host society still struggled to comprehend the hidden costs of becoming a travel destination that drew ten times its population in visitors each year. In ways that were difficult to quantify, the newly bridged province was a little less distant, a little less distinct, a little less of an island. Confronted with mass tourism's bridge-enabled tendency to homogenize, did Islanders cling even more tenaciously to what they felt made them different, what they considered unique, when marketing themselves to others? In its curious way tourism still held a mirror up for the host society to gaze at themselves. Who could say if they would continue to recognize the image they saw there. Or whether the reflection was true.

EPILOGUE

A Delicate Balance

since 2000

Vintage postcards give vanished features along the Island's coastline a certain immortality. Pulpit Rock at Kildare Capes, the Three Sisters near Campbellton, the Lone Rock at Cavendish, Table Rock near Bedeque – all live on in postcards even though the landmarks themselves have worn away. Of all these lost features, none achieved more celebrity than Elephant Rock.

Sometime around 1990, people spotted a pachyderm just offshore, not far from North Cape. Since Western Prince County was a corner of the Island that did not see many tourists, and the provincial government was always on the lookout for new ways to draw visitors there, tourism promoters made much of Elephant Rock. It first appeared in the visitors guide in 1993 as a highlight of the Island's "North by Northwest" tourist region. By 1996, Elephant Rock had worked its way onto the Prince Edward Island tourism road map and into its merchandizing, as visitors and Islanders alike went in search of the much promoted landmark. But a 1998 winter storm sheared the head and trunk off the rock, consigning the attraction to an elephant graveyard. By 2000, it sank from the visitors guide and map. *Sic transit elephantus.*[1]

Elephant Rock's brief career as a tourist attraction offers us a parable about fragility. When it began to disappear, efforts were made to shore up its trunk with discrete injections of cement, but they were no more resistant to wind and weather than the soft red sandstone and its overburden of soil. Elephant Rock's fate is a reminder of just how vulnerable the province's physical landscape is. In an era of climate change, on an island where tourism relies heavily on shorelines and farmscapes, that vulnerability is greater than ever. Sea level rise threatens familiar beaches and low-lying areas. Meanwhile, the circum-Island belt of inshore sea ice that insulates the shore from heavy winter surf is steadily thinning, accelerating coastal erosion. As David Wallace-Wells observes in *The Uninhabitable Earth*, not only is this century likely to put underwater "any beach you've ever visited," but "it will take thousands of years,

Figure 6.0 (facing page) ▪ Cover of the 2020 *Visitor's Guide.* Tourism PEI/Stephen Harris.

Figure 6.1 • Elephant Rock first appeared in the annual *Visitors Guide* in 1993, headlined the guide's West Prince section by 1996, and, its head and trunk having eroded away, disappeared completely from its pages by 2000. Such fleeting celebrity demonstrated the difficulty of long-term tourism planning. Climate change and COVID-19 likewise show that the sands are constantly shifting underfoot. Tourism PEI/Camera Art.

perhaps millions, for quartz and feldspar to degrade into sand that might replenish the beaches we lose."[2] Weather extremes, storm surges, wind, wave, and runoff: all fret the fabric of Island tourism's famous patchwork quilt.

The industry's intangible terrain, its culture and spirit of place, is no less fragile in this epoch of mass tourism, where even "authenticity" is a product that is bought and sold, and the tipping point between success and excess can only be identified once it is passed. As new realities press against long-held assumptions and tourism seeps deeper and deeper into the cracks of Island culture, tourism's trends and choices will have ever graver consequences for the host society.

Tourism began on Prince Edward Island in the middle years of the nineteenth century as a slender thread of possibility – an extended summer escape for the well-to-do. The thread thickened over the decades as new strands of attraction and compulsion gradually twined themselves around the evolving industry. As elsewhere in the Western world, much of the expansion came in the postwar era. The progression in government's sense of its own role in the industry mirrored larger changes, moving from benign, *laissez-faire* neglect through mild encouragement to a federally subsidized conviction that the state's role was to manage and direct tourism growth. The late twentieth-century emphasis on public–private partnership was less an ideologically and fiscally driven retreat from state intervention than a sorting out of roles. Although collaboration occasionally smelled like collusion, as with government's controversial investments in golf or its marriage of convenience with the Montgomery Estate, it was genuine and largely effective despite missteps.

Tourism, claims historian Hal Rothman, is the last resort of failed economies. While in places such as the cottage country of Ontario's Muskokas, where agriculture had withered in the thin, stony soils, or Bermuda, forced to reinvent itself several times, that might be true, Prince Edward Island, like many other destinations, has not given itself over entirely to tourism. Not yet.

By 2021, nearly fifty years after the prediction was first made that tourism would soon overtake agriculture as the most valuable industry in Prince Edward Island, it still has not done so.[3] Every time it seemed poised to reach the top, some circumstance kicked the ladder out from under its ascent. Much of the time, the culprit was the economic cycles that periodically buffet the Western world, thwarting one or more of tourism's basic prerequisites: leisure time, disposable income, inclination, and safe travel. After all, the Island's tourism industry, like the Island economy, is only a small wheel whirring inside a much larger one. Over the past two decades, newspaper headlines have predictably oscillated between "banner year" braggadocio and sober accounts of worrisome declines.[4] Observed from a distance, however, the overall narrative is one of growth. In the twenty plus years since the opening of the Confederation Bridge, Island tourism has proven stubbornly resilient.

Exactly how resilient and how much growth is difficult to gauge. Tourism officials argue that being an island with controllable points of entry has always made their statistical estimates the most accurate in the country.[5] Nevertheless, there is an indeterminate margin of error. The problem is not just that statisticians have for some time preferred to think in terms of "tourist parties" rather than individual tourists and not just because there have been periodic revisions to the multipliers they employ to extrapolate from survey samples to overall numbers. In the new millennium the definition of what constitutes a tourist has itself changed. It now includes intra-Island tourism: that is, Islanders visiting other parts of the province. In fact, tourism officials would rather not talk in terms of people but in terms of nights of accommodation booked, something tourist operators are now constrained to share.[6] That method makes a useful distinction between someone who stays four nights instead of two, but it does not account for day-trippers or for pleasure

Table 6.1 ▪ Estimated number of tourists, 1925–2019

1925	11,000
1935	<25,000
1940	c. 42,000
1951	c. 35,000
1954	c. 92,000
1958	>150,000
1960	208,507
1965	333,951
1970	572,680
1973	573,000
1976	583,016
1979	566,640
1980	619,924
1983	557,590
1988	715,600
1991	630,000
1996	788,300
1997	1,238,100
2000	1,179,300
2004	c. 960,000
2011	1,238,276
2013	1,297,522
2019	1,580,000

While controlled points of entry make PEI's tourism statistics more reliable than many other locales, they have always been based on extrapolations from available data and the application of changing formulas. These are based on estimates drawn from various provincial government sources.

visitors who stay in their own cottage or with friends. Nor can it easily catch the many who populate the burgeoning, as yet unregulated Airbnb universe. Given such considerations, the recent estimate of 1.58 million tourist visits for 2019, an increase of twenty-five per cent over the boom year of the bridge opening, should be taken as indicative but only roughly comparable.

Tourism's exact economic impact is similarly elusive, based as it is on the estimated sales of "tourism-related" industries without being able to break out domestic from tourist spending in those sectors. Which is only to say that tourism has never been a science. The exact numbers matter less than the fact of the industry's centrality. The gap in dollar value between it and agriculture, once gaping, is now small, and tourism directly employs far more people than farming.[7] Its share of the Island's GDP, currently running at 5–6 per cent annually, consistently ranks the highest of any province in Canada.

In riding out economic crests and troughs, Island tourism has not been forced to reinvent itself. It continues to project peace and certitude and help for pain. The "gentle island" of recent marketing campaigns echoes the slogans of a century ago. But that is not to imply that tourism has failed to renew itself or to sharpen the tools of the old summer trade. The industry has progressively been professionalized. Market analysis, for example, has reached new levels of sophistication. To the many past forms of categorization (income, origin, age, expectation) marketing consultants now use census records and postal code information to collect psychographic data that probe motivations and profile likes and dislikes among ever more specific subsets of the prospective clientele. Instead of marketing to particular regions, Island tourism targets specific readerships, user types, social media choices.[8] The industry does not set trends, it chases them. But when it catches up, the tourist lens soon magnifies what it has found, projecting values, attitudes, and views onto the backdrop of the host society.

Many of the "new" marketing strategies are actually reimaginings of older themes. For instance, the ongoing crusade to brand the province as "Canada's Food Island"[9] marks a gastronomic evolution rather than revolution. In the marketing lexicon of early Island tourism, the few food references used adjectives such as "plain," "plentiful," "fresh," and "wholesome," much in keeping with the province's overall image as a return to premodern innocence and childhood simplicity.[10] The postwar era's rapid deployment of drive-in canteens and summer-time restaurants trended more towards greasy burgers and soggy French fries to tempt the motor tourist palate, but the 1950s also began to repackage a local foodway for tourist consumption. The community lobster supper was a variation on more venerable, food-based gatherings: the "tea parties" and "pic-nics" of the nineteenth century and their near cousins, the "box social" and the church supper. The term "lobster supper" as a reference to a community event is practically nonexistent in the Charlottetown *Guardian* before the 1930s, but after 1945 dozens of communities began advertising annual lobster suppers, usually as a local fundraiser. They rallied neighbours to organize, supply, and stage them, and drew friends, relatives, expatriates, and other curious tourists to sample homemade food and a homey sense of belonging. The Roman Catholic parish of St Ann's in Hope River, just a few table-lengths from Cavendish, is usually credited with turning an annual event into a weekly, and then daily, one during tourism season; what began in 1963 as a short-term strategy to pay for their new church is still active today.[11] Other communities followed suit, and soon commercial lobster suppers were also offering reasonable facsimiles of authentic "down-home" experiences.

If the "traditional" lobster supper merely extended and repurposed an existing marketing trope, Food Island means to transform "fresh," "wholesome," and "sourced locally" into *haute cuisine*. The campaign has clear roots in the creation of a Culinary Institute in the 1990s within Holland College's Tourism and Hospitality Institute and before that, in 1988's tourism-sponsored "Culinary Masters" competition, which featured international chefs creating signature dishes from local foods.[12] The Island's food profile also received a significant boost after 1991 from American-born Michael Smith, chef and, more recently, co-owner of the upscale Inn at Bay Fortune (founded on the site of C.P. Flockton's nineteenth-century actors' colony). A string of successful cookbooks and television cooking shows (among them *The Inn Chef*, 1998–2001, and *Chef at Home*, 2004–15) brought Smith's sustainable cooking philosophy and its Island setting to audiences around the world.[13] Schooled by such programming, today's upscale travellers expect fine dining at their destinations. The promise of culinary delights may not by itself lure them to Prince Edward Island, but leaving a good taste in their mouths might well bring them back.

Event tourism has a comparable premise. Prince Edward Island has a long history of festivals and fairs with overt tourist overtones, not least among them Old Home Week's old-fashioned confection of agricultural exhibition, vaudeville, and amusement arcade and Summerside's annual Lobster Carnival, which dates from 1956. But the 2000s hatched a whole new generation of state-sponsored spectacles specially designed to attract tourists. The aforementioned Festival of the Fathers failed to put down roots, while a chronic lack of snow – and, in the end, sponsors – eventually put paid to Mill River's International Sled Dog Races.[14] Since 2005, unreliable winter weather has also plagued Charlottetown's modest version of *Carnivale*, the Jack Frost Festival.[15]

Music festivals have proven less weather-dependent than snow sculptures or sled dog races. The oldest is the Rollo Bay Fiddle Festival, which celebrated its forty-third anniversary in 2019.[16] The largest, the country-themed

Figure 6.2 ▪ Held each summer since 2009 – until the pandemic summers of 2020 and 2021 – the Cavendish Beach Music Festival demonstrates how PEI tourism continues to evolve, a blend of tradition and novelty. On the one hand, as the largest music festival in Atlantic Canada, attracting more than 60,000 visitors annually, it represents the province's new emphasis on event tourism. On the other hand, its country music theme relies on the Island's longtime identification with rural life.

Cavendish Beach Music Festival, dates only from 2009. While Rollo Bay's organizers, the Chaisson family, were motivated to preserve the Island's traditional fiddle culture, Cavendish Beach has been from the beginning a speculative, tourism-oriented, state-supported venture in country music promotion. The inaugural event received $1.1 million in provincial funding, $200,000 of it directly from the provincial tourism department.[17] Other Tourism PEI investments have tended to be one-off events. The biggest splash came when ABC's popular daytime talk show *Live! with Regis and Kelly* taped four episodes on location in Charlottetown in July 2010. The promotion cost the Department of Tourism and Culture $800,000 but allegedly generated $22.6 million worth of advertising.[18]

Although event tourism sometimes targeted the off-season, it played best in high summer. In contrast, the fastest growing element of Island (and global) tourism in the new millennium, cruise ship touring, took aim squarely at the local industry's steeply sloping shoulder seasons. Cruise ships had begun calling at Charlottetown as early as 1894, but their visits were so infrequent, often separated by decades, that when two Swedish American cruise ships, the *Gripsholm* and *Kungsholm*, made stops in Charlottetown in the late summer of 1969, they were considered something of a novelty. But during the 1980s, as cruise ship tourism began to gather way, Charlottetown became an occasional port of call for various cruise lines sailing itineraries that ran between New York or Boston and Quebec City or Montreal.[19] The numbers fluctuated

wildly from year to year: two visits in 1980, eleven in 1981; twenty-four in 1992, fifteen the next year.[20] It did not help Charlottetown's reputation as a destination when wind shear tore off one ship's gangway during a 1994 stopover.[21]

By 1996, when Charlottetown's Capital Commission produced a "Cruise Ship Tourism Impact Study" for Tourism PEI, the global cruise industry was booming. According to the study, the global industry had grown 70 per cent over the previous ten years, and 40 per cent in the past five. By 1999, experts predicted, cruise ships would carry seven million passengers annually and generate $50 billion in revenue. Here was a bandwagon – boat – worth jumping on. Since then Island tourism has aggressively courted the highly competitive cruise ship industry to make Charlottetown (or Summerside or Georgetown) a more frequent port of call by scrounging funds to upgrade port facilities, reorienting same-day tour packages for cruisers' convenience, and scaling downtown retail hours to accommodate cruise ship passengers. In 2000, eighteen cruise ships carrying 7,600 passengers docked at Charlottetown. Predicated on an average expenditure per passenger

Figure 6.3 • By the 2010s, Charlottetown had become a popular cruise ship destination. This is the MSC *Meraviglia*. Its listed capacity of 7,250 passengers and crew exceeds the number of tourists who visited the Island annually a century ago and would make it, when in port, the fourth-largest community in twenty-first-century Prince Edward Island.

of $110 per stay (about half that of other tourists), their visits pumped roughly a million dollars into the local economy, much of it in the spring and fall shoulder seasons. In 2017, the figures were sixty-eight ships and 90,820 visitors.[22] Two years later, a record ninety-six visits were scheduled, most of them after Labour Day, with a potential capacity of 206,715 passengers and crew.[23] On peak days in the fall of 2019 as many as four ships crowded the harbour, disgorging (if everyone landed) more than 8,000 visitors and crew onto the dockside.

Cruise ship passengers are now a familiar sight in twenty-first-century Charlottetown, crowding the "Hippopotabus" and horse-drawn wagons on downtown tours or wandering the thoroughfares, maps in hand, conferring on street corners. For tour operators, retail shops, and downtown restaurants they are an unalloyed good, injecting welcome cash into the shoulder season. For points east and west and for local tourist accommodations, the story is somewhat different. On average, the great floating hotels stay only for six to eight hours before weighing anchor, and of necessity (as well as choice) the tours their passengers take seldom range outside the familiar golden triangle that leads from Charlottetown out to Cavendish and back again by way of the Confederation Bridge. Even for the lucky few along their path, cruise ship spending continues to lag that of other tourists.

Cruise ships advocates rebut such criticisms by arguing that cruise visits constitute a sort of reconnaissance in force. "Cruise ship passengers are some of the most frequent travelers," the 1996 study claimed. "They also use cruises to identify areas for return visits. Industry statistics indicate that 50% of passengers fully expect to return to the same destination for another type of vacation." To date, however, there are no studies to suggest how many cruise ship passengers come back to Prince Edward Island for longer stays. The environmental consequences of so much cruise tonnage in Island waters is also beginning to draw attention: exhaust fumes, waste disposal, water consumption, carbon footprint, high-speed collisions with endangered right whales out in the sea lanes of the gulf. As yet, though, such concerns have not soured the romance between Island tourism and the cruise industry.

Cruise ship tourism has created a new tourist rite of passage for a new millennium even if the visitors' stays might be as short as millennials' supposed attention spans. Another day, another port. Passengers might be excused for conflating the destinations. One sunny morning in the spring of 2015, a straggle of cruise ship passengers strolled into town along Charlottetown's waterfront boardwalk, which led them directly past a floating restaurant.

A sidewalk ambassador held out his tray to the passing parade. "Would you like to sample some of our Island blue mussels? They're the best on PEI!"

An elderly woman looked up. "Where am I?" she asked.[24]

When the journey is more important than the destination, it is hard to imagine such transient visitors choosing to return for longer stays.

While tourism marketers hailed passing cruise ships, Greg and Linda Lowther eyed a different clientele. In the summer of 2003, they opened a four-star resort on a quiet side road near Cavendish, sparking passionate debate within the local community (and, via media coverage, beyond). The Oasis catered to "naturists," that is, nudists, and the local community was deeply divided over whether or not nudism was appropriate to the Island's tourism image. Both sides invoked the spirit of Anne of Green Gables to defend their positions. Still smarting from locals' snickering, one local councillor complained at a public meeting that the new resort made Cavendish "the laughing stock of the Island, perhaps the nation … it sickens me, I'm disgusted by it and again it's not the concept, it is where the concept is being set. Lucy Maud Montgomery never wrote a book about Anne in a brothel or Anne in a nudist resort." Leone Barton thought differently. "I'm sure if Anne were around today, she probably would try out the nudist resort," she said, evidently forgetting that Anne was never actually around.[25]

Although revealing about Islanders' ambivalent attitudes towards diversity, the controversy might be dismissed as a tempest in a hot tub. There was, after all, no law against naturist resorts and the province declined to make one. The Lowthers listened respectfully to their critics, then quietly went about their business. A year later, when they sought permission from the Resort Municipality to add a campground, the application was quietly approved.[26] Towards the end of that first public debate, however, local resident Harry Sim voiced a criticism that was more than skin deep. The resort council, he said, would have to start licensing businesses in order to prevent such developments in future. "As time goes on," he said, "you're losing control of your surroundings, you're losing control of your community."[27] His concerns went beyond issues of appropriateness to ones of appropriation. When it comes to tourism, who should – or can – control the storyline? And that question, in turn, strikes at the heart of larger issues. Tourism's commitment to perpetual growth poses challenges for the province's society and culture. They speak to the longstanding tensions between Islanders and tourism's principal actors, but as tourism continues its ascent, the challenges also raise fundamental questions about sustainability and agency.

"Cottages and cabins for the accommodation of tourists seem to be rising mushroom-like in the central part of the province," exclaimed "K." one hopeful June in a letter to the editor of the *Guardian*. "Circumspect people must have a premonition of the cornucopia to come in the near future."[28] The quote might have come from the early 1970s, perhaps, or the 2010s, when tourism recorded three consecutive years of 5 per cent annual growth, but it dates from 1938, when cottage life remained a novelty rather than a norm along the Island's coastlines.

It was urban Islanders and their expatriate relatives who generally occupied the first Island cottages, which were easy extrapolations from the adapted farmhouses that furnished many tourist accommodations in the late nineteenth century. Roughing it along the shore had obvious allure for the very few in the province that might be termed the "idle rich." Wealth, of course, is relative, and so were the cottage accommodations. They had fewer comforts but more privacy than the seaside resorts and accessed the same natural attractions: sea, sand, salt air, countryside. By the early years of the last century, as we have seen, Charlottetown's professional and middle classes found summer homes or built primitive cottages all around the perimeter of the city's harbour, from Keppoch to the lower reaches of West and North River but especially at Holland Cove near Rocky Point at the harbour's mouth. Those accommodations were primarily, though not exclusively, for locals. During the 1920s, meanwhile, L.M. Montgomery's celebrity encouraged local entrepreneurs in Cavendish to erect the first of many tourist bungalows and cottages there.

Over the following decades the cottage phenomenon inexorably spread across the province. Where lobster factories had once dotted the shoreline, now thousands of summer homes and cottage lots section off the shore fields of coastal farms, strung like beads along the water's edge or concentrated in subdivisions laid out like so much seaside suburbia. Their presence is, of course, merely an extension of a much larger North American trend, a great washing back of population towards what historian John Gillis terms the coastal ecotone.[29]

As the demand for shorefront drove up real estate prices across the continent, the demand for property on Prince Edward Island escalated rapidly in the 1960s. Indeed, it was a map exposing the extent of nonresident landownership that shocked the Campbell government into appointing a royal commission on the land in 1972. That, and ads from companies like the British Columbia-based Canada Land Fund, which offered prime Island waterfront so that buyers could "possess the best of nature's land … places of peace and solitude, away from the sounds and tensions of the city, the maddening crowd, night latches and bolted doors."[30] Subsequent legislation in 1973 required all purchases by nonresidents in excess of ten acres of land or 330 feet of shore frontage to have the approval of the Governor-in-Council. "We in Prince Edward Island," Premier Campbell told a federal–provincial conference in May 1973, "have no intention of allowing our province, through attrition, neglect or oversight, to end up in the hands of non-residents who have little interest in the communities of our province, little concern for the preservation of our way of life, little involvement in our Island institutions and who may simply view the province as a place either to spend a holiday or opt out of an urbanized society."[31] Of course, it was easy for a government to be tough with people who had no vote.

In practice, enforcement of the legislation was left to the government's discretion – and it was very discreet. During the balance of 1973, there were some 231 nonresident applications under the terms of the act; only thirty-eight of them were rejected.[32] That ratio set the trend for ensuing years. Apart from discouraging would-be purchasers, the legislation denied very few actual ones, although the rejections were usually significant.[33] The principal control over nonresident ownership turned out to be red tape not rejection and, by 1976, another 66,000 acres had passed into the hands of nonresidents. In 1982 a new Lands Protection Act actually halved the allowable limits on nonresident landownership to five acres and 165 feet of shore frontage before executive council endorsement was required.[34] But the issue was not rules so much as enforcement. In the absence of any integrated land use policy for the whole province, approvals continued to be pro forma. In the two-year period of 2006–07, according to the Charlottetown *Guardian*, 120 nonresident land applications came before the Island Regulatory and Appeals Commission (IRAC). It recommended approval with no conditions for 113 of them. Cabinet actually approved 116.[35]

Paper restrictions and periodic recession might curb but could not quench the off-Island appetite for Island water frontage. One of the predicted outcomes of the fixed link's completion in the late 1990s was an uptick in cottage construction. That came true with a vengeance. In the three years following the completion of the Confederation Bridge, 484 cottage construction permits were issued. Over the next two decades, the average number of new permits dwindled considerably, but the cumulative total still came to 1,384 by 2018, one hundred of them granted in the previous year.[36]

Demand predictably drove up prices. Between 1994 and 2004, the average cost of land along the North Shore of the province tripled. Property values continued to soar in succeeding years. By the 2010s, prime waterfront lots were priced beyond the means of most Islanders. Meanwhile, a cordon of private property restricted their customary access to many beaches.[37] Back in 1902, a writer in the *Examiner* had wryly predicted that it was the Island's "destiny" to have its shores, "one long street of summer hotels."[38] Substitute "cottages" for "hotels" and the statement begins to read like prophecy. Actually, if one travels by car, second-growth forest, another sign of pastoral decline, often hides the water view. Only from a boat is it possible to grasp the degree to which the Island's coastline has become cottage country. To cite just one, admittedly extreme example, historian Josh MacFadyen has looked at coastal land use change in the North Shore community of New London. In 1968, there were five properties along the New London waterfront. By 2012, there were over 150, ninety-two of them owned by nonresidents, including thirty-three Americans.[39]

The issue for Islanders goes well beyond physical access or even the fundamental alterations in the landscape engendered by these changing patterns of land ownership. Cottage subdivisions, as in the well-known example of Cousins Shore near Park Corner in the heart of Anne country, progressively mar the pastoral vistas that drew their buyers there in the first place.[40] Faced with accelerating coastal erosion born of global climate change, cottage owners complicate the problem (or simply move it down the shore) with makeshift breastworks and gabions. And as posttropical storm Dorian demonstrated in September 2019, being – literally – on the front lines of climate change is hazardous. More than twenty people had to be evacuated when a storm surge flooded Crystal Cove Campground in the aptly named Lower New Annan on Malpeque Bay. The same storm destroyed an estimated 80 per cent of the tree cover in the Cavendish Campground at Prince Edward Island National Park.[41] The coastal ecotone has become a vulnerable place.

Spoiled vistas, coastal crowding, environmental degradation, nonresident ownership: all speak to the question of sustainability, an especially pressing concern for small island states with finite shorelines and limited landmass. There is no formula for sustainability, though it is tied to a tourist destination's carrying capacity. In *Tourism: The Key Concepts*, Geoff Shirt defines sustainable tourism as "tourism development that harmonizes with the pre-existing economic, sociocultural and ecological situation" and posits multiple carrying capacity thresholds: physical (that is, the sheer number of visitors), infrastructural (where transportation networks or accommodations can no longer cope), environmental (after which irreparable damage is done), economic (the point at which local communities are adversely affected), sociocultural (causing active harm to the host society's culture, values, identity, and relationships), and, finally, perceptual (when tourists feel their experience of a place has been compromised).[42] In an attempt to quantify carrying capacity, Jerome L. McElroy has designed a "Tourism Penetration Index" for islands that is geared to the level of visitor spending per resident and visitor density per thousand permanent inhabitants.[43] The least developed islands, McElroy concludes, stating the obvious, tend to be the most pristine. Tourism there is small scale, the landscape is rural, and visitors stay longer. Of course, it also generates less revenue.

For Prince Edward Island, which has long sold itself as a quiet refuge from the hurly-burly and existential angst of modern life, becoming too popular carries palpable risks. How many people can "get away from it all" before they have essentially brought "it all" with them – especially if the bulk of them arrive all at once, in July and August? The answer is difficult to gauge, but other, older tourist destinations elsewhere have clearly reached the limits of their carrying capacity. In recent years, critics have coined the term "overtourism" to describe the corrosive social, cultural, and environmental consequences of too many tourists crowding the calendar and the tourist landscape.[44] Overtourism kills the thing it loves and in the process breeds visceral resentment among permanent residents marginalized and trivialized by its priorities. The tipping point comes when instead of tourism orbiting around its host culture, the surrounding culture comes to define itself in terms of tourism. That, too, is a question of sustainability. The society that plays perpetual host not only ends up feeling a certain hospitility towards its guests but also a species of self-loathing.

In the end, the province's cultural carrying capacity may be even more at risk than its physical environment. Tourists may hunger for authenticity but mass tourism also craves convenience, and that demands commodification. Commodification, in turn, is relentlessly reductionist, a process of selection and simplification that belies the diversity and complexity of any culture. And because Islanders, too, consume the province's tourism messaging, they run the risk of believing the simplistic, even ersatz, version of themselves that they see there.[45] That fact raises the stakes for tourism promoters honestly seeking a proper – and profitable – balance between necessary commodification and a debasing commercialism.[46]

The COVID-19 pandemic that swept across the world in 2020 violated one of the basic preconditions for tourism: safe travel. It starkly reminded host and visitor alike that tourism is dictated by external events, while exposing the global economic colossus's feet of clay. The Island's tourism industry reeled in 2020 and 2021 as the fallout from COVID-19 closed borders, branded cruise ships and airplanes as petri dishes for infection, and made Islanders cast a wary eye on strangers with out-of-province plates. Tourism statistics for the 2020 season made for grim reading. Instead of a hundred cruise ships, none. A 99.5 per cent plummet in bus tours. Bridge traffic down 42 per cent;

ferry traffic down 61 per cent; air travel down 81 per cent. Attendance at Green Gables down 96 per cent.[47] Even after tourist travel within a precarious "Atlantic Bubble" was authorized during the second half of that summer season, TIAPEI projected a decline in tourist expenditures of more than half for the year, including an 80 per cent drop in revenues among airports, hotels, attractions, and amusement parks.[48] How long would it take for tourism to recover? Having grown concerned in recent decades about the perils of too many tourists, the Island wondered when there would again be enough.

In the ideal world of travel planning, each day of a vacation opens like a storybook with the expectation of adventure and happy endings. After all, one of the defining principles of tourism is pleasure. Twenty-first century tourism plays to that desire with the current vogue for experiential tourism and authentic experiences. Of course, at some level, all tourist experiences are "authentic," especially, one might argue, experiences such as flight delays and cancellations, dismal weather, or shoddy accommodations. But in the language of advertising, the term expresses a tacit understanding that the experiences referenced will be both enjoyable and intrinsic to the culture being sampled. Except in rare instances, the reality is inescapably artificial. Activities designed for tourists are generally adapted from something typical or that was once typical. Like reality television, they mimic real life. There is a spectrum of authenticity, and visitors measure their experiences along what they know of that spectrum as well as their entertainment value. Most of them know, and do not mind, that they are merely scratching the surface of a culture. In any case, tourist destinations are inevitably a projection of visitors' hopes and desires as much as those of their hosts. And the performance of tourism – by both visitor and host – creates its own dynamic, hybrid culture that is in its own way unique.[49]

But the question of authenticity runs deeper even than that on Prince Edward Island, where tourism promotion has always sold a way of life that grew organically out of a natural landscape that was itself a product of human intervention. For the first time in its history, the pastoral landscape is itself at risk, and the danger runs deeper than the possibility of lasting environmental damage through overtourism, "inappropriate" development, or even climate change. The most potent threat to the pastoral landscape on Prince Edward Island is not really ecological but demographic. For the landscape that tourism has defined and marketed since the 1860s was not created by or even for tourists. It was the by-product of a rural people wresting a living from

Table 6.2 ▪ Number and acreage of farms, 1901–2016

Year	No. farms	% change from previous	Avg. acreage	Total farm acres/ acres in crops
1901	13,749		87	
1921	13,701	−0.004	89	1,220,000/461,000
1931	12,865	−6.1	93	1,190,000/497,000
1941	12,230	−4.9	96	1,170,000/470,000
1951	10,137	−17.1	108	1,100,000/426,000
1961	7,335	−27.6	131	960,000/391,000
1971	4,543	−38.1	171	780,000/351,000
1981	3,154	−30.1	232	700,000/391,000
1991	2,361	−25.1	271	640,000/380,000
2001	1,845	−21.9	350	650,000/434,000
2011	1,495	−19.0	398	590,000/411,000
2016	1,353	−9.5	425	575,000/400,000

There were almost 12,400 fewer farms on PEI in 2016 than in 1901 – a 90 per cent drop – and the average farm was almost five times larger. The Island's "patchwork quilt" farmscape is being transformed by farm consolidation and industrial agriculture: not just farms but also fields are fewer and bigger, monoculture is more common, and fewer families are connected to this land. All this has implications for the Island's culture – and for the image that the Island in turn can present to tourists.

their environment. Today, the figures in that landscape are rapidly vanishing. A century ago, two-thirds of Islanders lived on farms; today, 3 per cent do. Compounding the decline in farm population, the total number of Islanders has shot up in recent years. Between 2016 and 2018, the Island's rate of population growth led the country, rising in a way not seen in the province since the 1850s. The increase happened despite negative interprovincial migration. Most of the newcomers, 90 per cent, were new immigrants from diverse cultural backgrounds, and most of them settled in urban areas.[50]

Little more than a century ago, there were slightly fewer than 14,000 farms on Prince Edward Island, most of them family owned, most of them mixed operations, with an average size of eighty-seven acres. The most recent census puts the number at 1,353, most of them corporate enterprises, most of them specializing in one commodity, with an average farm size of 425 acres.[51] The demographic changes are mirrored in the physical landscape. Between 1931 and 2016, the number of acres being farmed in the province fell by more than half. Fields did just the opposite, as hedgerows were bulldozed to accommodate the heavy farm machinery of corporate agriculture.[52] During the Development Plan era of the 1970s, protesters had fought to save the family farm. Twenty years into the new millennium, it is essentially dead, and the traditional culture that it once fostered is arguably on life support. Almost imperceptibly, the seasonal cycles of farm work that once governed Island society have given way to the seasons of the tourist year.

The broken connection to the pastoral suggested by these physical and demographic trends – and, by extension, the broken link to the Island's history and traditional culture – has obvious implications for the province's tourism image. While to the casual observer the look of the land might seem the same, in both cultural and physical terms, the placid veneer of the pastoral landscape has grown perilously thin. As the gap steadily widens between the tourist face of Prince Edward Island and its actuality, the implications for tourism promotion are obvious. How many tourist seasons will pass before the only place that the Island's pastoral culture and landscape meet is within the glossy covers of next year's *Visitor's Guide*?[53]

On a sun-bathed Island beach, as the summer afternoon wears on, a child finds a wooden stick along the shore. With bold strokes, she prints a message in the wet sand near the water's edge, staking out her claim to this day, this place. A little while later, the family folds up their beach chairs, packs up their cooler and backpacks, shakes out their towels. The beach empties, car doors slam in the distance. There is the sound of a car engine, and then they're gone. Back on the shore, the rising tide will soon wash away her message, leaving a blank slate for the following day.

A tourist is, by nature, ephemeral, but tourism leaves permanent traces of its passage across a season, a landscape, a culture. "Just leave us the way you found us," the narrator of 1976's *Come In from Away* asks tourists. Today we know that's not possible. Tourism transforms. In his withering indictment of tourism in the American West, Hal Rothman labels it "a devil's bargain … Regions, communities, and locales welcome tourism as an economic boon, only to find that it irrevocably changes them in unanticipated and uncontrollable ways."[54] For Rothman, the arrival of tourism in a locale launches a linear progression that ends with outside capital subverting the local economy and the local culture transformed beyond recognition.[55] Economic success, paradoxically, brings social calamity.

For evidence on Prince Edward Island, Rothman might have looked at Cavendish. Its permanent population is currently just more than 300; on a given day in July or August, the population nears 7,500.[56] It combines the best – and worst – of tourism. The main road – the strip – features amusement parks, retail outlets, assorted attractions, and accommodations of every sort but also a national park with signature coastline scenery and a series of pastoral vistas. Government got so used to thinking of the North Shore region as a necessary unit of administration that in 1990 it bundled the adjacent communities of Stanley Bridge, Hope River, Bayview, Cavendish, and North Rustico into something called the Resort Municipality. What those adjacent districts all had in common was tourism.

But casting tourism's history as a morality tale suggests inevitability, in much the same way that Jerome McElroy's Tourism Penetration Index reduces a complicated and contingent relationship to a formula charting a preordained lifecycle. Perhaps it is better to plot tourism in a particular place as a series of points on separate but related continuums – social, cultural, economic, environmental – that allow us to calibrate the industry's impact over time. Just as no tourism trajectory is preordained, no tourism story is ever exactly the same.

Back in 1971, tourist Derwyn Evans of London, Ontario, wrote to offer Premier Alex Campbell some unsolicited advice about the Island's tourist industry. (Unlike the era's consultants, he did not charge.) After some loss-leader suggestions about expanding the number of B&Bs and promoting physical activities such as cycling, hiking, and horseback riding accompanied by a caution about the tyranny of the automobile, Evans outlined his "Five Principles Regulating Tourist Development in PEI." To encourage positive attitudes towards tourism, he wrote, "Do not undertake, promote, or encourage any endeavor that does not directly or indirectly benefit the people of P.E.I." In considering new infrastructure, "Do not build, undertake, promote or encourage any facility except that Islanders shall be the primary users of such a facility." As much as possible embed the tourism exchange in genuine culture: "Encourage institutions which permit a high degree of personal interaction between visitors and natives." Avoid "the paradox of the tourist trap"; do not destroy through reckless expansion the very assets that draw visitors in the first place. (Here he listed the Island's charms: "friendly people, beautiful scenery, country charm, interesting architecture, unmarred beaches.") Above all, "In no way encourage any one individual or mass of individuals to become totally dependent upon tourism. The individual entirely dependent economically upon tourism is placed in a subservient position."[57] It also, he added, invites economic disaster as the tourism industry periodically expands and contracts. It was good advice in 1971. It is good advice today.

History suggests that tourism's planners and promoters must seek a fine balance between the natural and the contrived, the authentic and the artificial, the spontaneous and the packaged, between being hosts and servants. They must learn the lesson of limits and the many meanings of sustainability. They must choose between courting mainland capital and losing their grip on the industry they are trying to grow. Even if we heed the advice of come-from-aways like Delwyn Evans, the choices are still ours to make, not once, but every day, every year. It will be well for Island tourism – but also for us – to choose wisely. Because Prince Edward Island tourism will continue, despite its challenges and regardless of the degree to which Islanders participate in shaping it. After all, who among us, seeing an island on a map or from a mainland shore, hasn't felt the pull to go there?

Notes

Abbreviations

ARDT	Annual Report, Department of Tourism, Government of Prince Edward Island, PEI Coll., Robertson Library, University of PEI, Charlottetown, PEI
Fleming diary	Diary of R. G. Fleming, 3698/2, Public Archives and Records Office of Prince Edward Island, Charlottetown, PEI
JLA	*Journal of the Legislative Assembly of Prince Edward Island*, PEI Legislative Documents Online, https://www.peildo.ca/
LAC	Library and Archives Canada, Ottawa, Ontario
LMM Coll.	L. M. Montgomery Collection, McLaughlin Archives, University of Guelph, Guelph, Ontario
PARO	Public Archives and Records Office of Prince Edward Island, Charlottetown, PEI
East Point NP, PC	File on proposed East Point National Park, file 01-07-P1, vol.1, Parks Canada, PEI Field Unit, Ardgowan Historic House, Charlottetown, PEI
PEI Coll.	Prince Edward Island Collection, Robertson Library, University of PEI, Charlottetown, PEI
PEILDO	PEI Legislative Documents Online, https://www.peildo.ca/
PEIMHF	Prince Edward Island Museum and Heritage Foundation, Charlottetown, PEI
TIAPEI	Tourism Industry Association of Prince Edward Island, Charlottetown, PEI

Introduction

1 George Brown to Anne Brown, 13 September 1864, in George Brown fonds, Library and Archives Canada [henceforth, LAC], http://heritage.canadiana.ca/view/oocihm.lac_reel_c1602/216?r=0&s=5. There is a transcript of this letter in *Canadian Historical Review* 48, 2 (June 1967): 110–12. See also P.B. Waite, *The Charlottetown Conference* (Ottawa: Canadian Historical Association, 1970).

2 *Ross's Weekly*, 9 June 1864. Throughout, all references are to Charlottetown newspapers unless explicitly stated otherwise.

3 This is based on the United Nations World Tourism Organization's longtime definition of the term. See Stephen L.J. Smith, "The Measurement of Global Tourism: Old Debates, New Consensus, and Continuing Challenges," in *A Companion to Tourism*, eds. Alan A. Lew, C. Michael Hall, Allan M. Williams (Malden, MA: Blackwell Publishing, 2004), 29. Interestingly, the UNWTO's website defines tourism simply as "the activity of visitors" but then cites a longer, more detailed definition. https://www.unwto.org/glossary-tourism-terms.

4 Smith, "Measurement of Global Tourism," 29.

5 The international literature on tourism is vast. We have benefited in particular from Dean MacCannell, *The Tourist: A New Theory of the Leisure Class* (New York: Shocken Books, 2013 [1976]); John J. Jakle, *The Tourist: Travel in Twentieth-Century North America* (Lincoln and London: University of Nebraska Press, 1985); John Urry, *The Tourist Gaze: Leisure and Travel in Contemporary Societies* (London: Sage Publications, 1990); Alain Corbin, *The Lure of the Sea: The Discovery of the Seaside in the Western World, 1750–1840*, trans. Jocelyn Phelps (London: Penguin Books, 1994); John Urry, *Consuming Places* (New York: Routledge, 1995); John Towner, *An Historical Geography of Recreation and Tourism in the Western World* (London: Wiley, 1996); Hal Rothman, *Devil's Bargains: Tourism in the Twentieth Century American West* (Lawrence: University Press of Kansas, 1998); Duncan McDowell, *Another World: Bermuda and the Rise of Modern Tourism* (London: Macmillan Education, 1999); Orvar Löfgren, *On Holiday: A History of Vacationing* (Berkeley: University of California Press, 1999); Shelley Baronowski and Ellen Furlough, eds., *Being Elsewhere: Tourism, Consumer Culture, and Identity in Modern Europe and North America* (Ann Arbor: University of Michigan Press, 2001); David Crouch and Nina Lűbbren, eds., *Visual Culture and Tourism* (Oxford: Berg, 2003); Margaret McClure, *The Wonder Country: Making New Zealand Tourism* (Auckland: Auckland University Press, 2004); John K. Walton, ed., *Histories of Tourism: Representation, Identity and Conflict* (Clevedon: Channel View, 2005); Dona Brown, *Inventing New England: Regional Tourism in the Nineteenth Century* (Washington: Smithsonian Books, 2007); John K. Walton, "Seaside Tourism and Environmental History," in *Common Ground: Integrating the Social and Environmental in History*, eds. Genevieve Massard-Guilbaud and Stephen Mosley (Newcastle: Cambridge Scholars Publishing, 2011), 66–87; Eric G.E. Zuelow, ed., *Touring Beyond the Nation: A Transnational Approach to European Tourism History* (Farnham: Ashgate, 2011); Peter Robinson, ed., *Tourism: The Key Concepts* (London and New York: Routledge, 2012); and Will B. Mackintosh, *Selling the Sights: The Invention of the Tourist in American Culture* (New York: New York University Press, 2019).

6 Important works on the history of Canadian tourism, including some not mentioned in the text, are Ian McKay, *The Quest of the Folk: Antimodernism and Cultural Selection in Twentieth-Century Nova Scotia* (Montreal and Kingston: McGill-Queen's University Press, 1994); Ian McKay and Robin Bates, *In the Province of History: The Making of the Public Past in Twentieth-Century Nova Scotia* (Montreal and Kingston: McGill-Queen's University Press, 2010); Patricia Jasen, *Wild Things: Nature, Culture, and Tourism in Ontario, 1790–1914* (Toronto: University of Toronto Press, 1995); Karen Dubinsky, *The Second Greatest Disappointment: Honeymooners, Heterosexuality, and the Tourist Industry at Niagara Falls* (Toronto: Between the Lines Press, 1995); James Overton, *Making a World of Difference: Essays on Tourism, Culture, and Development in Newfoundland* (St John's, NL: ISER, 1996); Michael Dawson, *Selling British Columbia: Tourism and Consumer Culture, 1890–1970* (Vancouver: UBC Press, 2004); Cecelia Morgan, *"A Happy Holiday": English Canadians and Transatlantic Tourism, 1870–1930* (Toronto: University of Toronto Press, 2008); Ben Bradley, *British Columbia by the Road: Car Culture*

and the Making of a Modern Landscape (Vancouver: UBC Press, 2017); Alan Gordon, *Time Travel: Tourism and the Rise of the Living History Museum in Mid-Twentieth-Century Canada* (Vancouver: UBC Press, 2017); Nicole Neatby, *From Old Quebec to La Belle Province: Tourism Promotion, Travel Writing, and National Identities, 1920–1967* (Montreal and Kingston: McGill-Queen's University Press, 2018); Ben Bradley, Jay Young, and Colin M. Coates, eds, *Moving Natures: Mobility and the Environment in Canadian History* (Calgary: University of Calgary Press, 2016); Ben Bradley and J.I. Little, eds., "The History of Tourism in Canada," special issue of *Histoire Sociale/Social History* 49, 99 (June 2016); and J.I. Little, *Fashioning the Canadian Landscape: Essays in Travel Writing, Tourism, and National Identity in the Pre-Automobile Era* (Toronto: University of Toronto Press, 2018).

7 Judith Adler, "Tourism and Pastoral: A Decade of Debate," in *The Garden Transformed: Prince Edward Island, 1945–1980*, eds. David Milne, Verner Smitheram, and Satadal Dasgupta (Charlottetown: Ragweed Press, 1982); Sheila Squire, "Ways of Seeing, Ways of Being: Literature, Place, and Tourism in L.M. Montgomery's Prince Edward Island," in *A Few Acres of Snow: Literary and Artistic Images of Canada*, eds. Paul Simpson-Housley and Glen Norcliffe (Oxford, ON: Dundurn Press, 1992), 137–47; Matthew McRae, "The Romance of Canada: Tourism and Nationalism Meet in Charlottetown, 1939," *Acadiensis* 34, 2 (Spring/Summer 2005): 26–45; and Matthew McRae, "New Nationalism in the Cradle of Confederation: Prince Edward Island's Centennial Decade," in *Celebrating Canada: Commemorations, Anniversaries and National Symbols*, eds. Raymond Blake and Matthew Hayday (Toronto: University of Toronto Press, 2018), 339–75.

8 Edward MacDonald, *If You're Stronghearted: Prince Edward Island in the Twentieth Century* (Charlottetown: Prince Edward Island Museum and Heritage Foundation, 2000); Alan MacEachern, *Natural Selections: National Parks in Atlantic Canada, 1935–1970* (Montreal and Kingston: McGill-Queen's University Press, 2001); Alan MacEachern, "Discovering an Island: Travel Writers and Tourism on Prince Edward Island," *The Island Magazine*, no. 29 (Spring/Summer 1991): 8–16; Alan MacEachern, "The Greening of Green Gables: Establishing Prince

Edward Island National Park," *The Island Magazine*, no. 45 (Spring/Summer 1999); Edward MacDonald, "Bridge Over Troubled Waters: The Fixed Link Debate on Prince Edward Island, 1885–1997," in *Bridging Islands: The Impact of Fixed Links*, ed. Godfrey Baldacchino (Charlottetown: Acorn Press, 2007), 29–46; Edward MacDonald, "A Landscape … with Figures: Tourism and Environment on Prince Edward Island," *Acadiensis* 40, 1 (Fall 2011): 70–85; Edward MacDonald and Alan MacEachern, "Rites of Passage: Marine Transportation and Tourism on Prince Edward Island," *Social history/Histoire Sociale* 49, 99 (June 2016): 289–306; Alan MacEachern, "The Landscapes of Tourism," in *Time and a Place: An Environmental History of Prince Edward Island*, eds. Edward MacDonald, Josh MacFadyen, and Irene Novaczek (Montreal and Kingston: McGill-Queen's University Press, 2016), 246–63; Alan MacEachern and Edward MacDonald, "Unwanted Guests: Postwar Tourism and Racism on Prince Edward Island," *The Island Magazine*, no. 82 (Fall/Winter 2017): 35–8; and Edward MacDonald and Alan MacEachern, "How Dolph and Bertha Learned to Like Tourism," *The Island Magazine*, no. 85 (Spring/Summer 2019): 20–7.

9 R.W. Butler, "The Concept of the Tourism Area Cycle Evolution: Implications for Management of Resources," *Canadian Geographer* 24, no. 1 (1980). TALC also became known as the Butler Model.

10 On islands, see particularly John R. Gillis, *Islands of the Mind: How the Human Imagination Created the Atlantic World* (London: Palgrave, 2004), as well as John Gillis, *The Human Shore: Seacoasts in History* (Chicago: University of Chicago Press, 2012); and Alain Corbin, *The Lure of the Sea: The Discovery of the Seaside in the Western World, 1750–1840*, trans. Jocelyn Phelps (London: Penguin Books, 1994). On islands' experiences with tourism, see McClure, *Wonder Country*; McDowell, *Another World*; and Fonda Taylor, *To Hell with Paradise: A History of the Jamaican Tourist Industry* (Pittsburgh: University of Pittsburgh Press, 1993).

11 On landscape appreciation, two down-to-earth Canadian starting points are Jasen, *Wild Things*; and Susan Glickman, *The Picturesque and the Sublime: A Poetics of the Canadian Landscape* (Montreal and Kingston: McGill-Queen's University Press, 1998). The literature on the benefits of the seaside is copious. See, for example, Corbin, *Lure of the Sea*;

John Beckerson and John K. Walton, "Selling the Air: Marketing the Intangible at British Resorts," in Walton, *Histories of Tourism*, 55–68; and Towner.

12 On antimodernism, see McKay, *Quest of the Folk*; David E. Shi, *The Simple Life: Plain Living and High Thinking in American Culture* (New York: Oxford, 1985); and T.J. Jackson Lears, *No Place of Grace: Antimodernism and the Transformation of American Culture* (New York: Pantheon Books, 1981).

13 Prince Edward Island, Departments of Tourism and Parks and Regional Industrial Expansion, *Resident Tourism Attitude Survey 1988* (Charlottetown: 1989), 8.

14 The phrase owes a debt to Brown, *Inventing New England*, which argues, "Tourism is not destiny, imposed on a community or a region by its geography or its history. Tourist industries were built by people," 205.

15 L.M. Montgomery, *The Selected Journals of L.M. Montgomery*, vol. 5: 1935–1942, eds. Mary Rubio and Elizabeth Waterston, 14 August 1938 (Toronto: Oxford University Press), 274–5.

16 Scott Lash and John Urry, *The End of Organized Capitalism* (Cambridge: Polity Press, 1987); and Mackintosh, *Selling the Sights*.

17 See, for example, Urry, *Consuming Places*, 129; and Richard Todd, *The Thing Itself: On the Search for Authenticity* (New York: Riverhead Books, 2008). The original quote is in Henry James to "My darling Mammy," from Florence, 13 October 1869, *The Letters of Henry James*, selected and ed. Percy Lubbock (New York: Scribner's Sons, 1920).

18 We found particularly helpful Jeremy Boissevain, ed., *Coping with Tourists: European Reactions to Mass Tourism* (Providence, RI: Berghahn Books, 1996).

19 This has been recognized: the first line of McRae's "New Nationalism" is "Prince Edward Island has always had something of a love–hate relationship with tourism," 339.

20 As in so many issues surrounding tourism, Prince Edward Islanders were not alone in feeling this way. Margaret McClure notes that New Zealand long considered tourism "'the darling industry,' a frivolous, inconsequential business on the edges of economic life, flirting in the wings while the real work of agriculture took centre stage." McClure, *Wonder Country*, 5.

21 From its title forward, Rothman, *Devil's Bargains* is good on this.

22 "Found Money," *Guardian*, 20 November 1923, 4; and Reigh Tinney, quoted in "P.E. Island Tourist Association Held First Annual Meeting," *The Busy East*, February 1925, 7.

23 Marian Bruce, *Saltwater Road: Tales of Travel on the Northumberland Strait* (Wood Islands, PEI: Wood Islands and Area Development Corporation, 2014), 48. In an email communication with author Edward MacDonald, Bruce corrected the timing of the comment to the early 1930s, rather than the 1940s.

Chapter One

1 *Islander*, 21 July 1871.

2 *Illustrated Historical Atlas of the Province of Prince Edward Island* (Philadelphia: J.H. Meacham & Company, 1880), 64, http://www.islandimagined.ca/meachams_atlas.

3 Meacham's *Illustrated Historical Atlas*, 52.

4 J.L. Holman file, 2603/1, Public Archives and Records Office of Prince Edward Island [henceforth, PARO].

5 "PEI Affairs," Toronto *Globe*, 13 July 1875, 2.

6 "The Governor General and Princess Louise at Seaside Hotel," reprinted from *Canadian Illustrated News*, in *Examiner*, 13 October 1879, 1. Somewhat different information about the visit is given in "Seaside Hotel, Rustico, PEI," 1 February 2011, PEI Heritage Buildings blog, http://peiheritagebuildings.blogspot.ca/2011/02/seaside-hotel.html; and Catherine Hennessey, "A Beautiful Summer Resort," Catherine Hennessey blog, 10 April 2002, archived https://ruk.ca/sites/ruk.ca/files/catherinehennesseyx.pdf.

7 *Canadian Illustrated News*, 24 August 1878, 125.

8 Newspaper clipping, no date, "Seaside Hotel Rustico, PEI"; and Michael O'Grady, "In the Footsteps of Jesse Walter Fewkes: Early Archaeology at Rustico Island," *The Island Magazine* 33 (Spring/Summer 1993): 10–16, http://vre2.upei.ca/islandmagazine/fedora/repository/vre:islemag-batch2-442/OBJ/05_In_the_footsteps_of_jesse_walter_fewkes_p_10-16.pdf.

9 J.L. Holman's nephew, R.T. Holman, became one of the Island's most successful businessmen but made no effort to reopen the Island Park.

10 A New Brunswicker, "A Visit to Prince Edward Island," *Examiner*, 13 July 1880.

11 Karl Baedeker, *The Dominion of Canada with Newfoundland and an Excursion to Alaska* (Leipzig: Karl Baedeker, 1900), 101, https://archive.org/details/cihm_32549. S.W. Silver and Co.'s *Handbook to Canada* called it "a very good hotel" and in James R. Osgood and Co.'s *The Maritime Provinces*, editor Moses F. Sweetser noted that it was "patronized by American tourists" and gave it a one-star rating. *Picturesque Canada* would refer to the islet in Summerside harbour as "the site of the 'Island Park Hotel'" – not mentioning, as the author must have known, that the hotel itself was closed. *Handbook to Canada: A Guide for Travellers and Settlers* (London: S.W. Silver and Co, 1881), 105, https://archive.org/details/swsilvercoshand01cogoog; *The Maritime Provinces: A Handbook for Travellers* 3rd ed. (Boston: James R. Osgood and Co., 1883), 179, https://archive.org/details/maritimeprovince02swee; and Rev. R. Murray, "Prince Edward Island," *Picturesque Canada: The Country as It Was and Is*, ed. George Munro Grant (Toronto: Belden, 1882), 865, https://archive.org/details/picturesquecanad02gran.

12 Benjamin, *The Cruise of the 'Alice May' in the Gulf of St. Lawrence and Adjacent Islands* (New York: D. Appleton, 1885), 7, https://archive.org/details/cihm_00134.

13 Canada, *House of Commons Debates*, 4th Parliament, 2nd Session: Vol. 1, 10 March 1880, 579, http://parl.canadiana.ca/view/oop.debates_HOC0402_01/588?r=0&s=1. Also, "Rustico, a French Canadian settlement is a splendid place for sea-bathing and has delightful scenery in its vicinity. It is frequented by the great and fashionable … In fact, Rustico for quietness and enjoyment, is the very queen of watering places." From the Montreal *Daily Post*, reprinted in *Herald*, 6 June 1883.

14 John Lawson, *Letters on Prince Edward Island* (Charlottetown: G.T. Haszard, 1851), 38, https://archive.org/details/cihm_63161.

15 *Colonial Herald*, 12 September 1840, 3.

16 A.E. Arsenault, president of PEI Tourist Association, "Was Island's First Tourist," *Guardian*, 24 August 1934, 13. See also Creelman MacArthur and C.W. Robinson, 25 April 1934, Canada, *Debates of the Senate of Canada*, 17th Parliament, 5th Session: Volume 1 (1934), 300. Cartier might be better

called the Island's first tourism promoter. His 1534 description of the land around Cape Kildare as "la plus belle qu'i soict possible de voir" has become the most blurbed description of the Island in more than a century of tourism literature, translated as "the fairest land 'tis possible to see." Ignore the choice of "'tis" as a likely translation of sixteenth-century French, and ignore too that Cartier called a number of places the finest he had seen – even after having seen Cape Kildare. See MacEachern, "Landscapes of Tourism," 247–8.

17 Piers Brendon, *Thomas Cook: 150 Years of Popular Tourism* (London: Secker and Warburg, 1991). On tourism's history generally, see Löfgren, *On Holiday*; and Towner, *An Historical Geography of Recreation and Tourism*.

18 Mackintosh, *Selling the Sights*, 11. See also Richard H. Gassan, *The Birth of American Tourism: New York, the Hudson Valley, and American Culture, 1785–1835* (Amherst, MA: University of Massachusetts Press, 2008); Cindy S. Aron, *Working at Play: A History of Vacations in the United States* (New York: Oxford University Press, 1999); and Brown, *Inventing New England*.

19 See Holman, *Sailstrait* blog; and PEI's Coastal Vessels and Ferries, http://www.islandregister.com/ship_data5.html, for more on PEI's early steamships.

20 On Americans in the mackerel fishery, see Edward MacDonald and Boyde Beck, "Lines in the Water: Time and Place in a Fishery," *Time and a Place*, 224–5; and Edward MacDonald, "The Yankee Gale," *The Island Magazine* 38 (Fall/Winter 1995): 17–25.

21 *Haszard's Gazette*, 13 July 1852, 2.

22 *Haszard's Gazette*, 24 May 1856, 5. Likewise, the colonial secretary believed that if given good steamer service American travellers might well visit, seeing that "they had almost exhausted all the places of interest in their own country." *Examiner*, 23 March 1857, 1.

23 Albert G. Catlin, Charlottetown, to Lewis Cass, Secretary of State, Washington, 1 October 1858, Despatches from the United States Consuls in Charlottetown, 3024/1, PARO.

24 *Ross's Weekly*, 9 June 1864.

25 Isabella Bird, *The Englishwoman in America* (London: J. Murray, 1856), 37, https://archive.org/details/englishwomaninaoobirdgoog.

26 *Haszard's Gazette*, 20 July 1852, 3, and 3 August 1852, 3.

27 "Shaw's Hotel National Historic Site of Canada," Canada's Historic Places, http://www.historicplaces.ca/en/rep-reg/place-lieu.aspx?id=12974.

28 Summerside *Progress*, 13 August 1866, 4. On Keefe and the Commercial, see Alice Gordon Green, *Footprints on the Sands of Time: A History of Alberton* (Alberton, PEI: Alberton Historical Group, 1980), 31–2.

29 Holman, "Civil War Blockade Runner was the First of the 'Boston Boats," *Sailstrait* blog, 27 January 2015.

30 "As Others See Us," reprint of Francis Proctor article in Cape Ann *Advertiser*, Gloucester, Massachusetts, in *Herald*, 26 August 1885.

31 "A Trip to P.E. Island, no.1," Halifax *Reporter*, undated, reprinted in *Patriot*, 23 August 1873.

32 "The Seaside Hotel," *Patriot*, 29 July 1878, 4.

33 *Islander*, 21 July 1871.

34 *Patriot*, 29 July 1878.

35 See Meacham's *Illustrated Historical Atlas*, 121, 142, 78, 126, 97, and 70 respectively. John Nelson, the original owner of the Seaside, was by this point managing the Lorne.

36 Charles MacKay, "A Week in Prince Edward Island," *The Fortnightly Review* 5, no. 26 (1 June 1866): 143; and Benjamin, *The Atlantic Islands*, 203.

37 *Islander*, 21 July 1871.

38 See, for example, "A Trip to P.E. Island," Halifax *Reporter*, reprinted in *Patriot*, 23 August 1873.

39 HF.79.15.3, PARO.

40 S.G.W. Benjamin, "Prince Edward Island," *Harper's New Monthly Magazine* 55 (September 1877): 545–54; and Benjamin, *The Atlantic Islands as Resorts of Health and Pleasure* (New York: Harper & Brothers, 1878), app. 2, 271, and 259, https://archive.org/details/atlanticislandsaoobenj. Benjamin was a renaissance man: besides being a travel writer, he was an accomplished marine painter, an art historian, and a one-time diplomat to Persia.

41 Thomas F. Anderson, Boston *Sunday Globe*, cited in *The Maple Leaf*, July 1911, 2.

42 Charles Dudley Warner, *Baddeck and That Sort of Thing* (Boston: J.R. Osgood and Co., 1874), 170–1, https://archive.org/details/baddeckandthatso2warngoog. Cape Bretoners did not so quickly forgive Warner's assessment of them; see McKay and Bates, *In the Province of History*, 262–3. J.I. Little explores American travel writers' more ambivalent responses to Cape Breton in "'A

Fine, Hardy, Good-Looking Race of People': Travel Writers, Tourism Promoters, and the Highland Scots Identity on Cape Breton Island, 1829–1920," *Acadiensis* 44, 1 (Winter/Spring 2015): 20–35.

43 On the rise of travel literature in Britain and the US, see James Buzard, *The Beaten Track: European Tourism, Literature, and the Ways to Culture, 1800–1918* (New York: Oxford University Press, 1993); Larzer Ziff, *Return Passages: Great American Travel Writing, 1780–1910* (New Haven: Yale University Press, 2001); and Gassan, *The Birth of American Tourism*, 70–84.

44 Examining PEI travel accounts and immigration promotional material of an earlier era, Boyde Beck writes that it "articulated and perhaps helped to shape the foundations for that sense of pride and patriotism that burned so fiercely in the breasts of so many Islanders during the years of the Confederation crisis." Beck, "'The Fairest Land That Might Possibly Be Seen': The Image of Prince Edward Island in Some Descriptive Accounts, 1750–1860," unpublished MA thesis, Queen's University, 1984, 26.

45 James Doyle, ed., *Yankees in Canada: A Collection of Nineteenth-Century Travel Narratives* (Downsview: ECW Press, 1980), 20.

46 The airplane and the Confederation Bridge have removed some of that power. In his classic *The Tourist*, Jakle wrote of flying, "It was not really travel at all; it was merely being sent in an enclosed capsule substantially divorced from outside reality," 178.

47 Warner, *Baddeck and That Sort of Thing*, 170.

48 Benjamin, *Atlantic Islands*, 190.

49 For example, Benjamin, *Atlantic Islands*, 198; and Warner, *Baddeck and That Sort of Thing*, 170.

50 See, for example, Martin V. Melosi, "The Age of Miasmas," part 1 of *The Sanitary City: Environmental Services in Urban America from Colonial Times to the Present* (Pittsburgh: University of Pittsburgh Press, 2008); and Gregg Mitman, *Breathing Space: How Allergies Shape Our Lives and Landscapes* (New Haven: Yale University Press, 2007).

51 "The Island as a Resort for Visitors," Summerside *Journal*, 14 May 1868.

52 "Prince Edward Island," *Cor. Boston Advertiser*, reprinted in *Patriot*, 6 December 1873.

53 *The Canadian Magazine* 17, 4 (August 1901): 388. Discussed in *Prince Edward Island Magazine*,

August 1901, 233–4, http://vre2.upei.ca/peimagazine/fedora/repository/peimag:228/-/%20peimag:228.

54 Benjamin, *Atlantic Islands*, 197. Benjamin believed that small islands were second only to sea voyages in promoting good health and assured readers that "No islands are included in these pages except such as are free from the visitations of yellow fever or persistent malarial and zymotic epidemics," 7.

55 Summerside *Progress*, 13 August 1866, 4.

56 Canada, Atlantic, and Plant S.S. Co, *Nova Scotia, Cape Breton, Prince Edward Island, and Newfoundland* (Buffalo: Matthews-Northurp, ca. 1890s), no pagination, https://archive.org/details/novascotiacapebroocana.

57 Fred Horne, *Human History, Prince Edward Island National Park* (Ottawa: 1979), 122, http://parkscanadahistory.com/series/mrs/352.pdf.

58 Murray, "Prince Edward Island," 866. Having said that, through the late nineteenth century there was somewhat more tourism interest in the Island's autumn than there is even today. Writer Anna L. Ward, for example, said that the fall was when PEI was "at its best." "The Garden of British North America," *Frank Leslie's Popular Monthly*, 1 August 1887, 183. But the season only stretched so far. Benjamin joked that PEI offered "special inducements to those who enjoy six months of snow." Benjamin, *Atlantic Islands*, 197.

59 Benjamin, *Cruise of the Alice May*, 9.

60 Baedeker, *Dominion of Canada*, 99.

61 Murray, "Prince Edward Island," 854. There are huge, long-developed literatures on the sublime and the picturesque. For valuable Canadian introductions to the concepts, see Jasen, *Wild Things*; and Glickman, *The Picturesque and the Sublime.*

62 Benjamin, *Atlantic Islands*, 198–9.

63 Murray, "Prince Edward Island," 853.

64 In *The Maritime Provinces*, Sweetser stated, "Some travellers have greatly admired the rural scenery of its suburban roads, but others have reported them as tame and uninteresting. The same conflict of opinion exists with regard to the scenery of the whole island," 177. Roland Barthes's line that "The picturesque is found any time the ground is uneven" seems appropriate here. Barthes, *Mythologies*, trans. Annette Lavers (New York: Hill and Wang, 1972 [1957]), 81.

65 See MacDonald, "Landscape … with Figures."

66 W. Fraser Rae, *Newfoundland to Manitoba through Canada's Maritime, Mining, and Prairie Provinces* (New York: G.P. Putnam's Sons, 1881), 115, https://archive.org/details/newfoundlandtom01raegoog.

67 Ward, "Garden of British North America," 183.

68 Benjamin, *Atlantic Islands*, 199.

69 Murray, "Prince Edward Island," 853. While difficult to measure, later travel accounts and promotional material seemed more willing to compare Prince Edward Island to American sites. An 1890s guide declared that "Those who have seen some of the more fertile sections of the Illinois prairies, with their undulating surface, scattering forests, wood-fringed streams, and prosperous farms, have seen an American reproduction of Prince Edward Island." *Nova Scotia, Cape Breton*, no pagination. A Canadian author spoke in 1908 of PEI's "unlikeness" to all other parts of the continent, and yet discussed it repeatedly in terms of the United States: Island oysters were "the luxury of American restaurants," for example, and sea gulls, oddly, were "like the sea gulls of Manhattan." Cyrus MacMillan, "Beautiful Prince Edward Island: The Second Acadie of the North," Toronto *Globe*, 25 July 1908, 2. Although MacMillan did not mention it in the article, he had grown up in Wood Islands, PEI.

70 Dawson, *Hand-Book for the Dominion of Canada*, prepared for the Meeting of the British Association for the Advancement of Science, at Montreal, 1884 (Montreal: Dawson Brothers, 1884), 101, https://archive.org/details/handbookfordomioosciegoog.

71 John Rowan, *The Emigrant and Sportsman in Canada* (London: E. Stanford, 1876), 186, https://archive.org/details/emigrantsportsmaoorowaiala.

72 See McKay and Bates, *In the Province of History*, esp. chapter 2.

73 Sweetser, *Maritime Provinces*, 177; and Withrow, 69. Sweetser had been quoting an earlier source himself, but since Withrow copied liberally from Sweetser throughout, it is reasonable to assume that is whom he was copying from here.

74 For example, Benjamin, *Atlantic Islands*, 201. The name of the Acadia Hotel in Grand Tracadie dictated it would take this theme furthest, opening its 1890s promotional booklet with two stanzas of "Evangeline." Acadia Hotel, *Prince Edward Island as a Summer Resort: Where It Is and How to Get There*

(Charlottetown: Acadia Hotel, 1893), frontispiece, https://archive.org/details/cihm_39938.

75 Warner, *Baddeck and That Sort of Thing*, 170.

76 For example, the editor of *The Canadian Courier* x, 2 (10 June 1911): 12; and editor of the *Canadian Magazine*, who also called it "the dingiest and most unprogressive city in the east," cited in *Prince Edward Island Magazine*, August 1901.

77 Canada, Atlantic, and Plant S.S. Co., *Nova Scotia, Cape Breton*, no pagination.

78 "To PEI," *Trades Journal*, 3 August 1887, 2.

79 Neil McLeod, "Prince Edward Island," *New England Magazine* 10 (1894): 768.

80 Benjamin, *Atlantic Islands*, 203.

81 Benjamin, *Cruise of the Alice May*, 17.

82 International Steamship Co. *The Sea Coast Resorts of Eastern Maine, New Brunswick, Nova Scotia, Prince Edward Isld, Cape Breton* (Boston: Rand Avery, 1892), 69.

83 New York *World*, reprinted in *Examiner*, 21 January 1879. The Island editor noted that to a New Yorker, "the sight of a cow would be a novelty" but admitted, "There are some poor districts on the Island."

84 J. Heber Hastam, "How Prince Edward Island Settled Its Land Question," *Arena* 16 (October 1896): 743; Intercolonial Railway and Prince Edward Island Railway of Canada, *Forest Stream and Seashore* (Springhill, NS: s.n., 1892), 156, https://archive.org/details/cihm_06075; and Rowan, *Emigrant and Sportsman*, 180.

85 Benjamin, *Atlantic Islands*, 203–4.

86 Benjamin, *Cruise of the Alice May*, 6 and 16–17.

87 Intercolonial, *Forest Stream and Seashore*, 154.

88 Acadia Hotel, *Prince Edward Island as a Summer Resort*, frontispiece.

89 Seaside Hotel register, HF.79.15.3, PARO. These numbers by necessity represent the visitors who signed the register, not all who stayed in the hotel. But a "John Smith" signature might represent a man alone, a husband and wife, or a family of ten. Our practice was to count each name (ex. "John Smith") as one; a family of unidentified size (ex. "John Smith and family") as four; and, of course, a family of identified size (ex. "John Smith, wife, and four children") by its identified size (in this case, six). There were 129 indecipherable addresses in the register.

90 "Picturesque Scenes in the East," *Canadian Courier* 2, 1 (1 June 1907): 18. Alexander Martin, M.P. for

Queen's, described PEI in 1908 as "becoming, perhaps the best summer resort in Canada. It was first taken advantage of by the Americans, but now also by people from all parts of Canada." Martin, 9 June 1908, Canada, House of Commons Debates, 10th Parliament, 4th Session, vol. 1, 10157, http://parl.canadiana.ca/view/oop.debates_HOC1004_05/939?r=0&s=1.

91 Canada, Dominion Bureau of Statistics, *The Maritime Provinces in Their Relation to the National Economy of Canada: A Statistical Study of Their Social and Economic Condition* (Ottawa: Government of Canada, 1934), cited in Andrew Hill Clark, *Three Centuries and the Island: A Historical Geography of Settlement and Agriculture in Prince Edward Island, Canada* (Toronto: University of Toronto Press, 1959), 121.

92 Allan A. Brookes, "Islanders in the Boston States, 1850–1900," *The Island Magazine* 2 (Spring/Summer 1977): 11.

93 See Brookes, "Islanders in the Boston States;" Patricia A. Thornton, "The Problems of Out-Migration from Atlantic Canada, 1871–1921," *Acadiensis* 15, 1 (1986): 3–34; Clark, *Three Centuries*, 122 and 244, n4.

94 "Our New York Correspondent," *Prince Edward Island Magazine*, April 1899, 82. Lucy Maud Montgomery later explained why she submitted *Anne of Green Gables* to a Boston publishing firm: "It was natural for a Prince Edward Island girl to send her manuscript to Boston rather than Montreal or Toronto, even if she had been rebuffed there before. All Maritime province ambition turns to Boston." *Chatelaine*, June 1928, 23.

95 Thomas F. Anderson, "With Our Next-Door Neighbors," Boston *Daily Globe*, 7 May 1911, SM12.

96 Andrew Robb, "Michael A. McInnis, *The Maple Leaf*, and Migration from Prince Edward Island," *The Island Magazine* 17 (Summer 1985): 15–19. Of 641 subscribers in 1909, just more than one-quarter listed Island addresses.

97 See, for example, *The Maple Leaf*, September 1910, 1; November 1912, 6 ("Visitor to the Island of 'Red Clay' Meets Old Friends. Finds Prosperity and Contentment on Every Side"); September 1913, 7.

98 "As Others See Us."

99 For example, in the House of Commons in 1934, PEI MP Creelman MacArthur differentiated between "the real tourist" and expatriates whom "We cannot

100 strictly classify ... as tourists, because they spend their vacations at the homes of relatives or friends." MacArthur, 25 April 1934, in House of Commons, *Debates*, 17th Parliament, 5th session, vol. 1, 300.

100 *Weekly Examiner*, 19 August 1881.

101 An 1886 party of twelve from Massachusetts, for example, includes two "Mrs" and six "Miss."

102 "As Others See Us."

103 See, for example, *Canadian Presbyterian* 11, 37 (12 September 1883), 588; Francis Procter, Gloucester *Advertiser*, reprinted in *Herald*, 26 August 1885; and "Hope" letter to the editor, Toronto *Globe*, 18 October 1886, 4.

104 Don, in *Saturday Night*, reprinted in *The Monetary Times, Trade Review and Insurance Chronicle* 28, 9 (31 August 1894): 288.

105 Holman, "Civil War Blockade Runner."

106 Ward, "Garden of British North America," 183.

107 PEI, *Debates and Proceedings of the House of Assembly*, 1871, 67.

108 "The New Hotel," *Herald*, 2 September 1885.

109 Toronto *Globe*, 5 August 1872, 2.

110 *Herald*, 2 September 1885.

111 *Daily Examiner*, 26 August 1887.

112 "After 1900, there was a discernible falling off in the popularity of the travel narrative as a literary genre in the United States." Doyle, *Yankees in Canada*, 19.

113 Intercolonial, *Forest Stream and Seashore*, 151. This served as the opening to the PEI section of subsequent editions of this book through 1908 and as the opening of the railways' *Prince Edward Island: The Garden of the Gulf* as late as 1913.

114 Acadia Hotel, *Prince Edward Island as a Summer Resort*.

115 W.H. Crosskill, *Prince Edward Island, Garden Province of Canada: Its History, Interests, and Resources, with Information for Tourists, etc.* (Charlottetown: Murley & Garnhum for the PEI government, 1899) https://archive.org/details/cihm_03629.

116 Crosskill, *Prince Edward Island*, 72.

117 The Scotch Highlander "never changes," he wrote, and Acadians are "clannish, and stick to their own language and peculiar costume; they live on potatoes and fish, marry in their teens, and seem to have no ambition to improve their condition in life." Rowan, *Emigrant and Sportsman*, 186.

118 Acadia Hotel, *Prince Edward Island as a Summer Resort*, 2, 3, 5.

119 Acadia Hotel and Acadia Spring, *The North Shore of Prince Edward Island* (no publishing information, 1905).

120 *Examiner, Prince Edward Island Illustrated* (Charlottetown: Examiner, 1897), 44–5. https://archive.org/details/cihm_93627.

121 Jesse T. Lazear to Charlotte C. Sweitzer, 25 August 1901, Series 1, Philip S. Hench Walter Reed Yellow Fever collection, Claude Moore Health Sciences Library, University of Virginia. https://search.lib.virginia.edu/catalog/uva-lib:2222252.

122 PEI Development and Tourist Association, *Beautiful... Prince Edward Island* (Charlottetown: PEI Development and Tourist Association, n.d. [ca. 1905?]), 13. https://archive.org/details/cihm_53319. The booklet is mistakenly dated here as having been published in 1893.

123 Acadia Hotel, *Prince Edward Island as a Summer Resort*, 19.

124 "Traveller," *Examiner*, March 1902, cited in "Tourist Section," *Guardian-Patriot* Centennial Souvenir Edition 1873–1973.

125 *Prince Edward Island Magazine*, July 1902, 180. For a full run of the magazine, see http://vre2.upei.ca/peimagazine/. See more tourism boosting, for example, on July 1899, 166; June 1899, 199; and July 1902, 183.

126 *Prince Edward Island Magazine*, July 1900, http://vre2.upei.ca/peimagazine/fedora/repository/peimag:135/-/%20peimag:135.

127 Editor, "Town and Cities," *Canadian Magazine* 17, 4 (August 1901), 389. Not until 1931 did the capital get its first-rate hotel, the Charlottetown – built by CN Railway, a representative of the next dominant transportation technology.

128 *Guardian*, 30 August 1899, 6.

129 Edna L. Dixon, "Rambling and Memories: How Can We Forget," 1983, PARO 4196. See also Reg Thompson, "Food and Travel in PEI's Bygone Days," CBC Radio, 17 August 2019, https://www.cbc.ca/news/canada/prince-edward-island/pei-bygone-days-dutch-thompson-1.5245982; and *Guardian*, 6 March 1909, 5.

130 *Dun and Bradstreet Reference Books* (Toronto: Dun and Bradstreet of Canada, 1875–1905).

131 Sweetser, *Maritime Provinces*, 175.

132 *Prince Edward Island: Information Regarding Its Climate, Soil, and Resources, Suitability for Summer Visitors and Tourists …* (Ottawa: MacLean, Roger & Co., 1888), 15, https://archive.org/details/cihm_12147. An earlier edition of this booklet, from 1883, promoted PEI principally for settlement or investment, and only in the second edition was "*Suitability for Summer Visitors and Tourists*" added to the title. See https://archive.org/details/cihm_12146.

133 See Thompson, "Food and Travel."

134 International Steamship, *Sea Coast Resorts*, 69. Even of the Island's hotels it was said, "They are homes; and it is this quality of homelikeness that more than compensates for the lack of electric bells and elevators." McLeod, "Prince Edward Island," 767.

135 A.B. Warburton to William Owen, no date, box 2 no.215 and no.220, Owen family papers, PARO 3744.

136 Seaside Hotel register, HF.79.15.3, PARO. The register was not used for the 1903 season, and the hotel was not opened in 1904 or 1905. The numbers from Prince Edward Island, the other Maritime provinces, and Massachusetts saw the biggest drop over time, while those from Ontario and Quebec remained steadiest.

137 Judith Tulloch, "Alexander McDonald and Dalvay-by-the-Sea," *The Island Magazine* 35 (Spring/Summer 1994): 10–15; and Dalvay-by-the-Sea Hotel, http://www.historicplaces.ca/en/rep-reg/place-lieu.aspx?id=4308.

138 Ward, "Garden of British North America," 183.

139 Toronto *Globe*, 31 July 1901, 2.

140 See Linda M. Peake, "Establishing a Theatrical Tradition: Prince Edward Island, 1800–1900," *Theatre Research in Canada* 2, 2 (Fall 1981): 117–32, https://journals-lib-unb-ca.proxy1.lib.uwo.ca/index.php/TRIC/article/view/7511; Adele Townshend, "Drama at Abells Cape," *The Island Magazine* 7 (Spring/Summer 1979), 33–7; Reginald Carrington Short, "The C.P. Flockton Comedy Company," *The Island Magazine* 11 (Spring/Summer 1982), 23–8; "Bay Fortune Notes," *Guardian*, 1 March 1899, 7; and *Guardian*, 7 February 1899, 7.

141 "Summer Visitors," *Guardian*, 30 April 1901, 2. Writer Henry F. Coombs had said much the same in the *Guardian* a decade earlier: "Houses of the Shaw class at Brackley Point are more likely to pay than expensive structures, which cost a large sum to keep up. The bulk of the tourist travel that will come as far east as P.E. Island are people of limited means." *Guardian*, 6 May 1891, 2.

142 "Summerside to Make Progress," *Guardian*, 12 March 1903, 8.

143 On New England's first Old Home Weeks, see Brown, *Inventing New England*, 135–42.

144 Some Islanders conceived the appeal of an Old Home Week strictly in social terms. Janetta MacPhail of Orwell wrote the *Guardian* that it would "promote long-remembered family reunions" and a "healthful, delightful, and in some cases even romantic renewal of old friendships." MacPhail, "The Old Home Week," *Guardian*, 26 June 1903, 1; and *Guardian*, 26 June 1903, 2. But others interested in developing the tourist trade recognized that it promised a clear focus for marketing: the *Guardian* noted that "there are enough of the Island's sons and daughters now abroad to make the biggest weeks' tourist business that was ever yet done by the railways and steamboats in northeastern North America." *Guardian*, 26 July 1902, 4. The newspaper recognized potential social results, too: "And it is not too much to hope that at least some of those who come only for a week may decide to remain for the balance of their lives."

145 See "In 'Garden of the Gulf': Prince Edward Island to Have an 'Old-Home' Reunion," Boston *Globe*, 12 June 1904, 28; "Prince Edward Island's Old-Home Week," Boston *Globe*, 12 July 1904, 11; the front-page coverage of *Guardian*, 11 July 1904 (including the banner headline "Summerside Extends a Hearty Welcome to the Island Sons"); and Summerside Improvement and Tourist Association, *Prince Edward Island: The Garden of the Gulf and Its Attractions – Programme of the Islanders Reunion Celebration* (publishing information not given: 1904). Whether the association negotiated a similar excursion rate for those travelling from Central Canada is unclear.

146 Summerside *Journal*, 13 July 1904.

147 *Guardian*, 28 May 1904, 5; 31 May 1904, 5; and 5 July 1904, 5. On Hughes, see "George Edward Hughes," Prince Edward Island Legislative Documents Online [henceforth, PEILDO], http://www.peildo.ca/fedora/repository/leg%3A25460.

148 *Guardian*, 2 May 1905, 1.

149 "Charlottetown to Have an Old Home Week," *Guardian*, 28 March 1905, 1. Note that the term "Old Home Week" was not associated with the Provincial Exhibition, as it is today. The exhibition dates to 1888 but only took up the name "Old Home Week" early in the Second World War.

150 *Guardian*, 29 April 1905, 1; *Guardian*, 8 June 1905, 4; and *Examiner*, 17 July 1905. The arrangement that was worked out with the Canadian Pacific Railway demonstrates the improvised nature of destination tourism in this era. The price for return tickets to PEI from Ontario or Quebec depended on how many others bought. If more than 300 tickets were sold, the return ride was free; if 50 to 300, the return from Montreal was free and they paid one-third for the rest; if 10 to 50, the return from Montreal was free and they paid two-thirds for the rest. The Plant Line steamer from Boston simply reduced its return fare from $18 to $11.

151 *Guardian*, 17 May 1906, 1.

152 *Examiner*, 17 July 1905. On where the expatriates were coming from, see "The Celebration of Old Home Week Begins," *Guardian*, 25 July 1905, 1 and 5.

153 *Guardian*, 10 July 1905, 2.

154 "Development and Tourist Assoc'n," *Guardian*, 16 May 1906, 1.

155 V Edward VII, Cap.20, *The Acts of the General Assembly of Prince Edward Island*, 1905 (Charlottetown: Queen's Printer, 1905), 83.

156 "Fire Destroys Seaside Hotel," *Guardian*, 15 January 1906, 1; and "Destruction of Acadia Hotel," *Guardian*, 17 August 1906, 1. They joined the Island Park Hotel, which had burned down in late 1904. "Island Park Hotel Destroyed by Fire," *Guardian*, 1 December 1904, 1.

157 Montgomery herself said that the community of White Sands was based on Rustico, and Montgomery scholar Shelagh Squire calls it "highly probable" the White Sands hotel was modelled on the foremost resort of the author's own childhood. Montgomery, *Selected Journals*, vol. 1: 1889–1910, 16 August 1907, 330–1; vol.2: 1910–1921, 27 January 1911, 40; and Shelagh Squire, "L.M. Montgomery's Prince Edward Island: A Study of Literary Landscapes and Tourist Development," unpublished MA thesis, Carleton University, 1988, 133.

158 Montgomery, *Anne of Green Gables* (Toronto: Seal, 1996 [1908]), 271–4.

Chapter Two

1 Lucy Maud Montgomery wrote her friend, "Do you know I was nearly run over by an *automobile* last night! Automobiles in Cavendish! There is no such thing as solitude left on earth!" Montgomery to Ephraim Weber, 8 October 1906, in Wilfrid Eggleston, ed., *The Green Gables Letters from L.M. Montgomery to Ephraim Weber, 1905–1909*, 2 ed. (Ottawa: Borealis Press, 1981 [1960]), 59. See Sasha Mullally, "'Daisy,' 'Dodgie,' and 'Lady Jane Grey Dort': LM Montgomery and the Automobile," *L.M. Montgomery and Canadian Culture*, eds. Irene Gammel and Elizabeth Epperly (Toronto: University of Toronto Press, 1999), 120–31.

2 On the ban, see PEI, *Journal of the Legislative Assembly* [henceforth, *JLA*], 1911, 58–60, http://www.peildo.ca/fedora/repository/leg:8904; *Guardian*, 25 March 1908, 1; Deborah Stewart, "The Island Meets the Auto," *The Island Magazine* 5 (Fall/Winter 1978): 9–14. On Smith and Agnew, see *Biographies of the Members of the Legislative Assembly*, PEILDO, http://www.peildo.ca/fedora/repository/leg%3Abiography.

3 *Patriot*, 14 April 1913.

4 McDowell, *Another World*, 68.

5 All but three were based in Charlottetown. See *McAlpine's Prince Edward Island Directory* (Halifax: McAlpine Publishing Co. Ltd, 1904 and 1909 eds.).

6 "Queen's County Guardian," *Guardian*, 11 June 1907, 7.

7 On Smith and Montgomery, see Mary Henley Rubio, *Lucy Maud Montgomery: The Gift of Wings* (Toronto: Doubleday, 2008).

8 "A 200,000 Club Formed in Prince Edward Island," St John *Sun*, 16 May 1907, 4.

9 *Guardian*, 11 June 1907, 1.

10 "Queen's County Guardian," *Guardian*, 17 July 1907, 7. Nine of the twenty-seven officers of the new organization had been in the executive of the provincial tourist association. Only Secretary W.H. Crosskill resigned. Although Reverend Smith continued to work on the club's behalf, for whatever reason, he was not listed as one of its officers.

11 *Guardian*, 28 March 1908, 1.

12 The very last reference to the Tourist and 200,000 Club is in "Queen's County Guardian," *Guardian*, 16 July 1908, 5. In 1909, Reverend Smith moved to Halifax and became an editor of the *Presbyterian Witness*.

13 *Guardian*, 29 November 1923, 4.

14 Crosskill, *Prince Edward Island*. As mentioned, Crosskill was a founding member of the provincial tourist association.

15 Alfred Lefurgey, 1 October 1903, Canada, *House of Commons Debates*, 9th Parliament, 3rd Session, vol. 6, 12840, http://parl.canadiana.ca/view/oop.debates_HOC0903_06/120?r=0&s=3.

16 Lefurgey, 7 July 1904, Canada, *House of Commons Debates*, 9th Parliament, 4th Session, vol. 4, 6229, http://parl.canadiana.ca/view/oop.debates_HOC0904_04/111?r=0&s=1; Edward Hackett, 5 July 1904, Canada, *House of Commons Debates*, 9th Parliament, 4th Session, vol. 3, 5929, http://parl.canadiana.ca/view/oop.debates_HOC0904_03/1013?r=0&s=1; and Alexander Warburton, 7 February 1910, Canada, *House of Commons Debates*, 11th Parliament, 2nd Session, vol. 2, 3189, http://parl.canadiana.ca/view/oop.debates_HOC1102_02/617?r=0&s=1.

17 Alexander Martin, 9 June 1908, Canada, *House of Commons Debates*, 10th Parliament, 4th Session, vol. 4, 10157, http://parl.canadiana.ca/view/oop.debates_HOC1004_05/939?r=0&s=2.

18 See, for example, *The Canadian Courier*, 10 June 1911, 12; 20 April 1912, 14; and 8 June 1912, 26; quote from the latter. Cooper returned again and again to the topic because of how his original article, written around 1900, was received: "The people were so angry at being given advice by a man 'from Canada' that when a second visit was planned some hot-heads talked of getting a few rotten eggs ready for the occasion," 10 June 1911, 12.

19 By comparison, the article listed thirty-nine in Ontario, seventeen in Quebec, eight in BC, two in Manitoba, and one in Saskatchewan. "Some Canadian Summer Resorts and Hostelries," *The Canadian Courier*, 1 June 1907, 33. On the Cliff and North Shore Hotels, see *P.E.I. Heritage Buildings* blog, http://peiheritagebuildings.blogspot.ca/2012/01/north-shore-hotel-malpeque.html.

20 Harry Tinson Holman, "'Our Quiet but Engaging Scenery': W.S. Louson and the Picturing of Prince Edward Island," *The Island Magazine* 80 (Fall/Winter 2016): 30–5; Harry Tinson Holman, *Straitpost: The Early Postcards of Prince Edward Island* blog, https://straitpost.wordpress.com/; Mary Ledwell, "The Louson Portfolio," *The Island Magazine* 29

(Spring/Summer 1991): 3–8, http://vre2.upei.ca/islandmagazine/fedora/repository/vre%3Aislemag-batch2-383/OBJ; and Mary Ledwell, "The William Steele Louson Fonds," *Archivaria* 34 (Summer 1992): 166–74.

21 See W.S. Louson, *Charlottetown, the Beautiful City of Prince Edward Island: The Capital of the Garden of the Gulf* (Grand Rapids, MI: James Bayne Co., for Carter & Co., Charlottetown, 1903), https://archive.org/details/charlottetownbea00lous; and W.S. Louson, *Prince Edward Island, The Garden of the Gulf* (Grand Rapids, MI: James Bayne Co., for Carter & Co., Charlottetown, ca. 1905).

22 "Looking for Building and Factory Sites," *Guardian*, 8 April 1912, 2.

23 "A Publicity Agent," *The Island Farmer*, 12 June 1912, 4.

24 Mr Bradley, "Meeting of Anti-Automobilists," *Guardian*, 20 August 1914, 1.

25 Premier J.A. Mathieson to J.E.B. McCready, 26 August 1912, Publicity Agent fonds, 4502/1, PARO.

26 Norman Lambert, "Auto on Probation on Prince Edward Island," Toronto *Globe*, 22 November 1913, 12.

27 "Farmer," letter to the editor, *Patriot*, 14 March 1908.

28 D.L. MacKinnon, letter to the editor, *Guardian*, 16 March 1908, 2. Similar sentiment may be found, for example, in Benjamin Clow, "The Auto Question," letter to editor, *Guardian*, 3 April 1912, 2; and "The Automobile Question," letter to the editor, *Guardian*, 10 April 1912, 2.

29 *The Maple Leaf*, August 1908, 3.

30 For example, the Calgary *Albertan* stated, "If the Legislature now executes a man for insisting that the world moves, its fame should be complete" (cited in *Guardian*, 14 April 1908, 2); and *The Canadian Courier* called PEI "the funniest spot on earth" and urged it to "stop grumbling and make the most of its exceptional opportunities" (3, 18 [4 April 1908]: 6). Callbeck has suggested that the 1908 Automobile Act "probably cost the province a great loss in tourist dollars and gained it great publicity abroad." Lorne C. Callbeck, "Economic and Social Development Since Confederation," in *Canada's Smallest Province: A History of P.E.I.*, ed. Francis W.P. Bolger (Charlottetown: Centennial Commission, 1973), 350. As interesting an idea as that is, there is no evidence to support it.

31 "What Became of the Tourist," *Guardian*, 10 September 1910, 14. A Vermonter writing in the

Guardian offered the general opinion that "On my return to my native Island this year I find much complaint regarding the falling off of tourist travel." He pinned the blame in part on the car embargo. "Hotels and Automobiles," letter to the editor, *Guardian*, 20 August 1910, 8. However, others said that tourist numbers were actually rising. Estella Howard, "A Woman's Letter on Autos," letter to the editor, *Guardian*, 25 April 1912, 2.

32 Alan MacEachern, "Canada's Best Idea? The Canadian and American National Park Services in the 1910s," *National Parks Beyond the Nation: Global Perspectives on 'America's Best Idea,'* eds. Adrian Howkins, Jared Orsi, Mark Fiege (Norman: University of Oklahoma Press, 2016), 51–67.

33 Deborah Stewart notes that 1913 was the year the North American production of automobiles surpassed that of buggies and wagons. Stewart, "Island Meets the Auto," 11.

34 Progress, "Do You Want a Bigger, Better and Busier State of Affairs for Your Island Home? Read This and Answer," advertisement, *Guardian*, 30 March and 2 April 1912, 9.

35 "The Automobile Bill," *Guardian*, 12 April 1913, 9. Three members of the delegation, Benjamin Rogers, W.F. Tidmarsh, and James Paton, had been members of the defunct provincial tourist association.

36 Katherine Dewar, "John A. Dewar: The Principled Maverick," *The Island Magazine* 43 (Spring/Summer 1998): 3–7; and Sasha Mullally, "The Machine in the Garden: A Glimpse at Early Automobile Ownership on Prince Edward Island, 1917," *The Island Magazine* 54 (Fall/Winter 2003): 16–25. Tuesdays, Thursdays, Saturdays, and Sundays – that is, farmers' market, shopping, and church days – remained car-free.

37 Samuel Jacobs, 10 March 1930, Canada, *House of Commons Debates*, 16th Parliament, 4th Session, vol. 1, 461, http://parl.canadiana.ca/view/oop. debates_HOC1604_01/463?r=0&s=1.

38 MacDonald, *If You're Stronghearted*, 56.

39 Douglas Baldwin, *Land of the Red Soil: A Popular History of Prince Edward Island* (Charlottetown: Ragweed Press, 1990), 120. PEI continued to have the lowest automobile ownership rate in Canada for decades.

40 F.W. Hyndman, letter to the editor, *Patriot*, 23 March 1908.

41 The first advertisement in the *Guardian* for automobile insurance is one for Hyndman's firm, 18 May 1914, 2.

42 A.E. Farrow, "The Auto Question," letter to the editor, *Guardian*, 2 May 1912, 2.

43 PEI, Executive Council, *Minutes*, 22 July 1913.

44 W.L. Crosman, "Observations of a Vacationist on Prince Edward Island," *The Maple Leaf*, September 1913, 6.

45 The first reference we have found was by PEI Lieut. Gov. G.W. Howlan, speaking at the *Proceedings at the Unveiling of the Monument to Sir John A. Macdonald, G.C.B. at Ottawa, July 1st 1895* (Ottawa: Govt. Print. Bureau, 1895), 19, https://catalog. hathitrust.org/Record/100255869. The nickname does not appear in the *Guardian* until 1907.

46 "Jubilee of Confederation," *Guardian*, 9 December 1913, 2.

47 *Guardian*, 27 December 1914, 2.

48 "Confederation Jubilee Meeting," *Guardian*, 1 January 1914, 5 and 7; and "Premier Borden Will Co-operate in the Confederation Celebration," *Guardian*, 15 January 1914, 1. On Bartlett, see *BookLives*, http://booklives.ca/islandora/object/booklives:376.

49 "To Celebrate Confederation Jubilee," *Guardian*, 6 January 1914, 1.

50 "Confederation Jubilee Meeting," *Guardian*, 1 January 1914, 5. See also Premier J.A. Mathieson, "Celebrating Confederation," *The Canadian Courier*, 23 May 1914, 8–9 and 16; and "Provincial Legislature Makes Good Beginning," *Guardian*, 13 March 1914, 1. MacLean was referencing another pressing issue, the decanal adjustment in the distribution of seats in the federal House of Commons. The Island's complement had already fallen from six to four, and now threatened – over its furious protests – to become three. A face-saving compromise ultimately fixed the Island's permanent representation at four members.

51 "Confederation Celebration, Register of Accommodations," *Guardian*, 4 August 1914, 2.

52 *Guardian*, 28 July 1914, 1.

53 "PEI Well Remembered in This Year's Estimates," *Guardian*, 29 May 1914, 1. Still, this sum is dwarfed by the $300,000 Canada had put toward the Quebec tercentennial in 1908. It is unclear how much the provincial government committed to the 1914 event.

54 "Confederation Celebration Postponed," *Guardian*, 4 August 1914, 1; and Simon Lloyd, "Confederation Celebration Postponed in 1914 after Outbreak of

First World War," *Guardian*, 4 August 2014, http://www.theguardian.pe.ca/News/Local/2014-08-04/article-3822816/Confederation-celebration-postponed-in-1914-after-outbreak-of-First-World-War/1.

55 The plaque is described in detail in *Guardian*, 13 August 1949, 22.

56 See, for example, "Many American Tourists Holidaying in Canada," Toronto *Globe*, 13 August 1915, 6; "Americans May Travel Unmolested in Canada," Toronto *Globe*, 11 May 1916, 8; and "Making it Easy for the Tourist," Toronto *Globe*, 11 July 1918, 7. Many of the same rumours arose again during the first years of the Second World War.

57 Statutes of Prince Edward Island, *An Act to Incorporate the Charlottetown Summer Resorts, Ltd*, 1913, cap. 40. See Holman, "Robert L. Cotton's Charlottetown Summer Resorts," *Sailstrait* blog, https://sailstrait.wordpress.com/2015/06/05/robert-l-cottons-charlottetown-summer-resorts/. The resorts' location can be seen in Cummins Map Co., *Atlas of Province of Prince Edward Island, Canada* (Toronto: Cummins Map Co., 1928), 67, http://www.islandimagined.ca/fedora/repository/imagined:208783.

58 The last five years of the 1910s have the five lowest recorded occurrences of "tourist" in their decade. Likewise, the first five years of the 1920s have five of the six lowest for their decade.

59 This is essentially the narrative described by Hon. John Sinclair (Queen's), 10 July 1924, Canada, House of Commons *Debates*, 14th Parl., 3rd Session, vol. 5, 4296.

60 Hyndman was speaking at the so-called Duncan Commission, the Royal Commission on Maritime Rights, and referring specifically to complaints about ferry service. "Royal Commission Continues Evidence," *Guardian*, 14 August 1926, 10.

61 More generally, see MacDonald and MacEachern, "Rites of Passage."

62 In 1928, a surprised group of 300 excursionists from Nova Scotia had to shorten their trip because they had nowhere to eat. "Tourist Traffic Discouraged," *Guardian*, 30 July 1928, 1.

63 "Tourist Traffic Discouraged," *Guardian*, 30 July 1928, 1.

64 Anne E. Nias, "Interviews with Authors," *Saturday Night*, 28 October 1911. The fictional interview is reprinted in full in Benjamin Lefebvre, ed. *The L.M. Montgomery Reader, vol. 1: A Life in Print* (Toronto:

University of Toronto Press, 2013), 110–13. On the early recognition of Cavendish as a literary shrine, see also Thomas F. Anderson, "With Our Next-door Neighbors," Boston *Daily Globe*, 7 May 1911, SM12, reprinted in Lefebvre, 98–100.

65 "P.E. Island Shrine," *Guardian*, 13 November 1926, 4. The editor was restating an argument made by author W.A. Stewart at the St James Literary Society the night before, a talk published on page 9 of the same newspaper.

66 Avonlea Restaurant advertisement, *Guardian*, 30 June 1928, 10; and Well Wisher, "This Restaurant Business" letter to the editor, *Guardian*, 16 July 1928, 3.

67 Montgomery to G.B. MacMillan, February 1928, in *My Dear Mr. M.: Letters to G.B. MacMillan from L.M. Montgomery*, eds. Francis W.P. Bolger and Elizabeth R. Epperly (Toronto: McGraw-Hill Ryerson, 1980), 130.

68 There were sixteen times as many cars in the US in 1920 as there had been in 1910, and the buy-in only kept climbing. The best telling of this era in automobile history remains Warren James Belasco, *Americans on the Road: From Autocamp to Motel, 1910–1945* (Cambridge, MA: MIT Press, 1979).

69 These figures are taken from Robinson, 20 April 1925, Canada, House of Commons *Debates*, 14th Parliament, 4th Session, vol. 3, 2238; "Prince Edward Island Tourist Association Held First Annual Meeting," *The Busy East*, February 1925, 7; "Tourist Traffic Brought Island $825,000 in 1925," *The Busy East*, May 1926, 28; and PEI Publicity Association, *Annual Report*, January 1929, A.E. Arsenault papers, 4135/21, 3, PARO. Islanders' own rate of car ownership was less than half the Canadian average in the mid-1920s, although the difference was shrinking. See "Of Interest to Motorists," Toronto *Globe*, 17 October 1925, 8; and "Automobile Traffic Is Vastly Increased," Toronto *Globe*, 13 September 1929, 3.

70 See Toronto *Globe*, 19 June 1920, 5. The *Guardian* described this merger as New Brunswickers having taken steps to create an association "all-provincial and genuinely alive in character." *Guardian*, 22 June 1920, 4.

71 It was immediately decided that the NSTA had been poorly structured at its creation, and it was absorbed by a more corporate Publicity Bureau. "'Canada's Ocean Playground': The Tourism Industry in Nova Scotia, 1870–1970," Nova Scotia Archives website,

https://novascotia.ca/archives/tourism/default.asp; and Michael Boudreau, "A 'Rare and Unusual Treat of Historical Significance': The 1923 Hector Celebration and the Political Economy of the Past," *Journal of Canadian Studies* 28, 4 (Winter 1993–94): 28–48.

72 Ernest R. Forbes, *The Maritime Rights Movement, 1919–1927: A Study in Canadian Regionalism* (Montreal and Kingston: McGill-Queen's University Press, 1979). Any exploration of Maritime tourism in this period must consider, and owes a debt to, McKay, *Quest of the Folk*; and McKay and Bates, *In the Province of History*.

73 "A Great Movement Started in the Tourist Association," *Guardian*, 28 January 1924, 1; Aubin Edmond Arsenault, *Memoirs* (Charlottetown: Island *Guardian*, 1951), 144–8, https://archive.org/details/memoirs000arseuoft; and Matthew McRae's, "Manufacturing Paradise: Tourism, Development and Mythmaking on Prince Edward Island 1939–1973," unpublished MA thesis, Carleton University, 2004, 25–8. McRae's is a rare and valuable historical study of tourism on midcentury PEI.

74 "1924 Old Home Summer for PEI," *Guardian*, 31 October 1923, 1; *Guardian*, 12 April 1924, 15; *Guardian*, 16 July 1924, 6; and "Annual Meeting of PEI Publicity Association," *Guardian*, 12 January 1926, 1 and 3. Boudreau notes that plans for a 1924 Old Home Summer in Nova Scotia were dropped in part over fears that returning expatriates might draw away other citizens with them – that the end result would be more outmigration. Boudreau, "Rare and Unusual Treat," 44. Interestingly, although the *Guardian* had no Old Home Week to write about for the remainder of the 1920s, its use of the term "old home" actually increased dramatically over the remainder of the 1920s, as it reported more and more on individuals visiting their "old home" in summertime.

75 See Arsenault, *Memoirs*, 144–8 and 155–6; and "Aubin Edmond Arsenault," Biographies of the Members of the Legislative Assembly, PEILDO, http://www.peildo.ca/fedora/repository/leg:27812.

76 "Tourist Ass'n to Continue Vigorous Work," *Guardian*, 11 January 1933, 1. President Arsenault praised MacFadyen for giving tourism a "personal touch" that set PEI apart. "Here too the tourist industry is not commercialized as in many other provinces." "Tourist Ass'n Annual Meeting," *Guardian*, 7 January 1931, 1. Tourism PEI has worked diligently in recent years to preserve, or resurrect, such an impression, whether in directing people to talk to named 1-800 operators ("Call Jill") or its 2017 "Ask an Islander" campaign (https://www.tourismpei.com/askanislander).

77 Arsenault, *Memoirs*, 146. On MacFadyen, see also Stanhope Women's Institute History Committee, *Stanhope: Sands of Time* (Stanhope, PEI: Stanhope Women's Institute, 1984), passim. Member of Parliament Robert Jenkins (Queen's) stated in 1929, "In our province we have a live publicity and tourist association doing a fine piece of work. A large quantity of literature is distributed each year and … the only expense in this regard being a small amount paid to an energetic lady secretary." Jenkins, 12 March 1929, Canada, House of Commons *Debates*, 16th Parliament, 3rd Session, vol. 1, 900, http://parl.canadiana.ca/view/oop.debates_HOC1603_01/902?r=0&s=3.

78 "Prospects Bright for Tourist Trade," *Guardian*, 7 January 1930, 1. For the sake of clarity, we will refer to it as the Tourist Association throughout.

79 "A Great Movement Started in the Tourist Association," *Guardian*, 28 January 1924, 1.

80 "Officers Elected for Ensuing Year," *Guardian*, 11 Jan 1929, 1.

81 "A Comparative Statement Showing Stewart and Bell Government Grants," *Guardian*, 24 June 1927, 7. The advertisement ran several times.

82 "Found Money," *Guardian*, 20 November 1923, 4.

83 "P.E. Island Tourist Association Held First Annual Meeting," *The Busy East*, February 1925, 7. The "golden harvest" image also appears in "A Great Movement Started in the Tourist Association," *Guardian*, 28 January 1924, 1.

84 "P.E.I. Tourist and Publicity Association Organized," *The Busy East*, April 1924, 27.

85 "Annual Meeting of the P.E.I. Publicity Association," *The Busy East*, March 1926, 14. Note that MP Ernest William Robinson (King's, NS) provided statistics that 36,000 tourists came to PEI in 1925, bringing in $750,000 in revenue. Robinson, 20 April 1925, Canada, *House of Commons Debates*, 14th Parliament, 4th Session, vol. 3, 2238.

86 *Guardian*, 13 June 1925, 1.

87 Dawson, *Selling British Columbia*, 66.

88 PEI, *JLA*, 1925, 73, http://www.peildo.ca/fedora/repository/leg:7270.

89 "Maritime Step Dancing and Fiddling Contest Now On," *Guardian*, 13 July 1926, 1; and "Mr & Mrs H.T. Holman Entertain Railway Men," *Guardian*, 27 July 1926, 1.

90 "P.E. Island Tourist Association Held First Annual Meeting," *The Busy East*, February 1925, 7.

91 PEI Publicity Association, *Fifth Annual Report*, January 1928, and Sixth Annual Report, January 1929, Tourist Association file, Aubin Arsenault papers, RG25/20, PARO.

92 "P.E. Island Tourist Association Held First Annual Meeting," 7.

93 PEI Publicity Association, *Sixth Annual Report*, January 1929, "Tourist Association" file, Aubin Arsenault papers, RG25/20, PARO; PEI Publicity Association letter for support, 8 February 1930, "Tourist Association" file, Aubin Arsenault papers, RG25/20, PARO.

94 "Busy Session of City Council," *Guardian*, 23 February 1933, 1.

95 Michael Power, cited in "Annual Meeting of PEI Publicity Association," *Guardian*, 12 January 1926, 1; and "An Interesting Discussion," *Guardian*, 13 January 1926, 3. Similarly, a stanza of a temperance poem in the *Guardian* a few years later ran,
    The Tourist Association sings
    Our City's praise and all good things
    When will they ever change their jig;
    Investigate all those blind-pigs,
    Where men in numbers spend the night,
    And in the morning get home tight.
    Wife of a Souse, "I Pray Thee, Bacchus," letter to the editor, *Guardian*, 19 March 1932, 1.

96 A.C. Saunders, 11 March 1926, from the *Patriot*, Speeches of the Legislature, Legislative Library Material, RG10, PARO. The date cited here, as in future citations of this source, refers to when the quote was made, not when it appeared in the newspaper.

97 George Nestler Tricoche, *Rambles Through the Maritime Provinces of Canada: A Neglected Part of the British Empire* (London: A.H. Stockwell, 1931), 169.

98 In 1929, American geographer F.A. Stilgenbauer wrote of Prince Edward Islanders as if he had discovered a rare and reclusive species: "Lack of travel and social intercourse beyond the local community causes the Islander to view the visitor with suspicion until his wants are made known. Visitors are occasionally threatened with arrest because of suspicion. When the Islander is satisfied one means no harm he will show his warm hospitality." Stilgenbauer, "The Geography of Prince Edward Island," unpublished PhD thesis, University of Michigan, 1929, 5.

99 Murray, *Picturesque Canada*, 854. "The country is gently undulating and there is not a mountain or very high hill in all the Island." Crosskill, *Prince Edward Island*, 27. "Though lacking the grandeur of mountainous scenery, the gently undulating landscape is an ever varied delight to the eye." J.E.B. McCready, *Prince Edward Island: A Summer Paradise* (Charlottetown: PEI Government and Maritime Stationers, 1913), 6.

100 McCready, *Prince Edward Island*, 7.

101 Crosskill, *Prince Edward Island*, 25; and McCready, *Prince Edward Island*, 33. Emphasis added.

102 Canada, Department of the Interior, *Prince Edward Island: Its Resources and Opportunities* (Ottawa: Natural Resources Intelligence Service, 1926), 59.

103 PEI Travel Bureau, *Prince Edward Island, Vacationland of Heart's Content* (Charlottetown: PEI Travel Bureau, 1939), back cover.

104 See, for example, James Murton, "'The Normandy of the New World': Canada Steamship Lines, Antimodernism, and the Selling of Old Quebec," in *Settling and Unsettling Memories: Essays in Canadian Public History*, eds. Nicole Neatby and Peter Hodgins (Toronto: University of Toronto Press, 2012), 419−53.

105 McKay, *Quest of the Folk*; McKay and Bates, *In the Province of History*; Gwendolyn Davies, "The 'Home Place' in Modern Maritime Literature," *Studies in Maritime Literary History, 1760−1930* (Fredericton: Acadiensis Press, 1991), 193−9; and Benedict Anderson, "Staging Antimodernism in the Age of High Capitalist Modernism," *Antimodernism and Artistic Experience: Policing the Boundaries of Modernity*, ed. Lynda Jessup (Toronto: University of Toronto Press, 2001), 97−103.

106 W.S. Ferguson, letter to the editor "Coming to the Isle of the Gulf," *Guardian*, 31 August 1906.

107 Compare, for example, its *Forest Stream, and Seashore* (1908) and *Prince Edward Island* (1913).

108 Arsenault address to the Rotary Club, *Patriot*, 28 September 1937.

286

Notes to pages 75−8

109 McCready, *Prince Edward Island*, 28.

110 PEI Travel Bureau, *Prince Edward Island, Vacationland*, 15.

111 Ian McKay, "Liberty, Equality and Tourism: D.C. Harvey, Prince Edward Island, and the Power of Tourism/History, 1931–1956," *Histoire sociale/Social History* 49 (June 2016): 263–89.

112 See Peter E. Pope, *The Many Landfalls of John Cabot* (Toronto: University of Toronto Press, 1997).

113 PEI Travel Bureau, *Prince Edward Island, Vacationland*, 12. Some scholarship continues to put the Island forward as a credible candidate for Erikson's landfall. See Gísli Sigurðsson, "Vikings on Prince Edward Island?" *The Island Magazine* 44 (Fall/Winter 1998): 8–13, http://vre2.upei.ca/islandmagazine/fedora/repository/vre%3Aislemag-batch2-581/OBJ.

114 See Brown, *Inventing New England*, 208.

115 Tourist Association manager Reigh Tinney, "Annual Meeting of P.E.I. Publicity Association," *The Busy East*, March 1926, 13.

116 Lucy Gertrude Clarkin, "Prince Edward Island, The Beautiful Garden Province," *The Busy East*, June 1924, 5.

117 Canada, Department of the Interior, *Prince Edward Island* (1926 ed.), 63; and (1927 ed.), 63.

118 PEI Tourist Association, *Annual Report*, 1928, 6.

119 P.W. Clarkin, cited in "Officers Elected for Ensuing Year," *Guardian*, 11 January 1929, 3; "Victoria Hotel Destroyed by Fire on Sunday," *Guardian*, 14 January 1929, 1; and "Tourist Association Activities," *Guardian*, 21 January 1929, 3.

120 Arsenault, *Memoirs*, 152–4.

121 "Tourist Ass'n Annual Meeting," *Guardian*, 7 January 1931, 1.

122 "Tourist Ass'n to Continue Vigorous Work," *Guardian*, 11 January 1933, 1.

123 Canada, *Sixth Census of Canada, 1921*, vol. 4 (Ottawa: 1929), 120–37; Canada, *Seventh Census of Canada, 1931*, vol.7 (Ottawa: 1930), 74–94.

124 "Prospects Bright for Tourist Trade," *Guardian*, 7 January 1930, 1.

125 Subscriptions fell from $2,931 to $1,288 between 1929 and 1933, a reduction from 50 to 26 per cent of the association's fundraising. "Officers Elected for Ensuing Year," *Guardian*, 11 Jan 1929, 1; and "Tourist Traffic Held Up Well," *Guardian*, 17 January 1934, 1.

126 Arsenault, "Open Letter to Mr R.H. Sterns," letter to editor, *Guardian*, 22 January 1935, 4; R.H. Sterns, "Open Letter to Mr Justice Arsenault from R.H. Sterns," letter to editor, *Guardian*, 25 January 1935, 4; "Tourist Prospects Bright for 1935," *Guardian*, 18 January 1935, 1. Sterns also (wrongly) accused M.K. MacFadyen's husband James, head of the PEI Motor League, of being on the Tourist Association payroll.

127 "The Late Mr Sterns," *Guardian*, 26 January 1935, 4.

128 See "Tourist Ass'n Annual Meeting," *Guardian*, 7 January 1931, 1; "Busy Year for the Tourist Ass'n," *Guardian*, 12 January 1932, 1; "Tourist Ass'n to Continue Vigorous Work," *Guardian*, 11 January 1933, 1. "Tourist Traffic Held Up Well," *Guardian*, 17 January 1934, 1; "Tourist Prospects Bright for 1935," *Guardian*, 18 Jan 1935, 1; and "Car Ferry and Telegraph and Telephone Communications" file, Aubin Arsenault papers, RG25/20, PARO.

129 See M.K. MacFadyen, cited in "Busy Year for the Tourist Ass'n," *Guardian*, 12 January 1932, 1.

130 See *Journals of the Legislative Assembly*, 1930–38, http://www.peildo.ca/.

131 Meighen, 26 April 1934, Canada, *Senate Debates*, 17th Parliament, 5th Session, vol. 1, 312. On the Senate Committee, see chapter 1 of Alisa Apostle, "Canada, Vacations Unlimited: The Canadian Government Tourism Industry, 1934–1959," unpublished PhD thesis, Queen's University, 2003.

132 *Guardian*, 31 December 1935, 11.

133 Leonard John Cusack, "The Prince Edward Island People and the Great Depression, 1930–1935," unpublished MA thesis, University of New Brunswick, 1972, 130.

134 Hyndman, cited in "Travel Bureau Holds Annual Meeting," *Guardian*, 23 November 1935, 1.

135 "Tourist Prospects Bright for 1935," *Guardian*, 18 Jan 1935, 1.

136 Dawson, *Selling British Columbia*, 90–100, esp. 97.

137 Canada, Senate, *Report and Proceedings of the Special Committee on Tourist Traffic* (1934), x. Much of the account which follows of the site selection is from MacEachern, *Natural Selections*, 40–6 and 73–85.

138 Campbell, 31 March 1936, from the *Patriot*, Speeches of the Legislature, RG10 vol. 102, PARO.

139 Campbell to Howe, 8 February 1936, RG84 vol. 1777, file PEI2 vol. 1, LAC; and PEI, Executive Council, *Minutes*, 17 March 1936, RG7 series 3, Box 12 no.2640, PARO.

140 An advertisement for the sale of Dalvay-by-the-Sea was posted in the *Guardian*, 21 June 1935, 6.

141 Harry T. Holman diary, 28 February and 12 March 1936, Holman papers, Acc.4420 vol.7, PARO.

142 Minister of the Interior T.A. Crerar to Premier Campbell, 31 March 1936, RG84 vol. 1777, file PEI2 vol. 1, LAC. The name of the federal agency in charge of national parks changed a number of times over the years. For the sake of simplicity, we will refer to it as the National Parks Branch until 1973, when it took its current name, Parks Canada.

143 "Pro Bono Publico," letter to the editor, *Guardian*, 8 June 1936. There was a distinctly paranoid strain to these arguments. "Inquirer" asked if the park was really for "the benefit of the tourist and the sightseer or the seeker after health or pleasure, or for the convenience of those who would make wassail on the contents of the kegs borne shoreward by the waters of the Gulf?" Letter to the editor, *Patriot*, 18 October 1937.

144 "Five-Point Resolution Passed Last Night at Farmers Meeting," *Guardian*, 20 May 1936, 3.

145 Holman diary, 17 June 1936, Holman papers, Acc.4420 vol.7, PARO.

146 Counterfactualists may ask how Prince Edward Island tourism history might have been different if the national park had been created in Mill River, St Catherines, or Brudenell.

147 F.H.H. Williamson memo, 23 March 1936, RG84 vol. 1777, file PEI2 vol. 1, LAC.

148 Editorial, "Dalvay-by-the-Sea," *Guardian*, 15 July 1936, 4.

149 Director R.A. Gibson to Deputy Minister of Mines and Resources Hugh Keenleyside, 29 January 1948, RG84 vol. 1781, file PEI16.2 vol.4, LAC.

150 Williamson and Cromarty report on PEI sites, 28 July 1936, RG84 vol. 1777, file PEI2 vol. 1, LAC. The bureau had erected signs pointing to "Avonlea Beach" and "Green Gables."

151 Williamson memo, 23 March 1936, RG84 vol. 1777, file PEI2 vol. 1 pt.2, LAC; and Williamson and Cromarty report on PEI sites, 28 July 1936, RG84 vol. 1777, file PEI2 vol. 1, LAC.

152 Williamson to Commissioner James B. Harkin, undated [1936], RG84 vol. 1777, file PEI2 vol. 1, LAC. See chapter 4 for a discussion of racism within the tourism industry.

153 PEI, Executive Council, *Minutes*, 21 September 1936, RG7 series 3, Box 12 no.2640, PARO.

154 Williamson to Deputy Minister of Interior James Wardle, 5 October 1936, RG84 vol. 1777, file PEI2 vol.2, NA.

155 This is described in greater detail in MacEachern, *Natural Selections*, 85–92.

156 Montgomery, 27 September and 15 October 1936, *The Selected Journals of L.M. Montgomery* vol. 5, eds. Mary Rubio and Elizabeth Waterston (Toronto: Oxford University Press, 2004), 93 and 99–100. Montgomery was living in a Toronto suburb at the time, and may in this instance have been responding to rumour, but her importance to the Island meant that she was kept apprised throughout the park's establishment, including by the premier himself. Two weeks before inspectors Williamson and Cromarty had submitted their report that summer, she had written, "The Gov't is going to purchase a site for a National Park in P.E. Island and it is possible that the Webb farm will be bought for it – or part of it. Because of *Anne* forsooth!! The thought is a terrible one to me. What change and heartache may it not mean … [W]hen I love a place is it not doomed?" Montgomery, 12 July 1936, *Selected Journals*, vol. 5, 80.

157 Campbell to Crerar, 12 November 1936, RG84 vol. 1777, file PEI2 vol.2, NA. The Webbs were also allowed to keep living in Green Gables until the end of 1945. See Fred Horne with assistance from Mary Burke, "Green Gables House Report," *Parks Canada Manuscript Report no. 352* (1979), 7, http://parkscanadahistory.com/series/mrs/352.pdf.

158 In 1932, *Montreal Star* writer Genevieve Lipsett-Skinner gave a detailed description of staying at the farm of "Jeremiah Blank" while vacationing in Cavendish. Reprinted as "'First Time Visitor' Gives Impression of Garden of the Gulf," *Guardian*, 20 September 1932, 9.

159 See Horne, "Human History, Prince Edward Island National Park," *Parks Canada Manuscript Report no. 352* (1979), 65 and 132–3, http://parkscanadahistory.com/series/mrs/352.pdf.

160 For example, "As I write this letter I can see from my kitchen window a bountiful field of waving grain on my farm, a field which next year and all the succeeding years will be barren because of the determination of the Campbell Government to establish what is now becoming known throughout the Province as 'Expropriation Park.'" "One of

the Dispossessed," letter to the editor, *Guardian*, 23 August 1937, 4.

161 Katherine Wyand, "Mrs Wyand and the Premier," letter to the editor, *Guardian*, 12 March 1938, 4. See also Wyand 1936-1961 file, RG84 vol. 1784, file PEI16.112.1, LAC.

162 Wyand, "Open Letter to Members of the Legislature," *Guardian*, 1 April 1938, 1.

163 On its naming, see MacEachern, *Natural Selections*, 86.

164 *Globe and Mail*, 25 May 1937, 10.

165 Wendell Kelly interview with Fred Horne, 8 June 1978, PEI National Park files, Dalvay.

166 Tourist Highways on PEI file, RG22 vol.728, file PEI60.1, LAC; PEI, *Public Accounts*, 1938, 76, PEILDO, http://www.peildo.ca/fedora/repository/leg%3A6466; and Campbell, *Patriot*, 21 March 1939, from the *Patriot*, Speeches of the Legislature, RG10 vol. 102, PARO.

167 On Thompson, see Kenneth Donovan, "'Thinking Down the Road': Stanley Thompson, Canada's Golf Architect, Artist and Visionary, 1893–1953," *The Nashwaak Review* vol. 14/15 (Fall 2004–Winter 2005): 252–302. On golf courses in national parks, including PEI National Park, see Elizabeth Liane Jewett, "Behind the Greens: Understanding Golf Course Landscapes in Canada, 1873–1945," unpublished PhD thesis, University of Toronto, 2015, ch.6.

168 R.A. Gibson to Williamson, 27 December 1937, RG84 vol. 150, file PEI313, LAC.

169 The barn proved too dilapidated, however, and a new clubhouse was built. RG84 vol. 150 and vol. 182, file PEI313, LAC; and RG84 vol. 151 and 182, PEI313.7, LAC.

170 S. Leonard Tilley, "Crerar Opens National Park as Part of P.E.I. Celebration," *Globe and Mail*, 20 July 1939, 1. The golf course became the focus not just of development in the park but of the PEI Conservatives' opposition to the park. In a speech published in the *Guardian*, for example, party leader W.J.P. MacMillan questioned why the government had spent so much on a park: "'For what? To build a Golf Course for the accommodation of you farmers and fishermen. You can't go to the courts to get a square deal ... but they're going to give you a Golf Course to compensate for everything!' (Laughter)." Then, in the spirit of the day, he said that Premier Campbell was worse than Hitler. "Conservative Leader Heard in Scathing Indictment of Moribund Liberal Regime," *Guardian*, 10 March 1939, 5 and 9.

171 Campbell, 22 March 1939, from the *Patriot*, Speeches from the Legislature, RG10 vol. 102, PARO.

172 See Dalvay file, RG84 vol. 1781, file PEI116.2 vol.3 (1939-1944), LAC. In 1938–39, the Parks Branch seriously considered turning Dalvay into a community centre or museum. RG84 vol. 1804, file PEI318 vol. 1 and vol.2, LAC.

173 Williamson to Percy "McCausland," 7 August 1940, RG84 vol. 1780, file PEI116, LAC; and, for example, MacAusland to Prime Minister John Diefenbaker, 25 January 1961, RG84 vol. 1779, file PEI2A pt.3, LAC.

174 RG84 vol. 1784, file PEI116.112.1 (1936-1952), LAC.

175 Supervisor, PEI Travel Bureau, *Annual Report*, 1940 (Summerside: Journal Publishing Company, 1941), 7. Emphasis in original.

176 Canada, House of Commons *Debates*, 20th Parliament, 1st Session, vol. 3, http://parl.canadiana.ca/view/oop.debates_HOC2001_03/404?r=0&s=3.

177 Montgomery to G.B. MacMillan, 1 April 1938, *My Dear Mr. M.*, 183.

178 Horne, "Green Gables House Report," 31.

179 MacEachern, *Natural Selections*, 73; and Horne, "Green Gables House Report," 7.

180 See, for example, Inflation Calculator website, http://inflationcalculator.ca/. The provincial public accounts cite expenditures of $106,204 between 1937 and 1939, http://www.peildo.ca/. A few additional, not expressly defined, settlements were made in the early 1940s.

181 Simpson to Minister of Mines and Resources Crerar, 24 February 1938, RG84 vol. 1777, PEI2 vol.5, LAC.

182 Juanita Rossiter, *Gone to the Bay: A History of the St. Peters Fire District Area* (2000), 139, http://137.149.200.109:8080/fedora/get/ilives:259552/PDF.

Chapter Three

1 The background information on the Flemings is culled from the period census records; Cummins, *Atlas of Prince Edward Island*; and the diary kept by Rudolf "Dolph" Fleming, 3698/2, PARO [henceforth, Fleming diary]. See also MacDonald and MacEachern, "How Dolph and Bertha Learned to Like Tourism."

2 See, too, "Expropriation Victims Petition Gov't," *Guardian*, 26 August 1937, 1. The group presented a

petition, signed by Fleming, protesting the denial of the right of appeal with respect to the expropriations.

3 Fleming diary, 6 October 1937.

4 Fleming diary, 11 November 1937 and 23 August 1938.

5 Fleming diary, 3 October 1938 and 19 July 1939. The planes were a Royal Canadian Air Force detachment from Halifax.

6 "National Park Is Officially Declared Open," *Guardian*, 20 July 1939, 1 and 3.

7 For instance, a *Guardian* editorial in 1920 urged the Historic Landmarks Association, precursor to the Historic Sites and Monuments Board, to formally register the Confederation Chamber in the Provincial Building. It appears, however, that the association was not reading the *Guardian*. See "Historic Landmarks," *Guardian*, 30 July 1920, 4.

8 The film, *Charlottetown, Cradle of Confederation*, was shown at Charlottetown's Prince Edward Theatre in the spring of 1926. Nothing else is known about its provenance or purpose. See *Guardian*, 3 April 1926, 14. In a simple keyword search of the digitized run of the *Guardian*, the phrase "Cradle of Confederation" appears just once before 1910, nine times during the 1910s, eleven in the 1920s, and twenty-seven over the course of the 1930s, the majority of the latter coming after 1936.

9 The following account follows closely McRae, "Romance of Canada."

10 In his analysis, McRae draws upon Daniel J. Boorstin's concept of "pseudo-events" in *The Image: A Guide to Pseudo-Events in America* (New York: Harper Colophon, 1964), and MacCannell, *The Tourist*.

11 It would be left to twenty-first century hair-splitters to carp about the alleged inaccuracy of the tourist-friendly metaphor. In the 1930s the term "Cradle" of Confederation was scarcely questioned.

12 Arsenault, *Memoirs*, 92.

13 McRae, "Romance of Canada," 31–2.

14 For more details, see McRae, "Romance of Canada," 32–6.

15 The minute is attached to a memo sent to Leo Dolan, director of the Canadian Travel Bureau, RG 20-A-9, vol. 1565, file T3252-13, LAC.

16 Apostle, "Canada, Vacations Unlimited," 4–18. The "CTB" became the "CGTB" – the Canadian Government Travel Bureau – during the Second World War. For the sake of simplicity, we will refer to the CTB throughout.

17 For the exchange between Dolan and Arsenault, see RG 20-A-9, vol. 1565, file T3252-13, LAC.

18 McRae, "Romance of Canada," 34.

19 McRae, "Romance of Canada," 35–6. *P.E. Island on Parade* had been around since at least 1936. (See "Annual Meeting of Summerside Board of Trade," *Guardian*, 22 January 1937, 7.) For the PEI booth at the New York World's Fair, see PEI Public Accounts, 1940, JLA.

20 Fragments of the newsreel footage are preserved as "Canadian News," National Film Board of Canada, Shot ID 6388, https://bit.ly/2PmEDJ8.

21 McRae, "Romance of Canada," 37–40.

22 The *Guardian* spoke in terms of "thousands of Islanders" and "hundreds of visitors." See "Pageant and Parade Mark Celebration" as well as "Historical Parade Is Huge Success," *Guardian* 18 July 1939, 1.

23 McRae, "Romance of Canada," 42.

24 Convention Proceedings of the Canadian Tourist Association, Charlottetown, 17–20 September 1956, Alex W. Matheson papers, RG 25.34, box 10, file 137: 36-39, PARO.

25 McKay and Bates, *In the Province of History*.

26 McKay, "Liberty, Equality and Tourism." In McKay's reading, Harvey's classical liberalism railed against the hucksterism of touristic history and the politics of commemoration. At the same time Harvey hoped to use public history to reach a broader audience with the principles of a history informed by classical liberalism: "religious freedom, political and social equality, intellectual openness and honesty, and idealization of freehold property."

27 McRae, "Romance of Canada," 35.

28 Quoted in "Post-Celebration Comment," *Guardian*, 28 September 1939, 4. The article, retitled "The Charlottetown Conference Revived," appeared in the September 1939 *Canadian Geographic Journal*.

29 "Address of Justice Arsenault on the Tourist Industry," undated newspaper clipping, *Patriot* [May 1940]. The Travel Bureau was subsequently attached to the Department of Industry and Resources.

30 "Summerside Board of Trade Annual Meeting," *Guardian*, 26 January 1940, 11. See, too, B. Graham Rogers to D. Leo Dolan, 12 January 1940, Canadian Travel Bureau fonds, RG 12-A-1, vol. 4236, file 3658-11, LAC: "The Government of Prince Edward Island is taking over the Prince Edward Island Travel Bureau

31 See "Provincial Boy Scouts Council," *Guardian*, 30 January 1941, 5.

32 For Summerside, see "S'Side Trade Board Committee Reports," *Guardian*, 22 January 1941, 9. For Charlottetown, "Board of Trade Officials Review Year's Activities," *Guardian*, 9 January 1941, 9. Curiously, the Charlottetown board claimed that *it* had "inaugurated, developed, and operated on a voluntary basis" the Travel Bureau.

33 The tourism spending numbers cited here were culled, by our colleague Boyde Beck, from the Public Accounts published with the annual *JLA*.

34 "Alberton," *Guardian*, 31 July 1945, 11; and "Premier King Sends Message to Prince County Electors," *Guardian*, 31 October 1939, 8.

35 *Guardian*, 3 February 1940, 8; and "Editorial Notes," *Guardian*, 13 January 1940, 4.

36 Unless otherwise noted, the following summary of Rogers's report is taken from Annual Report of the Supervisor, PEI Travel Bureau, 1940, PEI, *JLA*, 1941, PEILDO, http://www.peildo.ca/fedora/repository/leg%3A6337?startpage=&solrq=travel%20bureau.

37 The benefits of tourism as a local market for fishers and farmers became a recurring theme when promoting the industry to Islanders. In 1957, it even spawned a report for the Atlantic Provinces Economic Council. See W.J. Dalton, "The Tourist Industry and the Farm Economy," APEC, Halifax, 1957, SPC, RL, UPEI. Dalton calculated, using some very crude measurements, a value of $786,000 in 1956 to Island farmers from food sales to tourists. "From the above summary," he concluded, "it can easily be seen that the farmer has a vital stake in the tourist industry although he may never see a tourist."

38 On wartime tourism, see Michael Dawson, "'Travel Strengthens America'? Tourism Promotion in the United States during the Second World War," *Journal of Tourism History* 3, 3 (2011): 217–36.

39 Apostle, "Canada, Vacations Unlimited," 146–82.

40 Public Accounts, 1941, PEI, *JLA*, 1942, 13, PEILDO, http://www.peildo.ca/fedora/repository/leg:6208/-/%20leg:6208.

41 The Summerside office had been started by the Summerside Board of Trade. See "S'Side Trade Board Committee Reports," *Guardian*, 22 January 1941, 9.

42 "Tourist Gas Ration Cut," *Guardian*, 12 May 1942, 7; and Milton Derber, "Gasoline Rationing Policy and Practice in Canada and the United States," *Journal of Marketing* 8, 2 (April 1943): 143.

43 Speech from the Throne, PEI, *JLA*, 1944, PEILDO, http://www.peildo.ca/fedora/repository/leg:6056/-/%20leg:6056. See also, "Estimate of Revenue and Expenditure," *Guardian*, 17 March 1944, 7. For traffic figures, McRae, "Manufacturing Paradise," 64.

44 Speech from the Throne, PEI, *JLA*, 1944, PEILDO, http://www.peildo.ca/fedora/repository/leg:6056/-/%20leg:6056.

45 Gary Aitken, "The Guest Book: How Shaw's Hotel Changed My Life," *The Island Magazine* 71 (Spring/Summer 2012): 12–16.

46 "See Island Film," *Guardian*, 27 March 1942, 8. The members of the Island Legislature enjoyed a special screening the previous day in the Confederation Chamber. They gave it two thumbs up.

47 "P.E.I. Movie Wins Award," *Guardian*, 7 December 1942, 8. It was the only film from Canada to win an award, the newspaper noted of the third place finish.

48 "To Show Films," *Guardian*, 1 September 1942, 3. The tourist film was screened along with two war films.

49 For example, "Tourist Accommodation for the Summer," *Guardian*, 23 May 1943, 5.

50 The Liberal platform can be found in the *Guardian*, 7 September 1943, 10. For his remarks in the House, see "Premier Jones," *Guardian*, 18 February 1944, 7.

51 "Editorial Notes," *Guardian*, 7 August 1945, 4.

52 The following passage is largely excerpted from MacDonald and MacEachern, "Rites of Passage."

53 See Bruce, *Saltwater Road*, 24–43, 48–52.

54 MacDonald, *If You're Stronghearted*, 212–13. It also lost money, prompting calls for an increased subsidy.

55 These figures were 53,706 and 12,825, respectively. They were supplied to the Charlottetown Board of Trade by Graham Rogers, by then provincial director of Transportation. See 3147/9, PARO; and Board Minutes for 5 November 1946, 3147/3, PARO.

56 "Ferry Steamer Charlottetown Sinks Off N.S.," *Guardian*, 20 June 1941, 1; and Boyde Beck, *Prince Edward Island, An (Un)Authorized History* (Charlottetown: Acorn Press, 1996), 161–3. The only backup was a dirty, coal-burning scow named the SS *Scotia*.

57 According to a letter from the federal minister of transport. See Quarterly Meeting, Charlottetown Board of Trade, 14 April 1943, 3147/3, PARO.

58 For a summary, see Beck, *Prince Edward Island*, 135–40. See also "Maritime Central Airways Prepares to Take Over," *Guardian*, 21 November 1941, 8; and "Flight Cancelled," *Guardian*, 9 December 1941, 6.

59 "Wings Over the Maritimes," *Guardian*, 14 December 1946, 12. The airline carried 9,330 passengers in its first year, 32,000 in 1946.

60 "Maritime Central Airways Schedule of Operations," *Guardian*, 8 December 1941, 3; and "Transport Commission," *Guardian*, 19 July 1946, 3.

61 Numbers posted for MCA typically included passengers to the Magdalen Islands as well and sometimes lumped together arrivals and departures. These figures have been taken from annual reports of the Department of Industry and Natural Resources.

62 "Wealth Drawn from Sea and Soil: P.E.I. Attracts Tourists," *The Monetary Times*, August 1957, 68–73, in Alex W. Matheson papers, RG 25.34, box 10, file 137, PARO.

63 The two earliest references to the metaphor in the *Guardian* appear in CQ, "North Baltic and Vicinity" (18 June 1954, 11); and Mrs Gordon MacMillan, "A Country Garden" (14 February 1956, 11).

64 "To the Public," *Guardian*, 11 May 1946, 11.

65 Fleming diary.

66 As described, for example, in Jakle, *Tourist*, 183–9. According to Leo Dolan of the Canadian Government Travel Bureau, 96 per cent of tourists coming to Canada by 1954 were travelling by automobile. See Minutes of Special General Meeting, 16 March 1954, Tourism Industry Association of Prince Edward Island [henceforth, TIAPEI], 98-004, box 3, PARO.

67 "Tourist Association Director Stresses Value of Industry," undated clipping, May 1958, TIAPEI, 98-004, box 3, PARO.

68 McRae, "Manufacturing Paradise," 84.

69 These figures are drawn from the Public Accounts as tabled in the *JLA*.

70 Minutes of Special General Meeting, 16 March 1954, TIAPEI, 98-004, box 3, PARO.

71 Jones was writing to Leo Dolan of the CTB. Cited in McRae, "New Nationalism." See also McRae, "Manufacturing Paradise," 81. Jones was, it should

also be noted, given to deliberate overstatement, and at the time of writing Dolan found transportation issues far more urgent than tourist promotion.

72 J.E. Lattimer, *Economic Survey of Prince Edward Island* (Charlottetown: Department of Reconstruction, 1944). See also "Dr Lattimer's Report," *Guardian*, 5 February 1945, 4. For the creation of the department and its miniscule budget, see PEI, *JLA*, 1945, 13–14, 20, 133.

73 Lattimer, *Economic Survey*, 48.

74 "Interim Report of the Prince Edward Island Advisory Reconstruction Committee, Charlottetown, 20 July 1945," 232–3, PEI Collection, Robertson Library, UPEI [henceforth, PEI Coll.]. The tourism and transportation sections of the report remain closely connected, appearing in sequence and raising many of the same points. Its report is examined in detail by McRae, "Manufacturing Paradise," 72–7. Other recommendations included flying Union Jacks at Island schools to remind American visitors of our exotic otherness, rewarding rural beautification efforts, and bridge building to open up the Island's south shore to Charlottetown-based tourists.

75 "An Act to Regulate and License Inns and Restaurants," 11 Geo. VI (1947), cap. 18. An earlier piece of legislation from 1938 and amended in 1939 gave the Lieutenant Governor in Council blanket authority to set regulations and fees for licensed tourist accommodations but did not force premises to be licensed. (See "An Act for the Licensing and Regulation of Establishments for the Reception of Tourists, Acts of the General Assembly of the Province of Prince Edward Island, 2 Geo. VI [1938], cap. 25 and 3 Geo. VI [1939], cap. 50.) Licence fees in the 1947 legislation were initially set at $5 for hotels with ten or more rooms or cabins, $3 for smaller establishments, and $1 for tourist homes. There were fines for noncompliance with the act.

76 "The Appropriation Act," 11 Geo. VI, cap 1 (1947).

77 "P.E.I. Innkeepers Association Holds Annual Meeting," *Guardian*, 28 June 1947, 9. See "An Act to Incorporate the Prince Edward Island Innkeepers Association," 11 George VI, cap. 53. It is not clear whether its founding was a response to, or catalyst for, the government's tourist strategy.

78 In fact, among the association's declared objects in its act of incorporation was "to promote and advance

the facilities offered by its member to Tourists and the Travelling Public."

79 Among its founders was Sally M. Rodd. Both Leta Andrews and Senator Elsie Inman served as president during the 1950s and on stepping down each was made honorary president in recognition of her achievements. For more on women's role in the association, see McRae, "Manufacturing Paradise," 108–10.

80 McRae, "Manufacturing Paradise," 113.

81 "Annual Report of the Department of Health and Welfare, 1948," PEI, JLA, 1949.

82 "Report of the Division of Sanitary Engineering," "Annual Report of the Department of Health, 1954," PEI, JLA, 1955, 93–4. The establishments were given a year to come up to code.

83 "Annual Report of the Department of Health, 1957," PEI, JLA, 1958, 119.

84 "Public Accounts of the Province of Prince Edward Island for the year ending 31 March, 1948," PEI, JLA, 1949; "Public Accounts of the Province of Prince Edward Island for the Year Ending 31 March, 1949," PEI, JLA, 1949, 188.

85 Unless otherwise indicated, these figures are taken from the provincial public accounts, as published in the JLA.

86 "Lengthy Discussion," Guardian, 24 April 1952, 15.

87 "Loans under Plan for Tourist Accommodation," Guardian, 17 March 1953, 5. Simply adding up the loan statistics published in the public accounts suggests a total of just over $211,000 for the period 1948–54.

88 "Need Motels Says Premier as Controversial Tourist Accommodation Bill Read," Guardian, 30 March 1954, 1, 8; "Answers Tabled in Legislature," Guardian, 30 March 1954, 5.

89 Quoted in "Need Motels Says Premier," Guardian, 30 March 1954, 1.

90 The loan ceiling had been put in place in 1949 but only after a $32,000 loan had been made. See "Need Motels Says Premier," Guardian, 30 March 1954, 1, 8; and "Answers Tabled in Legislature," Guardian, 30 March 1954, 5.

91 "The Tourist Accommodation Loans Act," 3 Eliz. II, cap. 36. Terms were up to fifteen years at an annual interest rate of no less than 4.5 per cent.

92 "$156,134 Reduction," Guardian, 31 March 1954, 9.

93 Rodd received some $40,000, launching the family on the path to a regional hotel chain. (See Executive Council Minutes, 18, 24 February 1954.)

94 Minutes of General Meeting, 16 November 1959, PEI Tourist Association, 98-004, box 3, PARO.

95 "An Act to Amend the Tourist Accommodation Loans Act," 9 Eliz II, cap. 4; JLA, 1960, 137. Stewart low-balled the existing ceiling, which had been raised to $450,000 only the year before. See "An Act to Amend the Tourist Accommodation Loans Act," 9 Eliz II, cap. 41. It is no coincidence that the new government ran a record deficit in 1959–60 of $6.7 million. See Walter R. Shaw fonds, 3688, file 217, PARO.

96 "Public Accounts of the Province of Prince Edward Island for the Year Ended 31 March 1961," PEI, JLA, 1962. An undated list of "Tourist Accommodation Loans" from this period lists 128 in all, ranging from the $305 afforded Bernard Doiron to the $50,500 lent to Summerside tourist operator Vaughn Groom. Ten loans were for less than $1,000, thirty-three totalled between $1,000 and $5,000. The bulk of the loans, eighty-five of them, exceeded $5,000, of which thirty-two were for $20,000 or more. See "Tourist Accommodation Loans," Walter R. Shaw fonds, 3688, file 204, PARO.

97 "Tourist Industry Marching Ahead at Record Speed," undated newspaper clipping, TIAPEI, 98-004, box 3, PARO.

98 As described in MacDonald and MacEachern, "Rites of Passage," parts of which are excerpted below.

99 "Transportation Problem Stressed," Guardian, 23 February 1939, 3.

100 "Annual Report of the Department of Industry and Natural Resources, for the Year Ending 31 March 1952," Transportation Division, PEI, JLA, 1953.

101 Between 1947 and 1959, the province spent $38.2 million on highway construction. See MacDonald, If You're Stronghearted, 238–40.

102 MacDonald, If You're Stronghearted, 241. For the 1960 figure, see annual reports of the PEI Department of Highways.

103 MacDonald, If You're Stronghearted, 240–1. See too Walter Shaw to Cyrus J. Gallant, 13 April 1965, Walter R. Shaw fonds, 3688, file 212, PARO. Originally a five-year agreement worth $15 million with a target of 438 miles of pavement, the program was ultimately extended over a period of eight years.

104 J. Walter Jones, "What the Arrival of the M.V. 'Abegweit' Means to the Province of Prince Edward Island," *Guardian*, 8 August 1947, section 2, 7.

105 "Thousands View 'Abegweit'; C.N.R. Accepts Ship," *Guardian*, 11 August 1947, 1.

106 Council Minutes, 20 April 1949, Charlottetown Board of Trade, 3147/8-1, PARO. The Council minutes show that the PEI Boards of Trade and the provincial government collaborated on their respective briefs.

107 Submission by the PEI Boards of Trade to the Royal Commission on Transportation, July 1949, 2, 4, PEI Coll.

108 Northumberland Ferries President R.E. Mutch kept up the pressure through appeals to the Charlottetown Board of Trade (of which he was a member), the Innkeepers Association, Island MPs, and, particularly, the premier's office. Much of the sparse correspondence still extant in the Premier Matheson papers (RG 25.34, PARO) concerns ferry issues. For the Board of Trade discussions, see board and executive minutes (3147/8-1 & 8-2, PARO). Appeals to the Innkeepers Association can be tracked in board minutes (RG 32, 98-004, box 3, PARO).

109 B. Graham Rogers to A.W. Matheson, 8 February 1956, Alex W. Matheson papers, RG 25.34, box 9, file 136a, PARO. Between 1933 and 1953 the accumulated debt was $15.5 million. For the "supplementary" quote, see, Matheson to Lionel Chevrier, minister of Transport, 11 December 1953, Alex W. Matheson papers, RG 25.34, box 6, file 84, PARO.

110 The sense of crisis is captured in the memos, letters, and telegrams tabled with the board minutes of the Charlottetown Board of Trade for August and September 1950, 3147/1, PARO.

111 "Statistics Transportation, 1941–1965," Walter R. Shaw fonds, 3688, file 225, PARO. The figures are complicated by, at various times, including the number of trucks and buses in the overall vehicle count. In marked contrast to the rapid rise in auto traffic, rail traffic edged upwards from 41,705 railcars in 1943 to 53,660 (both ways) in 1961.

112 There were hopes that the *Confederation* could operate in winter, but the first ice season disproved that notion. See John Edward Belliveau, Silver Donald Cameron, and Michael Harrington, *Iceboats to Superferries: An Illustrated History of Marine Atlantic* (St John's: Breakwater Books, 1992), 79.

113 "Tourist Industry Prospects," *Guardian*, 3 April 1952, 4.

114 "Province Reaped Big Tourist Crop," *Guardian*, 26 January 1961, TIAPEI, 98-004, box 3, PARO. The findings were extrapolated from 3,000 questionnaires, probably a more scientific result than the suspiciously round numbers of the previous year's guesstimate: 200,000 visitors spending $10 per head for a gross value of $2 million. See "Our Tourist Industry," undated newspaper clipping, TIAPEI, 98-004, box 3, PARO. By way of comparison, the Island's leading industry, agriculture, was valued at $23.9 million in 1961, three times the figure for tourism. See Walter R. Shaw fonds, 3688, file 215, PARO.

115 "Two Slogan Contest Winners," undated newspaper clipping; and minutes of semiannual meeting, 26 May 1956, TIAPEI, 98-004, box 3, PARO. See also "Plan Tourist Promotion at Meeting of Innkeepers," *Guardian*, 28 May 1956.

116 "Electoral," *Guardian*, 29 February 1956, 15. The Innkeepers Association was sufficiently outraged to save a newspaper clipping of his remarks. See "Tourist Industry," undated newspaper clipping of remarks made in Legislature by Dr George Dewar, TIAPEI, 98-004, box 3, PARO.

117 Mrs A.B. LePage to editor, *Guardian*, 3 March 1956, 4.

118 MacDonald to Inspector E.L. Martin, L Division, RCMP, 26 July 1956, Alex W. Matheson papers, RG 25.34, file 105, PARO.

119 D. Leo Dolan, "PEI Banquet Session, 15 September 1956," 36–9, 1956 Convention Proceedings of the Canadian Tourist Association, Charlottetown, 17–20 September 1956, Alex W. Matheson papers, RG 25.34, box 10, file 137. PARO.

120 Minutes of Special General Meeting, 15 December 1956, TIAPEI, 98-004, box 3, PARO.

121 This process can be tracked across 1956–58 in the minutes of meetings of the Innkeepers Association.

122 The initial decision to make the change came in December 1956. See Directors' Meeting, 8 December 1956, TIAPEI, 98-004, box 3, PARO. It took two legislative steps. In 1957, "An Act to Amend an Act to Incorporate the Prince Edward Island Innkeepers Association," 6 Eliz., cap 47, changed the organization's objects and membership criteria. In 1958, "An Act to Amend an Act to Incorporate the Prince Edward Island Innkeepers Association," 7 Eliz II, cap. 40, tinkered with the wording of several clauses while officially renaming the association.

123 The association's activities are neatly summarized in McRae, "Manufacturing Paradise," 111–14.

124 "Let's Make It Province-Wide," *Guardian*, 26 July 1951, 4.

125 The war against ragweed can be traced in annual reports of the Department of Agriculture, newspaper reports, and the Island's successive promotional booklets. See, for example, "Will Launch All-Out Campaign to Eliminate Ragweed in PEI," *Guardian*, 7 May 1952, 1; "Efforts Being Made to Stamp Out Ragweed," *Guardian*, 24 September 1953, 5; "Sees Great Attraction in Ragweed Free Province," *Guardian*, 10 July 1956, 1; "Few Havens from Ragweed," *Guardian*, 17 August 1957, 4; and "Minister Pays Tribute to Federal Agriculturalists," *Guardian*, 8 March 1957, 1.

126 The shift was not announced but can be tracked in the public accounts tabled for the period.

127 "Editorial Notes," *Guardian*, 12 February 1951, 4.

128 A graduate of St Dunstan's College, Fraser began his career with the *Guardian*, before working as editor-in-chief for CBC's International News Service, as branch manager for the British United Press, and editor of *The Ensign*, a Catholic bi-weekly. For biographical details, see "Georgetown and Vicinity," *Guardian*, 20 November 1948, 8; "Changes in Provincial Civil Service Announced," *Guardian*, 20 January 1951, 1; "Mr. Fraser's Resignation," *Guardian*, 27 September 1957, 4; and McRae, "Manufacturing Paradise," 92–4.

129 1956 Convention Proceedings of the Canadian Tourist Association, Charlottetown, 17–20 September 1956, Alex W. Matheson papers, RG 25.34, box 10, file 137, PARO. D. Leo Dolan, "PEI Banquet Session, 15 September 1956," 36–9.

130 When Fraser resigned in 1957, the association minutes recorded their genuine regret, and he was presented with a souvenir gift tray bearing a map of the Island. His return a year later was greeted as a "shot in the arm" for the tourist industry. See Minutes of Annual General Meeting, 20 November 1957; Directors' Meeting, 4 December 1957; and President's Report, AGM, 20 November 1959, TIAPEI, 98-004, box 3, PARO.

131 "Provincial Tourist Director Announces His Resignation," *Guardian*, 27 September 1957, 1. Within a year he was back with the provincial government, now as director of information. See "Returns to Gov't Service Here," *Guardian*, 3 September 1958, 1.

132 "Provincial Tourist Director Announces His Resignation," *Guardian*, 27 September 1957, 1. For an extended profile, see Matthew McRae, "Building Treasure Island: The untold story of George Fraser and the Prince Edward Island Travel Bureau," *The Island Magazine* 86 (Fall/Winter 2019).

133 See, for example, *Prince Edward Island*, reprinted from the *Canadian Geographical Journal* for April 1951; and Lloyd Shaw, *The Province of Prince Edward Island* (Ottawa: Canadian Geographical Society, [c.1947]).

134 This generalization is based on breakdowns of expenditures published yearly in the provincial public accounts.

135 "Excellent Publicity," *Guardian*, 3 July 1953, 4.

136 Annual Report, Tourist and Information Bureau, PEI, 1958, 6.

137 "Tourist Industry Announces Blanket Advertising Campaign," *Guardian*, 5 January 1957, 1. The campaign envisaged at least eight ads. The readership estimates (100 million for the newspapers and 60 million for the magazines) were reached by multiplying circulation numbers by a factor of four.

138 Annual Report, Tourist and Information Bureau, PEI, 1958, 2–5.

139 "Sees Good Prospects for Tourist Grant Extension," *Guardian*, 16 May 1957, 2.

140 Minutes of the PEI Innkeepers Association, 2 February 1950.

141 See McRae, "Manufacturing Paradise," 102; and "Tourist Industry Prospects," *Guardian*, 3 April 1952, 4.

142 "Report 30% Boost in Tourist Inquiries," *Guardian*, 18 May 1953, 5.

143 McRae, "Manufacturing Paradise," 102–4, provides further analysis of tourist comments.

144 Quoted in McRae, "Manufacturing Paradise," 95.

145 McKay, *Quest of the Folk*, 30.

146 MacCannell, *Tourist*.

147 Douglas Roche, "Prince Edward Island: The Garden Province of Canada," *Ensign*, 1 November 1956, 24–5, in Alex W. Matheson papers, RG 25.34, box 10, file 137, PARO.

148 David Macdonald to editor, *Guardian*, 23 September 1955.

149 Semi-annual General Meeting, 19 May 1959; and "Tourists Seek New Angles," *Patriot*, 20 May 1959, TIAPEI, 98-004, box 3, PARO. Leo Dolan of the Canadian Government Travel Bureau had told the Innkeepers much the same thing back in 1954: "[T]he people of this Island should retain their serenity and … never become a carbon copy of the United States." "Mr. Dolan Lauds Value of Vacation Dollar in P.E.I.," *Guardian*, 17 March 1954, 1.

150 Towner, *Historical Geography of Recreation and Tourism*, 6. See, too, Jakle, *Tourist*, 5.

151 Jakle, *Tourist*, 95.

152 Quoted in McRae, "Manufacturing Paradise," 95.

153 *Abegweit*, produced for PEI Tourist and Information Bureau by Patterson Productions, Ottawa (1953).

154 Copy in possession of Edward MacDonald. See also, *Screenculture*, Canadian Educational, Sponsored, and Industrial Film Archive, http://www.screenculture. org/cesif/node/2265.

155 Similarly, the seventy-minute rail journey from Winnipeg to the town of Winnipeg Beach was widely regarded as part and parcel of the tourist experience of the beach resort as well as the necessary prerequisite for mass tourism. See Dale Barbour, *Winnipeg Beach: Leisure and Courtship in a Resort Town, 1900–1967* (Winnipeg: University of Manitoba Press, 2011).

156 Annual Report, Department of Tourism (henceforth, ARDT), 1965, 19. How they came up with the figure is not indicated, although the 1958 report noted that the film was distributed through film councils, universities, and libraries, as well as making excellent filler for television stations.

157 Annual Report, Department of Industry and Natural Resources, PEI, *JLA*, 1955.

158 "Island's Season Hits New High in Tourism: Gain in Travel Here Exceeds 12 Per Cent," undated newspaper clipping [September 1958], TIAPEI, 98-004, box 3, PARO.

159 MacEachern, *Natural Selections*, 172–3.

160 Charles E. Linkletter, Summerside, to A.W. Matheson, 26 June 1958; and Matheson to Linkletter, 15 July 1958, Alex W. Matheson papers, RG 25.34, box 9, file 133, PARO. Linkletter went ahead anyway, creating a Summerside landmark in the process, and the incoming Conservative government renewed the province's accommodation loans strategy.

161 McRae, "Manufacturing Paradise," 106.

162 R.L. Cotton to A.W. Matheson, Memo re Suggested Public Parks under Provincial Ownership, 31 January 1956, Alex W. Matheson papers, RG 25.34, box 7, file 103, PARO. Cotton offered up to $50,000 to purchase, develop, and, if necessary, support the intended parks.

163 Cotton to Matheson, 31 January 1956. See also, "Annual Report of the Department of Industry and Natural Resources, 1959," PEI, *JLA*, 1960.

164 ARDT, 1964, 3.

165 MacDonald, *If You're Stronghearted*, 274.

166 Will R. Bird, *These Are the Maritimes* (Toronto: Ryerson, 1959). The Island merited fifty-eight of its 330 pages. For more background on Bird, who was also a prolific journalist and popular novelist, see McKay and Bates, *In the Province of History*, 130–99.

167 McKay and Bates, *In the Province of History*, 157.

168 Bird, *These Are the Maritimes*, 192–3.

169 Bird sums Islanders up in this way at the end of his trip: "In Prince Edward Island they have more time for you, are more courteous, live in the past, want very much to be of help. By and large they did not seem to be readers like Nova Scotians, did not bother much with world events. Island events mean much more in their lives." See Bird, *These Are the Maritimes*, 328–9.

170 Bird, *These Are the Maritimes*, 220.

171 As noted in McRae, *Manufacturing Paradise*, 115–16.

172 Bird, *These Are the Maritimes*, 216–17.

173 Bird, *These Are the Maritimes*, 230.

174 Bird, *These Are the Maritimes*, 232–3.

175 Bird, *These Are the Maritimes*, 240–8.

176 Hope McBride Hambly, "Red-Soil Summers," *The Island Magazine* 67 (Spring/Summer 2010): 31–7. The McBrides vacationed at Stanhope for several weeks each summer from 1951–53.

177 "Wealth Drawn from Sea and Soil," 69.

178 McRae, "Manufacturing Paradise," 6.

179 Fleming diary, entries for 11, 16, 18 December 1953; 22, 23, 26 February 1954; 29, 30 April 1954; 27, 28 May 1954.

180 Fleming diary, 20 July 1954.

181 Fleming diary, 5 February and 10, 19 July 1955; and 28 May, 26 June 1956.

182 Fleming diary, 5, 6 10 August 1957; 10 July 1958; and 15 July 1959.

183 Fleming diary, 16, 22 July 1959.

184 Fleming diary, 28 June 1961.

185 Fleming diary, 15 June 1960.

186 That is, Rockwell's "Going and Coming" cover of *The Saturday Evening Post*, 20 August 1947.

187 Fleming diary, 4 October 1962; and "Obituary," *Guardian*, 29 October 1962, 12.

188 See Bertha's entries in the Fleming diary, which she sporadically continued after her husband's death.

189 Telephone interview with Megan Skinner, North Rustico, 9 February 2019. As a teenager, Megan's husband Bud (Bertha's grandson) annually helped Bertha ready her tourist accommodation for much of the 1960s.

190 Minutes of Directors' Meeting, 8 December 1956, TIAPEI, 98-004, box 3, PARO; and "PEI Innkeepers Want Separate Dept. for Tourist Industry," *Guardian*, 15 November 1956, 1. The government's reticence to invest in tourism is reminiscent of New Zealand's in the same period. See McClure, *Wonder Country*, 185–8.

191 General Meeting, 12 November 1959, Charlottetown Board of Trade, 3147/1, PARO.

Chapter Four

1 For details about the methodology, see Acres Research and Planning, Ltd, *Development Planning for Prince Edward Island: Recreation–Tourism* (Toronto: Acres Consulting, 1967), vol. 1, 27, vol. 2, A-1, T-1; and ARDT, 1965, 15. The survey teams took a catholic approach to defining tourists: "All visitors coming to the province were considered to be tourists since they were spending money away from their usual place of residence." See Acres, *Development Planning*, vol. 1, 27.

2 ARDT, 1965, 7 and 15.

3 Adler, "Tourism and Pastoral," 133.

4 See, for example, "Tourist Industry Marching Ahead at Record Speed," *Guardian*, 27 February 1963, 3A.

5 Jakle, *Tourist*, 306.

6 ARDT, 1964, 4–5.

7 ARDT, 1967, 15. Lest he be accused of self-promotion, Fraser added, "This assessment comes from impartial [though unnamed] observers."

8 The comparative provincial figures were provided in ARDT, 1965, 17. The budget numbers and their proportion to the total provincial budget are derived from the PEI *JLA*.

9 Elements of this discussion are adapted from MacEachern, "The Landscapes of Tourism," 343–5.

10 *Memo to Mom* (c.1963), Canadian National Railways.

11 *Abegweit* (1954), produced by the PEI Tourist and Information Bureau and Patterson Productions, Ottawa.

12 This list draws on ARDT, 1964; and *ScreenCulture*. The ca.1952 *This World of Ours* feature, titled *Prince Edward Island*, was coproduced by Dudley Pictures Corporation, New York/Beverly Hills, and the PEI Travel Bureau.

13 In its first year of release, *Holiday Island* played to an estimated audience of nearly 102,000 people in 1,499 screenings, all but thirty-two of them in Canada or the United States, and was aired at least once on Canadian television. It also played regularly on the Northumberland Strait ferry crossings. See Memo, George V. Fraser, Deputy Minister of Tourist Development, to Alex Campbell, 30 January 1969, Alex B. Campbell papers, 25.36, 1968–69, file 1090-2b, PARO.

14 William Chafe, *The Unfinished Journey: America since World War II*, 3rd ed. (New York: Oxford University Press, 1995), 99, cited in Neal Gabler, *Walt Disney: The Triumph of the American Imagination* (New York: Vintage Books, 2006), 480.

15 Gabler, *Walt Disney*, 18.

16 L.M. Montgomery, "Prince Edward Island," in *The Spirit of Canada, Dominion and Provinces, 1939: A Souvenir of Welcome to H.M. George VI and H.M. Queen Elizabeth* (Montreal: Canadian Pacific Railway, 1939).

17 Acres, *Development Planning*, vol. 1, 123.

18 This point is made in Adler, "Tourism and Pastoral," 134.

19 Brochures for Canadian National Parks, filled with white, nuclear, heterosexual families, implied the same thing. See MacEachern, *Natural Selections*, 164.

20 A version of this episode was published as MacDonald and MacEachern, "Unwanted Guests." Although the Island press spelled his name "Phils," his obituary renders his surname as "Phills." See "James A. Phills, MD, Sr.," Montreal *Gazette*, 3 March 2010.

21 "Resort Refuses Rooms to Negro," *Guardian*, 1 September 1962, 5; "Physician Claims He Was Refused Rooms at Resort," *Evening Patriot*, 1 September 1962, 1. The Phillses subsequently found lodgings at the Charlottetown Motel. As if it

made the offense less excusable, both newspapers took pains to point out that Dr Phills was a native Maritimer.

22 "Discrimination Widespread Here?" *Evening Patriot*, 4 September 1962, 1; "Racial Discrimination to Be Aired by Ass'n," *Guardian*, 5 September 1962, 3.

23 Don MacLeod, "Government Orders Probe of Discrimination, Montreal Sends Protest: Shaw Offers Apology," *Evening Patriot*, 5 September 1962; Don MacLeod, "Gov't to Probe Discrimination," *Guardian*, 6 September 1962, 2. Both newspapers were by then owned by the Thomson media chain, and their reporting of this incident shared a writer and, largely, content.

24 "Unfounded Rumors," *Evening Patriot*, 7 September 1962, 4. The editorial denied leaking the story to CP.

25 "Not to Our Credit," *Guardian*, 5 Sept. 1962, 4. It returned to the theme the next day in "Prompt Reaction," *Guardian*, 6 September 1962, 4.

26 "Here Lies the Shame," *Evening Patriot*, 5 September 1962, 4.

27 "Rumours Are Unfounded Says Tourist Minister," *Guardian*, 8 September 1962, 2.

28 "Well, Now, Mr. Stewart…," *Guardian*, 9 September 1962, 6.

29 "Tourist Promotion Plans Discussed by Association," *Guardian*, 3 November 1962, 1, 5; "Tourist Spending Near $10 Million," *Evening Patriot*, 3 November 1962, 1, 3.

30 Minutes of Annual General Meeting, 2 November 1962, TIAPEI, 98-004, box 3, PARO.

31 See Jim Hornby, *Black Islanders* (Charlottetown: Institute of Island Studies Press, 1991). Hornby briefly recounts the Phills incident while assessing the recent experience of the Island's Black community (96–101). Incidents of racism towards the Island's immigrant Lebanese and Chinese communities are recognized but generally played down in David Weale's *A Stream Out of Lebanon: An Introduction to the Syrian-Lebanese Emigrants to Prince Edward Island* (Charlottetown: Institute of Island Studies, 1988); and Hung-Min Chiang, *Chinese Islanders: Making a Home in the New World* (Charlottetown: Island Studies Press, 2006). See, too, Laura Lee Howard, "Let Them In but Keep Them Out: Liminality and Islandness of the First Born Chinese Islanders," unpublished MA thesis, University of Prince Edward Island, 2010.

32 R. Reymond to Editor, *Guardian*, 7 September 1962, 6. Reymond purchased the Stanhope Beach Inn in 1948 and began leasing Dalvay-by-the-Sea from the National Parks Branch in 1959. See W.F. Lothian, *A History of Canada's National Parks*, (Ottawa: Parks Canada, 1976), vol. 1, chapter 3, http://parkscanadahistory.com/publications/history/lothian/eng/vol1/chap3.htm.

33 MacEachern, *Natural Selections*, 166. As Reymond was still fox farming in Southport, near Charlottetown, at the time, he would have less reason to know about a previous incident in 1942 when a visitor complained to parks staff that Jews were allowed to stay at Dalvay-by-the-Sea. On that occasion, the park superintendent confirmed the presence of Jews, saying Dalvay's concessionaires "would not accept them if they could avoid it."

34 See *Guardian*, 12 July 1958, 7; and "Armstrong and His Band Please Large Audience," *Guardian*, 25 July 1958, 2.

35 The story is recounted, although the timing is muddled, in David Weale, "Satchmo," *Red* 5 (Fall/Winter 2012–13): 28. Our thanks to members of the McMillan family, whose helpful recollections confirmed the essential details of this story. According to family lore, a furious Dr McMillan promptly phoned Prime Minister John Diefenbaker to condemn the behaviour of a Crown corporation. Emails from Charles McMillan, John McMillan, and Maura Davies to MacDonald, October 2015.

36 Annual Report, Department of Industry and Natural Resources, PEI, 1962, 36–41.

37 Donald J. Savoie, *Visiting Grandchildren: Economic Development in the Maritimes* (Toronto: University of Toronto Press, 2006), 82–5. This summary amends the one provided in MacDonald, *If You're Stronghearted*, 267. There is a surprising level of disagreement in published sources when it comes to dating the various acts and agencies.

38 David Milne, "Politics in A Beleaguered Garden," in Smitheram, Milne, and Dasgupta, *Garden Transformed*, 45.

39 "Heavy Crop," undated newspaper clipping, Walter R. Shaw fonds, 3688, file 204, PARO. Some simple math suggests that the spending estimate should total just over $15 million, so the figure was evidently adjusted.

40 ARDT, 1965, 7.

41 Minutes, Annual General Meeting, 18 November 1965, TIAPEI, 98-004, box 3, PARO.

42 Acres, *Development Planning*, vol. 1, 47. The researchers did not provide any figure of their own for the total number of visitors, but working back from an expenditure of $5.8 million, with the average stay put at four days, and the average outlay at $6 per day per tourist, the total number of visitors works out to about 241,600, a far cry from the Department of Tourist Development's figure of 377,606.

43 Hartwell Daley, "Who's Right about P.E.I. Tourist Revenue?" undated newspaper clipping, c.1967, TIAPEI, 98-004, box 3, PARO. The rumoured discrepancy was even more worrisome, Daley added, when one considered that the Department of Tourist Development habitually claimed that its estimates were conservative.

44 Minutes, Annual General Meeting, 1 November 1967, TIAPEI, 98-004, box 3, PARO.

45 Acres, *Development Planning*, vol. 1, 14–15.

46 Acres, *Development Planning*, vol. 1, 28. The tabular breakdown in volume 1 provides slightly different figures for American tourists.

47 This paragraph summarizes findings found in the Acres, *Development Planning*, vol. 1, 29–37 and 103–6.

48 Acres, *Development Planning*, vol. 1, 105–6.

49 Acres, *Development Planning*, vol. 1, 33.

50 Acres, *Development Planning*, vol. 1, 79 and 82. As the report put it, "The fact that operators build motels where people go and people go where the motels are located, whereupon new motels are built – explains the present distribution."

51 Acres, *Development Planning*, vol. 1, 37–9, 47. Motel guests had the shortest average stays of all tourist types but as a group spent the most per day. The second largest accommodation group, nearly 20 per cent of the sample, paid nothing, since they stayed with friends and relatives.

52 Acres, *Development Planning*, vol. 1, 24–5 and 42–4.

53 Acres, *Development Planning*, vol. 1, 24.

54 Acres, *Development Planning*, vol. 1, 19–23. Kings County had 18,300 acres rated as class 1 or 2 (a whopping 14,100 acres in class 1); the figure for Prince County was 12,300 acres (5,100 acres in class 1, most of them around West Point and on the barrier dune system of Hog Island on Malpeque Bay). The map of

Land Capability for Recreation produced in 1968 for the Canada Land Inventory from Acres' assessment defined class 1 as "shoreland with very high capability to generate intensive family bathing and beach activities, fronting and providing access to a water body suited to family bathing and beach activities, fronting and providing access to a water body suited to family boating, and with a backshore suited to organized camping." The general description goes on to observe, "The abundance of Class 1 and 2 coastal areas is outstanding, unique not only regionally but nationally." (Copy in possession of author.)

55 Acres, *Development Planning*, vol. 1, 96. Desperate Travel Bureau staff were driven to canvassing private homes for emergency accommodations.

56 Acres, *Development Planning*, vol. 1, 96.

57 This paragraph summarizes data from the Acres, *Development Planning*, vol. 1, 63–82. The quote is from 63.

58 Acres, *Development Planning*, vol. 1, 78–82.

59 Acres, *Development Planning*, vol. 1, 94.

60 Acres, *Development Planning*, vol. 1, 109.

61 Acres, *Development Planning*, vol. 1, 101, 107.

62 Acres, *Development Planning*, vol. 1, 107.

63 Acres, *Development Planning*, vol. 1, 102. The estimates were predicated on replacement of the ferry service at Borden by a promised causeway by 1972, with a 20 per cent spike in visitation the following year.

64 Acres, *Development Planning*, vol. 1, 125.

65 Acres, *Development Planning*, vol. 1, 117–18.

66 Acres, *Development Planning*, vol. 1, 122.

67 The parallel regional story is summarized in Martha Elizabeth Walls, "Confederation and Maritime First Nations," *Acadiensis* 46, 2 (Summer/Autumn 2017): 155–76. An Island overview is provided by Louis Pellissier, "The Native People of Prince Edward Island," in *Readings in Prince Edward Island History*, ed. Harry Baglole (Charlottetown: Department of Education, 1976). For the decline of Mi'kmaw handicrafts, see "Natives Maintain Tradition of Basket Weaving," *Evening Patriot*, 22 March 1986, 3.

68 Executive Council Minutes, Province of PEI, 25 March 1960, PARO.

69 "Indians' and First Settlers' Contribution Outlined to H&S," *Guardian*, 17 November 1962, 5.

70 Interview by author with Catherine Hennessey, Charlottetown, 3 September 2020.

71 "Notice of Granting of Letters Patent," *Royal Gazette*, 9 April 1960.

72 The original corporation appears to have sold the business in 1974, made its last return in 1986, and dissolved in 1990. The successor corporation, having formed in 1974, made its last return in 1999 and dissolved in 2003, the Village "no longer open to the public." See PEI Business, Corporate Registry, Registration no. 2260 and no. 2261.

73 See, for example, *Guardian*, 29 July 1930, 6; 30 July 1957, 11; and 25 July 1962, 3.

74 "Lennox Islanders Open New Handicrafts Centre," *Guardian*, 17 July 1973, 5; "Lennox Island Band Members Produce Objects of Beauty," *Guardian*, 25 February 1974, 2. In the photograph accompanying the first article, Chief Jack Sark is shown wearing what appears to be a Plains style headdress rather than the traditional Mi'kmaw version.

75 "Lennox Island Museum 'Needs' Development," *Guardian*, 14 February 1983, 2.

76 "Basket Making 'A Dying Art,'" *Guardian*, 14 February 1983, 2.

77 "Island a Mecca This Year for Steady Tourist Influx," *Guardian*, 20 August 1953, 8. See also "Many Visitors to Confederation Chamber in 1950," *Guardian*, 2 January 1951, 5; "Record Number Sign Visitors Book," *Guardian*, 3 January 1952, 5; and "International Air Cadets Complete Visit to Island," *Guardian*, 25 July 1958, 11.

78 MacDonald, *If You're Stronghearted*, 276.

79 Frank MacKinnon to Eric Harvie, 14 January 1959, G1/1304, Frank MacKinnon papers, Glenbow Museum and Archives.

80 The most detailed account of the founding of the Fathers of Confederation Memorial Buildings, now known as the Confederation Centre of the Arts, is Edward MacDonald, *Cradling Confederation: The Founding of the Confederation Centre of the Arts, Charlottetown* (Charlottetown: Confederation Centre of the Arts, 2013). The condensed version offered here borrows heavily from that publication.

81 For its part, the government of Prince Edward Island agreed to provide and prepare the proposed building site. See W.R. Shaw to Frank MacKinnon, 5 November 1962, MacKinnon papers, G1/1313, Glenbow Museum and Archives.

82 MacKinnon later implied that the bigger challenge might have been the attitude of small-minded Island- ers. "There was vicious and shabby local criticism of the very idea of a Centre," he remembered. MacKinnon to Edward MacDonald, 18 February 2004.

83 For more details and discussion, see MacDonald, *Cradling Confederation*, 28–9 and 44–5; and McRae, "New Nationalism," 345–7.

84 Diary of Dorothy Cullen, Charlottetown, 1 September 1964, photocopy in possession of authors.

85 "Address of the Honourable Walter R. Shaw, Premier of PEI to the Prime Minister of Canada and the Premiers of the Provinces at the Commemorative Ceremonies Honoring the Fathers of Confederation, September 1, 1964," 3688, file 92, PARO.

86 The most complete account of the 1964 Centennial celebrations is McRae, "New Nationalism," 349–56.

87 Minutes, Annual Meeting, 2 November 1962, TIAPEI, 98-004, box 3, PARO.

88 McRae, "New Nationalism," 355–6.

89 McRae, "New Nationalism," 352–3.

90 *The Hundredth Summer*, National Film Board of Canada, 1964.

91 McRae, "New Nationalism," 352.

92 Quoted in McRae, "New Nationalism," 348 and 355. Of course, the committee was also keen to show that its half a million dollars in funding had been well spent despite the absence of measurable revenues.

93 ARDT, 1964, 1–3; and McRae, "New Nationalism," 354–6. The annual report disingenuously attributed a drop-off in business along the North Shore on poor summer weather rather than the competing pull of Centennial events.

94 President's Annual Report, 1964, TIAPEI, 98-004, box 3, PARO.

95 McRae, "New Nationalism," 350.

96 McRae, "New Nationalism," 355.

97 President's Annual Report, 1964, TIAPEI, 98-004, box 3, PARO.

98 McRae, "New Nationalism," 347.

99 Ambridge to Eric Harvie, 9 September 1963, MacKinnon papers, G1/1273, Glenbow Museum and Archives.

100 Quoted in Frank MacKinnon, *Honour the Founders! Enjoy the Arts* (Charlottetown: Confederation Centre of the Arts, 1990), 38.

101 Jack MacAndrew, Director, Public Relations, Confederation Centre of the Arts, 2 November 1967, memo re "P.E.I. Tourist Association Meeting," Campbell papers, 25.36, 1967–68, file 1048, PARO.

102 MacDonald, *Cradling Confederation*, 19.

103 Jesuitical arguments were made by the Shaw government in submissions to Ottawa to explain why it should not be held to its pledge. See, for example, the undated memo in Walter Shaw papers, 3688, PARO.

104 Working with the Confederation Centre, the Shaw government had squeezed a $100,000 annual operating grant out of Ottawa in 1965. In 1966, the federal cabinet reluctantly agreed to up the amount to $175,000 per year, provided the province matched the grant. The new money reduced the centre's operating deficits to manageable proportions. See Edward MacDonald, "Cradling Confederation: The Origins of the Confederation Centre of the Arts," a research report prepared for the National Vision Task Force, Confederation Centre of the Arts, 2004.

105 President's Annual Report, 1964, TIAPEI, 98-004, box 3, PARO.

106 As recounted by Tom Symons. See Edward MacDonald, "Summer Islander," in *Tom Symons, A Canadian Life*, ed. Ralph Heintzman (Ottawa: University of Ottawa Press, 2011), 343.

107 According to Guinness World Records: see J. Kelly Nestruck, *Globe and Mail*, 10 March 2014. Of course, Guinness did create the category especially for the production.

108 This section is adapted from MacDonald and MacEachern, "Rites of Passage," 20–3.

109 Annual Report, Department of Highways, PEI, 1968, 45.

110 "Statistics Transportation, 1941–1965," WSF, 3688, file 225, PARO. The statistics for July–August traffic are from 1965 but can be taken as normative.

111 Summary – P.E.I. Ferry Service, 1966 Traffic, Campbell papers, 25.36, 1966–67, file 1108, PARO.

112 David Hinks, "Prince Edward Island Transportation Systems," Canadian Transportation Commission Research Branch, Directorate of Transport Industries Analysis, Report no. 20-77-7, July 1977; and MacDonald, *If You're Stronghearted*, 304.

113 John H. Gill to Minister of Tourism, 18 September 1969, Campbell papers, 25.36, 1968–69, file 1090-4, PARO.

114 M. Frank, Toronto, to Campbell, dated 27 August 1971, Campbell papers, 25.36, 1971, file 1090-4, PARO.

115 Mrs A.W. Faux, Perth, Ontario, to Campbell, 26 July 1971, Campbell papers, 25.36, 1971, file 1090-4, PARO. The Faux family had already waited 3.5 hours in line at Tormentine on their way to the Island. It was their second visit to the province in three years and perhaps their last.

116 Mrs B.M. Bayne, Montreal, to Campbell, 30 August 1968, Campbell papers, 25.36, 1968–69, file 1090-4. PARO

117 A. Walthen Gaudet, Secretary, PEI Tourist Association, to Alex B. Campbell, 1 June 1967, Campbell papers, 25.36, 1967–68, file 1048, PARO.

118 Campbell to Lyman Wood, Victoria, 29 October 1968, Campbell papers, 25.36, 1968–69, file 1090-4, PARO.

119 Editorial cartoon from Halifax *Chronicle-Herald*, reproduced in Copthorne MacDonald, *Bridging the Strait: The Story of the Confederation Bridge Project* (Toronto: Dundurn, 1997), 40.

120 See ARDT, 1966, 9–10. Tourism was up 20 per cent until August, but the season ended with only a 4 per cent overall increase.

121 Press Release, 10 October 1969, Campbell papers, 25.36, 1968–69, file 1090-2b, PARO.

122 "New Ferry Purchased for Borden Operation," *Guardian*, 23 January 1969, TIAPEI, 98-004, box 3, PARO.

123 Notes for Throne Speech, 1969, Campbell papers, 25.36, 1968–69, file 1090-2b, PARO.

124 "Northumberland Strait Crossing, Presentation of Brief by Province of PEI to Federal Government of Canada," 23 October 1968, Campbell papers, 25.36, 1968–69, file 1131-2, PARO.

125 Bird, *These Are the Maritimes*, 192.

126 "The Northumberland Strait Crossing, Briefing Session," Department of Public Works, Canada, Charlottetown, 14 July 1966, Campbell papers, 25.36, 1967–68, file 1063c, PARO.

127 It is hard to imagine that the Canso Causeway, completed in 1955, did not play into the causeway movement on Prince Edward Island. See Del Muise and Meaghan Beaton, "The Canso Causeway: Tartan Tourism, Industrial Development, and the Promise of Progress for Cape Breton," *Acadiensis* 37, 2 (Summer/Autumn 2008): 39–69.

128 The account here borrows from MacDonald, *If You're Stronghearted*, 293–5.

129 Acres, *Development Planning*, vol. 1, 102. As of 1967, the projected completion date was 1972.

130 Press Release, Prime Minister's Office, 8 July 1965, Campbell papers, 25.36, 1967–68, file 1063c, PARO.

131 "Notes on Northumberland Strait Crossing Feasibility Study Meeting," 17 August 1968, Campbell Papers, 25.36, 1968–69, file 1131-1, PARO.

132 "Opinion with Jack McAndrew," [undated, 1968], Campbell papers, 25.36, 1967–68, file 1063a, PARO.

133 "Northumberland Strait Crossing, Presentation of Brief by Province of PEI to Federal Government of Canada," 23 October 1968, Campbell papers, 25.36, 1968–69, file 1131-2, PARO.

134 The most informed version of events is offered in H. Wade MacLauchlan, *Alex B. Campbell, the Prince Edward Island Premier Who Rocked the Cradle* (Charlottetown: Prince Edward Island Museum and Heritage Foundation, 2014), 89–98.

135 One of the authors acknowledges partial responsibility for this reading. See MacDonald, *If You're Stronghearted*, 302.

136 MacDonald, *If You're Stronghearted*, 298–9 and 342. The actual ratio over the life of the plan was heavily weighted towards the federal side, something in the order of 3:1.8. According to the *Canadian Annual Review*, 1983, 283, the totals to that time were $301 million from the federal government and $186 million from the Island government.

137 MacDonald, *If You're Stronghearted*, 303.

138 *Agreement Covering Development Plan for Prince Edward Island* (Ottawa: Department of Regional Economic Expansion, 1970), 39.

139 ARDT, 1968, 9. By way of comparison, estimated tourist spending had nearly doubled between 1960 and 1968.

140 "The Plan," *Tourist Talk*, March [1969], TIAPEI, 98-004, box 3, PARO.

141 Walford MacEwen, Kensington, to Campbell, 1 October 1969, Campbell papers, 25.36, 1968–69, file 1090-3. PARO.

142 Boyd Bernard, Tignish, to Campbell, Campbell papers, 25.36, 1968–69, file 1090-3, PARO.

143 ARDT, 1970, 14. Besides preparing and executing relevant projects within the recreation–tourism component of the Development Plan, the unit was mandated to work with other departments as well as the general public.

144 Project Planning Associates Ltd, Toronto and Halifax, "West Prince County PEI Tourist and Recreation Plan," Progress Report Number 3, 30 October 1970, 2, in Campbell papers, 25.36, 1969–70, file 1090-1, PARO.

145 These details and those that follow are contained in "Policy and Program: Recreation and Tourism Sector," Department of Environment and Tourism, 15 December 1971, Campbell papers, 25.36, 1972, file 1090-2, PARO.

146 Caroline Spankie, Tourist Development Planning Unit, "Progress Report: Programme: Recreation–Tourism Sector," February 1971, Campbell papers, 25.36, 1971, file 1090-2, PARO. The scenic loops were also routed so as to include as many as possible of the twenty-three provincial parks, which were scheduled for their own trial by rationalization.

147 "Policy and Program: Recreation and Tourism Sector," Department of Environment and Tourism, 15 December 1971, Campbell papers, 25.36, 1972, file 1090-2: 11-13, PARO.

148 Acres, *Development Planning*, vol. 1, 108.

149 By way of illustration, the overall budget for the Department of Tourist Development, which was responsible for developing the resort complexes, more than doubled between 1969 and 1970, from $913,000 to $1.97 million. Nearly half of its capital budget (46 per cent) was earmarked for the Brudenell project. Ottawa's share of the total was 75 per cent.

150 Back in the fall of 1968 the province had signed a contract with the Atlantic Development Board to fund a motel at Brudenell Provincial Park. Agreement between ADB and Province, 24 September 1968, Campbell papers, 25.36, 1971, file 1090-1, PARO.

151 See, undated [1969] memo from Fraser to Campbell, and follow-up memo, 12 September 1969, Campbell papers, 25.36, 1968–69, file 1090-1, PARO.

152 As the tourism department's annual report noted in 1971 (23), the new Brudenell Resort would "encourage private enterprise to develop more attractions in the Kings County area and … thereby create a tourist destination centre in Prince Edward Island."

153 The conflict is noted in APEC, "History of the PEI Comprehensive Development Plan," 73, PEI Coll.

154 For the chronology, see Official Program for opening of Brudenell Resort, 16 July 1971, Campbell papers, 25.36, 1971, file 1090-1, PARO. For the cost estimates, see Memorandum, Richard Higgins to Doug Cameron, re "Cost to Date for Brudenell and Mill River Complexes," 9 July 1971, Campbell papers, 25.36, 1971, file 1090-1, PARO. ARDA grants accounted for $351,225 of the total cost, ADB contributed

155 $318,901, and cdp funding provided the rest, $356,287 actual, and $531,800 projected.

155 Higgins to Cameron, 9 July 1971, Campbell papers, 25.36, 1971, file 1090-1, PARO.

156 J.E. Belliveau speech to PEI Tourist Association, 19 May 1971, Campbell papers, 25.36, 1971, file 1090-2, PARO.

157 Kirbys to Campbell, 29 November 1971, Campbell papers, 25.36, 1971, file 1090-2, PARO.

158 Letter to the Editor [*Toronto Star Weekly*, undated, 1972], Campbell papers, 25.36, 1972, file 1090-2, PARO.

159 Cobb's article, "Tourist Traps, Billboards and a Plaster Kangaroo," was reprinted in Ottawa *Citizen*, 15 November 1971, https://news.google.com/newspapers?nid=2194&dat=19711115&id=170yAAAAIBAJ&sjid=wOwFAAAAIBAJ&pg=6661,4793236&hl=en.

160 G.O. Best, University of Toronto Law School, to Campbell, 16 November 1971, Campbell papers, 25.36, 1971, file 1090-4, PARO.

161 See also Catherine Hennessey, "Marc Gallant, 1945–1994," 28 July 2000, archived https://ruk.ca/sites/ruk.ca/files/catherinehennesseyx.pdf. Ironically, Gallant got his artistic baptism as a child selling his pictures to tourists on the beach at North Rustico.

162 Adler puts it less colloquially: "taste is socially situated." "Tourism and Pastoral," 137.

163 Elizabeth T. Greenlee, Director of Humanities, Laurel School, Cleveland, to Campbell, 15 November 1972, Campbell papers, 25.36, 1972, file 1090-4, PARO. She concluded her letter by begging that he not let Prince Edward Island be "turned into a copy of Honkytonk Isle U.S.A."

164 George Meikle, President, Summerside Board of Trade, to Alex B. Campbell, 13 December 1967, Campbell papers, 25.36, 1967–68, file 1048, PARO.

165 Campbell to Bonnell, 23 April 1971, 30 July 1971; and Don Hoyt, Island Information Services, to Campbell, 16 July 1971, Campbell papers, 25.36, 1971, file 1090-1, PARO.

166 J.E. Belliveau, Speech to PEI Tourist Association, 19 May 1971, Campbell papers, 25.36, 1971, file 1090-2, PARO.

167 Minutes, Semiannual Meeting, 26 April 1967, TIAPEI, 98-004, box 3, PARO.

168 See "ATL 2701," Wikipedia, https://en.wikipedia.org/wiki/ATL_2701; and Anthony Reinhart, "The Irving Whale Rides Again," *Globe and Mail*, 11 December 1907, http://www.theglobeandmail.com/news/national/the-irving-whale-rides-again/article699708/.

169 Draft Speech from the Throne, 1972, Campbell papers, 25.36, 1972, file 1090-2, PARO.

170 Perhaps for that reason, "Environment" was removed from the department's name in 1975 in favour of the Department of Tourism, Parks, and Conservation.

171 The mission statement for the Department of Tourist Development's new Planning Unit already emphasized that all projects must preserve the Island's "natural environment," its "prime tourist resource." See, ARDT, 1970, 14.

172 The Island's stringent signage regulation had a parallel in at least one other tourist island, Bermuda, which back in 1911 had passed an Advertisements Regulation Act banning "unsightly advertisements" from that colony to avoid spoiling its tourist ambience. McDowell, *Another World*, 69–70.

173 As recorded in Adler, "Tourism and Pastoral," 136–7.

174 MacDonald, *If You're Stronghearted*, 335.

175 Milton Acorn, "The Island," in Acorn, *The Island Means Minago: Poems from Prince Edward Island* (Toronto: NC Press, 1975), 47–8.

176 The most detailed account is Ryan O'Connor, "Agrarian Protest and Provincial Politics: Prince Edward Island and the 1971 National Farmers Union Highway Demonstration," *Acadiensis* 37, 1 (Winter/Spring 2008): 31–55.

177 McRae, "New Nationalism," 359.

178 Jessie Ramsay to Campbell, 21 June 1971, Campbell papers, 25.36, 1971, file 1090-3, PARO.

179 K.B. Jenkins, Stanhope Bay Road Camping, to Campbell, 4 September 1970, Campbell papers, 25.36, 1970, file 1090-3, PARO. See also, Jenkins to Campbell, 15, 21 December 1966, Campbell papers, 25.36, 1966–67, file 1018, PARO; Jenkins to Campbell, 1 October 1970, Campbell papers, 25.36, 1970, file 1090-3, PARO.

180 Kathryn Wood, Dunrovin, Victoria, to George V. Fraser, Deputy Minister of Tourism, 9 September 1968, Campbell papers, 25.36, 1968–69, file 1090-1, PARO.

181 Chesley W. Clark, President, and Executive of Cavendish Resort Association to Campbell, 8 October 1969, Campbell papers, 25.36, 1968–69, file 1090-1, PARO. Meanwhile, the association complained that its appeal for financial assistance to build a convention centre in Cavendish was being given the cold shoulder.

182 John A. Morley, Assistant Director of Parks and Provincial Recreation Planner, to Campbell,

23 December 1969, Campbell papers, 25.36, 1968–69, file 1090-1, PARO.

183 McDowell, *Another World*, 98 and 196–8.

184 The ad is reprinted in Harry Baglole and David Weale, eds., *Cornelius Howatt: Superstar!* (Summerside: [the authors], 1974), 130. One of the authors, a high school student at the time, remembers his indignation at being told how to be nice to strangers.

185 For more on the Brothers and Sisters of Cornelius Howatt and their attitude to the Development Plan, see MacDonald, *If You're Stronghearted*, 318–19.

186 Baglole and Weale, *Cornelius Howatt*, 99. Matthew McRae ably covers this ground in "New Nationalism," 361–6.

187 Baglole and Weale, *Cornelius Howatt*, 103.

188 Indeed, it was being labelled "quaint" by a tourist that transforms the Pie-Faced Kid from "sidewalk ambassador" to the "Scourge of Tourism." See Baglole and Weale, *Cornelius Howatt*, 132.

189 Baglole and Weale, *Cornelius Howatt*, 151–3.

190 Summerside *Journal-Pioneer*, 6 April 1973. The image was reproduced in Baglole and Weale, *Cornelius Howatt*, 82–3, and the transition noted in its text.

191 Baglole and Weale, *Cornelius Howatt*, 150.

192 From Elaine Harrison, *I am an Island that Dreams* (Fernwood, PEI: Elaine Harrison & Associates, 1974).

193 Baglole and Weale, *Cornelius Howatt*, 191. Simon had published *No Island Is an Island: The Ordeal of Martha's Vineyard*, earlier in 1973.

194 The issue is summarized in several places. This account is based on MacDonald, *If You're Stronghearted*, 307–8.

195 ARDT, 1973, 4.

196 *Prince Edward Island: Come in from Away* (dir. William Rhodes, MPI Productions/PEI Department of Tourism, Parks, and Conservation, 1976).

197 The tourist focus of the 1967 Centennial was Expo '67 in Montreal. On Prince Edward Island, tourist traffic rose in 1967, but spending dipped, probably because visitors' stays were shorter than usual. See ARDT, 1967, 7.

198 MacLauchlan, *Alex B. Campbell*, 247; McRae, "New Nationalism," 361.

199 These figures combine McRae, "New Nationalism," 361; and MacLauchlan, *Alex B. Campbell*, 246.

200 Depending on how you counted them. The tabled figures for 1972, previously pegged at 685,422

visitors, had been downgraded without explanation to 523,000, allowing 1973 to set a new record. ARDT, 1973, 25.

201 MacLauchlan, *Alex B. Campbell*, 246–7.

202 MacDonald, *If You're Stronghearted*, 320–1.

203 Press release, 23 January 1970, Campbell papers, 25.36, 1970, file 1178, PARO.

204 Brochure, PEI Heritage Foundation, Campbell papers, 25.36, 1970, file 1178, PARO.

205 Campbell to Donald K. Martin, Charlottetown, 18 February 1972, Campbell papers, 25.36, file 1178, PARO.

206 As summarized in MacLauchlan, *Alex B. Campbell*, 247.

207 Telephone conversation with Catherine Hennessey, Charlottetown, 2 December 2015.

208 Individually, if not collectively, they probably did; several former members, including Brother Baglole, were working for the Heritage Foundation by that time.

209 Baglole and Weale, *Cornelius Howatt*, 222.

210 Campbell to C. Bruce Fergusson, Chair, Historic Sites and Monuments Board, 21 September 1966, Campbell papers, 25.36, 1966–67, file 1075, PARO.

211 "Province House National Historic Site of Canada," Parks Canada, http://www.pc.gc.ca/apps/dfhd/page_nhs_eng.aspx?id=580.

212 There are seventeen examples preserved in the premier's files.

213 Pinto to Campbell, 12 September 1969, Campbell papers, 25.36, 1968–69, file 1090-4, PARO.

214 Proctor to Campbell, 22 August 1969, Campbell papers, 25.36, 1968–69, file 1090-4, PARO.

215 Davies to Campbell, 13 July 1972, Campbell papers, 25.36, 1972, file 1090-4, PARO.

216 Saunders to Campbell, 24 August 1970, Campbell papers, 25.36, 1970, file 1090-4, PARO.

217 Baglole and Weale, *Cornelius Howatt*, 183–4.

218 Summerside *Journal-Pioneer*, 1 November 1973.

219 D.A. Macdonald, Moncton, to Chrétien, 2 June 1969, Proposed Parks, PEI, East Point National Park, file 01-07-P1, vol. 1, Parks Canada, Ardgowan National Historic Site, Charlottetown [henceforth, East Point NP, PC]. Macdonald first offered to donate his 180-acre property as early as 1962. Walter Dinsdale, Department of Northern Affairs and Natural Resources, to J. David Stewart, Provincial Secretary, 24 September 1962, 2617/3, PARO.

220 Chrétien to Macdonald, 23 June 1969, East Point NP, PC.

221 J.R.B. Coleman to R. Gordon Robertson, Deputy Minister, 30 January 1962, RG84, vol. 1963, file U2.11, vol. 1, LAC.

222 MacEachern, *Natural Selections*, 223–4.

223 C.L. Merrill, "Shoreline Reconnaissance, Prince Edward Island," July 1964, Campbell papers, 25.36, 1966–67, file 1058, PARO.

224 These developments can be traced in the epistolary exchange between the two levels of government between 1964 and 1966. See 2617/3, PARO.

225 Acres, *Development Planning*, vol. 1, 22.

226 See East Point, PEI, Wallet 1, file 01/07-P1, PC. The unique natural features were explored in more detail in a follow-up survey in 1970. See "Shoreline Reconnaissance, Prince Edward Island, North Shore, June 1970."

227 This last point is contained in Arthur Laing to Walter Shaw, 28 January 1966, 2617/3, PARO.

228 Shaw to Laing, 22 February 1966, 2617/3, PARO.

229 See Shaw to David Macdonald, MP Egmont (in West Prince), 15 February 1966, Confidential, 2617/3, PARO. Shaw was also suspicious because his government's offer to enlarge the proffered park site at Cedar Dunes had mysteriously disappeared before reaching the minister responsible, delaying negotiations for six critical, preelection months. See J. David Stewart to Arthur Laing, 19 June 1965; Shaw to Laing, 7 January 1966; and Laing to Shaw, 28 January 1966, 2617/3, PARO.

230 William L. Meggison to Keir Clark, Minister of Municipal Affairs, 21 September 1966, Campbell papers, 25.36, 1966–67, file 1058, PARO. Of the ninety-four properties and 13,600 acres that Meggison examined, he estimated that 900 acres were in a state of high cultivation, 9,000 "average," and 1,300 in a "poor state of cultivation." The remaining 2,400 acres were given over to woods, bush, and marsh.

231 "Proposed New Park, Briefing Material," undated [c.1969], East Point, East Point NP, PC.

232 A.E. Breau, "Minutes of Charlottetown Meeting of October 10, 1969 between the National and Historic Parks Branch and the Province of Prince Edward Island," East Point NP, PC. Breau thought $1 million the more accurate estimate, working from the rough math of 8,000 acres at no more than $100 an acre.

233 As Premier Campbell explained to Kenneth Birtwistle, of the Cavendish Resort Association, the amount of money involved was "out of proportion" to the province's financial ability "to meet the priorities for tourist development." See Campbell to Birtwistle, 19 April 1971, Campbell papers, 25.36, 1971, file 1090-3, PARO. For the province's parlous financial situation in 1966–67, see MacDonald, *If You're Stronghearted*, 295–6.

234 Campbell memo to Lorne Bonnell, Minister of Tourist Development, 15 August 1966, Campbell papers, 25.36, 1966–67, file 1018, PARO.

235 The various permutations in the funding formula can be traced in "Note to File," L.H. Robinson, Halifax, 16 October 1969, re Proposed Park – PEI; John Rae to Andrew Wells, 28 April 1970, East Point NP, PC.

236 Note to File, L.H. Robinson, Halifax, 16 October 1969, East Point NP, PC.

237 John I. Nicol to Regional Director, Atlantic Region, "Draft Position Paper for Possible Discussion with P.E.I. Government," 3 December 1971, East Point NP, PC.

238 Field Notes of Neil Munro, Regional Planner, 3 August 1972, East Point NP, PC.

239 According to the federal government, it had spent $3.97 million on the PEI National Park between 1958 and 1964 alone. See Arthur Laing to Walter Shaw, 21 April 1966, 2617/3, PARO.

240 Campbell papers, 25.36, 1966–67, file 1058, PARO.

241 "East Point Park," *Evening Patriot*, 9 October 1965, Campbell papers, 25.36, 1966–67, file 1058, PARO.

242 Eastern Kings Board of Trade, "Alternative Proposal for Second P.E.I. National Park," 16 June 1966, Campbell papers, 25.36, 1966–67, file 1058, PARO; and Shaw to Laing, 21 June 1966, 2617/3, PARO.

243 In the end, the southern boundary of the park was modified to skirt MacDonald's property. See National Park Boundary Plan, National and Historic Parks Branch, Department of Indian Affairs and Northern Development, 9 April 1970, East Point NP, PC. It is not clear whether he requested the change. The adjustment may also have been influenced by the province's decision around this time to develop a fisheries museum at nearby Basin Head.

244 L.H. Robinson, Regional Director, Atlantic Region, National Parks Branch, to Hector Hortie, Deputy Minister of Development, 2 October 1969, East Point NP, PC.

245 The census of 1971 counted 822 inhabitants in Lot 47, which encompassed the proposed boundaries of

the park. According to Michael A. O'Grady, *From Grass Roots to Grim Reapings: A History of the Prince Edward Island Rural Development Council* (Charlottetown: Institute of Island Studies, 1997), 49, about 1,000 people were affected by the project.

246 Campbell to Chrétien, 30 May 1972, East Point NP, PC.

247 Copy of Proposed Agreement, attached to a letter from John Rae, Executive Assistant, to Andrew Wells, Executive Assistant to the Premier, PEI, 28 April 1970, East Point NP, PC.

248 See Campbell to Lorne Bonnell, Bruce Stewart, and Hector Hortie, Deputy Minister of Development, 3 September 1970, Campbell papers, 25.36, 1969–70, file 1090-1, PARO; and Chrétien to Campbell, 22 September 1970, East Point NP, PC. Parks agreed to explore the eastward extension of PEI National Park but was predisposed to find against it. A.E. Breau, Regional and Town Planner, Halifax, to P.A. Thomson, Acting Regional Director, 12 November 1970, East Point NP, PC.

249 Chrétien to Bonnell, stamped 2 March 1972, East Point NP, PC.

250 Alex Campbell to Jean Chrétien, 30 May 1972, East Point NP, PC.

251 The "life tenancy" option went through several drafts between late 1971 and 1973. See, for example, John I. Nicol to Regional Director, Atlantic Region, "Draft Position Paper for Possible Discussion with P.E.I. Government," 3 December 1971, East Point NP, PC; and L.H. Robinson to P.B. Lesaux, Assistant Director (National Parks), 4 January 1972, East Point NP, PC. The Parks Branch was not inclined to offer life tenancy provisions unless the province insisted.

252 Comment made by Fred Cheverie, who was part of the local protest, at a public lecture on the East Point National Park episode: Edward MacDonald, "The Prospect of Development: The Pursuit of a Second National Park on Prince Edward Island," Parks Canada Lecture Series, UPEI, 23 October 2012.

253 Dorothy Eber, "Will Success Spoil Prince Edward Island?" *Maclean's*, 15 October 1966, 28 and 35–6.

254 The study was conducted by Traveldata Ltd, of Toronto, Montreal, Boston, and Cleveland "to determine the potential for development of Fall travel to the Maritime provinces." See W.E. Belliveau, Tandy Advertising, to Campbell, 25 February 1972, Campbell papers, 25.36, 1972, file 1090-2, PARO.

255 Robert Schurman, Minister of Environment and Tourism, to W.H. Wilkes, Chairman of the Board, Tandy Advertising Ltd, Toronto, 23 June 1972, Campbell papers, 25.36, 1972, file 1090-2, PARO. The implied connection between the decision and Tandy's pessimistic assessment is speculative. The motives were no doubt complicated. However, it probably did not help that Tandy also had aggressively lobbied for the province to restore its promotional budget, which had been slashed in half. See Tandy Advertising, "Prince Edward Island: Tourism," 11 February 1972, Campbell papers, 25.36, 1972, file 1090-2, PARO.

256 Summarized in Adler, "Tourism and Pastoral," 145–6.

257 Adler, "Tourism and Pastoral," 147.

258 From 583,016 in 1976, the estimated tourist numbers fluctuated up and down, bottoming out at 530,197 visitors in 1984. According to H. Spierenberg, *Historical Statistics of Prince Edward Island* (Charlottetown: Queen's Printer, 2007), which measures "tourist parties," the record tourism numbers of 1975 were not surpassed for twelve years.

259 Although no one remarked it at the time, this pattern of initial, rapid growth followed by relative stagnation is actually standard for most tourist destinations.

Chapter Five

1 "Heritage balloon illustrates height," *Evening Patriot*, 12 March 1981, 1.

2 The references and quotes in this passage come from Stevenson & Kellogg Ltd, "The Greater Charlottetown Urban Area Opportunities Study," 3 vols., prepared for DREE, Province of PEI, and City of Charlottetown, December 1973, vol. 2, 71–2 and 77, PEI Coll. The "rainy-day city" reference is in vol. 3, 71.

3 Spatial Planning Inc., "Preliminary Market Analysis, Hotel–Convention Centre, Charlottetown, Prince Edward Island," prepared for Dale Corporation, 7 July 1980, personal collection of Catherine Hennessey; and "Hotel–convention centre proposed for Charlottetown," *Guardian*, 5 July 1980, 2.

4 For details about the intended height of the building and the demonstration, see *Prince Edward Island Heritage Foundation Newsletter* 11, 1 (May 1981): 2; interview with Catherine Hennessey, Charlottetown,

21 October 2019; interview with John Rankin, Charlottetown, 21 October 2019; and "Heritage balloon illustrates height," *Evening Patriot*, 12 March 1981, 1.

5 Catherine Hennessey, the architect of the balloon stunt, recalls that a backroom meeting at city hall on the day of the protest endorsed the reduced height requirement. Interview with Hennessey, 21 October 2019. There was a public meeting on the project on 17 March, five days later, but public opinion was mixed, and the height issue was simply referred to planning board. See "City Council ponders complex height," *Evening Patriot*, 18 March 1981, 1. However, public concerns over scale was later cited as one reason for reducing the building's height, "Council approves hotel–convention complex," *Guardian*, 24 March 1981; and "Complex design changing," *Guardian*, 28 May 1981.

6 Stevenson & Kellogg, "Charlottetown Urban Area Opportunities Study," vol. 1, 81.

7 See "Group proposes $18 million Center for City," *Guardian*, 16 April 1980. Even before the project was approved, estimates had escalated to $26.5 million. "Hotel–convention centre proposed for Charlottetown," *Guardian*, 5 July 1980, 2; and "Officials await news on funding for project," *Guardian*, 18 December 1980.

8 Chris Wood and Barbara MacAndrew, "An island's season of discontent," *Maclean's*, 16 September 1985, 13–14, https://archive.macleans.ca/article/1985/9/16/an-islands-season-of-discontent#!&pid=12; *JLA*, 26 February 1985, 147–8; and Wayne Thibodeau, "Prince Edward changes hands," *Guardian*, 12 August 1999, A1. It opened as a Hilton, was bought by the province and operated independently, was acquired by Sheraton, then passed to Canadian Pacific, which would operate it for the next fourteen years, before transferring ownership to Delta.

9 "PEI business greats honored," Summerside *Journal-Pioneer*, 7 January 2004, 1. Two years earlier, Dale was honoured by the City of Charlottetown for his career as a developer.

10 Tourism Marketing Branch, Marketing Plan, 1979–80, Department of Tourism, Parks and Recreation, PEI Coll.

11 The same concerns about tourism trends and present capacity were echoed in Peat, Marwick & Partners, "Tourism study for PEI," Department of Development and Tourism, Parks and Conservation, Montreal, 1979, PEI Coll.

12 The numbers tabled in the marketing plan for combined air and auto travel totalled 584,331 visitors in 1975 and only 587,486 in 1978.

13 On tourism as an extractive industry, see Rothman, *Devil's Bargains*, 13.

14 See, for example, "Tourism comes of age," *APEC Newsletter* 22, 4 (May 1978).

15 Tom McMillan, "Report from Parliament: Special Tourism Issue," April 1985, PEI Coll. On the other hand, McMillan declared, "in Canada, as a whole, tourism is in deep trouble."

16 The figures are taken from the annual reports of government's tourism division. The numbers are converted into "tourist parties" in Spierenberg, *Historical Statistics of Prince Edward Island*, 99.

17 Bill MacDonald, "Santa Claus Drives a Winnebago: Myths of Prince Edward Island Tourism," *New Maritimes*, September 1983: 10–11. He identified three myths: chronic over-statements about actual tourist spending, an emphasis on the number of tourism-related jobs rather than their quality, and an exaggeration of the industry's actual benefits.

18 1988 Resident Tourism Attitude Study, 10 March 1988, report for Department of Tourism and Parks and DRIE, PEI Coll.

19 To cite just one influential example, consultant Alistair Morrison's 1980 assessment of tourism infrastructure argued that "too much emphasis has been placed in the past upon the question of tourism and conservation and not enough upon the planning and improvement of the industry for the benefit of all Islanders and visitors." See Alastair M. Morrison, "Tourism Plant Analysis Study," 2 vol. (Charlottetown: Department of Tourism, Industry and Energy, 1980).

20 This estimate is based on a cursory scan of the holdings in the PEI Collection, UPEI. The actual number is likely much higher.

21 Canada–PEI Cooperation Agreement on Tourism Development, 30 October 1991, Vertical File, PEI Coll.

22 The early 1970s Department of Environment and Tourism clung to its environmental connection as Tourism, Parks and Conservation (1975). After a Progressive Conservative interlude as Tourism, Industry and Energy, it reverted to Tourism and Parks in 1986, then Tourism, Parks, and Recreation

(1991). For most of the 1990s, it was Economic Development and Tourism, then, incongruously, Fisheries and Tourism (1998).

23 Again, more details can be found in the annual reports of the provincial government's tourism division. Tourism's total ordinary expenditures for 1979–80 came to $4 million. A decade later it was $8.1 million. It is more difficult to extract tourism spending from the annual departmental reports for the 1990s, but in 1998–99, with government's tourism activities largely concentrated in its Crown corporation, Tourism PEI, the ordinary operating budget came to $9.4 million.

24 For the hiring of a full-time general manager, see minister's message, ARDT, 1973. Also, interview with Jim Larkin, Charlottetown, 29 August 2019.

25 As noted in Smith Green & Associates, "Northumberland fixed crossing: potential impacts on PEI tourism," background document for Question J: Bridge concept assessment supplement, Public Works Canada, 1989, 6. The number of actual regional associations varied according to their health. ARDT, 1988, for example, references twelve associations.

26 ARDT, 1982.

27 In her introduction to the 1989 Tourism Media and Marketing Plan, provincial Minister Nancy Guptill bemoaned the loss of $1.2 million in annual federal funding when the latest ERDA subagreement covering tourism lapsed. It is hard to tell whether philosophy or funding issues persuaded the Department of Tourism to privatize its Convention Bureau in 1987. See ARDT, 1987, 9.

28 These figures are cited in Economic Development Strategy Background Papers, PEI, May 1994, PEI Coll.

29 See, for example, Smith Green & Associates, "Northumberland fixed crossing," 5–6.

30 "Partners in Marketing: 1988 Tourism Marketing and Media Plan and Three Year Marketing Strategy, 1988–90," esp. 6–7, PEI Coll.

31 ARDT, 1988.

32 This was predicated on a three per cent per annum increase in tourism visitation.

33 Tourism 2000: A Statement on Tourism Development, PEI Coll.

34 In his assessment of Tourism 2000, Larry Peach noted that of 1,600 tourism plans lodged with the World Tourism Association, only two-thirds had actually been carried out. See Peach, "Tourism Planning in Prince Edward Island: A Framework for Evaluation," unpublished MA thesis, Simon Fraser University, 1995, 10.

35 "Tourism … A Partnership for the Future," Report of the PEI Task Force on Tourism to the Cabinet Committee on Government Reform, January 1993, iii, PEI Coll.

36 Interview with Jim Larkin, Charlottetown, 29 August 2019. For a reference to one of the failed attempts, see "Looney tax angers tourism group," *Guardian*, 31 March 1990, 6.

37 See "Furious tourism association quits government committees," *Guardian*, 15 March 1990, 1; "Liberals under Fire for Room Tax," *Guardian*, 16 March 1990, 3; and "Guptill defends 'looney tax,'" *Guardian*, 28 March 1990, 3. The minister pledged to spend the resulting revenue on tourism marketing, but the act did not stipulate that.

38 "An Act to Repeal the Room Tax Bill," 1991, c. 37, s. 1, *JLA*, 107 and 142.

39 Wayne Thibodeau, "Room tax coming to aid tourism," *Guardian*, 1 December 2006, A1.

40 Interview with Jim Larkin, Charlottetown, 29 August 2019.

41 ARDT, 1987, 10.

42 Tourism Operators Survey, Department of Tourism and Parks and DRIE, 1989, PEI Coll.

43 The statistics are patched together from three sources: the ARDT, 1981; Five-Year Strategic Action Plan for P.E.I.'s Tourism Industry Technical Report, Randolph Group, December 1995, 2–14, PEI Coll; and Smith Green & Assoc., "Northumberland fixed crossing."

44 See Iris Phillips, "Grading system possible for tourism facilities," *Guardian*, 21 March 1986, 3; and interview with Jim Larkin, Charlottetown, 29 August 2019.

45 ARDT, 1994–95.

46 "Tourism Disaster," John Brewer to Editor, *Guardian*, 12 March 1992, 3.

47 This is the opinion of TIAPEI's general manager at the time; interview with Jim Larkin, Charlottetown, 29 August 2019.

48 Consider, for example, the dissection of target audiences in the media plan prepared for Enterprise PEI by Media Buying Services Ltd of Toronto, February 1995, PEI Coll.

49 Maritime Market Study prepared for Tourism Department of Prince Edward Island, Atlantic Trends Ltd, April 1986, PEI Coll.

50 To cite just one example, the durable auto corridors of the 1970s (Lady Slipper Drive, Blue Heron Drive, the King's Byway) were eclipsed in the mid-90s by six day-tour regions meant to extend visitors' stays even as they catered to the growing number of tourist sites across the province. These were North by Northwest (which became the more evocative "Sunsets and Seascapes"), Hills and Harbours, Bays and Dunes, Ship to Shore, Evangeline, and Charlotte's Shore.

51 For the record, these were the Beaches (that is, the stretch of shoreline that encompassed the National Park beaches at Stanhope, Brackley, and Dalvay), Cavendish, Charlottetown, Evangeline, Kensington, New London, South Shore, Summerside, West Prince, Southern Kings, and East Kings.

52 Such punning wordplay rippled through almost every promotion. The training program offered to hospitality sector employees turned a folksy exclamation into two defining descriptors: "Goodness. Gracious." Provincial parks were "Naturally Entertaining." TIAPEI's members were "the people vacations are made of." Scottish heritage buffs were encouraged to take "The Road to the Isle." For those of Irish descent, Prince Edward Island was "akin to Ireland."

53 ARDT, 1998–99.

54 Introduction to Highlights of the 1987 Marketing/ Media Plan and Three Year Marketing Strategy, Department of Tourism and Parks, 1987, PEI Coll.

55 Highlights of the 1992 Marketing and Media Plan, Department of Tourism, Parks, and Recreation, PEI Coll.

56 ARDT, 1994–95, 10.

57 The figure for 1993 was 20 per cent. See Randolph Group, "Five-Year Strategic Plan for PEI's Tourism Industry: Technical Report," December 1995, PEI Coll.

58 See Randolph Group, "Five-Year Strategic Plan." The most dramatic increase, 62 per cent, occurred between 1982 and 1988. See "Highlights of the 1989 Marketing Plan and Three Year Marketing Strategy, 1989–91, Department of Tourism, Parks, and Recreation, PEI Coll.

59 According to the Randolph Group's estimates, the Maritimes' share of pleasure visits declined from 52 per cent in 1990 to 33 per cent in 1994. Also, "Half of visitors to Province come from Maritimes: study," *Guardian*, 12 April 1986, 3.

60 The harder it was to get to the province in terms of distance or ease of travel, the longer visitors tended to stay and the more they spent. Ontarians spent more than Nova Scotians. New Englanders spent more than Ontarians. Japanese spent more than either. See, for example, Randolph Group, "Five-Year Strategic Plan," 2–8.

61 Calvin Trillin, "'Anne of Red Hair': What Do the Japanese See in *Anne of Green Gables*?" in Gammel and Epperly, eds., *L.M. Montgomery and Canadian Culture*, 216.

62 For just one among many consultants' reports that flagged the emerging DINK demographic of aging baby boomers, see Randolph Group, "Five-Year Strategic Plan," 3.

63 Randolph Group, "Five-Year Strategic Plan," 2–24.

64 The subsidized extension of the Confederation Centre's Summer Festival run is referenced in consecutive annual reports of the department of tourism in the late 1980s.

65 ARDT, 1998–99, 18. In the early '70s, camping had been the most popular accommodation choice. See Stevenson & Kellogg, "Charlottetown Urban Area Opportunities Study," vol. 3.

66 Statistics tabled for 1993 to 1997 in Tourism PEI's 1998 marketing plan suggested that between 80 and 90 per cent of visitors spent time sightseeing. Between 40 and 60 per cent visited friends and relatives, even if that was not the chief motivation for travel.

67 Accommodations, restaurant meals, and retail shopping regularly accounted for about 85 per cent of pleasure tourist expenditure in the 1990s. Spending on attractions averaged 8–12 per cent.

68 Alastair M. Morrison, "Tourism Plant Analysis Study," 2 vol. (Charlottetown: Department of Tourism, Industry and Energy, 1980), vii.

69 Richard Judd, *Second Nature: An Environmental History of New England* (Amherst: University of Massachusetts Press, 2014).

70 In fact, it was possible to be both a conservationist and a preservationist, and rather than a binary, the natural history advocates represented a broad continuum of values. For more on the evolution of a natural history sensibility during this period, see Rosemary Curley, "Wildlife Matters: A Historical

Overview of Public Consciousness of Habitat and Wildlife Loss on Prince Edward Island," in MacDonald, MacFadyen, and Novaczek, *Time and a Place*, esp.128–39.

71 See Smith Green & Assoc., "Green tourism opportunities study," PEI Department of Tourism and Parks, Charlottetown, 1993, PEI Coll., 1; and Highlights of the 1989 Marketing Plan and Three Year Marketing Strategy, 1989–91, PEI Coll.

72 Smith Green & Assoc., "Green tourism opportunities study," 1.

73 Smith Green & Assoc., "Green tourism opportunities study," 56–7.

74 Smith Green & Assoc., "Green tourism opportunities study," 7.

75 Curley, "Wildlife Matters," 136.

76 Parts of the account rely on MacDonald, *If You're Stronghearted*, 369; and also draw on Curley, "Wildlife Matters," 135–6.

77 These details are drawn from the original plan, tabled in 1981 and summarized in M.D. Simmons, "Environmental impact assessment proposed Greenwich development, St Peter's Bay" (Halifax: Maritime Resource Management Service, 1981), PEI Coll. The original developers were from British Columbia, but both the principals and the exact details of the resort development changed over time. For example, the original vision of a 200-room hotel and 400 "residential units" morphed into a plan for largely condos.

78 The parabolic sand dunes, with their associated counter ridges, called *Gegenwälle*, are considered very rare in North America. As they slowly migrate eastward along the peninsula, they have gradually swallowed up the adjacent countryside. See "Greenwich," Prince Edward Island National Park, https://www.pc.gc.ca/en/pn-np/pe/pei-ipe/visit/greenwich.

79 Simmons, "Environmental impact assessment," 38–40.

80 "Anderson Backs Greenwich Project," *Guardian*, 19 March 1981, 1. The speaker, Don Anderson, was not only a local resident but closely tied to agriculture as general manager of the PEI Potato Marketing Board. Although his comment was made in 1981, it is representative of local views over the long course of the controversy.

81 For useful summaries of the issue's tortuous windings, see Susan Hornby, "Fragile dunes at center of development controversy," *Guardian*, 17 March 1981, 3; and Nancy Willis, "Greenwich Dunes system now part of National Park," *Guardian*, 9 February 1998, A2.

82 Willis, "Greenwich Dunes system." Cardigan MP Lawrence MacAulay, minister of labour, was instrumental in brokering a deal to resolve the issue while salvaging some prospect of development in his home community of St Peters. Nancy Willis, "In safe hands: Parks Canada begins developing Greenwich," *Guardian*, 21 November 1998, A1.

83 Mike Gauthier, "Greenwich ecolodge scrapped," *Guardian*, 21 December 1999, A1. For discussion of, and reaction to, plans for development within and on the fringes of the Greenwich annex, see Wayne Thibodeau, "Greenwich project said scaled back: Document outlined plans for dozens of new businesses including health spa, convenience store and art gallery, says Sharon Labchuk," *Guardian*, 27 October 1999, A3; and Nancy Willis, "Hotel threat to new National Park, say environmentalists," *Guardian*, 19 October 1999, A3.

84 Jacques Whitford Environment Ltd and Smith Green & Assoc., and Ecologistics Ltd, "Rail lands development study, Prince Edward Island" report prepared for Department of Tourism, Parks and Recreation, June 1993, 10, PEI Coll.

85 ARDT, 1991–92.

86 Progress on the rail conversion was regularly reported in the annual reports of the Department of Tourism and Parks. Funding came from ERDA agreements but also 50:50 cost-shared programs partnering the provincial government and Human Resource Development Canada.

87 Most famously articulated in MacCannell, *Tourist*. For a contemporary take on the meaning of, and search for, authenticity, see Ilinka Terziyska, "Interpretations of Authenticity in Tourism," *Science & Research*, 4 (2012), https://www.researchgate.net/publication/280304792_INTERPRETATIONS_OF_AUTHENTICITY_IN_TOURISM; and "Why tourists thirst for authenticity – and how they find it," *The Conversation*, 25 November 2016, http://theconversation.com/why-tourists-thirst-for-authenticity-and-how-they-can-find-it-68108.

88 See John Eldon Green, *A Mind of One's Own* (Charlottetown: Tangle Lane Press), 254–5. Green would soon be the principal in Smith Green &

Associates, which produced some of the most influential reports on tourist-related issues such as the expected impact of construction of a fixed link and the proposal to create what became the Confederation Trail.

89 DPA Group Inc. "Report on the Economic Impacts and Opportunities, the Cultural Industries in Prince Edward Island," 3 vol., Charlottetown, 1988.

90 There was little intention of drawing tourists from Ireland itself, although reacquainting Islanders with their Irish heritage did lead to an enduring connection with the tourism board in County Monaghan, the greatest single source of Irish emigration to PEI in the nineteenth century.

91 For a brief backstory on the founding of the College of Piping, see "How the College of Piping Began," College of Piping and Celtic Performing Arts of Canada, https://collegeofpiping.com/about-us/history/.

92 A comparable process is described for nineteenth-century Ireland in Susan Kroeg, "Cockney Tourists, Irish Guides, and the Invention of the Emerald Isle, *Eire-Ireland* 44, 3/4 (Fall/Winter 2009): 200–28.

93 "Today in History," Summerside *Journal-Pioneer*, 27 June 2001, 2.

94 Darlene Shea, "Remembering the dinner theatre 'La Cuisine à Mémé' at Tuesday Talk in Miscouche," Summerside *Journal-Pioneer*, 13 August 2018. For more about Barachois and its impact, see Megan Forsyth, "From Kitchen Party to the Stage: The Legacy of Barachois," *The Island Magazine*, 87 (Spring/Summer 2020): 4–12.

95 "Today in History," Summerside *Journal-Pioneer*, 12 July 2005, 4.

96 ARDT, 1987–8, 10. The job was cost-shared on a 50:50 basis with the secretary of state and was part of an ongoing strategy to grow tourism in the largely Acadian region.

97 For example, in 1997 Frank Turgeon's play *Gabriel and Evangeline, the Musical* began a successful run at the Carrefour Theatre in Charlottetown. See "Lovers' Tale Hits the Stage," *Guardian*, 26 June 1997, B6.

98 See "Competition unfair for Island Indian crafts," *Guardian*, 16 May 1984; "Natives Maintain Tradition of Basket Weaving," *Evening Patriot*, 22 March 1986, 3.

99 For an account of the enterprise's early growth, see "Minegoo basket production centre marks third anniversary this month," *Guardian*, 16 February 1988,

5. For the centre's closure, see Barbara Jadis-Bruised Head, *Frank Jadis: A Mi'kmaq from the John Jadis Clan* (Scotchfort: [the author], 2017), 70–1.

100 Mike Nesbitt, "Lennox Island gets boost with Ecotourism Complex," *Guardian*, 26 July 2004, A1.

101 For example, Rothman, *Devil's Bargains*, 11–12. McKay, *Quest of the Folk* makes much the same argument in its treatment of cultural selection.

102 This paragraph is adapted from MacDonald, *If You're Stronghearted*, 368.

103 Quoted from Ghiz's public speech in *Powerful Dreams, Powerful Memories: Final Report of the Confederation Birthplace Commission*, October 1991 (Charlottetown: Queen's Printer, 1991), 4. The commission chair was a returned expat and policy advisor, Wendy MacDonald.

104 Ghiz, *Powerful Dreams, Powerful Memories*, 5–6.

105 "Confederation Landing Park and Peakes Parking Lot," CADC, http://cadcpei.com/projects/confederation-landing-park-peakes-parking-lot/.

106 "CN Car Shop / Founders Hall," Projects, CADC, http://cadcpei.com/projects/cn-car-shop-founders-hall/.

107 Doug Gallant, "Tourism Agencies merge to market Charlottetown," *Guardian*, 1 April 2006, B8.

108 Doug Gallant, "Festival of the Fathers finished," *Guardian*, 4 August 2006, A5.

109 For more on Founders' Hall, see Edward MacDonald and Sasha Mullally, "On National Heritage, Grand Narratives, and 'Making History Fun': Founders' Hall, Prince Edward Island and the Story of Canada." *International Journal of Heritage Studies* 13, 3 (2007): 288–94.

110 MacCannell posits five stages in site sacralization: naming, framing and elevating, enshrinement, mechanical reproduction, and social reproduction. MacCannell, *Tourist*, 43–5.

111 See Elizabeth Waterston, "Lucy Maud Montgomery," in *The Clear Spirit: Twenty Canadian Women and Their Times*, ed. Mary Quayle Innis (Toronto: University of Toronto Press, 1966), 219. There is a considerable literature on how Montgomery's fiction markets the Island landscape. See, for example, Janice Fiamengo, "Towards a Theory of the Popular Landscape in *Anne of Green Gables*," in *Making Avonlea: L.M. Montgomery and Popular Culture*, ed. Irene Gammel (Toronto: University of Toronto Press, 2002).

311

Notes to pages 226–33

112 There were Hollywood film adaptations of Montgomery's Anne novels in 1919, 1934, and 1940, along with animated or made-for-television series dating from 1952, 1956, 1958, 1972, 1975, and 1979 on British, American, Canadian, and Japanese broadcasting systems. None of them filmed on Prince Edward Island. See Anne of Green Gables adaptations, Internet Movie Database, https://www.imdb.com/list/ls063123798/; and *The Canadian Encyclopedia*, https://www.thecanadianencyclopedia.ca/en/article/anne-of-green-gables.

113 The Provincial Parks system also supported filming. See ARDT, 1996–97, 17.

114 See "Emily of New Moon shoots second season," *Guardian*, 29 May 1997, C3; ARDT, 1996–97, 23.

115 Sally Cole, "A Musical Is Born," *Guardian*, 18 June 1999, C1; Doug Gallant, "Emily proves she has what it takes," *Guardian*, 2 September 1999, A3; "Confederation Centre getting ready for new theatrical season," Summerside *Journal-Pioneer*, 25 May 2000. The decade was sprinkled, too, with smaller productions, such as *The Strike at Putney Church,* that played off lesser-known Montgomery works; the Confederation Centre hosted a production of this play. One of its troupe, Hank Stinson, adapted no fewer than three musicals from Montgomery novels, *The Blue Castle, Rainbow Valley*, and *Emily of New Moon.* See "Montgomery's Writings Still Inspirational," *Guardian*, special insert, 10 June 2002.

116 As the 1992 Marketing and Media Plan argued, Anne of Green Gables was "an international icon."

117 Inbound First-Time Visitors Survey, Auto-Recreation Vehicle Only, Department of Tourism and Parks and Department of Regional Economic Expansion, May 1986, PEI Coll.

118 Journalist Calvin Trillin describes them as "Young Office Ladies," that is, "women in their late teens and twenties who are doing office work for a few years before they marry and begin a family." See Trillin, "'Anne of Red Hair,'" 216.

119 Kate Taylor, "Anne of Hokkaido," *Globe and Mail*, 6 July 1991, Section C-1, XZ1 MS A098063, File 2, L.M. Montgomery Collection, Guelph McLaughlin Archives, University of Guelph [henceforth, LMM Coll.]. In all, the ten Anne titles had sold 13 million copies by 1991.

120 Both Taylor, "Anne of Hokkaido," and Trillin, "'Anne of Red Hair,'" make this point. See also Douglas

Baldwin, "L.M. Montgomery's Anne of Green Gables: The Japanese Connection," *Journal of Canadian Studies/Revue d'Etudes Canadiennes* 28, 3 (1993): 123–33.

121 In seconding this assessment, Trillin references anthropologist Claire Fawcett, herself a Montgomery scholar, who favours the triumph of family loyalty over Anne's individuality in explaining the character's appeal. Trillin, "'Anne of Red Hair.'"

122 Micki Moore, "CanLit's Keeper," *Sunday Sun*, 4 September 1994, 52, XZ1 MS A098063, file 3, LMM Coll.

123 See Roger March, "How Japan Solicited the West: The First Hundred Years of Modern Japanese Tourism," 7–8, www.inboundtourism.com.au › western-travel-in-japan-1868-1964. The motive was in part to ease Japan's burgeoning balance of trade surplus.

124 See Highlights of the 1987 Marketing/Media Plan and Three Year Marketing Strategy, 1987–89; and ARDT, 1986–87.

125 The figure is cited in Hugh A. Mulligan, "Anne of Green Gables Finds Countless Kindred Spirits in Japan," *Los Angeles Times*, 21 December 1997.

126 "Scholars, Fans Flock to Author L.M. Montgomery's Home This Summer," Guelph *Mercury*, 22 July 2000, box 005D, XZ1MSA09035, LMM Coll.

127 See, for example, Randolph Group, "Five-Year Strategic Plan," 2–7.

128 *Green Gables Area Plan Concept* (Environment Canada), XZ1 MS A098120, LMM Coll.; and Peach, "Tourism Planning," 150. The average daily visitation in the mid-1980s was 2,600 people and the average length of stay 2.5 hours.

129 "Scholars, Fans Flock," Guelph *Mercury*, 22 July 2000, box 005D, XZ1MSA09035, LMM Coll.

130 "Economic Impact Tourism 1996," Research Division, Enterprise PEI, [n.d.], PEI Coll.

131 See Horne, "Human History," 129–35, 142–3; and Fred Horne, "PEI National Park Gulf Shore Parkway Realignment Environmental Impact Study: Cultural-Historical Concerns," August 1986, 10–17, PEI Coll.

132 Nancy Rootland, *Anne's World, Maud's World: The Sacred Sites of L.M. Montgomery* (Halifax: Nimbus Press, 1996).

133 This list is culled from successive issues of the annual *Visitors Guide*. For another example of ubiquity, see *Prince Edward Island Handbook* (Charlottetown:

Imageworks PEI, 1998), which contains more than thirty Montgomery-based ads or references in a little more than one hundred pages.

134 The account given here is based on the following sources: Throwback Thursday, *Island Morning*, CBC Radio, 9 July 2020 (story originally aired July 1995); interview with Anne Putnam by Mitch Cormier, *Island Morning*, CBC Radio, 27 August 2020; interview with Anne Putnam by Edward MacDonald, Charlottetown, 23 August 2020. Putnam and McNevin brought the T-shirt back into production in August 2020, advertising through Facebook.

135 Although the heirs considered that they had inherited copyright upon Montgomery's death in 1942, in fact, the author had sold her rights to her publisher, L.C. Page, in 1920 to settle a bitter legal dispute.

136 "Anne's Road to Avonlea Could Lead to Courtroom," *Toronto Star*, 6 March 1994, A16, XZ1 MS A098063, file 3, LMM Coll.

137 Deborah Jones, "Trouble in Anne Country," *Globe and Mail*, 13 March 1993.

138 "Authority to Control Anne of Green Gables," *Globe and Mail*, 19 May 1994, C1.

139 Trademark Licensing, Government of PEI, https://www.princeedwardisland.ca/en/information/innovation-pei/trademark-licensing.

140 "Authority to Control Anne of Green Gables," *Globe and Mail*, 19 May 1994, C1. According to the Anne Authority's current website, royalties are payable at the discretion of the Authority.

141 For the number of licensed products, see The Anne of Green Gables Licensing Authority, Government of PEI, http://www.gov.pe.ca/anne/list.php3. For the legal questions surrounding the Anne Authority's dual protection/profit mandate, see Andrea Slane, "Guarding a Cultural Icon: Concurrent Intellectual Property Regimes and the Perpetual Protection of Anne of Green Gables in Canada," *McGill Law Journal* 56, 4 (June 2011): 1011–55, https://www.erudit.org/en/journals/mlj/2011-v56-n4-mlj1817631/1005851ar/.

142 "Anne's Road to Avonlea Could Lead to Courtroom," *Toronto Star*, 6 March 1994, A16.

143 The quote comes from a 1992 brochure promoting the Off Stage Theatre Company. Courtesy of Donald Moses. The review ran from 1991 to 1997.

144 See Randy MacDonald, "Review of *Annekenstein*," *A Bit More Detail* blog, 27 June 2016, https://abitmoredetail.wordpress.com/2016/07/27/review-annekenstein/; and "Return of 'Annekenstein,'" *Guardian*, 24 June 2016.

145 Rob MacDonald, quoted in an email communication from Cameron MacDonald, 26 August 2019.

146 Ramsay provided the story of the plate's creation to blogger Peter Rukavina. See "The Truth About the Anne License Plate," 13 August 2007, *Ruk* blog, https://ruk.ca/content/truth-about-anne-license-plate. See "Province Scraps Anne of Green Gables, Confederation Bridge License Plates," *Guardian*, 15 July 2013.

147 Quoted in "Car-Plate Debate Stirs Foes of 'Anne of Green Gables,'" *Ottawa Sun*, reprinted in *Buffalo News*, 20 September 1992, https://buffalonews.com/1992/09/20/car-plate-debate-stirs-foes-of-anne-of-green-gables/.

148 Tom Killorn, "Extend PEI's tourism season, put more tourists in rural areas," *Guardian*, 6 April 2000, A3. The report was prepared by the Randolph Group and Enterprise Management Consultants for the TIAPEI and ACOA.

149 For the environmental history of Canadian golf courses, see Jewett, "Behind the Greens."

150 ARDT, 1988–89, 10; as well as the annual report for 1992–93, which is quite explicit about the intention.

151 In 1998, *Golf Digest* magazine gave Crowbush a prestigious five-star rating. See Dave Stewart, "The Links Awarded Five-Star Rating," *Guardian*, 28 July 1998, A3.

152 See ARDT, 1991–92, 18; and ARDT, 1993–94, 22.

153 The 1994 golf strategy cited two earlier studies commissioned by Golf PEI. The first, in 1991, laid out a marketing strategy and development opportunities. The second, by the PEI Marketing Agency, assessed the experience of adults golfing while on vacation. Those studies discovered that the base of local members as well as the number of rounds played was declining on Prince Edward Island.

154 The statistics cited here, as well as the recommendations, are culled from KPMG Management Consulting et al., "A Golf Strategy for Prince Edward Island, Canada," 1994, PEI Coll.

155 KPMG et al., "Golf Strategy." The main recommendations can be found on 34–8.

156 ARDT, 1997–98, 17; Tourism PEI Act, Bill No. 56, 48 Eliz. II, 1999.

157 ARDT, 1998, 21.

158 For a list of courses, see *Guardian*, 23 April 2003, special section, 9.

159 KPMG et al., "Golf Strategy," 1.

160 "World-class hotel in works near Crowbush golf course," *Guardian*, 9 July 1998, A1; and Danielle Gauthier, "Government 'Secrecy' About Proposed Resort Bothering Liberals," *Guardian*, 10 July 1998, A3.

161 In a case of historical synchronicity, the Rodd family had opened the first motel in the province in the 1950s and had been early leaders in the PEI Innkeepers Association.

162 The tortuous path from first announcement to completion can be traced through the Island press. See, in particular, Tyler Waugh, "Plans finalized for first-class Crowbush Resort," Summerside *Journal-Pioneer*, 30 November 1999, A1; Andy Walker, "Strait Crossing dropped from Crowbush development," Summerside *Journal-Pioneer*, 26 May 2000, A1; Steve Sharratt, "Crowbush tees off with five-star hotel," *Guardian*, 30 December 2000, A3; and "Crowbush Resort Opens," *Guardian*, 29 June 2002, B8.

163 For the expansion to the resort in anticipation of increased visitation, see "Province proposes Brudenell hotel," *Guardian*, 19 March 1998, A1; and Danielle Gauthier, "Rodd chosen to expand Brudenell," *Guardian*, 13 August 1998, A1.

164 Criticism came from the opposition Liberals, of course, but soon from the media and, eventually, the province's auditor general. See Ron Ryder, "Milligan slams golf deal: Liberal says Tories pay Brudenell upkeep," *Guardian*, 3 December 1998, A1; and Wayne Thibodeau, "PEI auditor general criticizes sloppy bookkeeping, bad loans," *Guardian*, 28 March 2002, A1.

165 The government also paid nearly $500,000 for used equipment that, the auditor general noted, it might have bought new for only a few thousand dollars more. See Andy Walker, "Golf equipment no deal: auditor," Summerside *Journal-Pioneer*, 14 April 2001, 3.

166 Wayne Thibodeau, "College to pick up golf facility: Holland College to announce it has bought Brudenell Golf Academy from businessmen," 9 December 2000, A1. In its first two years of operation, it had already rung up $775,000 in deficits.

167 Ron Ryder, "Golf Digest rates Dundarave among country's top courses," *Guardian*, 17 April 2002, A3; and Jim Day, "Golfers not flocking to Dundarave golf course," *Guardian*, 24 July 2003, A1.

168 "Investment in golf looks like a winner," editorial, *Guardian*, 26 July 2003, A6.

169 Ryder, "Golf Digest rates Dundarave."

170 Day, "Golfers not flocking."

171 Jim Day, "PEI Golf Missing the Cut," *Guardian*, online edition, 10 February 2015 (updated 30 September 2017).

172 "Growth in tourism, golf, not in sync – report," *Guardian*, 21 May 1999, B1.

173 Highlights of the 2000 Tourism Marketing Plan, Department of Economic Development and Tourism, 1999, PEI Coll.

174 Cited in Ian Munro, op ed, "Provincially Owned Golf Courses Continue to Bleed Red Ink on PEI," *Guardian*, 17 February 2015. See also "PEI Named Undiscovered Golf Destination of the Year," Summerside *Journal-Pioneer*, 20 November 2010, A3. In commenting, a local golf spokesperson preferred to think "Canada's No. 1 Golf Destination" was just undiscovered at an *international* level.

175 Day, "PEI Golf Missing the Cut."

176 The following relies on MacDonald, *If You're Stronghearted*, 376–81; Edward MacDonald, "Bridge Over Troubled Waters: The Fixed Link Debate on Prince Edward Island, 1885–1997," in *Bridging Islands: The Impact of Fixed Links*, eds. Godfrey Baldacchino and Annie Spears (Charlottetown: Acorn Press, 2007), 29–46; and MacDonald and MacEachern, "Rites of Passage," 305–6.

177 David Hinks, "Prince Edward Island Transportation Systems," Canadian Transportation Commission Research Branch, Directorate of Transport Industries Analysis, Report no. 20-77-7, July 1977, PEI Coll.; and MacDonald, *If You're Stronghearted*, 304.

178 These were Omni Systems, proposing a rail tunnel; Northumberland Bridge Builders; and Nova Construction (later, Abegweit Crossing), which began with a hybrid bridge/causeway/tunnel concept but later advocated a bridge.

179 David Milne, "Prince Edward Island," in *Canadian Annual Review*, 1986, 317.

180 For the formation of Friends of the Island, see "Friends Seek More Information on Fixed Link," *Guardian*, 28 November 1987. The best summary

314

Notes to pages 240–5

of the Friends' position is found in its submission to the *Environmental Assessment Panel Reviewing the Northumberland Strait Project: Compilation of Submissions*, vol. 3 (Charlottetown: Queen's Printer, 1990), PEI Coll.

181 Ian G. Johnston, "The Politics of the Link: An Examination of the Fixed Connection in Prince Edward Island," unpublished MA thesis, St Mary's University, Halifax, 1995, 115–6.

182 See, for example, Martin Dorrell, "The Media and the Fixed Link," in *Crossing that Bridge: A Critical Look at the PEI Fixed* Link, ed. Lorraine Begley (Charlottetown: Ragweed Press, 1993), 136–45.

183 The group was probably referencing Smith Green & Assoc., "Northumberland fixed crossing," 12. Smith Green found that many Nova Scotians had a negative attitude towards an Island vacation because of expected ferry lineups, and he noted that ease of access had been listed in a 1982 exit survey as the third most important factor in deciding on a vacation destination.

184 "Fixed Link Main Concern for TIAPEI," *Guardian*, 4 March 1987.

185 Dorrell, "Media and the Fixed Link," 136.

186 Smith Green & Assoc., "Northumberland Fixed Crossing," 14, cited the figure as 71 per cent.

187 "Marine Atlantic Brief," *Environmental Assessment Panel*, vol. 2.

188 See "The PEI–NB Fixed Link: Will It Ever Become a Reality?" Summerside *Journal-Pioneer*, 17 November 1987.

189 Smith Green & Assoc., "Northumberland Fixed Crossing," 14.

190 Kevin Walker, "Islanders 'Need' More Information on Fixed Crossing, *Guardian*, 10 December 1987.

191 Begley, *Crossing that Bridge*, 114–21.

192 For example, "Time for a Causeway?" *Evening Patriot*, 3 April 1985, 4.

193 "Resident Tourism Survey," Department of Tourism and Parks and DRIE, March 1989, PEI Coll. The provincial government also commissioned a study more focused on the potential impact of the Fixed Link.

194 John Crossley, "Prince Edward Island," *Canadian Annual Review*, 1990, 209.

195 The panel had interpreted its "environmental" mandate quite broadly. To deal with the most substantive of its reservations, that a bridge would impede the flow of ice through the strait, causing

a whole raft of problems, Public Works convened a special "ice panel," which decided that a bridge would pose no appreciable risk.

196 Details about the cost and construction of the bridge are based on Macdonald, *Bridging the Strait*.

197 The announced cost for the completed structure was $840 million. According to provincial estimates, 70 per cent of that total had been spent on PEI. The figures are quoted in the 1998 edition of the *Prince Edward Island Annual Statistical Review*.

198 Most preconstruction models had projected an increase of 125,000 to 145,000 visitors per year if the link was built. See Five-Year Strategic Action Plan for PEI's Tourism Industry Technical Report, Randolph Group, December 1995, PEI Coll. For the recorded increases, see ARDT, 1998–99, 17; and ARDT, 1999–2000, Appendix G: Tourism Economic Impact 2000. The 1996 figure had been 788,300 visitors. For the 2004 declension, see Doug Gallant, "Dark Days for Tourism on Island," *Guardian*, 27 November 2004, A1.

199 Cited in Institute of Island Studies, "A Place to Stay?" 33.

200 See *Prince Edward Island Annual Statistical Review*, 1998. Nova Scotia and New Brunswick, which usually supplied about a quarter of the pleasure travel to Prince Edward Island, showed the biggest jump, going from 22 per cent in 1996 to 30 per cent in 1997. The proportion of tourists from Ontario also rose steeply, from 18 per cent to 24 per cent. Curiously, the percentage of American tourists fell back to 23 per cent of the total in 1997 from 29 per cent in 1996. In 1998, it fell again, to 18 per cent.

201 David Weale, Charlottetown, interviewed by Edward MacDonald, 14 March 1999. Weale had been the most visible opponent of the fixed link, even running against arch-advocate Tom McMillan in the 1988 federal election.

Epilogue

1 This section is adapted from MacEachern, "The Landscapes of Tourism," 259–60.

2 David Wallace-Wells, *The Uninhabitable Earth: Life After Warming* (New York: Tim Duggan Books, 2019), 61.

3 Although disputed claims that tourism had surpassed agriculture in value were made in the wake

315

Notes to pages 246-55

of the 2002 tourism season – just before a major tourism downturn. See Jim Day, "Tourism Leaps Past Agriculture as PEI's Top Money-Maker," *Guardian*, 30 November 2002, A3.

4   To cite just two examples, see "Cavendish faces bleak summer, traffic in Resort Municipality down dramatically," *Guardian*, 11 July 2003, A5; and "String of record tourism years on P.E.I. comes to an end: Island still exceeds one million overnight stays for second straight year," CBC News, 31 January 2019, https://www.cbc.ca/news/canada/prince-edward-island/pei-tourism-numbers-1.5000539.

5   Interview with Cheryl Paynter, CEO Tourism PEI, and Chris Jones, Department of Tourism and Culture, 5 June 2017.

6   Interview with Paynter and Jones, 5 June 2017.

7   In 2016, for example, the province's annual statistical review put total farm receipts at $483.5 million, while tourism revenues were guesstimated at $430 million, including both resident and nonresident tourists.

8   Interview with Paynter and Jones, 5 June 2017.

9   See, for example, "Whetting Appetites," *Guardian*, 28 November 2015, A3.

10 As late as 1953's promotional film *Abegweit*, for example, visitors were being told they could get "home-baked bread, cream, butter, and fresh eggs from the nearby farm."

11 *St. Ann's Parish History, Hope River, PEI* (1993), 29–30.

12 For the "Canada's Food Island" initiative, see, for example, "A Food Island," *Guardian*, 16 March 2015, A3. For the "Culinary Masters," see ARDT, 1988–89. In 1997, the Culinary Institute expanded into new quarters in the former PEI School of Nursing. See Nigel Armstrong, "Newest school worth noise of construction," *Guardian*, 14 October 1997, A5. The Culinary Institute in turn could trace its origins to a committee formed in the late 1970s. See "A good idea produces success," Lloyd C. McKenna to editor, *Guardian*, 6 February 1998, A7. For the deficiencies of Island restaurant cuisine, see Robert Brennan, "Delivering on a Promise: We sell ourselves as 'One of the World's Great Islands,' but are we?" *IslandSide* 3, 6 (July/August 1991): 18–25.

13 For background about Smith, see "Michael Smith (chef)," *Wikipedia*, https://en.wikipedia.org/wiki/Michael_Smith_(chef); "Island television production company a partner in new Chef at Large series," *Guardian*, 12 January 2002, C3; "The Inn Chef,"

Wikipedia, https://en.wikipedia.org/wiki/The_Inn_Chef; "Island inn featured on cooking show: The Inn Chef with Michael Smith at the Inn at Bay Fortune begins today on Life Network," *Guardian*, 22 September 1998, C1; Heather Clarke, "Chef Michael Smith and wife, Chastity, revolutionize dining on PEI," Halifax *Chronicle-Herald*, 19 September 2019, https://www.thechronicleherald.ca/more/robert-simmonds/chef-michael-smith-and-wife-chastity-revolutionize-dining-on-pei-242641/.

14 Wayne Thibodeau, "Dogs mush through slush," *Guardian*, 2 March 1998, A1. The race was cancelled four times in its first nine years, and lack of snow was a constant worry. See, for example, "Sled dog races canceled," *Guardian*, 26 February 1999, A3. The event ran yearly from 1991 until 2005, with no race in 2004. See "No sled dog races at Mill River this year," Summerside *Journal-Pioneer*, 20 January 2006, 2.

15 The inaugural festival, deemed a great success, was nevertheless christened with the headline "Weather ravages Jack Frost festival, but volunteers work tirelessly to save it," *Guardian*, 12 February 2005, A3.

16 Katherine Hunt, "Family, friends and fiddles," Summerside *Journal-Pioneer*, 18 July 2018, A4.

17 "Funding hits sour note," op ed, Summerside *Journal-Pioneer*, 6 June 2009, A4. The other $900,000 came through a federal–provincial infrastructure program.

18 "Awaiting the Results of Regis and Kelly," editorial, *Guardian*, 17 July 2010, A14; "Economic impact of Regis, Kelly in millions," *Guardian*, 11 November 2010, A5.

19 "1894 Excursion from New York and Boston was the real beginning of Charlottetown as a cruise ship port of call," *Sailstrait*, https://sailstrait.wordpress.com/2021/05/05/1894-excursion-from-new-york-and-boston-was-the-real-beginning-of-charlottetown-as-a-cruise-ship-port-of-call/. The *Orinoco* returned the next summer, but the experiment ended there. See also, "First Cruise Ship Visited More Than A Century Ago," *Sailstrait*, https://sailstrait.wordpress.com/2017/09/18/first-cruise-ship-visited-more-than-a-century-ago/. ARDT, 1969, 10.

20 ARDT, 1981; Capital Commission of PEI, "Cruise Ship Tourism Impact Study," Tourism PEI, 1996, PEI Coll.

21 "Cruise Ship Impact Study," 14.

22 ARDT, 2017–18, 12.

23 "Cruise Schedule," Port of Charlottetown, http://portcharlottetown.com/cruise/cruise-schedule/.

The total included 144,645 potential passengers. By way of comparison, overall tourism numbers for 2019 were 1.58 million visitors.

24 Observed by one of the authors from the balcony of their apartment in downtown Charlottetown.

25 Wayne Thibodeau, "Nudist resort under attack," *Guardian*, 22 July 2003, A1. For weeks afterwards, local newspapers were well populated with op eds, letters to the editor, additional reporting, and questionable puns about the resort.

26 "PEI nudist resort given permission to add campground," *Guardian*, 15 December 2004, A5.

27 Thibodeau, "Nudist Resort Under Attack."

28 K. to editor, "Clifton and Tourists," *Guardian*, 8 June 1938, 4.

29 John R. Gillis, "Muddying the Waters of Environmental History: Islands as Ecotones," in *Time and a Place*, 19–35.

30 Quoted in MacKinnon, *Between Two Cultures*, 177.

31 Quoted by Campbell's speech writer Andrew Wells (who may well have written the words he was citing) to William Reed, Maine, 12 November 1973, A.B. Campbell Papers, PARO RG 25.36, Box 5, file 1124A. This paragraph and the next adapt text from MacDonald, *If You're Stronghearted*, 350–1.

32 See ARDT, 1973–74, 26.

33 According to the figures for 1972–76, of 1,070 petitions, 911, 85 per cent, were approved. Cited in Esther Kienholz, *The Land-Use Impacts of Recent Legislation in P.E.I.: An Analysis of the Land Development Corporation and Non-Resident Ownership*, Land Use in Canada Series, No. 18 (Ottawa: Environment Canada, 1980). Despite the high rate of approvals, Kienholz felt that the legislation was achieving its ends.

34 Cited in Isabelle Gallant, "The Disappearing Landscape," *Guardian*, 19 July 2008, A2. See also PEI Lands Protection Act, Legislative Counsel Office, https://www.princeedwardisland.ca › sites › default › files › legislation.

35 Gallant, "Disappearing Landscape."

36 *Prince Edward Island 41st Annual Statistical Review, 2014*, 71, http://www.gov.pe.ca/photos/original/2014statsreview.pdf; and *Prince Edward Island 45th Annual Statistical Review, 2018*, 75, https://www.princeedwardisland.ca/en/publication/annual-statistical-review.

37 A point made in Eric Kipping, "We're losing access to our shore," op ed, *Guardian*, 28 July 2008, A7.

38 "Traveller," *Examiner*, March 1902, cited in "Tourist Section," *Guardian-Patriot* Centennial Souvenir Edition 1873–1973.

39 We are grateful to Josh MacFadyen for sharing this data from his work-in-progress "Time Flies: Landscapes and Change on Prince Edward Island, 1935–2020."

40 Gallant, "Disappearing Landscape."

41 Colin MacLean, "More than 20 people rescued from Dorian," Summerside *Journal-Pioneer*, 8 September 2019, https://www.theguardian.pe.ca/news/local/more-than-20-people-rescued-from-campers-as-water-surged-into-crystal-beach-campground-sunday-349906/; Shane Ross, "Cavendish Campground closes for season after 'significant change to the landscape,'" CBC News, PEI, 9 September 2019, https://www.cbc.ca/news/canada/prince-edward-island/pei-national-park-cavendish-closed-hurricane-dorian-1.5276029.

42 Geoff Shirt, "Carrying Capacity," in *Tourism: The Key Concepts*, 22–6.

43 Jerome L. McElroy and Courtney E. Parry, "The Characteristics of Small Island Tourist Economies," *Tourism and Hospitality Research* 10, 4 (July 2010). McElroy and Parry concentrated on warm water islands in the Mediterranean and Caribbean, an admittedly different tourism environment from cold-water islands such as Prince Edward Island.

44 See, for example, "How Tourists Are Destroying the Places They Love." *Der Spiegel Online*, http://www.spiegel.de/international/paradise-lost-tourists-are-destroying-the-places-they-love-a-1223502.html; "The Dutch War on Tourism," *The Atlantic*, September 2019 issue, https://www.theatlantic.com/magazine/archive/2019/09/the-war-on-tourists/594766/; Wendy Rose, "Is tourism a trap for Atlantic Canadians?" *Guardian*, 11 June 2019, https://www.theguardian.pe.ca/news/now-atlantic/is-tourism-a-trap-for-atlantic-canadians-320569/.

45 This passage is adapted from MacDonald, "A Landscape … with Figures," 84.

46 McRae, "Manufacturing Paradise," 6, defines the dilemma in different but congruent terms: "Thus a great paradox was created: tourism became the central feature of the plan to modernize Prince Edward Island, but at the same time required the

Island to retain its underdeveloped rural character. Tourism was simultaneously weaving and unravelling the garden myth it depended upon for its success."

47 These statistics are culled from "Tourism Indicators," Department of Economic Growth, Tourism, and Culture, 30 November 2020, https://www.princeedwardisland.ca/sites/default/files/publications/202011tourismindicatorsrptfin4.pdf; and *Prince Edward Island 47th Annual Statistical Review, 2020*, 18–19.

48 TIAPEI 2021 Provincial Pre-budget Submission, https://www.tiapei.pe.ca/news/tourism-industry-association-of-pei-makes-2021-pre-budget-submission.

49 See Mike Crang, "Cultural Geographies of Tourism," in Lew, Hall, Williams, *Companion to Tourism*, 75. For a damning indictment of the tourist-host dynamic, see Rothman, *Devil's Bargains*, 13. The commodification of experience, he argues, "shatters historical distinctions between the real and the unreal by producing faux replicas of experience independent of the activity from which they derive."

50 Kevin Yarr, "Immigration drives PEI population past 150,000," CBC News, https://www.cbc.ca/news/

canada/prince-edward-island/pei-immigration-population-growth-1.4309170.

51 The statistics on agriculture are cited in *Prince Edward Island 44th Annual Statistical Review, 2018*, 81, https://www.princeedwardisland.ca/en/publication/annual-statistical-review.

52 *Historical Statistics of Canada*, Section-Agriculture, General Statistics. See http://www.statcan.gc.ca/pub/11-516-x/sectionm/M1_11-eng.csv and http://www.statcan.gc.ca/pub/11-516-x/sectionm/M23_33-eng.csv.

53 The foregoing paragraphs update and extend a passage in MacDonald, "Landscape ... with Figures," 84–5.

54 Rothman, *Devil's Bargains*, 10.

55 Rothman, *Devil's Bargains*, 11–12, 27.

56 Census Profile, 2016 Census, Statistics Canada, https://tinyurl.com/yfn23vxz; "Cavendish, Prince Edward Island," *Wikipedia*, https://en.wikipedia.org/wiki/Cavendish,_Prince_Edward_Island.

57 Derwyn G. Evans, London, Ontario, to Campbell, 6 March 1971, Alex B. Campbell Papers, PARO 25.36, 1971, file 1090-2.

Index

Page numbers in italics refer to illustrations.

Abegweit, 143; translated, *61*
Abegweit (ferry), 117–18, *117*, 127, 131, 165, 244, 249
Abegweit (film), 53, 128, 142, 316n10
Abegweit Sightseeing Tours, *191*
Aboriginal Ecotourism Strategy, 230
Acadia Hotel, 39, 44, 46–8, 53, 59
Acadian Pioneer Village, 228
Acadians, 35, 46, 79, 101, 228–9, 279n117, 311n96
accommodations, 48, 80, 104–5, 114–15, *128*; in Charlottetown, 26–7, 43, 49, 59, 203–5; in PEI National Park, 92–3; provision by Islanders, 80–1, 134–6; in rural PEI, 49; statistics, 154. *See also* cabins; campgrounds; cottages; motels; *and specific properties*
Acorn, Milton, 180
Acres Report, 139, 144, 152–5, *152*, 172, 297n1
Acres Research and Planning Ltd, 139–40, 149, 152–5, *152*, 169
Adler, Judith, 7, 177, 199
Advisory Reconstruction Committee, 113
Agnew, John, 55
Agricultural Rehabilitation and Development Act / Agricultural and Rural Development Act (ARDA), 148, 175
agriculture, 267–8, *267*

agriculture vs tourism, 180, 255–6
air travel, 111
Aitken, Gary, 108
Aitken, Gordon, 108
Alberton, 23, 24, 48, 173, *plate 3*
Ambridge, Douglas, 162
Anderson, Thomas F., 29
Anglo Rustico, 17. *See* Rustico
Annekenstein, 238, *plate 7*
Anne of Green Gables Licensing Authority, 237–8
Anne of Green Gables (novel), 53, 67–8, *70*, 87, 132, 163, 233–9; licence plate design, *plate 7. See also* "Topless Anne"
Anne of Green Gables – The Musical, 160, 163–4
anti-tourism. *See* "hospitility"
Apostle, Alisa, 106
Armstrong, Louis, 147
Arsenault, Aubin E., 72–3, *73*, 78, 82, 98–9, 102
Atlantic Canada Opportunities Agency (ACOA), 210
attractions. *See specific attractions*
authenticity, 126, 225–6, 266
autocamping, 80–1
automobile ban, 55–6, 61–4, 282n30
automobiles, 69, 71, 79–80
Avonlea Cottages, 90
Avonlea Restaurant, *71*, 90

baby boom, 112, 128, 139
Baedeker guide, 19, 32

Baglole, Harry, 183, 185
Bartlett, Major A.A., 64
Basin Head, 189
Bates, Robin, 101, 131
Bay Fortune, 50–1, *51*, 257
Bayne, Mrs B.M., 166, *167*
beaches: absence from tourism promotion, 59; access to, 264; as attraction, 4, 9, 12, 20, 22, 25–6, 87, 94, 126, 143, 176, 179, 217, 220, 269; environmental threats, 253–4. *See also specific locations*
Beach Grove Inn, 82
Beaconsfield Historic House, 189
Belfast Cove, Eldon, 130
Belliveau, Ned, 175–8
Benjamin, S.G.W., 19, *27–8*, 29, 31, 34, 36, 38
Benson, Edgar, 170
Bernard, Boyd, 172
Bernard, John, 157
Best, G.O., 176
Bird, Will R., 130–4, 168
Birthplace Explored Commission. *See* Confederation Birthplace Commission
Birthplace of Confederation. *See* Cradle of Confederation
Blue Heron Drive, 174, 309n50. *See also* scenic drives
boards of trade. *See* Charlottetown Board of Trade; Eastern Kings Board of Trade; Summerside Board of Trade

Bonnell, Lorne, 177, 197

boosters, 56, 73, 84, 94. *See also* tourism promotion

Borden, 67–8, 111, 165–7, 244–5, 251

Boughton Island, 222

Bovyer, George, 22–3, *23*

Bovyer, William, 22–3, *23*

Brackley, 23, *24*, 37, 88, 90, 92, 108, 144

Brackley Beach, 3, 48

Brackley Beach Hotel, 38

Brackley Point, 26

Brecken, Frederick, 20

Brooks, A.B., 176

Brothers and Sisters of Cornelius Howatt (BS-CH), 183, *184*, 185–6, 189, 191

Brown, Anne, 3

Brown, George, 3

Brudenell Provincial Park, 174

Brudenell Resort, 174–5, 177, *178*, 182, 242–3

Brudenell River, 130

Burke, Carl, 111

Burlington, 132–3

Butler, R.W., 7

cabins, *66*, 90, 115–16, 262, 292n75. *See also* accommodations

Cabot, John, 79

Cameron, Jack, 144, 146

Campbell, Alex B., 166–7, 170, 174, 177, 188–90, 193, 196, 198, 263, 269

Campbell, Norman, 164

Campbell, Thane, 82, 85–8, 98–9, 155, 188

campgrounds, 129, 130, 151, 181, *181*, 198, 213, 218; public vs private, 154. *See also* accommodations; camping

camping, *128, 129*, 130, *181*, 299n54, 309n65

"can ban," 180. *See also* environmental issues

Canada's Garden Province (film), 108

Canadian Association of Tourist and Publicity Bureaux, 72, *73*

Canadian government, 58, 83–4, 107, 168–70, 245–8, *plate 6*; funding PEI tourism, 65, 91, 99, 124, 160–1, 187,

210, 248. *See also* Agricultural Rehabilitation and Development Act / Agricultural and Rural Development Act (ARDA); Atlantic Canada Opportunities Agency (ACOA); Comprehensive Development Plan; Confederation Centre of the Arts; Economic Regional Development Agreements (ERDAS); Fund for Rural Economic Development (FRED); National Parks Branch; Parks Canada

Canadian Government Travel Bureau. *See* Canadian Travel Bureau

Canadian National Railways, 80, 83, 111, 117–18, 142

Canadian Tourism Association, 110, 112

Canadian Travel Bureau, 83–4, 99, 107, 120, 127

Cape Traverse, 48

Capital Commission (Charlottetown), 231–2, 259

Carr, David, 26

Carson, Rachel, 178

Carter & Co., 60

Cartier, Jacques, 21, 79, 275n16

Cavendish, 9, 20, 70–1, 87–90, 132, 219, 262, 269

Cavendish Beach Music Festival, 258

Cavendish Resort Association, 182

Cavendish Resort Municipality, 235, 261, 269

Centennial, Canadian, 143, 160, 304n197; effect on tourism, 158, 161, 300n93. *See also* Charlottetown Conference

Centennial Celebration Act, 187

"centennialitis," 158–9

Chafe, William, 143

Chambers, Bob, 166, *167*

Charlottetown, 35–6, 59, 162–3, 219; accommodations in, 80, *81*, 151, 203–5, 279n127; centennial, *133*, 159; as cruise destination, 258–60; and tourism levies, 212

Charlottetown (ferry), 82, 111

Charlottetown Airport, 100

Charlottetown Board of Trade, 84, 117, 137

Charlottetown Conference, 3–4; 1914 anniversary, 64–5; 1939 anniversary, 99–102, *100*; 1964 anniversary, 158, 160–2; 1989 anniversary, *221*, 227; souvenirs, *plate 3. See also* Centennial, Canadian

Charlottetown Development and Tourist Association, 52

Charlottetown Driving Park, *109*

Charlottetown Hotel, 80–1, *81*, 147

Charlottetown Summer Resorts, *66, 66*

Chrétien, Jean, 192, 197

Clarke, Dennis L., 161–2

Clarkin, Lucy Gertrude, 80

Clements, Gilbert, 223

Cliff Hotel (Stanhope Beach Inn), 42, 48, 59

climate change, 254, 264. *See also* environmental issues

Cobb, David, 176

Cobbett, William, 44

Coghlan, Charles Francis, 50

College of Piping and Celtic Performing Arts, 227

Commercial House, 23, 31

Committee of Dispossessed Landowners, 89–90, 93

Comprehensive Development Plan, 13, 140, 170–5, 180, 183–4, 187–8, 194–5, 198, 200, 208

Confederation. *See* Cradle of Confederation; Fathers of Confederation

Confederation (ferry), 119, 232

Confederation Birthplace Commission, 230

Confederation Bridge, 244, 247–51, *249. See also* fixed link

Confederation Centre of the Arts, 159–63, *160*, 218

Confederation Landing Park, 232

Confederation Players, 227

Confederation Trail, 224–5, *224*, 232

Cook, Thomas, 10, 21

Cooper, John A., 59, 282n18

320

—

Index

Corby Croft, 166
cottages, 50, 66, 71, 90, 92–3, 95, 116, 128, 133, 150, *152*, 173, 242, 262–4. *See also specific cottage developments*
Cotton, Robert L., 57, 129–30, 175
Covehead, 22, *23*
COVID-19, 4, 265–6
Cradle of Confederation, 64, 98–101, 225–7, 231–2
Cradle of Confederation (film), 98, 290n8
Craig, Robert, 158
Crerar, Thomas, 98
Cromarty, W.D., 86–7
Crosskill, W.H., 44, 57, 77
cruise ships, 258–61, *259*, 316n19
Cudmore, Don, 212
Cuisine à Mémé (play), 228
Culinary Institute of Canada, 257
Cullen, Dorothy, 161
Cullen, Eugene, 113
cultural tourism, 226–7
Curley, Rosemary, 222

Dale, Bernie, 203–5
Daley, Hartwell, 148–9
Dalvay, 87–8, 92, 129
Dalvay Beach, 166
Dalvay-by-the-Sea, 85–7, *85*, 91, 146
Davies, J.A., 190
Dawson, Michael, 6
Dawson, S.E., 35
DDT, 178
DeBlois, George, 85–6, 88
Deighen, Greg, 243
Dennis, W.H., 83
Department of Tourism (PEI), 12, 149, 156, 205, 212–14, 247, 258; budgets, 141, 302n149; creation, 137; nomenclature, 179, 208, *209*, 303n170, 308n27; promotes ratings program, 212–14; relations with TIAPEI, 208–12; and tourism awareness, 207
Depression. *See* Great Depression
DeRoche Pond, 222
Development Plan. *See* Comprehensive Development Plan

Dewar, George, 119
Dewar, Katherine, *plate 5*
Dewar, Mae, *plate 5*
"Diary of a Young Charlottetonian," 41
Dicks, Captain Edward, *85*
Diefenbaker, John, 158–9, 168–9
Diercks, George, 223
Diercks, Phyliss, 223
Disney, Walt, 143
Dolan, D. Leo, 99, 120, 122
Doyle, James, 30
DPA Group, 226
Dubinsky, Karen, 6
Dun and Bradstreet, 48–9
Dundarave (golf course), 242
Dundee Apartment Motel, 147

Eastern Kings Board of Trade, 195–6
East Point, 193, *195*
East Point National Park proposal, 192–8, *195*. *See also* PEI National Park
Eber, Dorothy, 198
Economic Regional Development Agreements (ERDAS), 208
Elephant Rock, 253, *254*
Emily of New Moon (book), 233
Emily of New Moon (play), 239, 312n115
Emily of New Moon (television series), 203, 215, 233
environmental issues, 155, 176–80, 253–4, 264
environmental tourism. *See* green tourism
Eptek Exhibition Centre, 189
European and North American Railway, 24
Evangeline, 35, 79, 277n74, 311n97
Evangeline (region), 228–9
Evans, Derwyn, 269
event tourism, 257–8
expatriate tourists, 12, 20, 40–4, 52, 79, 104, 120, 125, 199, 217, 278n99; as cottage owners, 262; encouraging outmigration, 41, 285n74; as tourist ambassadors, 20. *See also* Old Home Week

Fathers of Confederation, 3–4, 21, 26, 158, 160–1, 227
Fathers of Confederation Memorial Building. *See* Confederation Centre of the Arts
Faux, Mrs A.M., 165
federal government. *See* Canadian government
Fergusson, C. Bruce, 190
ferries, 67–9, 82–3, *83*, 110, 116–19, 139, 164–6. *See also specific ferries*
ferry traffic, 82, 104, 110–11, 118–19, 125, 165, 244. *See also* transportation
Festival of the Descendants, *221*, 227
Field, Alan, 127
First World War and tourism, 67–8
Fisher, John, 112
fixed link, 168–70, *169*, 244–50, 248, *249*. *See also* Confederation Bridge
Fleming, Bertha, 97, 134–6
Fleming, Cornelius, 97
Fleming, Dolph, 97–8, 112, 134–6
Flockton, C.P., 50, *51*, 257
Florida Hotel, 48
Follows, Megan, 233
food tourism, 256–7
Forster, W.E., 83
Fort Amherst, Rocky Point, 79, 156
Founders' Hall, *231*, 232
Fraser, George V., 121–7, *122*, 129, 137, 139–41, 174
Friends of the Island, 245, 247–8
Fund for Rural Economic Development (FRED), 148–9

Gallant, Lennie, 235
Gallant, Marc, 176
Gallant, William M., 186
Garden of the Gulf, 34, 126, 238
Gaudet, Walthen, 146
Ghiz, Joe, 230, 248
Gibson, R.A., 91
Gill, John H., 165
Gillis, John, 262
Glencourse Summer Resort, 26, *plate 2*
Glover, Patsy, *178*
"golden triangle," 151, 219

golf, 91–2, 175, 239–45, *241*
Golf Links PEI, 240, 242–3
Gordon, Alan, 6
Government of Canada. *See* Canadian government
Government of PEI. *See* PEI government (and tourism)
Grand Tracadie, 44, 46, 48, 53, 59, 85
Gray Lord, Margaret, 101
Great Depression, 82–3
Green, John Eldon, 226
Green Gables Bungalow Court, *128*, 129
Green Gables House, *70*, 87–91, *92*, *93*, 132, 134, 235–6. See also *Anne of Green Gables* (novel)
Greenlee, Elizabeth T., 177
green tourism, 220–1, *221*
Greenwich, 222–4, *222*
Gregor's-by-the-Sea, 92, 144–5
Griffin, Diane, 222
Gripsholm (cruise ship), 258

H.R. Dickie Ltd, 223
Hampton, 48, 55
Harris, Robert, *37*, *66*, *plate 1*
Harrison, Elaine, 185
Harvey, D.C., 79, 102
Harvie, Eric, 159
Haszard, Helen, *plate 3*
Hayward, William, 161
Hennessey, Catherine, 188, 307n5
heritage, 79, 186–9; tensions with tourism, 203–5, 222, 307n5
heritage tourism, 5–6, 102, 157, 186–9, 210, 213–14, *221*, 225–9, 311n90. *See also* Charlottetown Conference; cultural tourism; Mi'kmaq; natural heritage
Hilton International, 203
Hodgson House, 48
Holiday Island (ferry), 167
Holiday Island (film): (1948), 143; (1967), 127, 143, 156, 297n13
Holiday Island (slogan), 119, 185, 250
Holland Cove, 66, *66*, 262
Holman, A.H., 146
Holman, Harry T., 85–6

Holman, James L., 17–19, *19*. *See also* Island Park Hotel
Holman's Island, 17, 19–20, 174
Hood, John, 57
Hope River, 257
Hornby, Jim, 146
"hospitility," 10, 75–6, 183–6, 199, 239, 304n184
hotels. *See* accommodations; *specific properties*
Howe, C.D., 85, 98
Hughes, George, 52, 55–7
Humphrey, R.S., 129
Hyndman, F.W., 63
Hyndman, J.O., 67, 84, 116

Indigenous tourism. *See* Micmac Indian Village; Mi'kmaq; Minegoo Arts and Crafts Society
information booths. *See* tourist information booths
Inn at Bay Fortune, 257
Innkeepers Association. *See* PEI Innkeepers Association
Intercolonial and PEI Railway, 38, 44, *45*, 78
International Sled Dog Races, 257
intra-Island tourism, 23, 41–2, 255
Irish heritage, 46, 227
Irving Whale, 178
Irwin, Archibald, 47, 52, 57
Islanders for a Better Tomorrow, 246–7
Island Nature Trust, 220, 222
islandness, as tourist experience, 8, 30–2, 118, 166; and passage over water, 126–8, 131, 247, 250–1
Island Park Hotel, 17–20, *19*, 53, 174
Island Regulatory and Appeals Commission, 263

Jack Frost Festival, 257
Jakle, John, 127, 141
James, Henry, 10
Japanese tourism, 148, 234–5, 309n60
Jenkins, Keith, 181–2
John Hamilton Gray (ferry), 167
Johnson, Margaret, 157

Johnstone, Lt Col Ernest, *132*, 133. *See also* Woodleigh Replicas
Jones, J. Walter, 109, 113–14, 117–18

Kane, Lorie, 240
Keefe, John C., 23, 31. *See also* Commercial House
Kensington and Area Tourist Association, 180–1
Keppoch, 49, 262
Keppoch Beach Hotel, 42
Kings Byway, 174, 309n50. *See also* scenic drives
Kings County, 302n152; attitudes towards tourism, 199; recreation/ tourism potential, 153; share of tourists, 219
Kirby, John, 176
Kirby, Judy, 176
Kitten Clubs International, 177, *178*
knockers. *See* "hospitility"
KPMG Management Consulting, 240–2
Kungsholm (cruise ship), 258

Labobe, Irene, 157
Lady Slipper Drive, 173, 309n50. *See also* scenic drives
Lake of Shining Waters, 9, 70, 236
landscape, as tourist attraction. *See* pastoral image
Lansdowne Hotel, 48
Lantz, Jeff, 243
Larkin, Jim, 212, 246
Lash, Scott, 10
Lattimer, Dr J.E., 113
Lazear, Jesse T., 47
Lefurgey, Alfred, 58
Lefurgey, J.E., 51, 57
Leitch, John C., 26
Lennox Island, 157, 229. *See also* Mi'kmaq
LePage, Mrs A.B., 119–20
L'Étoile de mer, 228
Linkletter, Charles, 129
Links at Crowbush Cove, The, 240, 242
Little, J.I., 6–7
Live! With Regis and Kelly, 258

L.M. Montgomery (ferry), 167
lobster suppers, 135, 227, 256–7
Longfellow, Henry Wadsworth, 35, 228
"looney tax," 212
Lord Selkirk (ferry), 133
Lorne Hotel, 26, 42, *plate 2*
Louson, W.S., 59–60, *60. See also*
  postcards
Lover's Lane, *plate 4*
Lowther, Greg, 261
Lowther, Linda, 261

MacArthur, Creelman, 83
MacAusland, Avonna, 119
MacAusland, Percy, 90, 93
MacCallum, Betty, 95
MacCannell, Dean, 126
MacDonald, Alexander, 50, 87
MacDonald, Bill, 207
MacDonald, Daniel J., 196
MacDonald, David, 126
MacDonald, Earle, 120
Macdonald, Major D.A., 192
MacDonald, Rob, 238
MacEwen, Walford, 172
MacFadyen, Josh, 264
MacFadyen, M.K. "Minnie," 72–3, *73*,
  82, 193
MacInnis, Gordon, 210
MacIsaac, Martha, *203*, 215, 233
MacKinnon, Frank, 125, 158–9
MacLean, A.A., 65
MacMillan, W.J.P., 98
MacNevin, Dale, 236–7
Macphail, Andrew, 62
Macphail, Lloyd, 195
MacRae, Andrew, 145, 148
Maddix, Robert, 228
Maloney, John, 156
Malpeque, 48
Maple Leaf, The (magazine), 40, 64
Marine Atlantic, 244–9
Maritime Central Airways, 111,
  292n61
marketing levies, 212
Marks, Dorothy, 247
Marquis of Lorne, 18, 26
Matheson, Alex W., 115, 118, 129, 136

Mathieson, J.A., 61
McBride, Hope, 133–4
McCallum, Herbert, 90
McCallum, Neil, 26
McCallum's Hotel (Brackley Beach
  Lodge), 26, *37*, 90
McCarthy, Hamilton, 65
McCready, J.E.B., 60–1, 65, 77
McElroy, Jerome L., 265
McInnis, Michael A., 40
McKay, Ian, 5, 78, 101, 126, 131
McMillan, Eileen, 147
McMillan, Dr Joe, 147
McMillan, Tom, 206, 246–7
McRae, Matthew, 7, 98, 112, 114, 134,
  161–2, 180, 187
Meggison, William L., 194
Meighen, Arthur, 83
Memo to Mom (film), 127, 142
Meraviglia (cruise ship), 259
Mi'kmaq, 46, 61, 148, *147*, 156–7, 229–30
Mi'kmaw handicrafts, *61*, 229, *229*
Michelin Travel Services, 213
Micmac Indian Village, *147*, 156
Miller, Leslie, 210
Mill River Resort, 174–5, 182, 242
Milne, David, 245
Minegoo Arts and Crafts Society, 229
Miscouche, 161
Mitchell, Martin, *147*, 156
Montague, 62, 133, *plate 3*
Mont Carmel, 228
Montgomery, Lucy Maud, 9, 67–8, *70*,
  89, 143–4, 163, 237–8, 288n156
motels, 115–16, 151, 154, 172, 174, 218,
  299n50, 314n161. *See also*
  accommodations
Moses, David, 238
Mulroney, Brian, 210, 245
Muraoka, Hanako, 234
Murphy, Conn, *191*
Murphy, Mrs Leo, 95
Murphy, Shirley, *191*
Murray, Rev. R., 32–4, 76
music festivals, 257–8, *258. See also*
  event tourism
Mutch, R.E., 110
Mutch's Hotel, 42, 48

Nash, Frederick, 57
National Parks Branch, 85–94, 146.
  See also Parks Canada
natural heritage, 192. *See also* green
  tourism
Neatby, Nicole, 6
Nelson, John, 25. *See also* Seaside
  Hotel
Newbery, Arthur, 65
New England, 22
New London, 88, 264
Newson, John, 17, 25–6. *See also*
  Seaside Hotel
Nicol, John I., 194
nonresident land ownership, 186,
  262–4, 316n7
North Cape, 253
North Rustico, 97, 161
North Shore, 3, 26, 46–7, 88, 94, 131,
  144–5, 179, 192, 219;
  accommodations situation on, 92,
  115; cost of property on, 263; and
  discrimination, 144–5; as focus for
  tourism, 20, 50, 70, 77, 151, *152*, 220;
  overcrowding on, 192, 264;
  unregulated development on, 193,
  236. *See also* Cavendish Resort
  Municipality; PEI National Park
North Shore Hotel, 26, 48, 59
Northumberland Ferries Ltd, 110, 244
Nova Scotia Railway, 24

Oasis Resort, 261
Ocean House hotel. *See* Seaside Hotel
Offstage Theatre Company, 238
Old Home Week, 12, 20, 51–3, 57–8,
  72, 74, *109*, 257, 280n144,
  281nn149–50, 285n74
Orton, Ron, 178
Orwell Corner, 189
outmigration, 20, 40–1, 52, 79, 195, 217
Overton, James, 6
overtourism, 10, 192, 198–9, 265–6
Owen, William, 49–50

Park Corner, 9
Parks Canada, 191–7, 222–5, 232.
  See also National Parks Branch

323

Index

pastoral image: landscape, 4, 8, 12, 30, 32–5, *45*, 59, 106, 123–6, 131–2, 141–4, 176, 193, 215–16, 234; culture, 8–9, 11, 77–8, 102, 126, 154–6, 180, 225; threatened, 247, 264, 266–8
Pearson, Lester B., 160, 168
PEI Centennial (1973), 184–5, 187, *188*
PEI Development and Tourist Association, 52, 55, 57
PEI government (and tourism), 12, 44, 137, 148; and accommodations, 59, 80, 114–15, 129, 173, 204–5, 218, 296n160; assumes control over, 12–13, 94–5, 200, 255; attitude towards, 112–13; creates provincial park system, 129–30; and golf, 239–43; and heritage, 188–9; position on fixed link, 248; and Province House, 190–1; regulation of, 114, 137, 174, 180, 237–8; relations with private sector, 90, 114, 181–2, 208–11, 226; spending on, 82, 91, 103–4, 107, 114–15, 141, 308n23; strategies, 171–2; support/lack of support for, 52, 58–61, 75, 103, 105, 200; takes over Tourist Bureau, 102. *See also* Charlottetown Conference; Department of Tourism (PEI); golf; PEI National Park; transportation; tourism planning; tourism promotion
PEI Heritage Foundation, 188–9, 203–4
PEI image. *See* pastoral image
PEI Innkeepers Association, *113*, 114, *120*, 121, 125
PEI National Park, *89*, 89–92, 222–4; competes with private sector, 181; development of, 91–2, 94, *128*, 129, 192; expropriation for, 88–9; golf course, 289n170; opening of, 97–8, 100; opposition to, 89–91; selection of, 85–8, 288n156. *See also* East Point National Park proposal
PEI Tourist Association: (1905 on), 52, 55–7; (1923 on), 72–5, *73*, 77–8, 80–3, *83*, 102; (1958 on), *113*, 121, 136, 145–6, 149, 161–3, 166, 168, 176,

178–80, 200, 285n77. *See also* PEI Innkeepers Association; PEI Travel Bureau; Tourism Industry Association of PEI (TIAPEI)
PEI Travel Bureau, *54*, 83, *97*, 98, 102–3, 105, *122*, 125–7
Phills, James A., 144–5
Pinto, Joseph A., 190
Plan, the. *See* Comprehensive Development Plan
Pleasant View Hotel, 48, 55
Point Pleasant Summer Hotel, 26
Polley, Sarah, 233
Pope, James C., 43
Port Hill, 48, 189
Port Hill House, 48
postcards, 32, 59–61, *60*, 78, 165, 253
Pownal, 48
Prince County, 173, 219, 253
Prince Edward Hotel, 203–5, *204*
Prince Edward Island: as Acadia, 35; history in travel literature, 78–9; people described, 38, 46; rural life, 36–7; as undiscovered, 4, 22, 46–7; weather, 31
Prince Edward Island (ferry), 67, *68*, *69*, 71, 111, 167
Prince Edward Island: Come In from Away (film), 186
Prince Edward Island Magazine, 47–8
Prince Nova (ferry), 110
Princetown, 26
Proctor, John E., 190
professionalization, 9–10, 200, 212–14. *See also* PEI government (and tourism)
Profitt, Wendell, 130
Prohibition, 67
promotional films, 127–8, 142–3, 156, 186. *See also specific films*
promotional literature, 38–9, 44, 46, 50, 61, 61, 76–8, 123, 127, 144, 148, 215–16, 220, 235, 276n44, 277n69, 295n125. See also *Visitors Guides*
Prouds's Parkhill Cottages, 133
Province House (Confederation Chamber), 78, 98–101, 104, 132, 158, 161, 190–1, 225, 232

provincial parks, 129–30
Putnam, Anne, 237

Queen Elizabeth II, 160, 164
Queen Hotel, 59

race and racism, 144–7
Rae, W. Fraser, 34
ragweed, 121, 124, 295n125
Rail Lands Development Corporation, 225
Ramsay, Baxter, 238
ratings systems, 212–14
Reid, W.W., 121
Reymond, Raoul, 146
Ritchie, Donald, 234
roads. *See* transportation: by road
Roads to Resources Program, 117
Robinsons Island, 17, 25
Roche, Douglas, 126
Rocky Point, *147*, 156
Rodd, Sally, 115
Rodd, Wally, 115
Rogers, B. Graham, 103–5, 108–9, 121
Rollo Bay Fiddle Festival, 257–8
Rossiter, Leo, 148
Rothman, Hal, 255, 268
Rowan, John, 35, 46
Royal Commission on Land Use and Land Ownership (1972), 186, 262–3
Rustico, 9, 17–20, 25, 48, 53, 88

St Ann's, 257
St Peter's, 95, 224
Saunders, A.C., 75–6
Saunders, Philip, 190
Savage Harbour, 177
scenic drives, 173–4, 309n50, *plate 9*
Schurman, Robert, 179
Scotia II (ferry), 167
Scots heritage, 46, 227–8
Seaforth, 48
Seaside Holiday (film), 127
Seaside Hotel, 17–20, *18*, 25–6, 28–9, *28*, 48, 50, 53; guest register, 39, 41–2, 278n89
Second World War and tourism, 105–6, *106*, 108–10

324

Index

Senate Committee on Tourist Traffic (1934), 83
Shaw, Gordon, 162
Shaw, Neil, 23–4, *24*, 26
Shaw, Walter, 136, 140, 148, 161, 168, 193
Shaw's Hotel, 23–4, *24*, 26, 32, 48, 92, 108
Sheepcote Cottage, *66*
Shirt, Geoff, 265
shoulder season, 153, 198–9, 218
Sim, Harry, 261
Simon, Anne W., 185
Simpson, Christianna, 90
Simpson, Jeremiah, 70–1, 90, 94
"Smiling Father" (Centennial logo), 185, *188*, *plate 3*
Smith, Edna, 48
Smith, Matthew, 55
Smith, Michael, 257
Smith, Rev. Edwin, 57
Smith, Stephen L.J., 4
South Shore, 182
souvenirs, *133*, *plate 3*
Spankie, Caroline, 174
Squire, Shelagh, 7
Stanhope Beach Inn, 82, 146
Stanhope Campground, *128*
Stanhope, 26, 42, 48, 59, 82, *128*, 133
steamship travel, 22
Sterns, R.H., 82
Stevenson and Kellogg, 203–5
Stewart, J. David, 115, 136–7, 145–6, 148, 159, 161
Stewart, William, 75
Strait Crossing Inc. (SCI), 248
Strathgartney Provincial Park, 130
Sullivan, Kevin, 233–4, 237
Summerside, 17, 19, 51, 59, 131, 219; airport, 111; hosts Old Home Week, 51–2; museum in, 189; resorts in, 17–19, 174, 293n96, 296n160; part of "golden triangle," 151, 219; supports provincial tourist association, 72–4, 80; supports tourism levies, 212; travel bureaus, 107, *plate 5*; in travel literature, 36
Summerside Board of Trade, 102–3
Summerside Improvement and Tourist Association, 51, 57–8

Summerside Lobster Carnival, 257
Sweetser, Moses, 35

Tandy Advertising, 175, 198–9
Taylor, Earle, *147*, 156
themes, promotional, 220–1, 227, 240
Thomas, Peter, 157
Thompson, Stanley, 91, 97
Thornton, Sir Henry, 80
Tignish, 172
Tinney, Reigh, 72, 74
Toombs, Roy, 97
"Topless Anne," 237–8, *plate 7*
tourism: activities, 143, 151, 218–21, 230, 266, 269; in Canada, 83; definition of, 4; employment, 153, 199; funding, 112, 226, 258, 308n27; health benefits, 31–2; historiography (Canada), 5–7; history, 21; in Maritimes, 71–2; in Nova Scotia, 78, 101; revenue, 4, 104, 119, *120*, 149, 206, 291n37, 294n114, 315n3; spending, 171, 308n23; theory, 7; visitor numbers, 42, 78, 84, 101, 119, 122, 149, 200, 206, 224, 249, *256*, 299n42, 306n258
Tourism 2000, 210–11
tourist associations, 12, 51, 211, 213. *See also specific associations*
Tourism Area Life Cycle (TALC), 7
Tourism Industry Association of Prince Edward Island (TIAPEI), *113*, 200, 209–13
Tourism PEI (1999>), 240, 258–9, 285n76
Tourism Penetration Index, 265
tourism planning, 107, 139–40, 148–54, 193, 199–200, 210, 307n19. *See also* Acres Research and Planning Ltd; Comprehensive Development Plan
tourism promotion, 8, 13, 58–9, 78, 105, 109, 123–4, *128*, 141–4, 266; cooperative marketing, 124–5; of 1939 Charlottetown Conference anniversary, 100; promotion with Atlantic provinces, 124, in Quebec, 84; by Tourist Association, 121.

See also promotional films; promotional literature; *specific promotions*
Tourism Quality Services, 213–14
Tourist Accommodation Loans program, 114–16
tourist demographics, 214–15, 217, 234–5, 315n200
tourist information booths, *107*
Tourist Roads Programme, 91
tourist spending, *120*, 149, 171, 206, 249–50, 307n17. *See also* tourism: revenue
tourist traffic, 84, 103–4, 107–8, 119, 140, 149–51, 162, 200, 206, 235, 249–50, 256, *256*, 306n258
tourists: American, 22, 24, 38–9, 104; Central Canadian, 39; intra-Island tourism, 23, 41–2, 255; from Maritimes, 39. *See also* Japanese tourism; tourist demographics
Towner, John, 127
Townshend Woodlot, 189
Tracadie Bay, 42
Tracadie Beach, 26
tractor demonstration, 180
TransCanada Highway, 130, 151
transportation, 43; by air, 111, 266, 276n46; by rail, 20, 24, 40, 43–4, *45*, 58–9, 67, 69, 224, 281n150; by road, 55–6, 84, 91, 117, 131, 181, 277n64; by water, 67, 71, 82, 84, 101, 103, 110–11, 115–19, 127–8, 133, 164–8, 244–9, 266, 315n183. *See also* automobiles; ferries; scenic drives
travel writing, 29–30, 44
Tricoche, G.N., 76
Trillin, Calvin, 217
Trudeau, Pierre, 170
Turgeon Commission, 118
200,000 Club, 57

Urry, John, 10, 226

Vacationland (ferry), 167
Victoria Hotel, 59, 80–82, *81*
Victoria-by-the-Sea, 161
visitors. *See* tourism: visitor numbers

Visitors Guide, 122–3, *123*, 141–2, *142*, *203*, 213, 215–17, *252*, 253, *254*, *plates 8–9*

Walker, Hal, 242
Wallace-Wells, David, 253–4
Warburton, A.B., 49–50
Ward, Anna L., 50
Warner, Charles Dudley, 29, 31, 35, 76
Weale, David, 183, *184*, 185, 250
Webb, Ernest, 70, *70*, 89–90, 92

Webb, Myrtle, 70, *70*, 89–90, 92
West Point, *203*
Williamson, Frank H.H., 86–8, 93
Winsloe, 115
winter: as barrier to travel, 116; tourism in, 257; in travel literature, 32
women, *42*, 66; as accommodation providers, 81, 136; among Japanese tourists, 234, 312n118; in pastoral landscape, 36, 78; in tourism workforce, 153, 199; in tourist

associations, 114, 136, 293n79; as tourist demographic, 41–2
Wood, Kathryn, 182
Wood Islands, 110, 165, 251
Woodleigh Replicas, *132*, 133
World War I. *See* First World War and tourism
World War II. *See* Second World War and tourism
Wyand, Katherine, 70, *71*, 90–1, 93